Boomtown Portsmouth

The World War II Transformation of a Quiet New England Seaport

Rodney K. Watterson

Boomtown Portsmouth by Rodney K. Watterson
Copyright © 2016
All rights reserved.

Published by Piscataqua Press
An imprint of RiverRun Bookstore, Inc.
142 Fleet Street | Portsmouth, NH | 03801
www.riverrunbookstore.com
www.piscataquapress.com
ISBN: 978-1-944393-33-5

Cover Photo: *Portsmouth Market Square (circa 1939/40)*.
Courtesy Thom Hindle Collection.

Printed in the United States of America

To Susan

With many thanks for the patience and understanding
shown over many years in granting me endless hours of our
retirement time to pursue a dream.

TABLE OF CONTENTS

ILLUSTRATIONS

PHOTOS

TABLES

FIGURES

ACKNOWLEDGMENTS

The origins of this book can be traced back to research done for a doctoral dissertation at the University of New Hampshire. I want to thank the members of that dissertation committee: my dissertation advisor, Kurk Dorsey, and committee members Jeffrey Bolster, Ellen Fitzpatrick, Gary Weir, and Carole Barnett. That dissertation and several more years of research, writing, and rewriting have resulted in two books: *32 in '44: The Building of the Portsmouth Submarine Fleet in World War II* (U.S. Naval Institute Press; 2011) and this one, *Boomtown Portsmouth: The World War II Transformation of a Quiet New England Seaport*.

Topping the list deserving recognition for contributions to this book is my copy editor, Joal (Jody) Hetherington. In addition to her excellent editing, she proposed many revisions to make this engineer's writing more reader-friendly. Thanks to her, much redundancy has been eliminated and many details have been moved to notes in order to move the narrative along. I appreciate her invaluable contributions and the helpful writing seminar I experienced in the process.

My technical background encourages the use of graphs, tables, and pictures instead of lengthy discussion to make some points, greatly complicating the publisher's task. Much credit goes to Kellsey Metzger at Piscataqua Press for accommodating my seemingly endless requests for format revisions in an effort to place the many illustrations in this book with the appropriate text.

Thanks to Richard Winslow, author of many Portsmouth

Navy Yard and other local histories, who offered suggestions and encouragement during my search for a publisher; to Karen Desrosiers for reading a very early manuscript draft and providing comments; and to Tom Hardiman, the Keeper at the Portsmouth Athenaeum, for his wise counsel and seemingly endless knowledge of all things Portsmouth.

Among the archivists deserving thanks for their assistance with the many boxes, binders, and photographs that I pored through during my visits to their facilities are Joanie Gearin at NARA Waltham, MA; Patrick Osborne at NARA College Park, MD; Nancy Mason, special collections assistant at the Milne Special Collections and Archives at the University of New Hampshire; Carolyn Marvin, Portsmouth Athenaeum research librarian; Nicole Cloutier, special collections librarian at the Portsmouth Public Library; and Elizabeth Farish and Amanda Breen at the Strawbery Banke Museum. They could not have been more accommodating during my visits to their archives.

I am especially grateful to the individuals who consented to be interviewed by me for this book: Stan Davis, Jim Dolph, Eileen Dondero Foley, Mel Low, Dan MacIsaac, Claire Flanagan Papatones, Bea Randall, William Tebo, Frederick White, Harold Whitehouse, and Percy Whitney. Their contributions rounded out volumes of research and added greatly to the content of the book. Thanks also to Tammi Truax for drawing my attention to interviews she had conducted for her Tea for Two columns in the *Portsmouth Herald* that I might find useful. Similarly, Elizabeth Farish and Amanda Breen provided Strawbery Banke Museum oral histories for the Abbott Store Project that had application to this book.

Harold Whitehouse and Claire Flanagan Papatones graciously provided and approved the use of several personal photographs. I am also indebted to Gregory Mallory at the Boston Consulting Group for approving the use of the graph "Construction Times for All U.S. Submarines Built during World War II" and Pete Payette of http://www.northamericanforts.com for approving the use of the chart "Portsmouth Harbor Forts."

Thanks also to Thom Hindle for granting permission to include the Portsmouth Market Square (circa 1939/40) photo from the Thom Hindle Collection in the book and for the cover of this book.

After successfully counseling me through my first two books, Molly, my loyal project assistant, did not make it through this one. As a final tribute to the world's greatest golden retriever, I want to thank her for fourteen years of companionship, thousands of walks on the beach, and hundreds of sunrises that I would have missed.

Most importantly, I want to thank Susan, my high school sweetheart and wife of fifty-five years, for proofreading numerous drafts of this and my previous books, offering many recommendations and much encouragement. With great appreciation and much gratitude, I dedicate this book to her.

INTRODUCTION

This is a story of boomtown Portsmouth. War wrote it. War has brought a mushroom growth to Portsmouth similar to those towns that sprang up in our Far West when gold and other precious metals were discovered. At times developments here have been little less hysterical in tempo.

Portsmouth Herald,
26 May 1942,
"Boomtown Portsmouth
Finds It Has Special Needs"

The Portsmouth Social Protection Committee's report to the mayor, prominently displayed on the front page of the 14 July 1944 *Portsmouth Herald*, sounded the alarm. Not about the war, which was then at fever pitch, or even the all-too-real threat of U-boats stealing into home waters. In fact, a decoding device would have been helpful to interpret the *Herald*'s message. The article lamented "vice conditions" that needed to be corrected to prevent the spread of "social diseases," and called for "transient girls" to be kept away from "exposure places" and taxi drivers to cease acting as "producers." Curiously, the words *prostitute* and *venereal disease* did not appear in the report—although the city's high venereal disease rate, a condition the U.S. Navy attributed to excessive prostitution in the city of Portsmouth, was precisely the issue. Such was the city's reluctance to acknowledge one of the consequences of the World War II mobilization of Portsmouth Navy Yard.

Portsmouth was in the midst of perhaps the most dramatic

and drastic transformation it had ever experienced, one that would permanently shape its future in all manner of ways. As Milton Bracker noted in his 5 October 1941 *New York Times* article about the city, "Thus what was basically a prosperous New England port, steeped in history and thriving as a summer resort, has been transformed swiftly into a war-production area with the only newcomers being yard workers, soldiers, and sailors. There is no one in the city whose life has not been altered by the transformation."[1] The once-quiet seaport and popular tourist destination was galvanized into a boomtown when employment at Portsmouth Navy Yard quadrupled to more than 20,000 employees and hundreds of millions of defense dollars poured into the yard and seacoast New Hampshire region. Mobilization brought many booms—in population, economy, infrastructure, skilled labor, and female workers, plus less welcome spikes in environmental pollution, prostitution, and venereal disease—creating many challenges and opportunities.

New Hampshire's population and economic centers shifted toward the seacoast as employment and production peaked at the yard. The local economy flourished, commerce thrived, household incomes soared, and infrastructure development struggled through fits and starts to accommodate the thousands of immigrants seeking employment at the shipyard. Industrial training programs reversed a prewar shortage of skilled workers, and women filled vacated industrial jobs when the men went off to war. In November 1944, a Democratic victory overturned the long-standing Republican government in the city of Portsmouth— including the election of the first female mayor in the state of New Hampshire. These wartime events transformed Portsmouth not just for the war, but for all time. The city would never again be the quiet seacoast tourist town that it was before the war.

The wartime implementation of rationing, conservation, and recycling programs brought dramatic but less permanent lifestyle changes. Housewives stood in long lines to purchase rationed items, home thermostats and speed limits were reduced to save fuel, and everything from tinfoil to kitchen fats was recycled to support the war effort. These extraordinary homeland commitments and sacrifices, so vigorously prosecuted during the war, faded quickly when the war was over — but not so quickly from the memories of those who were there.

The harbor and civil defense systems established to protect the region featured prominently in the city's World War II makeover. The U.S. Army operated an elaborate harbor defense system centered on a half dozen restored forts and an underwater protective barrier of hydrophones, mines, and an antisubmarine net. Civil defense volunteers staffed observation posts to scan the skies for enemy aircraft, patrolled neighborhoods to enforce dimout and blackout regulations, and planned for unimaginable disasters. Both the harbor and civil defense systems were deactivated once victory was certain. Little evidence of the civil defense system remains, and the remnants of the harbor defenses are now mostly hidden from view amid the placid greenery of waterfront parks and recreation areas.

The conversion of tranquil Portsmouth into an active Navy liberty town, with all the positives and negatives that entails, was another temporary transformation, although traces of it persisted for a decade or more after the war. Businesses and bars in downtown Portsmouth prospered. The active bar scene stimulated the economy, attracted prostitutes or wayward girls (depending on one's viewpoint), and challenged local law enforcement officials. Naval officers demanded that city authorities clean up their town; city officials resisted, believing their city was much less wicked than advertised. The Navy gained the upper hand in this tug-of-war about the time the real war entered its final stages in the summer of 1944. The end of the war brought a greatly reduced military presence to the region, far fewer sailor squabbles in downtown Portsmouth, and a smoothing out of contentious relations between city officials and officers at the navy yard.

The environmental consequences of mobilization were, unfortunately, not nearly as transitory. The shipyard's practice of using hazardous solid industrial wastes as landfill to reclaim marshlands peaked during the war, and continued after, with long-lasting effects. Forty years later, the EPA declared the contaminated landfills Superfund sites, requiring millions of restoration dollars. The dumping of shipyard and other manufacturers' industrial waste effluents directly through uncontrolled sewers contaminated local waters, giving rise to pollution concerns and early cleanup efforts that continue to this day. These environmental calamities, as well as hazardous working conditions such as workers handling asbestos without protection, were part of the downside of the yard's record-setting wartime production.

Portsmouth's exploding population was not unique: boomtowns sprang up near shipyards, industrial sites, and military bases all across the United States. But unlike many that busted immediately after the war, Portsmouth managed to sustain the effects wrought by its stunning transformation from a region characterized by modest rural population growth and minimal industrial development to a bustling center. Having prospered and grown in many positive ways during the war, Portsmouth's leaders were determined their city would not boom and bust. Left heavily dependent on continued high postwar shipyard employment to preserve wartime gains, local leaders mounted a determined effort to save their shipyard as the war wound down, a scene successfully repeated numerous times since then.

Library shelves are full of history books exploring the role of New Hampshire and/or Portsmouth, especially during the colonial and early American periods. World War II home-front histories of the region, however, are surprisingly scarce. Among the books and sources that have been invaluable in providing information and background are Philip N. Guyol's quantitative and comprehensive *Democracy Fights: A History of New Hampshire in World War II* (1951);[2] Barbara McLean Ward's *Produce and Conserve, Share and Play Square: The Grocer and the Consumer on the Home-Front Battlefield during World War II* (1994), depicting day-to-day life in Portsmouth during the war;[3] the personal testimonies related in the documentary *World War II Homefront New Hampshire* (1994);[4] Harold Whitehouse's delightful anecdotal autobiography, *Home by Nine: The Real Story of Portsmouth's South End;*[5] and Jack P. Wysong's excellent history of the Portsmouth Harbor Defense System, *The World, Portsmouth, and the 22nd Coast Artillery: The War Years 1938–1948.*[6] This author's *32 in '44: Building the Portsmouth Submarine Fleet in World War II* (2011) is a study of the mobilization of Portsmouth Navy Yard.[7] However, all these works treat isolated aspects of Portsmouth's World War II experience, such as rationing or harbor defense, with little or no integration. Making use of considerable original research, this book builds on these subjects. More importantly, it introduces numerous previously unaddressed wartime Portsmouth topics — civil defense, economics, pollution, politics, skilled workers, women's contributions, infrastructure development, community activism, and the city's experience as a Navy liberty town — to provide a complete picture of Portsmouth's World War II experience.

Material presented in this book draws heavily from many archives and primary sources. Brief discussions of the five most valuable primary sources, listed below, may be found in the endnotes:

• *Portsmouth and National Defense* (1 August 1941) collects in one booklet a twelve-part series addressing anticipated changes due to mobilization that appeared in the *Portsmouth Herald* over the summer of 1941.[8]

• The lengthy *Survey of Health and Welfare in the Portsmouth Defense Area* (August 1943), coordinated by the New Hampshire State Planning and Development Commission, provides a snapshot of conditions existing in Portsmouth one and a half years into the war, from population change to health to recreation, and an outline of the perceived future needs of the city.[9]

• The Portsmouth War Records (1946–47), compiled immediately after the war in response to a state request that communities document their wartime experiences, provide fresh insights and timely recollections before they became outdated memories or secondhand accounts.[10]

• The Portsmouth Council of Defense Records, part of the Milne Special Collections at the University of New Hampshire Library, offer a detailed chronological and topical history of local civil defense, from blackout drills to the handling of unexploded bombs to the counting of casualties.[11]

• The front-page articles and editorials of the *Portsmouth Herald* (1939–46) lend a real-time appreciation to the facts, adding narrative, details, names, faces, editorial criticism, and subplots to the often-cold data of the other sources.

Collectively, the above sources provide a comprehensive picture of the evolving transformation of Portsmouth during the war.

This book is two narratives. The first half describes life in Portsmouth immediately before and during the war. It contrasts the calm of prewar Portsmouth with bustling wartime Portsmouth, emphasizing the shipyard mobilization, liberty town experience, harbor and civil defense, and a home front steeped in volunteerism and self-sacrifice. The last half of the book examines the consequences of the activities and events explored in the earlier chapters — in particular, booms in population, prosperity, infrastructure, pollution, skilled workers, and women's contributions to the workplace. The book closes with two important end-of-the-war developments: the election of a female Democratic mayor, Mary Dondero, after many years of male Republican rule; and the determined efforts of local officials to preserve the city's wartime gains by putting pressure on Washington and extracting promises to keep the shipyard open and well supplied with work. The dawn of female political leadership and this active community support of the shipyard were the precursors of practices that have served the city well in the postwar years. Throughout the book, Portsmouth's wartime experience is placed in context with concurrent state and national events, and juxtaposed with the experiences of other wartime boomtowns.

Mobilization is frequently presented as a straight-line event that kick-started American industry and won the war. However, mobilization was far more complex and multidirectional than that. Strong forces were set in motion, which did indeed win the war, but these forces also swept across the nation and reverberated through all levels of society. Lives and communities changed forever — some for the good, some for the worse. Portsmouth is one of the success stories.

CHAPTER I
PORTSMOUTH BEFORE THE WAR

> It is not strange that this district has become the
> main gateway for travelers in New England who
> seek the calm, the inspiration, and the beauty of its
> summers. . . . Nevertheless, we have often
> wondered why, with its strategic location,
> [Portsmouth] has not developed into a more
> populous center.
>
> Wallace Nutting
> *New Hampshire Beautiful, 1923*

Placid and picturesque, rather underdeveloped and seemingly in no rush to change things, prewar Portsmouth was the anchor of a region of rural farmland in southern Maine and along the brief New Hampshire seacoast. The area was a true American melting pot with conclaves of ethnic neighborhoods: Italian was the native tongue in Portsmouth's North End and French was as common as English in many nearby towns. Neighborhoods were well established and newcomers stood out. Considering the traditional staid New England mind-set — good fences make for good neighbors — the region did not appear to be a particularly welcoming environment for tens of thousands of immigrants looking for work at the shipyard. Nevertheless, it was.

Tourism had become an economic mainstay of the region, popular among summer visitors attracted to its beaches, boating waterways, and resort hotels; farming and employment at the navy yard were the other primary sources of income. Lacking skilled workers, the area had not been able to attract much industry — a circumstance that somewhat tempered the local effects of the Great Depression, which were far more severe for families living in urban and industrialized communities. Despite rising tensions and disturbing news from abroad, locally there was strong public sentiment for neutrality, similar to the mood that prevailed across most of the nation. War was a distant concern, but gradually creeping closer. A relative calm prevailed; life was good.

The Calm

The coming upheaval was all the more dramatic given the many years of stability and normalcy that preceded World War II. Portsmouth and the seacoast communities of New Hampshire and southern Maine prospered during the late nineteenth and early twentieth centuries when Victorian beach resorts attracted hordes of summer-by-the-sea vacationers. New Castle's Wentworth Hotel, built in 1873, and other grand resort hotels at Rye Beach, Hampton Beach, York Beach, and elsewhere filled with tourists as soon as the weather warmed each season. A photo of Hampton Beach's 1915 Carnival Week (photo 1) depicts the congested confusion that reigned as visitors flooded in from Boston and other cities, swelling the population of the seacoast resort towns. For a change of pace, vacationers could take convenient trolleys from the beaches straight into Portsmouth, where the shops tempted them with attractive wares. Wallace Nutting's *New Hampshire Beautiful* (1923) described why tourists found Portsmouth so appealing:

It is not strange that this district has become the

13

main gateway for travelers in New England who seek the calm, the inspiration, and the beauty of its summers. . . . Portsmouth itself has appealed to us as the most pleasing of all small shore cities. . . . To those who love at once the old and picturesque together with some signs that Americans are not dead, Portsmouth appeals strongly. . . . It may be as well that Portsmouth is no larger. Nevertheless, we have often wondered why, with its strategic location, it has not developed into a more populous center.[1]

Although certainly no metropolis in 1923, the Portsmouth area had experienced a modest population bump during World War I, which leveled out between 1920 and 1940 (ultimately peaking during World War II; see figure 1).[2] This

Photo 1: Postcard of Carnival Week at Hampton Beach (1915).
Courtesy Hampton Historical Society, Hampton, NH.

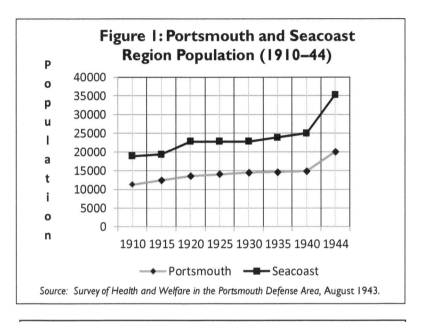

Figure 1: Portsmouth and Seacoast Region Population (1910–44)

Source: Survey of Health and Welfare in the Portsmouth Defense Area, August 1943.

Table 1: Portsmouth Area Urban versus Rural Population Distribution (1930 & 1940)			
	1930	1940	% Increase
Urban (Portsmouth)	14,495	14,521	1.8%
Rural Farms	1,201	1,701	41.6%
Rural Non-farms	9,513	11,755	19.1%
Total	25,209	27,977	

Source: Survey of Health and Welfare in the Portsmouth Defense Area, August 1943

bump was primarily the result of a boost in Portsmouth Navy Yard employment, which grew from 1,450 in 1916 to 5,500 in 1918, and the startup of two other shipyards, Atlantic Corporation Shipyard and Shattuck Shipyard.[3] Between 1930 and 1940, however, the region's rural character reasserted itself: urban Portsmouth barely grew at all, while there was a spike in the population on farms and a significant increase in rural non-farming communities as well (see table 1).[4] Immediately prior to World War II, the few arriving

Photo 2: Farm field between Spinney Road and Islington Street (circa 1910–30). It is unknown why the African-American workers are so well dressed. Courtesy Portsmouth Athenaeum.

newcomers were settling in rural communities rather than Portsmouth proper. This reflected the trend throughout New Hampshire: the rural population of the state climbed from 41.3 percent of the total population in 1930 to 42.4 percent in 1940, while industrialization languished.[5]

The rather bucolic nature of even the city itself is evident in the recollections of those who lived there. Don Ricklefs, born at the old Portsmouth Hospital in 1918, grew up in the Plains neighborhood, less than a mile from North Church and Market Square in the city center. Yet his memories of growing up between the wars are primarily rural, of "a happy childhood; hunting rabbit, fishing and swimming, picking blueberries and going to school." [6] He attended Plains School—a one-room schoolhouse. His grandparents lived in a house on Middle Street, a working farm at the time.

Louise Flynn-McGee is another with "happy and carefree" childhood memories of growing up between the wars on Portsmouth's Maplewood Avenue. In 1904, her grandmother bought a 65-acre parcel of land when the Frank Jones estate was divided into three parts and sold off; Flynn-McGee spent most of her life living on that land in one spot or another. Interviewed by Tammi Truax for the *Portsmouth Herald* in 2007, Flynn-McGee offered details of a relaxed, almost rustic existence. According to Truax, "She and her brother grew up in the old farmhouse that still stands on Maplewood Avenue though then it was a working farm with a huge barn that is gone, and was surrounded by undeveloped land . . . [which] served as a site for Audubon walks where people could come see blue heron and egrets in their natural habitat."[7]

The American Guide Series *New Hampshire: A Guide to the Granite State* (1938) spoke to Portsmouth's lack of industry and harbor traffic as war clouds were gathering in Europe:

> Apart from the Navy yard, Portsmouth is not an industrial city. . . . Popular as a resort, the city doubles its population each summer. . . . This influx of summer visitors adds to the prosperity of the city, which even in winter is the shopping center for a large area. . . . The port . . . is occupied now only by an occasional naval vessel, small yachts, or a barge bringing in gypsum and taking out scrap iron. Portsmouth still hopes that it will again become a busy harbor.[8]

In the late 1930s, Portsmouth remained a nonindustrial tourist destination with an underutilized harbor. Things were about to change.

Less than a month before the attack on Pearl Harbor in 1941, Frederick D. Gardner, chair of Portsmouth's finance committee and a member of the city planning board, reiterated the "city's long-time modus operandi of making a living off past glories, the navy yard, and summer tourists." Gardner wrote, "Since the passing of our heyday as a shipping center, shortly after privateers went out of business following the war of 1812, we have dozed rather peacefully, with the exception of a slight disturbance during World War I, dreaming of the glories of the past and in fact publicizing our landmarks of the past to attract tourists in the summertime. After we caught them, then we damned them for blocking traffic all summer, then heaved a sigh of relief when we got rid of them so we could go back to making a living off the navy yard workers until another summer rolled around." Local residents of today might argue that little has changed since then: Portsmouth residents still highlight past glories to attract summer tourists, who are damned for causing traffic jams that annoy year-round residents, and the shipyard continues to be the economic engine that drives the local economy.[9]

Occasional prewar initiatives to promote industrialization met with little success. In an effort to stimulate interest in bringing new industries to Portsmouth, the front page of the 2 September 1939 *Portsmouth Herald* announced the formation of the Portsmouth Industrial Association. According to the article, "The lack of diversified industries in our city has been felt by everyone with business interests for some time."[10] One week later, an editorial condemned a lack of public support for the new association and noted a "much too prevalent feeling of smug, complacent self-satisfaction as far as community problems are concerned."[11] The *Herald* article accused community leaders of possessing a "defeatist attitude, inertia, and lethargic do-nothingness which has sounded the death knell of the Chamber of Commerce, civic development, [and] industrial progressiveness."[12] In the fall of 1939, there was no groundswell of public support for increased industrialization, let alone for a behemoth shipyard in their backyard. Residents were apparently happy with the status quo.

Photo 3: Aerial view of Portsmouth suburbs (1948), showing the outskirts of the city to be open fields and farmland. Memorial Bridge to Kittery is in upper right corner. Courtesy Portsmouth Athenaeum.

Meanwhile, the small navy yard across the river had become part of the economic and social fabric of the region. *New Hampshire: A Guide to the Granite State* (1938) noted:

> The United States Navy yard, possessor of a stirring history, is the backbone of modern Portsmouth. . . . The Navy yard contributes much to the town, both financially and socially. The naval families are a distinct section of the population, and their presence adds much to the gaiety of the city. Balls and entertainments in the best naval tradition attract many of the townspeople and give the city a sophisticated air not common in New Hampshire. The sailors have their moments as in any seaboard town, and *occasionally too-happy hedonists are escorted to their quarters by naval police* [emphasis added].[13]

In the not-too-distant future, the streets of downtown Portsmouth would be flooded with more "too-happy hedonists" than the local bars and law enforcement officers could handle.

A 30 December 1939 *Portsmouth Herald* editorial took inventory of recent local events and anticipated the next year with confident optimism. Enthusiastic about the growing shipyard employment, the editorial pushed again for the new industry that had met with lukewarm support a few months earlier: "We have had a most excellent 1939 as a whole. The stores report excellent business during the Christmas season. The prospects for work at the navy yard are as bright if not brighter than a year ago. There are more men working there now than at any time since the close of the [First] World War." The editorial continued, "The possibilities for new industries seem bright, and more industries mean more people living in this city which means more business for the merchants. . . . Who knows what the new year may bring? We cannot tell, but we can be ready for whatever may benefit the community as a whole. . . . The turbulent 30s are passing and we are entering the 40s. We welcome the new-year that marks the beginning of a new decade."[14] Things were unraveling in Europe in December 1939, but locally business was improving, employment was up, and there was hope for attracting limited new industry and workers to the city. Things were calm and the future looked bright. Assuming the city's newspaper accurately reflected the mood and attitude of the local residents, neither had a clue about what 1940 would bring.

What it brought was massive mobilization when Congress passed the nation's largest-ever naval appropriations bill in June 1940 — and much of that money started flowing toward Portsmouth Navy Yard. It was followed the next month by another bill four times larger than the previous one, and hundreds of millions of defense dollars surged toward the local navy yard. Neutrality was on the way out and the military's presence in the region was burgeoning. Hundreds of young sailors were reporting to the navy yard to join their new submarines. Soldiers began arriving to staff the revived harbor fortifications. The war drums were beating louder; the calm was gone.

Neutrality Fades

A series of five Neutrality Acts between 1935 and 1939 sought to distance the United States from entangling events in Europe that might lead to another war. These acts had their roots in the public's lingering dissatisfaction with the outcome of the last war. Mobilization historian Maury Klein wrote, "The bitter, wholly unsatisfying outcome of that

Photo 4: Portsmouth Market Square (circa 1939/40).
Courtesy Thom Hindle Collection.

experience [the post–World War I recession] deeply scarred the memories of that generation, many of whom were leaders in every field of American life by 1939. Many, if not all of them wanted no more of war, bailing out Europe from its eternal conflicts, or 'blood profits' for bankers and munitions makers."[15] The nation's ugly experience with the last war clouded every discussion about preparations for the next one; Portsmouth was no exception. Daily during the late 1930s, the editorial page of the *Portsmouth Herald* boldly proclaimed a three-point platform, the first point of which was "Keep the United States of America out of War." Representative Styles Bridges (R-NH), and many of his constituents, strongly shared that antiwar view. Bridges believed the surest way to keep the peace was to mind our own business.[16] President Franklin D. Roosevelt gradually made the Allies' business our business, to the dismay of Bridges and others.

This isolationist stance began to shift in the fall of 1940

when Congress enacted the Selective Service and Training Act, much to the dismay of partisans of neutrality, requiring sixteen million American men between the ages of twenty-one and thirty-six to register for a lottery for military service. This was the first time the government had drafted men during peacetime. A draft had become necessary because few volunteers came forward in June 1940 when Congress initially raised the Army's personnel quota to 375,000 men. At the time, the U.S. Army ranked eighteenth in the world with barely 250,000 men, trailing such military powers as Spain, Portugal, Holland, and Belgium, and lagging far behind Germany's army of six million to eight million highly trained and well-equipped soldiers. The ranks of the U.S. Army urgently needed to be increased; the draft was the reluctant answer.[17]

The draft boards exempted the physically unfit, deferred agricultural and industrial workers engaged in vital defense jobs, and exempted conscientious objectors from combat duty. The boards found nearly half the men who reported unfit for military duty. According to Klein, "The main reasons included bad teeth (20.9 percent), poor eyesight (13.7 percent), heart and circulatory problems (10.6 percent), and venereal diseases (6.3 percent). Another 10 percent failed to measure up to fourth-grade educational standards."[18] Those "fortunate to qualify" enlisted for just one year, meaning their discharges would occur in the fall of 1941 — as it turned out, just months before the attack on Pearl Harbor.[19] The timing was not good. The attack brought an urgent need for more draftees and the immediate relaxation of the standards. The relaxation of standards never reached some men, such as Harold Whitehouse's father, who, with six children and an essential job at the shipyard, remained exempt from the draft for the entire war.[20]

In late 1940 and into 1941, however, strong sentiments for

neutrality and isolationism persisted until there was no other choice. In January 1941, with Great Britain under heavy bombardment, a poll conducted by the *Portsmouth Herald* showed that 32 percent of the readers favored no help at all for Britain, 18 percent favored limited help short of war, 28 percent favored all help short of war, and 22 percent favored all help possibly including war.[21] The poll followed an FDR fireside chat in late December during which he voiced strong support for Great Britain. Contrary to the president's convictions, and with war seemingly inevitable, fully 78 percent of the local citizenry wanted no part of helping Great Britain if it might lead to war. Portsmouth was not an anomaly: most of the nation held similar views.

Despite the rejection of direct military involvement, citizens were beginning to show concern and support for the British people through the Bundles for Britain program. This initiative, founded by Mrs. Walls Latham on 15 January 1940 in New York City, organized women to make bandages, sew and knit a variety of clothing, and collect used clothing and other needed items for residents of war-torn England. A local Hampton chapter began to meet weekly in January 1941 for sewing parties and fund-raising events.[22] One year later, with the war under way, the organization became Bundles for America, and the volunteers began shipping their sewing products to service members.

Meanwhile, in the summer of 1941, proposed enlistment extensions roused the ire of the isolationists, who were outraged at the idea of breaking promises to the draftees. The House of Representatives, reflecting these sentiments, barely passed the bill in August 1941 by a cliffhanger vote of 203–202.[23] The bill passed the Senate and FDR endorsed it, prolonging enlistment terms from twelve to thirty months. Had the bill not passed, the release of some 987,000 draftees would have cut the Army's manpower by 50 percent at a time when the Axis's armies were on the move through Europe — and just three months before Pearl Harbor. Congress, which had already authorized billions of dollars for defense, remained highly reluctant about committing soldiers to more than twelve months of service.

This was not the first time FDR had run afoul of the isolationists. For the past year he had been seeking ways to aid Great Britain. He did so very carefully, not wanting to risk the ire of Congress or jeopardize his third campaign for the presidency. His decision to escort Allied transatlantic convoys in the summer of 1940 had drawn some criticism. A few months later, on 2 September 1940, he took a bolder step when he bypassed Congress and ordered, on his own executive authority, the delivery of fifty surplus destroyers to Great Britain in exchange for naval bases in Newfoundland and Bermuda and ninety-nine-year leases on additional bases in the British West Indies. The destroyers were, however, "less seaworthy than expected" and "by the end of the year only nine of the promised fifty had reached Britain."[24] Despite its reputation as a submarine-only yard, Portsmouth contributed in at least one small way to the refurbishment of the destroyers bound for Great Britain. In January 1941, the yard shipped fifty nozzles to Philadelphia Navy Yard for the "destroyers 'turned over' to Great Britain" to fulfill a request from the British Purchasing Commission.[25] A few months later, the yard provided much more impressive support when British submarines began arriving at the shipyard for overhaul under the Lend-Lease program.

Lend-Lease Comes to Portsmouth

FDR, more confident about gaining congressional support for aid to the Allies after his reelection in November 1940, announced in his annual message to Congress on 6 January

1941 that he was preparing a Lend-Lease Bill with the intent of making the United States the great arsenal of democracy. The bill provided the Allies with the support needed to continue the fight against the Axis—FDR's response to Churchill's urgent request for "an immense and continuous supply of war materials and technical apparatus of all kinds."[26] Previously, trade with the Allies had been on a cash-and-carry basis, with "carrying" being done by the purchaser's ships. Lend-Lease authorized the president "to sell, transfer, exchange, lend, lease, or otherwise dispose of arms and other equipment and supplies to any country whose defense the president deems vital to the defense of the United States."[27] Congress passed the bill on 11 March 1941 and later expanded it to include provisions for the overhaul of British ships in United States shipyards. Portsmouth Navy Yard was one of those shipyards.

Lend-Lease marked the end of the gradual erosion of the Neutrality Acts of the 1930s, as well as a point of no return for the United States. Initially funded to $7 billion, the commitment would grow to $50 billion: $32 billion went to Great Britain, $11 billion to the Soviet Union, $3 billion to France, and $1.5 billion to China. FDR argued that Lend-Lease was akin to loaning your neighbor your garden hose when his house was on fire. FDR added, "I don't want $15 — I want my garden hose back after the fire is over."[28] Senator Robert Taft (R-OH) was less certain of reciprocity. He said, "Lending war material is much like lending chewing gum. We certainly do not want the same gum back."[29] Taft's analogy was the more accurate one.

On 18 March 1941, one week after Congress passed the Lend-Lease Act, the *Portsmouth Herald*, in a major departure from its longtime commitment to neutrality, replaced the antiwar plank in its platform with one calling for "a united effort in behalf of the Democratic nations to win the war and establish a just and lasting peace."[30] Referring to a recent address in which FDR called for a total victory, the newspaper reported, "After serious reflection, we sadly have realized that, on Saturday last, President Roosevelt delivered the funeral oration on the number one plank in our platform and with sincere regret it is herewith buried." A sketch of an R.I.P. tombstone drove home the point. The editorial continued, "By implication, if not by his actual words, the president declared war without benefit of Congress and in surroundings hardly befitting such a serious occasion. There was no specific statement that our Army and Navy would be sent to battle, but it is obvious that if they are required to achieve the total victory for which the president calls they will be used. That is only a matter of time. The dice are thrown. The hand has been put to the ploughshare. There is no sense in thinking of what might have been. This is total war and we are in it."[31] FDR's efforts to reverse the nation's antiwar sentiment had reached Portsmouth, New Hampshire.

On 27 May 1941, the *Herald's* editor took the next step and demanded an end to the neutrality deception the president's administration had been practicing: "This is War. Anyone who had a last lingering doubt about the future course of the United States should have it no longer. Our course is clear. . . Let us no longer be deceived by words—by leases that are more than leases; by lending that is more than lending; by patrols that are more than patrols; and in this speech by an 'unlimited emergency' that is actually war."[32] With those words, the *Herald* summarized well U.S. foreign policy for the first half of 1941. Lend-Lease, which had moved the nation much closer to war, had also moved British submarines much closer to the Portsmouth shipyard.

Lend-Lease originally targeted arms, ammunition, foodstuffs, and other supplies for shipment to the Allies. In

March 1941, FDR extended Lend-Lease to include the repair of British vessels in American shipyards.[33] Immediately after the announcement, the local newspaper speculated, "The new $3,000,000 dry dock to be built at the Portsmouth Navy Yard might at some future date be used for repairs to British or other Allied destroyers. . . . [It] has been rumored in Portsmouth ever since the announcement of the construction was reported."[34] The rumors were partially correct. British warships—not destroyers, but submarines—would soon be overhauled at Portsmouth. In early May 1941, the yard received notice from the chief of naval operations that a British submarine "will arrive the latter part of May and will enjoy a priority ahead of new construction."[35] Not only had Lend-Lease been extended to the repair of British submarines, the repairs would take precedence over the orders the yard had recently received for fourteen new submarines. During the last half of 1941, higher-priority repairs to British submarines delayed the yard's production ramp-up for the new construction.

Despite the expansion of Lend-Lease, there were limits. Following guidance from the secretary of the Navy, the Bureau of Ships advised the commandants of navy yards that items not normally provided to our own vessels were not to be supplied to foreign vessels using Lend-Lease funds. This had particular application to foodstuff for officers' messes. A Bureau of Ships letter of 18 August 1941 stipulated, "In view of the fact that United States naval officers pay for the food used in their messes, it is considered improper to accept charges against Lend-Lease funds for furnishing food for the officers of the visiting British naval vessels."[36] Had it not been for this monumental decision, the final $50 billion price tag for Lend-Lease would have been a few dollars higher.

Starting in late May of 1941 and continuing through the rest of the year, three British submarines, HMS *Truant*,

Pandora, and *Parthian*, and one Free French submarine, *Surcouf*, were overhauled at Portsmouth Navy Yard.[37] The *Surcouf*, which had escaped to Britain when France fell, was operating under British control. Repairs to all four fell under the auspices of the British Advisory Repair Mission, located in Washington, DC. Curiously, no mention of the British submarines appeared in the *Portsmouth Herald* until 21 September 1941. On that date, a front-page article with a Washington dateline revealed that United States shipyards were currently repairing more than a dozen British ships, including the British submarine HMS *Pandora* in Portsmouth. An editor's note indicated, "This has been common knowledge in Portsmouth for many weeks, but the *Portsmouth Herald*, in co-operation with the Navy Department's request, has refrained from publishing it." Neither the *Portsmouth Herald* article nor the press release from Washington mentioned the *Surcouf*, which was also in Portsmouth at the time. If the *Pandora*'s stay at the shipyard had been "common knowledge," the *Surcouf*'s visit must have been even more obvious: it was the world's largest submarine at the time,[38] with a displacement of four thousand tons, two eight-inch guns, an airplane, and "more decks than the average city hotel has floors."[39] More than twice the displacement of the fleet-type submarines built at the navy yard at the time, the *Surcouf* could hardly have transited up the narrow confines of the Piscataqua River to the shipyard unnoticed. Yet the Free French submarine was at the yard for several weeks before the press mentioned it, and then only after authorization by the U.S. Navy. Such was the world of secrecy and intrigue that surrounded events at Portsmouth Navy Yard in the fall of 1941.

The nation may have been embracing the Allies in late October 1941, but it was still not about to go to war. The bloodless exchange of fire between a German U-boat and the destroyer USS *Greer* in early September 1941 heightened tensions, but did not provoke war. Neither did the U-boat attack on the USS *Kearny* a month later, which killed eleven sailors. The 30 October 1941 sinking of the USS *Reuben James* by a German U-boat, killing more than one hundred Americans, pushed FDR and the nation to the brink of war — but no further. What would it take? Two factors were delaying the inevitable: 1) Germany was reluctant to start a war with the United States because her invasion of Russia was not going well on the eastern front, and the last thing she needed was another war on the western front; and 2) the United States was determined to avoid war at all costs short of an outright attack or invasion. Meanwhile, British submarines were transiting in and out of Portsmouth Harbor and the Japanese were eyeing Pearl Harbor.

A 24 June 1941 *Portsmouth Herald* editorial, "The Portsmouth of Tomorrow," presented a vision for the city that included "moderate industrialization . . . highways with dividing strips and no left turns . . . banishment of the unsightly clutter of billboards . . . restriction of business development to designated sites . . . increased happiness-giving recreation . . . many small, inexpensive, yet solid and attractively-designed homes, each with its plot of land . . . many small private industries, utilizing the products of nearby farms in new ways."[40] Nowhere was there any mention of a shipyard that was about to expand fourfold and spark a population boom that would lead to frantic housing construction and massive infrastructure development. In mid-1941, given their preference, Portsmouth's leaders apparently would have chosen a less chaotic path for the future of their city than that which emerged during World War II.

By late 1941, all pretense of neutrality had disappeared and mobilization was well under way at the navy yard.

Thousands of new employees were being hired, millions of defense dollars had found their way to the yard, and scores of American sailors were arriving weekly to crew the newly constructed submarines. These sailors were mixing in downtown Portsmouth with British and French sailors, an influx of Army personnel delegated to operate the harbor defense forts, and marines assigned to the shipyard. Local bars were buzzing with action; a tempest was brewing on the streets of Portsmouth.

The British crews were mixing with more than other servicemen. On 23 September 1941, the marriage of a local girl, Mercie Tarbell Clay, to Lieutenant Lyndon Walford of the HMS *Pandora* received considerable press coverage, including a picture of four *Pandora* sailors rope-pulling an open automobile holding the newlyweds. The picture caption, "It's an Old British Custom," explained that, lacking a horse and buggy, the sailors were doing their best to uphold a British tradition of transporting the couple in a formal and dignified manner from the church—St. John's Episcopal Church in Portsmouth.[41] As it turned out, pulling the car was safer than riding in it for the *Pandora* sailors. While returning from the wedding reception in New Castle later that day, six of them were injured in an automobile accident. The "convertible sports coup was badly smashed" when the operator, a *Pandora* sailor, lost control after crossing the New Castle bridge and skidded nearly 150 feet before hitting a tree. A local hospital treated the injured for various lacerations and bruises before releasing them.[42] The Lend-Lease program, and the *Pandora* wedding party, were alive and well in Portsmouth.

Throughout the punishing, drawn-out Battle of Britain, as the bombardment begun in mid-1940 became known, Winston Churchill urgently pressed Roosevelt for help and sought the United States's involvement in the war. FDR was willing but cautious, given the prevailing antiwar sentiment. The latter half of 1940 and most of 1941 saw the nation slowly drawn into Churchill's camp through evolving commitments. As seacoast residents watched British submarines navigate the Piscataqua River in the summer of 1941, it had to be obvious that there was not much more the nation could do to aid the Allies short of outright confrontation and hostilities.

While local concerns about the threat of an approaching war mounted, local teenagers were typically much more oblivious. Harold Whitehouse wrote, "In the eighth grade, we took a subject called geography. We were shown where Poland and Czechoslovakia were and brought up to date on what Germany was doing. We knew the Germans invaded Czechoslovakia, and we knew what the Nazis were. We followed it fairly close, but all us kids figured it was so far away. We'd look at the globe and turned it around to see where the United States was at the farther end of the world, and it wasn't of much interest to us."[43] With his parents not home on December 7, the interruption of his favorite radio program, *The Shadow*, was more an annoyance for Whitehouse and his brother than an alert. "I kept moving the dial to another station to see if we could get the program again. . . . We didn't even know where Pearl Harbor was or what the issue was," Whitehouse wrote. He quickly learned what the issues were when his parents got home. "It was very, very quiet at dinner. . . . It was from then on that everybody talked about the war and the war effort and everybody became very patriotic."[44] Any youthful innocence and naiveté about global events evaporated in many homes in a matter of hours.

Pearl Harbor ended all ambivalence. Overnight, people's

attitudes shifted from cautious optimism about the possibility of avoiding war to the stark realization that they were in one. There were many questions: What next? Where do we go from here? How do we get there? In his essay "Home Front," James W. Wensyel described how the attack instantly caused the nation to unite in purpose and turn to FDR for guidance: "Following news of the attack, Americans from Maine to Oregon waited for President Roosevelt to speak. Party affiliation and political philosophy no longer mattered. He was the president, and all Americans looked to their chief executive (and trusted him) to lead the nation in this time of crisis. In Washington, DC, hundreds instinctively walked to the White House, where FDR was meeting with his Cabinet. Standing quietly before the darkened Executive Mansion, they began to sing, softly at first but then more strongly, 'God Bless America' and other patriotic songs."[45] Shortly after noon on 8 December, in an address to a joint session of Congress and the nation, FDR condemned the Japanese attack and requested an immediate declaration of war.

The Senate complied, voting eighty-two to zero for war against Japan. The House of Representatives concurred, with one exception: Congresswoman Jeannette Rankin of Montana voted against war. Rankin, the first female member of the House of Representatives, had also voted against war with Germany in 1917, making her the only member of Congress to vote against both World War I and World War II. Republican efforts "to change her mind to make the vote unanimous were unsuccessful."[46] (Rankin, elected in 1916 in a state where women already had suffrage, also had the unusual distinction of being the only woman to vote in favor of giving women the right to vote when she supported the passage of the Nineteenth Amendment in 1919; she served a single term, then was returned to Congress in 1940 for one more term.) With Rankin's one disapproving vote, Congress declared war on Japan; Germany and Italy declared war against the United States three days later. The waiting was over. The country was at war.

According to Eileen Dondero Foley, who was a young woman at the start of the war, Pearl Harbor immediately changed the city. As she recalled, "There were buses on the square at six o'clock. There were three shifts. Everybody was everywhere. Business was booming. . . . Men came in from everywhere. . . . We had all the branches of the military here. The USO was booming. . . . It was a complete military city."[47] The transformation of Portsmouth and nearby communities had begun. Portsmouth was bustling with strangers and servicemen, large construction projects were under way at the yard, and all of a sudden there were no housing vacancies in the area. Where would it all lead? How would the city adjust to accommodate the hordes of workers flocking to the area? In a newly chaotic world, there was only one certainty: the calm scene that had prevailed since the early 1920s was gone forever.

CHAPTER 2
NAVY YARD MOBILIZATION

The enemy has struck a savage, treacherous blow.
We are at war, all of us: there is no time now for
disputes or delay of any kind. We must have ships
and more ships, guns and more guns, men and more
men—faster and faster. There is no time to lose.
The navy must lead the way. Speed up—it is our
navy and your nation.

Secretary of the Navy Frank Knox
11 December 1941

E ven as the urgency and pace of work ratcheted up at the shipyard, few could have foreseen the nearly miraculous transformation that mobilization was to bring about. Portsmouth, the nation's smallest navy yard, had constructed on average fewer than two submarines a year during the 1930s—yet by the end of the war, it would have produced some seventy-nine submarines, including thirty-two in the year 1944 alone, an astonishing clip never matched before or since by any other shipyard. The cover of the program for a 13 May 1944 state music festival held in Portsmouth by no means overstated the case when it proudly proclaimed, "Portsmouth Built Submarines are Winning the War."[1]

The dramatic spikes in production and shipyard employment visible in Figure 2 certainly suggest that something extraordinary happened at the yard during World War II. In fact, thanks to innovation, leadership, and various other factors, the Portsmouth Navy Yard was perfectly

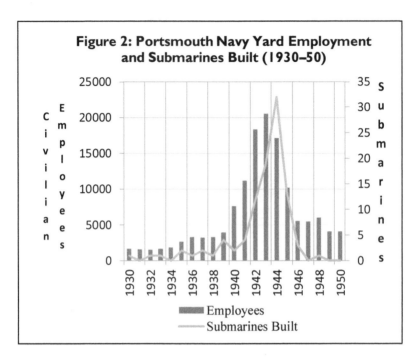

Figure 2: Portsmouth Navy Yard Employment and Submarines Built (1930–50)

poised to rise to the challenge of the war. (For a comprehensive analysis of events at the yard during the war, see the author's *32 in '44: Building the Portsmouth Submarine Fleet in World War II* (2011).[2])

Portsmouth's wartime production was part of a nationwide mobilization phenomenon. According to home-front historian James Wensyel, "By the end of the war, Americans had produced a staggering total of almost 300,000 planes, 87,000 ships and landing craft, more than 100,000 tanks and self-propelled guns, 47 million tons of artillery shells, and 44 billion rounds of small-arms ammunition."[3] These mind-boggling numbers dwarf the 79 submarines built by the yard—but the role those submarines played in winning the war was second to none. Portsmouth-built submarines sank 434 Japanese ships, totaling 1.7 million tons, about one-third of the Japanese tonnage sunk by United States submarines.[4] The nation's smallest navy yard came up big; few industrial facilities made more important contributions to winning World War II than Portsmouth Navy Yard.

Another shipyard that rose to the challenge was Henry J. Kaiser's new facility in Richmond, California, which produced Liberty ships at phenomenal rates. In 1941, it took eight months to produce a Liberty ship. Within two years, Wensyel notes, "Kaiser cut that time to fourteen days. A record time was set when workers at his Richmond, California, plant assembled the *Robert E. Peary* in less than five days." During its first year, Henry Ford's Willow Run plant produced only one B-24 bomber a day. By 1944, however, "streamlining increased production to one bomber

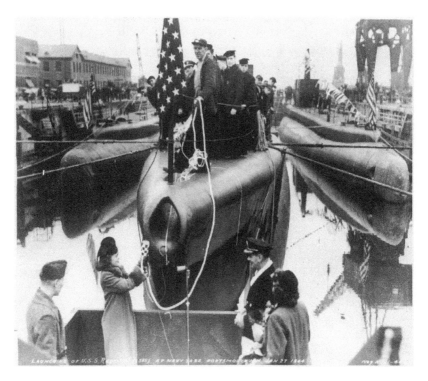

Photo 5: *Simultaneous triple launching of* Redfish, Ronquil, and Razorback *(1944). Courtesy Milne Special Collections and Archives, University of New Hampshire Library, Durham, NH.*

every sixty-three minutes. By war's end, 8,685 planes had rolled off the Willow Run assembly line." Like Portsmouth Navy Yard, these two facilities achieved unprecedented, if not unimaginable, production rates of critically needed war machines. [5]

On 27 January 1944, Portsmouth Navy Yard achieved two things no other shipyard ever had: it launched three submarines simultaneously, and it launched a fourth on the same day. *Ronquil, Redfish,* and *Razorback* lifted off their blocks in Dry Dock #1 at 1 p.m. (photo 5) and a few hours later the *Scabbardfish* slid down Building Way #4 into the Piscataqua River.[6] A congratulatory message from Secretary of the Navy Frank Knox acknowledged the feat: "In the launching of four submarines in a single day, the Portsmouth Navy Yard sets another record in the submarine program."[7] These four were among the record-setting thirty-two submarines the yard completed in 1944.[8]

The yard's performance is particularly impressive compared to its competitors (see table 2).[9] Portsmouth submarines spent much less time on building sites prior to launching and subsequently completed much sooner than

Table 2: Submarine Shipyard Schedule Performance (World War II)				
Shipyard	**Subs Built 1940–45**	**No. Bldg Sites 1941 1945**	**Shortest Bldg Pd**	**Shortest Time on Bldg Sites**
Portsmouth	79	5 9	173 days	56 days
Electric Boat	78	11 21	317 days	est. 8 mos.
Mare Island	17	2 8	273 days	192 days
Manitowoc	28	Side Launches	269 days	117 days

Sources: There are several sources for this table: 1) for Portsmouth, *32 in '44: Building the Portsmouth Submarine Fleet in World War II*; 2) for Electric Boat, John D. Horn, *Submarines and the Electric Boat Company*, Page V-3, Navy Department Library, Naval Historical Center, Washington, DC; and 3) for Mare Island and Manitowac, both *United States Naval Administration in World War II, Bureau of Ships*, 1946, Navy Department Library, Naval Historical Center, Washington, DC, 635–37, and David Randall Hinkle, editor-in-chief, *United States Submarines* (Annandale: Navy Submarine League, 2002), 11415.

those of its competitors. One Portsmouth-built submarine launched into the Piscataqua River just 56 days after its keel was laid and another required only 173 days to complete and be delivered to the fleet. No other submarine building yard came close to either of these accomplishments.

Figure 3, showing the construction time from keel laying to completion for all U.S. submarines built during the war, further highlights Portsmouth's outstanding performance. As can be seen from the dominance of green (Portsmouth's submarines) at the bottom of the chart, Portsmouth built almost all of the fifty most quickly delivered submarines. In addition, when compared to its competitors, the yard

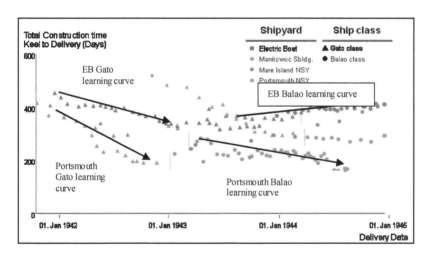

Figure 3: Construction Times for All U.S. Submarines Built during World War II. *Source* : Boston Consulting Group.

displayed steeper learning curves (*i.e.*, shorter construction times for follow-on submarines of the same class) for both the *Gato-* and *Balao*-class submarines, meaning Portsmouth continuously improved its processes and performance. The chart also reveals that Portsmouth delivered its first *Balao*-class submarine, which was greatly advanced over its *Gato* cousins, one year earlier (first green dot, January 1943) than the Electric Boat Company (first red dot, January 1944). This superior, deeper-diving submarine was a welcome addition to the Pacific Submarine Fleet. All of this is convincing evidence that Portsmouth Navy Yard was the premier builder of submarines for the U.S. Navy during World War II.

Success Factors

The war created an overarching crisis-filled environment that rallied yard employees and management to the common objective of increased production to defeat the enemy. But how much of the shipyard's success was due purely to the stimulation of war? Undoubtedly, the threat of war heightens an individual's performance, and twenty thousand heightened performances can produce extraordinary results. But there were a number of other, more definable factors that contributed to the yard's success.

Favored Between the Wars. Like so many "overnight" successes, Portsmouth's phenomenal performance actually rested on foundations that had been laid years, even decades earlier. Considerable expertise in submarine design and construction existed at the yard at the start of the war as the result of preferential treatment given it by the Navy Department during the 1920s and 1930s. Dissatisfied with its submarine acquisition process during World War I, the Navy sought to develop Portsmouth as an alternative to private shipyards for the design and construction of submarines. During the early years of submarine development, private builders Electric Boat Company and Lake Torpedo Company controlled the design of submarines with little or no input solicited — or accepted — from the Navy. According to naval historian Gary Weir, "The relationship between private shipbuilders and the navy before 1914 was essentially that of vendor and customer in the classic sense."[10] This situation continued during World War I. Many thought the motivations of private shipbuilders during the war had more to do with profiteering than providing the fleet with the submarines it needed.[11] In addition, the fleet wanted to define the operating capabilities and technologies designed into its submarines instead of buying a product that happened to be on the shelf. In short, the Navy believed it was paying too much for an inferior and ill-designed product.

Captain Andrew McKee, planning officer at Portsmouth during World War II, wrote an article in 1945 for the Society of Naval Engineers and Marine Architects in which he described the process the Navy used to wrest control of submarine design from the private yards. According to McKee, the Navy introduced Portsmouth to submarine construction in 1914 with a contract to build L-8 to the design of the Lake Torpedo Company, followed by a contract to build O-1 to the Electric Boat design in 1916. Once Portsmouth had gained experience with both competitors' designs, the Navy set up a design competition among the three shipyards: S-1 was assigned to Electric Boat, S-2 to Lake Torpedo Company, and S-3 to Portsmouth Navy Yard. Not surprisingly, the Navy preferred the Portsmouth design. Consequently, Electric Boat received no submarine orders during the 1920s, and Lake Torpedo Company folded in 1924 for lack of work. Meanwhile, the Navy strengthened Portsmouth's submarine design and new construction capabilities. Notes McKee, "For fourteen years, from 1919 until 1933, all the submarines ordered, and there were only nine . . . were built to plans prepared by Portsmouth." While Portsmouth's team had limited submarine design opportunities in the 1920s, Electric Boat and other yards had no opportunities at all.[12]

According to the Bureau of Ships' World War II self-history, "At one time or another during the period after World War I new construction disappeared from every navy yard except Portsmouth."[13] Unlike their counterparts at other navy yards, Portsmouth's naval architects, marine engineers, and experienced managers continued their employment despite a budget that was severely constrained by economic depression, politics, and foreign policy. Portsmouth not only survived, but also improved its design and production capabilities between the wars. As a result, the yard was more ready than most shipyards for the industrial mobilization galvanized by World War II.

Development of Sectional Construction. Submarine construction languished between the wars, thanks to

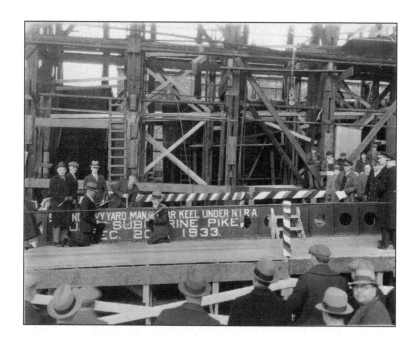

Photo 6: Keel laying for NIRA submarine USS Pike *(20 December 1933). Courtesy Milne Special Collections and Archives, University of New Hampshire Library, Durham NH.*

disarmament treaties, a strong bias toward neutrality, and very limited naval appropriations during the Great Depression. New Deal programs, however, channeled some funds and workers to shipyards when both were in short supply through traditional appropriations. Most noteworthy of these programs was the National Industrial Recovery Act (NIRA), which kick-started the nation's naval shipbuilding program in 1933.

Two NIRA-funded submarines, *Porpoise* and *Pike*, provided valuable submarine design and construction work for Portsmouth Navy Yard at a time when naval funding for new submarines was essentially nonexistent. The new sectional construction process that the yard used to build these submarines was one of the keys to the yard's record-

Photo 7: Submarine pressure-hull sections in Dry Dock #1 (1943). Courtesy Milne Special Collections and Archives, University of New Hampshire Library, Durham, NH.

setting production during World War II. This process required the construction of six or eight massive sections at various buildings in the yard and then transferring them by rail to the dry docks, where cranes lowered the sections to keel blocks for welding together. Prior to this, each vessel had been custom-built at a single building site. "A new method has been developed for the construction of submarines,"[14] declared a shipyard letter of 30 July 1934. "The submarines *Porpoise* and *Pike* are being constructed in sections. A section of the boat weighing approximately twenty tons is constructed at Building 96 and after it has been riveted and welded the section is moved by crane and railroad cars and placed on the building ways in Building 115. This method of constructing a large section and moving it as one piece to the ways has proven economical and more rapid than the method which was formerly used."[15] The shipyard refined the sectional construction process during the late 1930s by creating other independent erection sites in various buildings and adding content to the cylinders.[16] By the start of the war, Portsmouth had acquired considerable experience in sectional construction. When orders skyrocketed and mass production became the order of the day, Portsmouth was poised to capitalize on the revitalized naval rebuilding program when other shipyards were thankful just to go back to work.

Portsmouth was by no means the only submarine yard to employ sectional construction. In fact, during World War II, Electric Boat adapted a version of the process that included an "upside down" feature that rotated the pressure hull sections so that welders could "work upright instead of standing on their heads inside a rigid hull."[17] However, having been first with the process in 1934, Portsmouth Navy Yard had gone much further in perfecting it and adding content to the cylindrical sections before welding.

Streamlined for Submarine Construction. Portsmouth had another distinct advantage: focus. Unlike other navy yards (Boston, New York, Philadelphia, Norfolk, Charleston, Bremerton, and Mare Island), Portsmouth did not have to deal with multiple ship types or do much disruptive repair and overhaul work. The yard had essentially one mission: the construction of submarines. According to a 1944 industrial survey of the shipyard, "Any present judgment of the organization, administration, and control procedures of the Navy yard, Portsmouth, N.H., must give great weight to the development of the Yard, subordinating all other considerations to the demands of the war effort, *into a specialized construction activity for submarines only. All operating units have been streamlined for this sole purpose* [emphasis added]."[18]

Already primed to channel its resources and energies into one line of work, thanks to the Navy's efforts to develop the yard's submarine capabilities between the wars, Portsmouth was able to focus even more narrowly on just one thing — *new* submarines. Pearl Harbor and the West Coast shipyards were consumed by disruptive, high-priority battle repairs when the submarine war quickly moved to the Pacific theater. Portsmouth, however, was barely affected by these constraints, nor by the frequent shifting of workload priorities among different types of ships as the Navy's needs and strategic planning changed with the fortunes of the war. The yard's one unwavering mission during the war was to build as many submarines as possible — as fast as possible.

Despite expanding sixfold between 1940 and 1943, Portsmouth was the smallest navy yard in March 1943. At that time, Portsmouth had 20,500 employees, while the other navy yards averaged 38,000 employees.[19] A small shipyard with a singular mission, tailored to a well-defined, constantly increasing workload—Portsmouth had a distinct advantage over larger shipyards with a varied workload and frequent emergency work.

Decentralized Shipbuilding Environment. The yard benefited from a highly decentralized naval shipbuilding environment as well, meaning the naval authorities in Washington, overwhelmed by other matters, left the yard free to run its own show and make its own decisions. The Bureau of Ships, created in June 1940 concurrent with the passing of legislation that massively increased funding for naval construction, was soon consumed by the administrative burden of organizing a rapidly expanding bureaucracy while mobilizing the nation's shipbuilding industry to support the accelerated shipbuilding program.[20] Recognizing the bureau's excessive workload, Secretary of the Navy Frank Knox, in January 1941, directed navy yard commandants to operate independently of the Bureau of Ships to the maximum extent possible. He wrote, "During the present emergency, it is directed that Commandants of all Navy yards act with the full authority of the Bureau of Ships taking final local action to the greatest extent possible."[21] In essence, the navy yards became entrepreneurial operations; Portsmouth excelled under this environment.

Leadership. That independence certainly would not have been possible without outstanding leadership, starting at the top with the commandant, Rear Admiral Thomas Withers, one of the most respected leaders of the submarine community at the time. His immediate assignment prior to assuming command of Portsmouth Navy Yard on 10 June 1942 was Commander Submarines Scouting Force Pacific, which became Commander Submarine Force Pacific Fleet at the start of the war. Withers witnessed the attack on Pearl Harbor and directed the first deployment of United States

Photo 8: Rear Admiral Thomas Withers change of command (10 June 1942). Courtesy Milne Special Collections and Archives, University of New Hampshire Library, Durham, NH.

submarines after the attack. Withers had previously enjoyed a long and illustrious career in submarines. In 1928, at Commander Division 4 in New London, Connecticut, Withers had advanced the concept that U.S. submarines be used as independent commerce raiders, much as the Germans had done in World War I, rather than as scouting units in conjunction with fleet or coastal defense. For doing so, he receives credit for helping to change the direction of United States submarine policy. His concept of independent submarine operations required submarine designs with longer ranges, better sea-keeping ability, and improved habitability.[22] It was only logical that the Navy would assign one of its most innovative thinkers to head up the expanding submarine design organization at Portsmouth. He remained in command of the yard until late 1945.

The industrial manager, directly responsible for all aspects of production, was Captain H. F. D. Davis, an aggressive, hands-on waterfront manager whose initials were thought by many shipyard employees to stand for Hellfire and Damnation. The planning officer, Captain Andrew McKee, was an acknowledged expert in submarine design at the time. He subsequently enhanced that reputation and was promoted to rear admiral. In recognition of his technical contributions to the Navy, the submarine tender USS *McKee* (AS-41) was named after him, as was a prize for academic excellence at the Navy's nuclear power school. Combined with a highly qualified and experienced civilian management team, these three officers provided the yard with excellent leadership.

Innovative Practices. The yard's top-notch management team deployed three cutting-edge industrial practices to great success: 1) optimization of pre-launch construction on the building sites; 2) assembly line techniques, to the extent they could be applied to submarine construction at the time; and 3) empowerment of small teams with special training.

Portsmouth had a shortage of the most critically needed resource to accelerate production: building sites. Ramping up for the war, the yard added two traditional aboveground building ways, raising its total to five. During the first year of the war, the construction of a building basin and dry dock in which two submarines could be built side by side, and launched by floating them off their blocks, became key to Portsmouth's success.[23] Portsmouth had just nine building sites; its prime competitor, Electric Boat, had twenty-one. Necessity was very much the mother of invention as Portsmouth turned that shortage into an advantage by developing and optimizing pre-launch construction techniques, especially the building of submarines in the newly constructed dry dock and building basin. The yard could only achieve the desired building rates by forcing submarine hulls off the building sites very early in the construction schedule to make room for the next keels. Using a "push 'em off the ways" production strategy, submarines launched as soon as they were watertight. Much of the work normally done on building sites was completed pier-side. At least one submarine launched without the sail structure that encloses the periscopes and masts. Portsmouth launched submarines four times faster than Electric Boat. Any unnecessary occupation of a site by a submarine under construction was a luxury Portsmouth could ill afford. Early launches led to early deliveries, lower costs, and recognition of Portsmouth Navy Yard as the nation's preeminent builder of submarines.

The post-launch stepping of submarines through various berths for the completion of specific jobs was another highly efficient innovation. Newly launched submarines first had the sail and topside superstructure finished at one berth, the periscopes and masts installed at the next, the bow torpedo tubes completed and tested at yet another berth, the stern tubes completed and tested at another, and the final outfitting and dock trials completed at the last location. Other work, of course, took place at each successive berth in the process. The result was an assembly line of sorts, where the submarine stepped from berth to berth and small teams with specialized training reported to the same berth repeatedly to accomplish repetitive tasks.[24]

Decades before the radical management concept of using small teams of empowered workers was advanced by Dr. W. Edward Deming, the practice was flourishing in Portsmouth during the war. The yard was an environment tailor-made for a well-trained and self-motivated workforce with a homogeneous and repetitious workload. An empowered worker trained to accomplish the same job on submarine after submarine was highly productive, as well as an expert in his task. This practice also alleviated another concern: if a worker was drafted, his replacement could quickly learn the limited task with minimal disruption to the building process. For all of these reasons, Portsmouth Navy Yard made maximum use of special teams.

William Tebo, a high school teenager employed at the navy yard in 1944, recalled how he traveled from submarine to submarine on the building ways performing the few electrical jobs for which he was the "expert installer" with minimal supervision. One of his jobs was to wire the electrical distribution panel for the newly installed, and highly secret, shipboard radar. With the radar consoles and equipment concealed under wrappings and coverings, Tebo dutifully wired the radar electrical panels on submarine after submarine.[25] With limited electrical training, Tebo was able to provide a most useful and productive service to the yard during his six months of employment, prior to leaving for military service. Tebo was one of hundreds, if not thousands, of specialists on small teams scattered throughout all the trades.

———————

Record-setting production of submarines means very little if a shipyard sacrifices cost and quality for numbers. As it happened, cost and quality were as much a part of the Portsmouth success story as production. Dramatic cost reduction was a by-product of the yard's record-setting production and steep learning curves. By 1944, the yard required only 665,000 work hours to build a submarine, slashed from 2 million work hours in 1941.[26] In the shipbuilding industry, where time is money, a reduction in work hours means a proportional reduction in costs. By the end of the war, the yard was building submarines at one-third the cost in 1941.

During World War II, quality was not yet the quantitative

science it has since become. In the absence of statistical records and measurements typical of industry today, the testimony of the commanding officers and sailors who took the vessel to war best define the quality of a World War II submarine — and the archives are filled with such stories. One such testimony was provided by Dan MacIsaac TMI (SS) of the USS *Redfish* (SS-395), which suffered a depth charge attack by Japanese destroyers on 19 December 1944.

MacIsaac had been in the forward torpedo room after the sinking of the Japanese carrier *Unryu*, when three Japanese destroyers dropped seven depth charges off the starboard bow of the submerged *Redfish*. No one onboard was closer to the explosions. MacIsaac was thrown to the forward end of the compartment where he lay in the bilge, unconscious, for some period of time. The explosions cracked the pressure hull and damaged piping, torpedo tubes, and other equipment in the room. MacIsaac awoke to the sound of rushing water, realizing that he and his shipmates must quickly isolate the leaks as best they could if the submarine was to be saved. Using wrenches, rags, and whatever could be found, MacIsaac and his mates stopped the leaks. *Redfish* rested on the bottom of the East China Sea for four hours to avoid detection and further attacks. As soon as MacIsaac and his mates had gained control of the flooding, the commanding officer, Commander L. D. McGregor, came forward from the conning tower to assess the damage. More than sixty years later, MacIsaac remembered the captain's exact words when he stepped through the watertight door of the torpedo room and saw the damage to his submarine. "You can thank God that you are in a Portsmouth boat," he said. Such was the reputation of Portsmouth Navy Yard for building top-quality submarines.[27]

Submarine officers and crews also appreciated the latest fleet feedback and technological features Portsmouth incorporated into its submarines.[28] Portsmouth, a government yard, was much more receptive to change orders and late work than private yards. First-time installations of design changes require special attention and extra effort to ensure satisfactory performance and compatibility with other shipboard systems. They are typically costly and seldom trouble-free. Portsmouth Navy Yard's ability to routinely install design upgrades, while still achieving remarkable production rates and consistently high quality, reflects even more credit on the shipyard management and employees. Portsmouth not only delivered submarines much more quickly than its competitors, those submarines were more complete and technically superior to those produced by other shipyards.

Portsmouth Navy Yard's reputation for excellence grew with each passing year of the war. Early in the war, the Portsmouth-built USS *Kingfish* (SS-234) was completed in eight months on 20 May 1942; it was credited with sinking a Japanese freighter off southern Kyushu[29] on 1 October 1942 — just thirteen months after her keel had been laid. While other shipyards were having difficulty delivering submarines in thirteen months, *Kingfish* was built, steamed halfway around the world, and sank an enemy ship during the same period. The world began to take notice of the small navy yard building submarines on the banks of the Piscataqua River.

In September 1943, at the height of the war in the Pacific, the vice chief of naval operations, Admiral F. J. Horne, sent the following congratulatory letter to the shipyard: "The Secretary of the Navy revealed that the Japanese had lost one-third of their available tonnage up to 3 September 1943, and that seventy-seven percent of that tonnage loss was sunk by our submarines. Of the submarines contributing to these sinkings, forty percent were built by your Navy yard. This is, indeed, a record of which you can be proud."[30] The yard's reputation continued to grow until, at the end of the war, the shipyard's newspaper, the *Portsmouth Periscope*, celebrated the yard's wartime accomplishments with considerable pride:

> The war is over! And the part that Portsmouth played in the war is something that . . . every loyal workingman can look back on with a feeling of pride. . . . The Portsmouth submarine fleet was the scourge of the famed Japanese merchant ships. From the very darkest days of the war, Portsmouth started to swing at the little yellow men who had pulled the sneak attack on Pearl Harbor. . . . They rained submarines on the men who started this (for them) fatal conflict. . . . They slaughtered a Jap fleet that had had a free reign.[31]

If one can look beyond the emotion and racially charged language of the moment, the *Periscope* was accurate in reporting that Portsmouth Navy Yard had indeed played a significant role in the winning of the war.

CHAPTER 3
HARBOR DEFENSE

Mine in harbor exploded at 0400 hours. Large oil slick observed on water upon investigation at 0700 hours by personnel in mine yawl. Attempts to locate cause of explosion by divers failed to produce any positive results.

Portsmouth War Records
"Harbor Defense of Portsmouth"

The summer of 1940 was an anxious one for Americans: France had fallen and the blitzkrieg of Great Britain was under way. The Luftwaffe planes hauling bombs to London also carried the message that a cross-channel invasion by German troops was imminent. How long could Britain hold out? And if Britain fell, how could the war be constrained to Europe, or even the Atlantic Ocean? With war clouds gathering on the horizon, Charles T. McFarlane's *The Present War*, published in August 1940, spoke to the sudden realization that the United States might be Germany's next target:

Less than a year after Poland was invaded — how different the picture! Poland, Norway, Denmark, the Netherlands, Belgium, Luxemburg, and France in German hands! And all the fury of a victorious Germany supported by an Italy warlike under the leadership of Mussolini, to be turned on Great Britain in an

attempt to complete the kill! . . . Suddenly the
American peoples realized that if Great Britain
were defeated, and its fleet captured or driven
from the seas, the totalitarian powers of Europe
and Asia could strike at them.[1]

This nation's attention turned toward defense of the
homeland and the protection of its vital industrial assets.
Portsmouth Navy Yard, one of those vital assets, was also one
of the most vulnerable and easily reached by German attack.
The defense of Portsmouth quickly became a matter of high
national priority.

Three German threat scenarios roused the fears of
Portsmouth residents: shore bombardment from a surface
warship, an air attack, and a U-boat invasion of the harbor.
As long as the British fleet reigned supreme in the North
Atlantic, shore bombardment was unlikely. On the other
hand, the devastating saturation bombing then under way in
Britain made an air attack seem far more likely. Most
alarming, frequent and successful U-boat attacks were
already occurring just a few miles off the East Coast, raising
serious concerns about the possibility of a U-boat invasion of
Portsmouth Harbor that could wreak untold havoc on the
shipyard and local shipping. The U-boat concern was
twofold: enemy submarines could launch torpedo attacks on
ships, or use the same torpedo tubes to stealthily launch
mines into the harbor. The Portsmouth Harbor Defense
System was designed to deal with all three threats. While the
threats of a surface ship bombardment or an air attack waned
after the first year of the war, the fear that a U-boat might gain
entrance to the harbor persisted until late in the war.

A wealth of details, drawings, and photographs of the
upgrades to the harbor fortifications, with particular
emphasis on artillery, is gathered in Jack P. Wysong's *The*

World, Portsmouth, and the 22nd Coast Artillery: The War Years 1938-1948, a comprehensive account of the Portsmouth Harbor Defense System during World War II. This chapter builds on Wysong's excellent work by offering additonal information about the underwater defense system and the U-boat threat it was designed to meet.

The U-boat Threat

Early in the war, numerous sightings of German submarines off the East Coast, and the fiery damage they inflicted on coastal shipping, left no doubt in the minds of the residents of seacoast New Hampshire and southern Maine that U-boats could transit the Atlantic Ocean and reach the entrance of Portsmouth Harbor. Along the shores of Virginia and the Carolinas, according to historian Richard Lingeman, "flashes of explosions appeared against the night sky, and beaches became littered with the grisly flotsam and jetsam — bodies, charred lifeboats, empty lifebuoys and fish and water fowl that had died in oil-fouled waters."[2] German U-boats were essentially unopposed in the sinking of merchant shipping during the early stages of the war. Portsmouth Navy Yard, capable of producing large numbers of submarines, was an obvious threat to Germany's undersea dominance — and therefore a likely target. As the reports of U-boat successes multiplied, so did local fears about the damage an enemy submarine could do if it gained entrance to Portsmouth Harbor.

Offshore U-boat activity came as no surprise. A North Atlantic Naval Coastal War Diary entry for January 1942 explained, "The arrival of the [German] submarines in the waters off the east coast was not unexpected. . . . [I]t was responsible to assume that what the Germans had done with some success and with less efficient submarines in the last war, they would try to do again in this war." The commanding officers of German submarines quickly learned they were much less vulnerable operating against isolated coastal shipping than against open-ocean merchant convoys protected by Allied destroyers. The diary noted the increasing success of the escorted convoys: "The culminating of this steady progress came on December 15–16 [1941], when the Germans, in a prolonged attack on Convoy H.G. 76, lost four submarines while sinking only two ships out of a possible thirty-two." The coastal shipping lanes, crowded with merchant vessels and tankers running from northern ports to oil refineries in South America and the Gulf, offered much better odds for the U-boats—and so, potentially, did East Coast ports.[3]

A series of January 1942 Headquarters, North Atlantic Coastal Frontier reports must have raised local concerns and put nerves on edge. On 7 January 1942, the reports noted "strong indications that sixteen German submarines are proceeding to the area east of Newfoundland." A few days later, on 11 January, a U-boat sank a merchant ship off Cape Cod. The next day it was reported that four U-boats were known to be east of Nantucket Light moving westward, followed by a report that "[f]ive or six enemy submarines are moving between 30N and 50N [Portsmouth is at 43N latitude]." A 13 January log entry notes the closing of the ports of Boston, Portland, and Portsmouth because of the increasing submarine threat, adding, "About one hour after the ports . . . were closed, the first ship within the limits of the Frontier was sunk at 40-20N; 70-50W, sixty miles southeast of Montauk Point." From a Portsmouth resident's perspective, the war was immediately offshore in January 1942, much too close and well within reach of Portsmouth Harbor.[4]

Of the twenty-five Allied ships sunk in New England waters during World War II, twenty were sunk before

August 1942.[5] Included in that number were the troop ships *Cherokee* and *Port Nicholson*, with the combined loss of eighty-five lives, sunk by the U-87 on 15 June 1942, sixty-five miles east of the Isles of Shoals.[6] After an initial flurry of U-boat activity in New England waters during the first half of 1942, most of the action moved south and, for the most part, stayed there for the duration of the war.

The North Atlantic Naval Coastal War Diary recorded 13 ships sunk in January 1942, 14 in February, 23 in March, and 24 in April — most of these off Cape Hatteras and the Virginia coast. These areas and those off the coasts of the Carolinas, Georgia, and Florida proved to be the most productive U-boat hunting grounds. In total, German subs sank 172 ships off the East Coast in 1942.[7] It was not immediately obvious to those concerned with the defense of Portsmouth Harbor that most of this activity had shifted south by mid-1942. Fear was in the air and all were alert to the possibility of an attack.

U-boat attacks continued to ravage Allied shipping through March 1943. Notes historian Maury Klein, "During the first twenty days of March 1943 U-boats sank ninety-seven Allied merchant ships . . . twice the rate of new [U.S.] ships being built. The Germans lost only seven submarines, half the number coming out of [their] shipyards." The math was entirely in Germany's favor. However, by late spring 1943, the escort protection of convoys began to take its toll. "In May the Germans lost forty-one U-boats while sinking only fifty merchant ships, a devastating turnabout. By July the launching of new ships from American shipyards finally exceeded the tonnage lost since 1939." Before long, the former U-boat happy hunting grounds became burial grounds for many iron coffins — the slang term given to U-boats later in the war.[8]

Locally, there were numerous reported sightings of offshore threats. Oil slicks, possible enemy submarine sightings, and suspicious unidentified passing ships are the subjects of entries in the Portsmouth Harbor Defense Force log during the first two years of the war:[9]

4 Sep 42	Mine in harbor exploded at 0400 hours. Large oil slick observed on water upon investigation at 0700 hours by personnel in mine yawl. Attempts to locate cause of explosion by divers failed to produce any positive results.
25 Sep 42	Sub reported off Isles of Shoals. Depth charges were dropped by plane. Results not known.
9 Jun 43	Battle alert called. Unidentified vessel failed to stop or answer signals. Fired two warning shots. Vessel stopped. Navy intercepted and identified it as an Italian fishing vessel.
22 Jun 43	Sub sighted well inshore. Battle alert sounded. Sub disappeared. No shots.
30 Oct 43	Battery 951 fired examination round at Norwegian tanker which refused to stop and answer signals.

The 25 September 1942 incident off the Isles of Shoals may have been the same sighting reported by Rye resident Sandra Goss Munsey. Munsey wrote of a submarine sighting while standing watch with her grandmother at the Straw's Point observation post:

> One day when my grandmother and I were standing watch, a submarine could be seen slowly rising from the water directly east of our post [toward the Isles of Shoals]. By the time it had surfaced completely, it was evident from its

silhouette that it was a German. The phone call to the center confirmed that no U.S. submarines were known to be in the area. The Coast Guard patrol in the area also spotted the sub—and panicked. Running down to the edge of the shore, he fired his rifle. Naturally the sound carried quickly across the water. The sub immediately submerged. The skirmish was over. The probable cause for surfacing had been to dump garbage or recharge batteries. It wasn't the only sighting because other people along the NH coast reported observing the German sub, but it was "our sighting."[10]

Unfortunately, Munsey provided no date to permit correlation with the log entry, and the harbor defense log contains no confirmation of a U-boat sighting.

Munsey speculated that the submarine she observed might have surfaced to charge batteries. Although not widely known at the time, late in the war U-boats no longer had to surface to charge batteries, as did our submarines. The Germans had developed a snorkel system using a mast and exterior piping that provided a conduit for air to enter a submerged submarine, which allowed the diesel engines to be run submerged to charge batteries. Little airborne noise propagated from a snorkeling submarine, but a sonar array might detect the snorkeling engines; Portsmouth Harbor was heavily guarded with sonar hydrophones. The snorkel system was one of the more important advancements in submarine design that the United States gained from the study of captured German submarines at the end of the war.

Having witnessed the aircraft-equipped *Surcouf* at Portsmouth Navy Yard in the fall of 1941, local residents were aware that enemy submarines might not need to enter Portsmouth Harbor to inflict damage. If the French could build such a submarine, surely the more technically competent Germans were no less capable. In fact, unbeknown to most, the Japanese already had such a submarine. In November 1942, notes Richard Lingeman, the Japanese dropped incendiary bombs on an Oregon forest by launching "a modified Zero, equipped with pontoons, which was housed in a special watertight compartment on the submarine I-25."[11] The forest suffered little damage—but concern deepened: if the French and the Japanese had developed the capability to launch submarine-carried aircraft, why not the Germans? Late in the war, intelligence reports warned of an even more sinister threat: a newly developed class of U-boats capable of deck-launching V-1 flying bombs.[12] A submarine-launched attack plane or flying bomb outside Portsmouth Harbor would allow mere minutes for spotters to detect it and direct local batteries to the target. Rumors were rampant, the possibilities disturbing, and the unknowns frightening.

The most suspicious activity logged in the Portsmouth Defense Area Civil Defense Log Book occurred at 9:10 a.m., 2 February 1942: "Officer Hurley came in & reported about a spy car being around the beach flashing lights over the ocean—also having a machine gun in back of car."[13] Despite that report and the possibility of secret German agents roaming the seacoast, there was no follow-up entry in the log. Similar rumors about German "frogmen" coming ashore went unconfirmed in local records. There were, however, documented landings of German agents from offshore submarines on at least three occasions at other East Coast sites. On 13 June 1942, four German agents put ashore on Long Island from U-202. A few days later, on 17 June 1942, a second team of four agents—part of the same sabotage operation—landed near Jacksonville, Florida, from U-584. Authorities captured and tried all eight, and six were executed. Much later, on 29 November 1944, two agents put ashore at Bar Harbor, Maine, from U-1230. This incident, which occurred just a few hours' drive up the coast from Portsmouth, makes for a compelling story.

The two German agents, Erich Gimpel and a U.S. Navy deserter, William Colepaugh, came ashore at Bar Harbor with a mission to disrupt the Manhattan Project. The two eventually made their way to New York City, possibly passing through southern Maine and seacoast New Hampshire. While in New York, about a month after their arrival, Colepaugh lost his nerve and turned himself in to the FBI. The two men went to trial and received death sentences, but President Truman commuted their sentences after the war. Gimpel was deported, and Colepaugh was sentenced to Fort Leavenworth.[14]

The most decisive account of U-boat activity near Portsmouth is recorded in a 27 November 1945 letter from Assistant Secretary of the Navy John L. Sullivan to Laurence Shorey, who was secretary of the Portsmouth War Records Committee. Responding to Shorey's inquiry, Sullivan wrote, "On April 7, 1945, the German submarine U-857 was sunk by the US Destroyer Escort, GUSTAFSON, in position 42°22'N – 69°46'W. The sinking occurred at night, approximately 52 miles southeast of the Isles of Shoals, Portsmouth, New Hampshire, while the GUSTAFSON was on a routine patrol."[15] Beyond this single instance, research for this book found that all locally reported U-boat sightings and rumors of German frogmen coming ashore went unconfirmed. However, the threat was certainly very real, especially early in the war, making the upgrade of the Portsmouth Harbor Defense System a matter of urgency.

Pre-World War II Fort System

In fact, as World War II loomed, improvements had already begun at strategically important East Coast harbors, and by the time the United States entered the war, the upgrade of Portsmouth Harbor was in full swing. The Portsmouth Harbor Defense System, which fell under the purview of the U.S. Army, evolved to include numerous forts with large gun battery emplacements, an operations center, magnetic detection fields, sonar arrays, minefields, and an anti-submarine net. Fortunately, many of the necessary elements were already in place in the form of an inactive fort system left over from previous wars. The challenge was to expeditiously reactivate, augment, and update these fortifications to meet the needs of modern warfare.

Forts have guarded Portsmouth Harbor since colonial times. Fort Washington, Fort Sullivan, Fort Constitution (William and Mary), Fort Stark, and Fort McClary (figure 4) were among the earliest constructed. Locally it is common knowledge — less known or admitted in our nation's history books — that the first shots of the Revolutionary War actually occurred not far from downtown Portsmouth when colonists attacked Fort William and Mary (later Fort Constitution) in New Castle, New Hampshire, on the morning of 14 December 1774 to confiscate small arms and powder the British had stored in magazines. That afternoon and again the next evening, Portsmouth colonists attacked Fort Stark, also on the island of New Castle, to seize munitions and other stores. These attacks occurred four months before the "first" shots of the revolution fired at Lexington, Massachusetts, on

19 April 1775.[16] Portsmouth Harbor gained importance during the Revolutionary War with the emergence of the local shipbuilding industry, which constructed the first ships for the colonial navy. The establishment of the Portsmouth Navy Yard in 1800 and its growth in the years that followed created the need for a more substantial harbor defense system.

With the development of naval gunnery — longer-range rifled guns replaced smooth-bore cannons — the inner harbor forts (Sullivan and Washington) lost much of their strategic importance during the nineteenth century; Fort Washington, on Peirce Island, was in ruins by 1850. Fort Sullivan saw service through the Civil War before being dismantled in 1866 and eventually demolished in 1901. At Fort Stark, the original earthwork constructed in 1842 was replaced by a stonework fort in 1873, and its batteries were upgraded in the

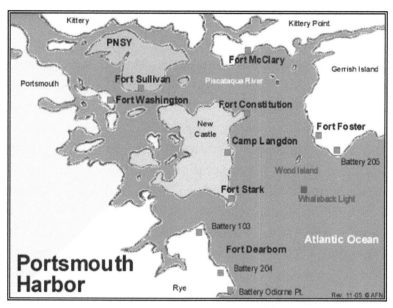

Figure 4: Portsmouth Harbor Forts.
Courtesy American Forts Network, www.northamericanforts.com.

early twentieth century. Following the Spanish-American War (1898), when improved defense of key harbors became a national priority, Forts Constitution and McClary were upgraded and Fort Foster constructed. However, all these forts were downgraded to caretaker status after World War I, when disarmament conferences and neutrality sentiments pushed the nation toward a reduced defensive posture.[17]

A mere twenty years later, all the remaining fortifications were once more teeming with activity. Forts Constitution, Foster, and Stark were reactivated as key elements of the Portsmouth Harbor Defense System, soon augmented by a new installation dubbed Fort Dearborn and the command headquarters constructed at Camp Langdon. Fort McClary became an adjunct of Fort Foster, its blockhouse serving as an observation post, and the former site of Fort Washington became an Army recreation center.[18]

World War II Fort Upgrades

In January 1940, Forts Constitution, Foster, and Stark were under the auspices of the 8th Coast Artillery Regiment, which was responsible for the harbor defense of Portland, some distance to the north. Of the regiment's one hundred men with caretaker assignments at various coastal forts, five were assigned to the Portsmouth Harbor forts. All that changed as of 1 February 1940, when the 22nd Coast Artillery was activated at Fort Constitution with command responsibilities for Portsmouth Harbor Defense. The unit moved to Camp Langdon, midway between Fort Constitution and Fort Stark, on 23 November 1940.[19]

According to the Portsmouth War Records, "On July 1, 1940, Capt. Lawrence M. Guyer assumed command of the forts in the harbor, and during the remaining months of 1940 small detachments of troops arrived. . . . Camp Langdon, the headquarters of the area, was built and well over 2,000 men were on duty at the Harbor Defenses at one time."[20] The officers and men reporting for duty with the 22nd Coast Artillery over the summer of 1940 found the batteries in a deteriorated, even dilapidated, condition. Most of the major batteries dated back to the turn of the century, and had not been exercised since World War I. The challenge was to quickly make them operational as a stopgap measure, while installing modern 6-inch and 16-inch batteries with much greater ranges and improved accuracy, able to compete with modern German warships and aircraft. (As it happened, by the time the new batteries were operational in the summer of 1944, they were no longer needed.)

The fortification upgrades fell into four major categories: mining operations, large gun batteries, harbor control, and administrative headquarters. Forts Constitution and Foster became the control centers for the harbor mining operations; Fort Dearborn, the only new fortification, became the site of the most formidable and modern batteries; Fort Stark monitored all harbor traffic and was the keeper of the gate for the anti-submarine net; and Camp Langdon served as the central base and administrative headquarters for the entire harbor defense system.

Fort Constitution's primary mission was to be "a Mine Operations Depot."[21] The care and maintenance of a minefield consisting of 182 mines, each weighing 3½ tons, was a major operation, and the fort expanded to a complex of eighteen assorted buildings, including a stowage facility with the necessary tracks and handling equipment to transfer mines to a loading dock. The fort did have one World War I battery of two 3-inch guns (Battery Hackleman) in service during World War II, but its two 8-inch guns (Battery Farnsworth) were removed well before the war started; that battery was used for mine cable stowage. The two inner lines (of three lines) of the minefield were controlled from Fort

Constitution.

Directly across the harbor on Maine's Gerrish Island, accessed by a new bridge and macadam road, Fort Foster rounded out the mining operations. The fort had three outdated and unreliable 10-inch guns (Battery Bohen), two 3-inch guns (Battery Chopin), and four 90-mm guns. Concrete casements were completed for two modern 6-inch guns (Battery Curtis), but the guns were never installed because the need for them had passed by the time the casements were ready. Guns, however, were not the strength of Fort Foster. The fort's crucial role was to monitor and control the outer line of mines in the harbor. In addition, the northern end of the anti-submarine net across the harbor anchored in the reef off Fort Foster.[22]

Fort Stark, as the site of the Harbor Entrance Control Post (HECP), became the nerve center of harbor defense where Army and Navy personnel served together to integrate the various organizations with harbor defense responsibilities. (As at Fort Foster, Stark's outdated 12-inch and 3-inch guns in Battery Hunter and Battery Lytle played a secondary role; its third battery, Hays, was decommissioned in 1942.) The HECP processed all intelligence reports, directed the movement of all craft in the harbor, and controlled the opening and closing of the anti-submarine net that stretched across the harbor entrance. Lobstermen and fishermen continued to ply their trades for most of the war with the help of the HECP to guarantee safe passage through the minefields and the net, anchored at the southern end of Fort Stark.[23]

Camp Langdon, which had been a military reservation and training area, became the headquarters for Portsmouth Harbor Defense. The camp grew into a small town, encompassing twenty barracks, seven mess halls, a fire station, a hospital, a theater, and a chapel. The diary of a recruit transferred from Fort Dix, New Jersey, in December

1943 suggests the camp was also a receiving depot for new recruits to complete two months of basic training before reassignment to other local commands: "This mess hall was a hell of a lot different than the one at Fort Dix. The places were set with plates-cups-silverware — even the coffee tasted like coffee. . . . The following afternoon Lt. Turner told us we were in Camp Langdon about 300 miles from New York. . . . 12/3/44 — We were taken to the range to fire our rifles. . . . 10 mile hike. . . .1/27/44 — Left Camp Langdon — [t]his was the day our basic training was over . . . arrived Fort Constitution."[24] With the construction of Camp Langdon and the upgrades to Forts Constitution and Stark, tiny New Castle became a formidable military installation with a complement of 1,500 servicemen, causing the town's population to explode from 500 to 2,000.[25]

The construction at all these fortifications roused little controversy — after all, these sites had long been government property.[26] The only new fort added to the system, Fort Dearborn, was a different matter entirely. When the government decided additional modern batteries were needed near Frost Point and Odiorne Point, things got a little dicey because the real estate belonged to private citizens — who, naturally, objected strongly to the forced sales that ensued.

Fort Dearborn grew from the Army's realization that an adequate defense of Portsmouth Harbor required more than the mere activation of the outdated World War I batteries. With the test-firing of Fort Foster's guns on 1 November 1941, all the existing batteries had been "proof-fired and ranged." The firing of Fort Foster's three 10-inch guns rattled dishes, windows, and doors as far away as Newburyport, Massachusetts. Worse yet, the guns did not automatically return to the load position; the crew had to manhandle the guns back to the firing position, and the carriages remained unreliable throughout the war. A harbor defense based on unreliable and outdated batteries that were outranged by German warships was a harbor defense in name only. Modern guns with much greater reliability and ranges were needed.[27]

Fort Foster had room for one new 6-inch battery, but there was no space available at any of the other forts without destroying existing batteries — thereby leaving the harbor and shipyard undefended for an extended period. An additional site was needed so that new batteries could be constructed without compromising the integrity of the harbor defense system. The planned additions included two batteries of modern twin 6-inch guns (one each at Fort Foster and Fort Dearborn) with a range of fifteen miles, and a battery of twin 16-inch guns at Fort Dearborn able to fire a 2,300-pound shell twenty-six miles out to sea. The new batteries were large construction projects involving thick reinforced concrete encasements with many rooms and multiple levels. Most of the new construction occurred at Fort Dearborn.

The site selected for Fort Dearborn was between Odiorne Point and Frost Point in Rye, New Hampshire, a tract of fashionable summer houses. In 1942, the federal government condemned and purchased all the land between the two points and gave the residents thirty days to pack up and leave. Resentful owners reluctantly complied. The Army's forced purchase of 265 acres included 90 acres of prime oceanfront real estate. The angry sellers questioned the Army's need for their land; many of their descendants still do. The fort began to take shape when the Army occupied the area in November 1942. In May 1943, the new base was christened Fort Dearborn after Hampton native and Revolutionary War hero Henry Dearborn, who was secretary of war during the Jefferson administration (1801–09).[28]

The reinforced concrete casements constructed on Odiorne Point for two 6-inch guns (Battery 204) and on Frost Point for two 16-inch guns (Battery Seaman) were not completed until the summer of 1944. Fort Dearborn also had four 155-mm guns able to engage close-in moving ships. The twenty buildings constructed at the fort included a gatehouse, barracks, officers' quarters, a chapel, a Post Exchange, and concrete buildings for the stowage of TNT for the harbor mines. Many of the soldiers lived quite comfortably in existing houses that the Army had purchased. The portion of Ocean Boulevard between Odiorne and Frost Point became the main passage through the new base. The Army closed the road to the public on 24 April 1942 and did not reopen it until some months after the end of the war.[29]

The various forts' batteries and buildings were behind guarded gates and out of view to the public. Another much more visible element of harbor defense was the strategic arrangement of sixteen coastal fire control stations positioned along the coasts of Massachusetts (four), New Hampshire (eight), and Maine (four) to provide accurate target bearing and range data for the batteries.[30] Some stations were easy to identify, such as the conspicuous eight-story Pulpit Rock Tower (photo 9) located on the coastal route immediately south of Odiorne Point and the Appledore Island Tower on the Isles of Shoals. Others were designed to be less obvious and blend into the countryside, such as the cottage-style station at Bald Head Cliff, the current site of the Cliff House resort.[31] Volunteer observers initially staffed the fire control stations to visually gather and transmit target range and bearing data to the batteries. However, the newly developed fire control radar quickly relegated them to a backup role. The stations continued to serve for the remainder of the war as civil defense observation posts.[32]

Photo 9: Pulpit Rock Fire Control/ Observation Tower (2014) and view from tower looking north up Route 1A toward the entrance to Portsmouth Harbor (above). Courtesy author's personal collection.

Underwater Defense System

———— ❧ ————

Minefields were not new to Portsmouth Harbor: mines had protected the harbor during the Spanish-American War and World War I. Once again during World War II, an elaborate array of mines—this time remotely monitored and activated—guarded the harbor, supplemented by an anti-submarine net. The Portsmouth Harbor system was part of the Eastern Sea Frontier passive defense network. A command diary entry for February 1942 describes early East Coast defense preparations:

> *Long before we entered the war*, plans had been made for the development of a system of *passive defense* for our coastline. Methods of cooperation between the Army and the navy had been devised, submarine nets and booms had been manufactured, locations for mine fields had been selected. Even before the war began, *minefields had been laid in the more important harbors and naval bases*. Immediately after December 7, the whole system of *passive defense* was greatly extended. Nets and booms were set in place, obstructions of all kinds were put across harbor entrances as fast as they could be manufactured, the areas of existing mine fields was increased and new fields were sowed farther out to sea [emphasis added].[33]

The mines protecting all the East Coast harbors were not contact mines; they were remotely controlled. Portsmouth Harbor, one of the nation's most important harbors, had its initial passive defense system completed in early 1941, long before the United States entered the war.

The coastal inshore mines, such as those planted in

Portsmouth Harbor, were the responsibility of the U.S. Army. The initial mines, which were designed to float about fifteen feet underwater, frequently broke free of their moorings, making them maintenance burdens. In 1943, the old mines were replaced with a heavier version that lay much more securely on the harbor floor.[34] Harrison "Workie" Workman, a lobsterman, son of a career Navy man, and resident of Portsmouth's South End, "served in 'the Army's Navy' from 1942 to 1945 . . . planting submarine mines in the Atlantic." Workman claimed to have been the first man drafted out of Portsmouth. When interviewed by Tammi Truax for a *Portsmouth Herald* article more than sixty years later, he said that laying mines for the Army was the most exciting period of his life.[35] Many Fort Constitution soldiers shared Workman's enthusiasm, planting and maintaining the 182 mines that protected the harbor.

In January 1942, at the peak of the U-boat threat, the Navy considered greatly expanding East Coast harbor defenses by installing contact minefields outside the remotely controlled inshore minefields. The chief of naval operations (CNO) proposed an ambitious program to plant contact mines between Cape Cod and Cape Ann to help protect Boston shipping, and a similar plan to augment the protection of New York Harbor. The start of this program was delayed about a month, initially to assemble enough minesweepers and patrol vessels to mount the effort, and later because of weather. On 21 February 1942, the commander of the Eastern Sea Frontier urged the CNO to reconsider his plan. Better to commit resources to offensive actions to keep U-boats well off the coast, the commander believed, than to plant extensive minefields needing to be monitored and patrolled by a large fleet of vessels to prevent friendly sinkings. He wrote, "Mine fields are a menace to friendly vessels. To require the Frontier to protect friendly vessels from its own weapons is a task that should be forced upon it by the enemy—not voluntarily adopted." The CNO agreed and suspended all preparations for laying the proposed contact minefields. Remotely controlled mines remained the primary defense of East Coast harbors. Observers in Fort Foster and Fort Constitution visually monitored, remotely controlled, and, on rare occasions, activated the mines in Portsmouth Harbor.

The following description of Portsmouth's mines comes from the personal diary of Frank Reda, a CPO assigned to the 22nd Coast Artillery and stationed at Fort Constitution in 1944. The sheer number and weight of the mines suggests the enormity of the effort required to install and maintain this element of harbor defense. "All together there are 13 groups with 14 mines in each, 182 mines. . . . A booster box contains 18 lbs of TNT. This sets off the main charge of the mine which contains 3000 lbs of TNT. . . . A mine which complete weighs 3½ tons—3000 lbs of TNT, case 3200 lbs and 100 lb weights on the bottom of the case . . . all together 7000 lbs."[36] The handling and maintenance of hundreds of these massive mines was probably much more demanding and dangerous than the nearby residents of New Castle appreciated at the time.

The minefields were part of a four-tiered harbor protection system (figure 5) that included magnetic loops, hydrophones, mines, and a thousand-yard gated anti-submarine steel mesh net. Portsmouth was fortunate to have a well-defined and comparatively narrow harbor entrance that could be protected with a physical barrier. An elaborate array of magnetic loops (shown as rectangular boxes) and sonar hydrophones (small numbers) ensured early detection of any underwater activity. This outer system stretched miles at sea from near Gerrish Island in Maine to immediately west of the Isles of Shoals and back to the coast of Rye, New

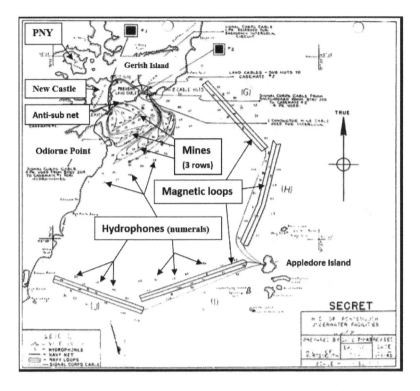

Figure 5: Portsmouth Harbor World War II Underwater Defense System. *Source:* http://fortwiki.com/Harbor Defense of Portsmouth - WWII Underwater Defenses (annotated for clarity).

Hampshire. This semicircle of protection monitored hundreds of square miles of ocean through which enemy submarines would have to transit to approach the harbor.

Well inside the outer magnetic loops (monitored from Appledore Island) and hydrophone arrays (monitored from Forts Foster and Stark) and immediately across the harbor entrance was a compact arrangement of three rows of mines—represented by the triangles on figure 5. The mines were grouped in fourteen individually monitored and controlled pods of ten to fifteen mines each, totaling 182 mines. Fort Foster operators controlled the outer row of

Photo 10: View from Fort Stark to Fort Foster (2015), the anchor points for the Portsmouth Harbor cross-channel anti-submarine net. Courtesy author's personal collection.

mines and Fort Constitution operators controlled the two inner rows. Orders to explode the mines came from the HECP at Fort Stark.

The final element of this formidable four-tier defense system was the anti-submarine net extended between Fort Stark in New Castle and the reef between Wood Island and Fort Foster in Maine. The net, which took a little over a year to install, was in place before the attack on Pearl Harbor. According to the Portsmouth War Records, "In the net was a large gate to allow the tankers, gypsum boats, submarines, and submarine tenders to pass through. The entrance to the harbor . . . was controlled through the Harbor Entrance Control Post at Fort Stark. . . . A small army L-boat was on duty at the gate to the net and this boat was in direct radio contact with the harbor defenses as well as the HECP. The net stretched nearly 1,000 yards across the harbor entrance and the gate was 150 feet wide. The net itself was composed of steel mesh and buoys with weights on the bottom of the harbor to hold it in place while the fast tides roared through. The gate was closed each night and the mines controlled at the harbor defenses were placed on contact as soon as the sun set." The war records speculate that "German submarines are believed to have attempted to penetrate the net, although there was no actual report of one having been seen despite the fact that several 'contacts' were made." Rumors and reports of suspicious contacts were frequent; confirmations were lacking.[37]

Locals patiently adapted to all the constraints in navigating the harbor, and fishermen and lobstermen pursued their trades despite the inconvenience of mines and the net. Fisherman William Marconi remembers, "And then when we had to go fishing here, they had gates out there . . . so you couldn't get through. Sometimes they wouldn't let us go through because they were . . . chasing a submarine out there. German submarines. They went after them. . . . They'd open them then you had to go to a certain place because they had mine fields all in the harbor. . . . They had buoys for us to go through. . . . You had to go way around instead of taking the shortcut. We had to go two miles out of our way to get through the minefields."[38] During the summer of 1945, the Army removed the minefields and net, restoring freedom of movement within the harbor.

U. S. Coast Guard Patrols

The U.S. Coast Guard, in conjunction with the Navy, shared responsibilities for harbor and coastal defense with the Army. The local Coast Guard detachment operated out of the Portsmouth Naval Base with responsibilities to guard the entire coast from Salisbury, Massachusetts, to Wells, Maine, including beach patrols in many sectors. Six large coastal picket boats patrolled offshore, six harbor picket boats patrolled around the navy yard, and additional patrol boats monitored the harbor entrance.[39]

In June 1942, a New Hampshire Coast Guard Auxiliary, consisting of approximately 300 civilian volunteers, was established to assist with the harbor and beach patrols. The auxiliary, known as the Temporary Reserve (TR), was organized in three flotillas—Hampton, Portsmouth, and Dover. The Hampton TR used dog patrols to monitor the beaches from Hampton River to the Army installations at Odiorne Point, and stood tower watches in the lifeboat station at Hampton Beach. The Portsmouth group was responsible for guarding the city's harbor and dock facilities and maintaining Piscataqua River patrols between Portsmouth's two bridges at night. The Dover contingent patrolled Great Bay and its river systems to protect the "back door of the navy yard," as well as the upriver petroleum stations and dock facilities. The three TR flotillas freed hundreds of active-duty Coast Guard personnel for combat duty. The flotillas remained active until November 1945.[40]

Activity at the various harbor defense units declined as the war progressed. By 1943, the war had moved on to distant theaters and the coastal threat had declined substantially. Construction slowed at the forts and the Army shipped resources originally designated for harbor defense elsewhere. Four months before Fort Dearborn's new 6-inch and 16-inch guns were completed and test-fired, a 4 February 1944 Harbor Defense Log entry signaled the beginning of the end: "Quite a day. Information of reduction received today. 34 officers authorized."[41] A farewell party for departing personnel occurred at Camp Langdon on 4 March 1944. The Army reassigned the men of the 22nd Coast Artillery at Camp Langdon to Camp Perry, Texas, "to earn their infantry badges."[42] The battle-hardened instructors there "were especially hard on them because of their previously safe and soft life stateside in the coast artillery."[43] The instructors apparently perceived duty with the harbor defense unit in New Castle, New Hampshire, to be less arduous than the overseas assignments drawn by other Army veterans. The Army announced on 25 July 1945 that all Atlantic Coast batteries had been returned to caretaker status.[44]

The Eastern Defense Command ordered the removal of all mines from Portsmouth Harbor on 20 March 1945. CPO Reda's diary provides details of the removal of Portsmouth's minefield, including the disposal of suspect mines at sea:

> April 2nd 1945. Back in camp. Orders had come in while I was on furlough to pick up the mine field. . . The [removed] TNT is stored at Fort Dearborn under guard. After it is placed in a box car and shipped to parts unknown. . . . [later] Soon this job will be complete as we only have 26 mines to go. *If a mine is brought in on a planter and is found to leak & be wet, this mine is taken out about 25 miles to sea then it is cut loose and dumped into the ocean.* So far we have been pretty lucky no one was hurt. In Portland they are way behind on picking up their mine field. We have completed the picking up of our entire mine field of 182 mines in record time [emphasis added].[45]

Based on Reda's description, there was probably not much competition for his highly dangerous job:

> Most of the mines when they are brought out still have from 5 to 20 lbs of TNT in them. This is where my job starts. I have to go down into the mine. As

small as I am, I have a tough time getting into the mine as the opening isn't so large. . . . I put on a face mask and scrape all the TNT loose. *Between you and I this is a very dangerous job.* I wear sneakers and use non-sparkable tools. I'm down in the mine for 15 to 20 minutes. If I make a spark I would blow myself and the entire fort up with me [emphasis added].[46]

Despite the hazards, the dismantling of the Portsmouth minefield concluded safely — although of course the final status of the mines dumped at sea remains unknown.

The Portsmouth harbor defense system had been a costly but necessary precaution — an insurance policy the nation was pleased not to redeem. None of the fort batteries ever fired in attack, although unidentified passing ships occasionally received warning shots. One mine exploded in Portsmouth Harbor, which resulted in an unexplained oil slick. Occasional reports of submarine sightings, presumed to be U-boats, went unconfirmed. There were, however, four confirmed U-boat sightings in May 1945. Shortly after V-E Day, hundreds of local residents lined the shores of the Piscataqua River to observe U-805, U-873, U-1228, and U-234, under the escort of U.S. destroyers, transit to the navy yard for close observation and selective stripping, as well as the processing of prisoners. The once-feared German U-boats had finally gained entry to Portsmouth Harbor — as surrendered vessels under the surveillance of the U.S. Navy.

CHAPTER 4
CIVIL DEFENSE

The business section is very dark now. . . . And yet you can look in the direction of the Navy yard from any place in the city and see the bright glow in the sky. Merchants and householders, although very cooperative, never cease to remind me of the bright lights on the navy yard and ask me what harm their 100 watt bulb in their window can do in comparison with that glow.

Gerald D. Foss
Chairman, Portsmouth
Civilian Defense
13 May 1942

Ask any civilian who lived through World War II about his or her most vivid homeland memories, and you will often hear stories of air raid sirens, blackout drills, and block wardens with armbands patrolling neighborhoods with flashlights. Civil defense trappings were very visible as millions of citizens from coast to coast participated in the effort. The public's enthusiasm for civil defense peaked at the start of the war and gradually waned as the war progressed—as did federal and local monetary support for the program. Civil defense requirements remained stringent for most of the war years, well after funding had been redirected to more urgent wartime needs overseas. The organization persisted through the efforts of loyal volunteers and contributors eager to do their part for the war effort.

Civil defense was a nationwide civilian volunteer

organization under the direction of the U.S. Army, whose primary purpose was the prevention, detection, and survival of an enemy air attack. At its peak, New Hampshire had about 30,000 civil defense volunteers, 1,500 assigned to the Portsmouth Defense Area, which was integrated with the Portsmouth Harbor Defense System. Volunteers staffed observation towers, patrolled neighborhoods, enforced dimout regulations, conducted blackout drills, and planned for dreaded enemy bombing attacks like those that had devastated Britain.

The Air Attack Threat

During the winter of 1941–42, many residents of seacoast New Hampshire and southern Maine, including senior officers at the Portsmouth Navy Yard, considered a German air attack highly probable. On the day before Christmas 1941, the shipyard's industrial officer, Captain H. F. D. Davis, reminded shipyard employees that they should be especially vigilant on Sundays and holidays because an attack would most likely come on those days.[1] In February 1942, a directive from Commandant Rear Admiral John D. Wainwright advised his managers to take precautions in anticipation of a possible bombardment: "The Axis Governments have used bombs ranging from 100 to 3000 pounds in their attacks on England"; consequently, he added, "vessels in the yard should be berthed singly if possible, and as widely dispersed as feasible, commensurate with dock space available and repair facilities along the docks."[2] Shipyard workers carried these warnings home, heightening public concerns about the possibility of an imminent attack. Harold Whitehouse's father, an employee at the yard, apparently spread the word to his family, because it was Harold's impression that "the enemy was right off the coast,"[3] ready to attack — an opinion shared by many of his neighbors.

New York City Mayor Fiorello La Guardia issued similar warnings to his constituents: "The war will come right to our cities and residential districts. At the present time, under the present relative position of the enemy, we may not expect long-continued, sustained attacks such as the cities of Great Britain have suffered, but we will be attacked—never underestimate the strength, the cruelty of the enemy—and we must prepare for that."[4] In March 1941, National Civic Patrol founder Natalie Hays Hammond of Gloucester, Massachusetts, warned a Hampton, New Hampshire, audience, "Americans should apply for their gas-masks before it is too late and should learn how to use them."[5] Fear was definitely in the air—the same air being scanned for German bombers by civil defense observers.

The attack on Pearl Harbor had raised serious doubts about the protection the wide Atlantic Ocean supposedly offered against a German attack. If the Japanese could mount an attack across the vast Pacific, who knew what the technologically superior Germans might be able to do? They did not possess a carrier navy like the Japanese, but the ingenious and industrially competent Germans had already crossed both the South Atlantic and the North Atlantic in the 1930s with the twelve-engine Dornier DO X aircraft, the largest heavier-than-air aircraft of its time.[6] What military applications might evolve from that advanced technology? If Germany carried the war to America's shores, as many assumed they could, the seacoasts of Maine, New Hampshire, and Massachusetts would be among the easiest targets to reach.

Civil defense posters soon warned, "This war is not like any other. It may reach your street—your home—at any moment. You may be fighting in this war tomorrow, or next week, or next month. Your government asks of you one simple thing, but one very important thing. . . . Learn and remember what to do if enemy planes and bombs come."[7] Coastal observation posts were quickly constructed from which volunteers searched the skies for enemy aircraft. Renovated and newly constructed batteries soon pointed seaward to engage perceived threats; blackout drills became common occurrences. In Concord, New Hampshire, workers painted the gold statehouse dome green to make it less visible to enemy planes.[8] The signs of war were everywhere; defense of the homeland had become a high priority for everyone. This nation could not afford to be surprised again.

Civil Defense Organization

This vast and far-flung operation certainly could not be left to chance. In 1941 the federal Office of Civilian Defense (OCD) was created to coordinate national defense through regional, state, and local offices. Home-front historian James W. Wensyel wrote of the OCD, "It organized most communities down to the block level, adding such expressions as 'block warden,' 'blackout,' and 'dim-out' to our wartime vocabulary. Volunteers studied aircraft identification silhouettes and stored sandbags, helmets, flashlights, buckets, and hoses for use in the event of an air raid. In mock attacks Civil Air Patrol planes dropped flour-filled dummy bombs or wardens threw firecrackers to simulate exploding shells."[9] In coastal New Hampshire and southern Maine, most of this activity occurred under the auspices of the Portsmouth Council of Defense, which included the New Hampshire towns of Portsmouth, New Castle, Newmarket, and Greenland and the Maine towns of Kittery and Eliot.

The New Hampshire State Council of Defense was created through legislation on 4 April 1941. The Portsmouth Council of Defense, created in November of that same year, was staffed twenty-four hours a day from 9 December 1941 until 22 February 1944.[10] OCD and the Portsmouth council had two arms: homeland defense and service. The defense corps received direction from the U.S. Army regarding procedures to prevent and respond to enemy attacks. The Portsmouth Defense Council's tasks primarily involved enforcing coastal dimout requirements, conducting blackout drills, preparing evacuation plans, and planning for dreaded disasters such as enemy bombardments and gas attacks. The service arm of OCD provided citizen support for homeland programs — victory gardens, war bond drives, salvage drives, conservation of resources for war, and consumer interest programs.

By December 1942, the state had established defense councils in 234 cities and towns throughout New Hampshire. There was no shortage of volunteers, but not all Americans were eligible initially to serve in the Civil Defense Corps. Residents of Portsmouth's North End, the city's Little Italy, must have been pleased to receive the 29 October 1942 memorandum from the New Hampshire State Council of Defense advising them, "After October 1942, aliens of Italian nationality will not be classified as enemy aliens, and accordingly will become eligible to become members of the Civilian Defense Corps."[11] With this notice, Portsmouth's pool of OCD candidates increased significantly.

The Portsmouth council's monthly Civilian Defense Report of 31 October 1942 shows the following staffing, 1,244 volunteers filling the positions indicated:[12]

Defense Council   3
Office Staff   7

Defense Corps		Service Corps	
Staff	7	Agriculture	1
Air Raid Wardens	360	Block Leaders	42
Auxiliary Firemen	82	Child Care	16
Auxiliary Police	37	Consumer	5
Decontamination	7	Housing	4
Demolition and Clearance	15	Nutrition	17
Drivers	31	Salvage	178
Emer. Food and Housing	167	War Bonds/Stamps	13
Emergency Medical	107		
Fire Watches	1		
Messengers	31		
Trainees	61		
Nurses' Aides	9		
Trainees	12		
Rescue Squads	31		

The preponderance of air raid wardens (33 percent) in the defense corps and salvage volunteers (65 percent) in the service corps suggests the importance of each of these responsibilities. This chapter focuses on the defense corps; Chapter 6, "Homeland Portsmouth," includes discussion about the service corps.

The nerve center for all civil defense activities, the Portsmouth Council Report Center, occupied the basement of a building to the rear of the First National Bank on Pleasant Street, immediately off Market Square. Ann Elaine "Mickey" McWilliams-Hussey was a volunteer at the report center. After graduating from Portsmouth High School in 1940, McWilliams-Hussey went to work in the heart of the city for Portsmouth Savings Bank; she also volunteered at the USO and the report center, both just a few blocks from her place of employment.[13] She and more than a thousand other volunteers staffed the Portsmouth Council of Defense.

Much of the council's daily activity involved the receipt and coordination of reports from a broad network of observers. A glance at the Portsmouth Defense Area Civil Defense Logbook for 1 January 1942 to 14 April 1942 reveals about a hundred entries a day documenting phone calls from post observers, other civil defense centers, and the Red Cross. Most of the calls reported routine setting and relieving of the watches at the various observation posts. Every two hours the Portsmouth Warning Center received a "white" report from the Boston Warning Center via Concord, meaning conditions were normal with no attack threats. The Portsmouth Warning Center operated out of the basement of the Masonic lodge on Middle Street.[14] A 20 January 1942 note from C. M. Sheppard, controller of the warning center, to the Portsmouth Report Center explained the coded threat-reporting system: "'White' report routinely given every two hours from Army headquarters in Boston to Portsmouth Warning Center and passed to Portsmouth Report Center. . . In case of an impending air raid, your report center will be given the color 'Yellow,' 'Blue,' or 'Red,' as it is flashed from Army Headquarters. Be prepared to act at once when any one of these colors is flashed to you."[15] The log for the first quarter of 1942 contained only "white" reports, reassuring everyone from the Army headquarters in Boston down to the local post observers in the Portsmouth Defense Area that conditions were normal. Despite elaborate preparations for an attack, and an occasional reported threat that was quickly dismissed, conditions remained normal for the duration of the war.

All blackout and air raid drills were coordinated from the Portsmouth Council Report Center. At its peak in late 1943, the center had a complement of eighty-four volunteers.

During the quiet periods, as few as two volunteers might be on watch. If a warning call was received, the staffing immediately expanded to include the chief air raid warden, the deputy chief warden, the blackout chairman, and representatives from the electric plant, fire department, and police department. After the first wave of arrivals, additional personnel reported to the center: phone operators, zone wardens, Red Cross workers and representatives from the water company, street department, and gas company. Thirty or forty volunteers with specific assignments quickly joined the original two watch-standers. In the case of a drill or reported threat, the center could go from quiet to chaos in a matter of minutes.[16]

One erroneously reported attack, just two days after Pearl Harbor, must have elevated the pulse rates of many Portsmouth residents. According to Laurence Shorey, secretary of the Portsmouth War Records Committee, "It was a false alarm, but [it] brought to Portsmouth the grim possibilities of what might happen as a result of the declaration of war the day before. . . . A report was received that enemy air raiders were approaching the country . . . coming down the Maine coast. . . . The ward system of spreading the alarm through the city was put into effect for the first time. . . . It worked admirably."[17] Officials had fully implemented Portsmouth's civil defense warning system, spreading fears and concerns about what the coming months might hold. German bombers never actually made an appearance over the seacoast; however, on two occasions in late 1941, Canadian bombers penetrated local airspace and landed in the Portsmouth suburbs. In the first instance, there is no mention of detection by the Civil Air Patrol; in the second, a Civil Air Patrol observer recognized the plane and aided in its emergency landing.[18]

Two months before Pearl Harbor, on 2 October 1941, a

twin-motored Royal Canadian Air Force Bolinbroke bomber flying a military mission out of Halifax lost its way while on a routine patrol off Nova Scotia and ended up "300 feet from the bedroom of Mr. and Mrs. Raymond Cash" on Winnicut Road in Greenland, New Hampshire. After dropping flares, and with "only a few minutes of gas supply left," the crew landed in an open field, and "came to their [the Cashes'] house to use the telephone." After welcoming their unexpected guests, Mrs. Cash served the men coffee. Adding more humor to this bizarre tale, when told they were in Greenland, the pilot, confusing the New Hampshire town with "the large island in the north Atlantic," reportedly "expressed his [negative] opinion of the navigator." The plane required repairs before being flown back to Canada.[19]

Two months later, on 16 December 1941, a second Canadian bomber visited Portsmouth when "another twin-motored Canadian bomber made a forced night-time landing at the Municipal Airport . . . with only 25 gallons of gasoline left in the tank." This time "a member of the Civilian Air Patrol, riding in an automobile, recognized it [the plane]" and quickly arranged to have the plane land "by the lights of over fifty automobiles." The next day the plane was refueled and returned to Canada. This event and the rumored German air attack, both occurring within days of the Pearl Harbor attack, fully exercised the city's civil defense system, as well as the nerves of Portsmouth residents.[20]

Funding Issues. The local council received direction from the State Council of Defense in Concord, New Hampshire, which fell under the jurisdiction of the U.S. Army Headquarters First Corps area commander in Boston. Tasks and requirements, and some limited equipment, flowed down the chain-of-command to the Portsmouth council—but little or no funding flowed with them. The council was forced to rely on the cooperation and financial support of local government officials to carry out its responsibilities. This arrangement, not surprisingly, proved to be problematic.

The council's projected equipment needs, established by the federal government, far exceeded the city's ability to provide. It was a classic example of a bureaucracy dictating requirements with little or no responsibility for fulfilling them. A 10 August 1942 letter from the chairman of the Portsmouth council, Gerald D. Foss, to the mayor and city council identified the following anticipated federal government support as a precursor to the additional support that would be required from the city:

Armbands	1200	Firemen's boots	40
Trailer pumps	4	Pump tank extinguishers	616
Steel helmets	300	Skid-mounted pumps	2
Firemen's helmets	40	Front-mounted pumps	2
Firemen's coats	40		

Foss added, "The federal government will also contribute gas masks, gas protective clothing . . . and most of the medical equipment." Much remained for the city to supply.

It took the city two months, until 10 October 1942, to decide what support to provide. The list below is just part of the "bare essential equipment" requested for air raid wardens, firemen, and decontamination squads in order "to protect lives and property in case of an attack," with the actual support provided by the city in parentheses:

Stirrup pumps	54 (42)	Helmets	150 (200)
Asbestos gloves/pairs	84 (48)	Faucet adapters	TBD (100)
First-aid kits	400 (400)	Firemen's coats	40 (24)
Gas rattlers (alarms)	400 (42)	Firemen's boots	40 (24)
Used trucks	3 (2)		

However, the city offered no assistance at all for many other requested items — buckets (350), hose (2,700 feet), clothesline (8,400 feet), bomb shovels (126), pairs of goggles (400), crowbars (84), axes (84), ladders (42), whistles (400), logbooks (42), brooms (100), and scrub brushes (24). The wide gap between the council's needs and the city's response forced the council to solicit support from local businesses and industries. For example, Chairman Foss noted, "The equipment used by Demolition crews, Emergency Food and Housing, and Rescue squads . . . is being donated by contractors, hotels, restaurants, and social agencies in this city." Civil defense was, to some degree, a bootstrap operation: as a last resort, determined and patriotic OCD volunteers often supplied some of their own equipment.

The limited funding and support provided early in the war by Portsmouth city officials dried up completely as the threat of an enemy attack subsided. Initially, Mayor Rowe empowered Foss to approve payment of routine bills. When Foss sought to continue this practice under the new mayor, Charles M. Dale, in January 1943, the mayor informed Foss he wished "to approve in advance bills for Civilian Defense expenditures other than small items." Throughout the remainder of the war, Foss obtained the mayor's prior approval for almost all purchases and forwarded the most minor of bills to him. Portsmouth Defense Council's purchases were carefully scrutinized, tightly controlled, and meager.[21]

Disaster Planning

The primary mission of the defense arm of the OCD was the protection of civilians in the case of an enemy attack. Most volunteers received local training qualifying them to perform their assignments; selected volunteers attended more formal and comprehensive training at the War Department Civil

Defense School at Amherst University. This ten-day school, taught by Army instructors of the Chemical Warfare Service, covered everything needed "to reduce the loss of life, injuries, and material damage that will result from the air raids which we hope will not come, but which we must expect and prepare to meet."[22] Camp Langdon offered other possibilities for training. On 4 May 1942, Foss wrote Lieutenant Colonel Harry E. Pendelton at Camp Langdon, "We [the Portsmouth Defense Council] have a decontamination squad of ten men for the city of Portsmouth in the event we ever get a gas attack . . . would like training from someone who knows about gas . . . [to] sniff some gases or, if possible, go through a gas chamber." The request to have trainees sniff gas and go through a gas chamber in nearby New Castle appears hideously peculiar in light of the tragic gas chamber happenings in Europe about the same time.

The Army generated a seemingly endless stream of literature to inform the public about the enemy's capabilities to deliver mass destruction; the Portsmouth council received more than a hundred Army "Protection Memoranda" in 1942. These memoranda, designed to educate the public, also served as gruesome reminders of the life-threatening tragedies that potentially awaited them. For example, Memorandum No. 104 of 24 October 1942 discussed "new types of incendiary and anti-personnel bombs used by the enemy," with detailed descriptions of firebombs, combination incendiary and high-explosive bombs, phosphorous-oil bombs, and thermal-pellet bombs. Protection Memorandum No. 50 (19 March 1942) required that "all unexploded and delayed action bombs" be reported immediately to the Office of Civilian Defense in Boston.[23] Protection Memorandum No. 46 (23 June 1942) provided guidance for personal protection during a gas attack: "War gases stay close to the ground, for they are heavier than air. To get out of a gassed area, simply walk against the wind or go upstairs."[24] These frequent sobering reminders of the looming threat kept the civil defense army of volunteers scanning the skies for the earliest possible doomsday warning.

Concord OCD headquarters passed warnings of an impending air attack via a network of telephone calls or messengers. Portsmouth received alerts direct from Concord and relayed the warnings to nearby Fort Stark; to Kittery, Ogunquit, Wells, York, and Eliot in Maine; and to New Castle, Rye, Greenland, Newington, and North Hampton in New Hampshire. Like Portsmouth, other "first-alert" towns — among them Dover, Somersworth, Rochester, Hampton, and Exeter — were responsible for notifying the smaller communities around them.[25] If all worked as intended, advance threat alerts (white, yellow, blue) would flow from the Boston Warning Center through Concord to the local warning centers prior to the final red alert, giving communities ample time to sound appropriate alarms.

Air raid alarms differed by locality. The nine Portsmouth schools had sirens — large canisters that looked like bird feeders — on their roofs.[26] The Newington alarm consisted of the ringing of the church bell and the blowing of the whistle of the Shell Gasoline Company. Concerned that the ice fishermen on Great Bay might not hear the signals, Reginald P. Kennard, chief air raid warden of Newington, requested the navy yard to fire a "small sized cannon" or "gun suitable for the warning."[27] In the town of Hampton, in the event of an attack, "church bells and the town bell would be rung and the police and fire chiefs would drive through town blaring their sirens."[28] In all cases, the "attack" signal was a three-minute-long warbling signal or series of short blasts. The "all clear" was a one-minute blast, two minutes of silence, a one-minute blast, a two-minute silence, and a one-minute blast.[29] The signals were standard; the noise sources delivering those signals varied according to whatever was available in each community.

Public air raid shelters in the city of Portsmouth were slow to be established. In November 1942, the city's planning board conducted an exhaustive survey of all buildings in the business section of the city and recommended creating three public air raid shelters, accommodating approximately a thousand people, in the basements of City Hall, South Church, and North Church. The report noted, "These basements are all provided with two exits and can be made safe from flying glass at a minimum expense."[30] Eight months later, in August 1943, needed upgrades remained unfunded for two of the buildings, and the third had merely been "marked with luminous signs with arrows on the street pointing to the direction of the air raid shelter." [31] Two years into the war, the support of city officials for civil defense was less than enthusiastic if significant costs were involved. Had the threat of attack not subsided so quickly, there might have been far more interest in providing suitable bomb shelters.

Meanwhile, schoolchildren were fingerprinted for identification purposes in the event of a bombing attack.[32] Sandra Goss Munsey recalls the day the Rye police chief and a state trooper came to the Rye elementary school to fingerprint everyone in her first-grade class: "I can remember being told that it was being done so that we could be identified if we became separated from our parents the way many English children had been. We had heard the stories of how English children had been moved inland and away from the cities for safety. No one made a big deal about it, so we were not frightened by the prospect. Of course, what was never discussed was the possibility of a direct attack. It was only much later that I realized that the fingerprints could be used to identify the dead and injured."[33] As the war progressed, defense preparations became highly cost-dependent. The completion of expensive bomb shelters languished while inexpensive efforts such as fingerprinting went forward.

Evacuation planning was another Portsmouth Defense Council responsibility. The Portsmouth evacuation plan, shown in figure 6, divided the city into eleven zones with an evacuation assembly site designated for each zone. The eleven zones were further divided into forty-two sectors. It was the council's intent to contact each home in all forty-two sectors to advise residents where to report in case of an evacuation. In May 1943, Foss reported to his superiors in Concord that the sector surveys had been completed in thirty-five of the sectors, but there was little hope of completing the task in all forty-two. The person in charge of the program had resigned and no replacement was available. Foss advised, "The program has been neglected because it appeared so hopeless." Portsmouth citizens apparently saw little threat of an enemy attack in May 1943, and even less need for an evacuation plan.

Ground Observation Corps

At the peak of the war, the Army Air Corps Ground Observation Corps (GOC) had 195 observation posts in New Hampshire manned by 17,000 volunteers.[34] Many posts were located in small towns along the vulnerable New Hampshire seacoast. Rye had two posts: one north of Wallis Sands and another at Straw's Point, just south of Rye Harbor. As Rye resident Sandra Goss Munsey recalls, "GOC members were all volunteers, mostly local women during the day, who worked in pairs scanning the sea and skies with binoculars. Their training involved memorizing the silhouetted shapes of

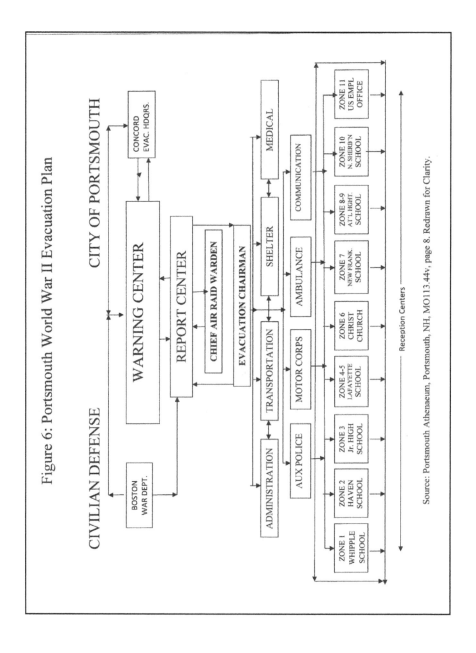

Figure 6: Portsmouth World War II Evacuation Plan

Source: Portsmouth Athenaeum, Portsmouth, NH, MO113.44v, page 8. Redrawn for Clarity.

airplanes and ships using flash cards a little larger than playing cards. Other cards provided an estimate of distance. An observer reported every passing aircraft and vessel, regardless of size, shape, or description, by telephone to a regional center where the movement of any particular craft could be tracked on a map."[35] The observation posts were often staffed by friends and family standing watches together.

Precautions against attack were not limited to coastal areas. Nationwide, the GOC attracted 600,000 plane spotters, who received training in identifying various types of German aircraft and their armament and capabilities. Models of German aircraft, often made by local students, were also popular identification aids. Bill Tebo volunteered for a Portsmouth High School program that had students craft model German airplanes for use by coastal lookouts. According to the number of models they built, the students received points toward honorary military titles that advanced them in seniority and importance. No compensation was involved; the reward was the personal satisfaction of contributing to the war effort.[36]

Aircraft identification quickly became something of a fad, part of everyday life for adults and children. Toy kits such as Plane Spotter advertised, "Is it a Republic P-47 or a Douglas DC3-A Flying Fortress or a Liberal Bomber? Every youngster from six to sixty wants to know. Everybody is interested in identifying planes." Another game, Spot'em, taught the identification of "96 leading war planes of the Allied Nations and the Axis." The manufacturers of the board game Spot-a-Plane reported, "Sales are soaring. We've never produced a faster selling game." Advertisements cited Parker Brothers' Warplane Game of Spotting as "Brand New and Popular in every City and Town." Even card players dealt from Bicycle decks featuring three different profiles of German planes.

Every box of Kellogg's Pep cereal contained an "authentic scale model" warplane assembly kit, a cardboard sheet of perforated plane parts, "suitable for silhouette identification." Plane identification wasn't just a crucial element of civil defense—it was also a profitable business.[37]

Harold Whitehouse acquired his knowledge of enemy aircraft from bubble gum cards, previously the province of baseball heroes: "We had these playing cards that we got from bubble gum and on the cards all the planes were identified that belonged to Germany and Japan. We'd play games and hold the cards up for just a second and we had to tell the specifics about a German plane or a Japanese [Z]ero, how fast they were or what kind of armament they had—you knew the statistics."[38]

A 6 June 1942 *Reader's Digest* article, "Are America's Civilians Ready for Attack?" told of civil defense preparations in Sheridan County, Wyoming—1,700 miles from the Atlantic seaboard and 900 miles from the Pacific coast. Some 3,000 of the county's total population of 19,000 people had enlisted in civil-defense activities. The entire town of Ranchester, Wyoming, with a population of 153, volunteered to serve in some capacity. The last man to volunteer reportedly signed on from his sickbed.[39] According to James Wensyel, "In Nebraska three ladies, each over seventy years of age, took turns serving as their town's 'plane spotter' every day of the war."[40] Everyone—men, women, and children—had a role to play, if they were willing.

In the summer of 1942, the entire nation was on guard. Wensyel wrote, "All across America, civilian defense seemed to be an area where Americans, anxious to help, could contribute to the war effort. A meeting to recruit OCD volunteers in Hannibal, Missouri, packed the armory with four thousand applicants, while another fifteen thousand waited outside. When the mayor of Northport, Alabama, galloped through the streets on horseback calling for volunteers, eighty percent of the town's 2,500 residents responded."[41] Civil defense had become a popular national pastime. If remote towns in Wyoming, Missouri, and Alabama were watching the skies and actively preparing for an enemy attack, Portsmouth, with a major industrial target in its backyard, had to be even more vigilant.

Reduced Lighting

In the seacoast area, that vigilance and enthusiasm faded somewhat when it came to the imposition of lighting requirements. The U.S. Army had two reduced lighting categories: dimouts and blackouts. Precautionary dimout measures established permanent reduced lighting standards for coastal areas, and directly affected day-to-day life on the seacoast. These requirements quickly became controversial: why, local merchants wondered, did they need to darken their storefronts with a shipyard ablaze with lights working three shifts just across the river? The public was much more compliant when it came to the occasional blackout drill or warning, which required the elimination of all light sources, than they were to the nightly enforcement of the dimouts.

Dimouts. Everyone was impacted by dimout regulations, which strictly governed everything from the routine lighting of businesses in downtown Portsmouth to seacoast homes and automobiles. Restrictions on sky glow and lights shining seaward were designed to protect against both surprise air assaults and submarine attacks; shipping silhouetted against a lighted background could be an inviting target to a periscope attack. Seacoast residents hung dimout shades or blackout curtains over the windows of their homes and dimmed their automobile lights by applying black electrical tape to the upper half of their headlights.[42,43] Every other streetlight was dark, and shields were installed on the ones in use to direct light downward.

Compliance was definitely not optional. The Portsmouth Defense Area followed the dimout regulations for New England as administered by U.S. Army Headquarters First Service Command in Boston. The designated dimout area for New Hampshire included "all the territory, including islands, lying south and east" of the major highways connecting the Maine–New Hampshire border to Dover, to Exeter, to West Windham, to the New Hampshire–Massachusetts border—roughly an arc extending twenty miles inland from the New Hampshire seacoast. The dimout area for southern Maine was similarly expansive, covering all areas south and east of the major highways connecting Gray to Sanford to North Berwick to the Maine–New Hampshire border.[44]

The regulations required controlled lighting "in coastal and metropolitan areas . . . to reduce permanently certain lighting, for the preservation of the commerce of the United States . . . from damage and destruction by enemy attack, for the prevention of enemy action against our shores, and . . . to reduce the dangers from hostile air operations." Consequently, "[a]ll lights of every nature and . . . source [with some exceptions for military bases, industries essential to the war effort, and the safety of automobiles, railroads, etc.] shall be permanently shielded, obscured, or reduced in intensity so that no light there from shall be visible from any point on the waters of the Atlantic Ocean. . . . If the lights thus visible cannot be so shielded or controlled, they shall be extinguished." Despite the apparent precision of the wording, the regulations left much to interpretation; dimout regulations became ever more controversial as the war progressed and the threat subsided. The Portsmouth Defense Council had the unenviable task of enforcing reduced-lighting requirements that local merchants thought were excessive and unfair.[45]

Much of the contention centered on a perceived inconsistency between the strictly enforced dimout demands on civilian establishments versus the more lenient practices of some industries and federal facilities such as the shipyard, where lighting was essential to support three-shift production of submarines. Merchants argued that it made little sense for them to go to great expense to darken their shops "with such bright lights burning at the Navy yard."[46] Nevertheless, Rockingham County officials vowed to make "every effort for dim-out perfection in Portsmouth" despite the fact that "the Navy yard and lighthouses stand out boldly in violation of the regulations."[47]

Major General Sherman Miles, commanding officer of the Headquarters First Corps Area, responded to this criticism on 19 May 1942: "The question of lights in the Navy yard and other Federal establishments is one of which we are all too well aware, and which we are trying to solve as expeditiously as possible. Work must continue, but you may be sure that steps are being taken to reduce the lighting to the minimum necessary."[48] Such assurances carried little weight with resentful local merchants, when federal establishments were essentially exempt from lighting reductions while they received warnings that "violations of these First Corps Area regulations are subject to federal prosecution."[49]

Things came to a head during the month of May 1942 when Portsmouth received an unsatisfactory report of dimout conditions from an Army inspector. In a letter to New Hampshire Governor Robert O. Blood, Gerald Foss, the defense council's acting chairman, took issue with the report. He wrote, "Mr. Redden has just informed me of the bad news it was your duty to relay concerning the dim-out in Portsmouth. I cannot agree with the report of the officer making the inspection, I have made three separate tours of the city myself seeking violations, the last one was last night, but yet have to find any illuminating signs of any size still glowing." Venting some of his frustration with the Army inspectors and the shipyard's noncompliant lights, Foss added, "The business section is very dark now. . . . And yet you can look in the direction of the Navy yard from any place in the city and see the bright glow in the sky. Merchants and householders, although very cooperative, never cease to remind me of the bright lights on the navy yard and ask me what harm their 100 watt bulb in their window can do in comparison with that glow. . . . I sincerely regret that we have caused you any trouble. If we are at fault, I want to know it, and I will take immediate steps to correct it. However, I dislike unsatisfactory reports when we are trying to comply unless they are justifiable." [50]

Major General Miles, not swayed by Foss's retort, wrote Governor Blood in late May 1942 to inform him that control of seacoast lighting required his attention because of "the unsatisfactory results so far obtained." According to Miles, "Street lighting must be materially diminished in the specified locations and communities. This applies particularly to the street lights themselves, and also to automobile headlights and such unnecessary lighting . . . at the entrances to movie houses, theaters, restaurants, etc."[51] Holding his ground, Foss expressed dissatisfaction with the Army's dimout specifications: "The specifications may be effective, but I doubt whether or not they are practical." According to Foss, "98% of the business establishments are satisfied to leave window lights entirely extinguished. . . . Several of them have told me that they would not expend any money to change their lights to comply with these suggestions."[52] Portsmouth merchants clearly thought Army inspectors were seeking perfect compliance with overly stringent regulations.

While continuing to press for relaxation of the commercial dimout requirements, the city proceeded to comply with the streetlight shielding regulations, which insisted that "the bottom of the shielding shall not be above a horizontal plane through the bottom of the source of the light."[53] In other words, the streetlight could only shine downward with minimal propagation to the side. On 28 May 1942, the shielding was reported complete on 75 percent of Portsmouth's streetlights with the remainder scheduled for completion the following week.[54] With the streetlights shielded and store lights extinguished, Portsmouth was a darkened city during the early months of the war.

Portsmouth had its fair share of chronic offenders against the lighting regulations. Albert Petrillo, owner of the Playland Penny Arcade on Daniel Street, "constantly violated the dimout regulations"; after repeated warnings, the authorities cited him for violations on 26 January and 17 February 1943. Petrillo reportedly "always promised to comply," but failed to do so.[55] The proprietor of the Jarvis restaurants in downtown Portsmouth was another repeat offender. The director of the State Council of Defense, Noel T. Wellman, reported that during the Portsmouth blackout drill on 9 December 1943, "this proprietor too hastily restored the lighted signs on both his restaurants." Wellman added, "It is my understanding that considerable trouble has been experienced with this concern during each blackout test, and although the proprietor is cognizant of the requirements, still he attempts to get away with something."[56] Many Portsmouth merchants complained about the dimout regulations; others such as these two openly defied them, with apparently little consequence. Despite a city ordinance that subjected blackout violators to "a fine not to exceed five hundred dollars or a sentence in the county jail not to exceed six months or both,"[57] research for this book, including a review of the Portsmouth police records for the war years, found no evidence of fines imposed or jail time served.

Burning and smoldering city dumps, typical of the era, were often in violation of the dimout regulations; Portsmouth's dump was no exception. The regulations required that all "bonfires, brush fires, dump fires, burning fields, and outdoor fireplaces and incinerators shall be completely extinguished."[58] On 15 December 1942, OCD observers reported the Portsmouth dump "blazing vividly at about 8:00 pm." When this was reported to the Board of Street Commissioners, the board "agreed to extinguish the fire," but admitted that it was "almost an impossibility" to do so. A 2 February 1943 inspection report noted that the fire "could not be seen" because of a heavy snowfall, but ten days later, it was again "burning vividly at 8:15 pm." The city dump remained in violation of the dimout regulations until they were lifted in late 1943.[59]

Even the chickens had dimout issues. Lighted chicken coops had to comply with dimout regulations for "the proper methods for dimming poultry houses," which required that all "openings which have any light behind them . . . be screened by curtains, shades, blinds, or paint for not less than the upper three-quarters of their open area." Compliance, as reported by Maurice Eugley, owner of a poultry-raising plant in North Reading, Massachusetts, restricted ventilation in his coops to the detriment of the health of his chickens — and it was expensive. He certainly saw no need to adorn his chicken coops with curtains or shades. Headquarters First Service Command investigated the complaint in December 1942 and suggested Eugley hang "bagging or other cheap materials . . . from beams a short distance removed from the windows," which "should allow ample circulation of air." Alternatively, "a coat of white-wash or white paint on the windows should supply a satisfactory covering when the interior lights are of low intensity. In this treatment, however, interior lights should be shielded to prevent their shining above the horizontal when windows are opened for ventilation." All this for a chicken coop! The dimout regulations, whose applicability ranged from naval shipyards to chicken coops, required constant clarification and frequent revision, generating much bureaucratic paperwork.[60]

The dimout regulations remained in effect until December 1943, at which time Portsmouth removed the cones around its streetlights, restoring the city to its "prewar brilliance, ending a dimout of the lights, which has lasted about a year and a half." At the time, the New Hampshire Gas and Electric Company expressed concerns about being able to restore "the cones within the required 24 hour limit in the event of a return to dimout restrictions." Councilman Glenn A. Rice opined, "It was not probable that they would be needed again and that the more light would aid local public safety facilities." Less than two years into the war, routine concerns for public safety had supplanted concerns about an enemy attack. [61]

Blackouts. Unlike the dimout regulations, the blackout rules left little to interpretation—the rules were black and white. Enforcement knew no compromises; the regulations allowed no light leaks of any description. The organizing and conducting of blackout drills was the Portsmouth Defense Council's most important responsibility.

Blackout drills started in the seacoast area more than a year before the United States entered the war. The first shipyard blackout drill occurred on Sunday, 8 September 1940, and the first Portsmouth blackout drill on Sunday, 27 October 1940. After the establishment of the Portsmouth Defense Council in November 1941, blackout drills of the entire seacoast became common. On 29 March 1942, all the towns in Rockingham County held a trial blackout.[62] On 31 October 1942, the Portsmouth Defense Council reported that it had conducted three blackout drills to date, the most recent on 27 October.[63] In Hampton, Herb Casassa, a member of the Men's Auxiliary Police, patrolled local streets to ensure everyone obeyed the blackout rules. According to Casassa, "Along the seacoast and inland all buildings had to have blackout curtains on the east, north and south sides [the most probable direction of an attack], or otherwise insure that lighting didn't show."[64] The Coast Guard went so far as to

Photo 11: Portsmouth blackout drill (circa 1942). The upper half of the photo shows Market Square dimly lighted. The bottom half shows the same view during a blackout drill. The few light leaks are circled. Courtesy Portsmouth War Records, Portsmouth Library.

cover all lighted buoys in the harbor during blackouts.[65]

While dimout regulations were actively challenged from the earliest stages of the war, violations of the blackout regulations were initially rare. An otherwise very successful drill on 27 August 1942 resulted in two reported violations and some mild profanity. The first violation involved a Hill Transportation Company supervisor, Mr. Borque, who felt it necessary to get to the navy yard to coordinate the dozens of buses that would be involved in the shift change during the drill. Stopped by five different sector wardens during his automobile trip from Rye to the navy yard, Borque reportedly told the last warden "to go to hell." The second offense involved a Mr. James Lamont, who, when asked to extinguish his house lights, responded, "I will when I am damn good and ready." Borque's violation highlighted the need for better identification and coordination of personnel authorized to move about during blackout drills. Lamont's violation illustrated nothing more than the rebellious nature of some individuals in the face of authority—even when threatened with fines or jail time.[66]

Blackout violations proliferated as the war progressed and the perceived need for caution and preparedness waned. Chairman Foss, in a 4 June 1943 report about the most recent drill, described a public that had lost much of its enthusiasm: "The results of the surprise test blackout on Wednesday night were the poorest they have ever been in this city. The personnel mobilized quickly and tried to cope with the offenders but there were too many to catch them all in such a short period. The stores and restaurants were very slow in blacking out. . . . Police and wardens were helpless to cope with the situation. Whether it was carelessness, indifference, or plain ignorance I don't know."[67] By the end of that year, the drills were a thing of the past.

OCD Phased Out

The public was eager to relax dimout procedures and other civil defense practices well before the Army was willing to do so. The Portsmouth council, caught in a balancing act between its constituents and the U.S. Army, found it challenging to serve both masters. As public support for discontinuing the unpopular OCD restrictions grew in early October 1943, FDR interjected himself into the debate. Seeking to stem the rising tide, he declared, "The time has not come for demobilization of civilian defense."[68] Perhaps not — but it was inching closer.

On 6 October 1943, Governor Blood noted that the Army had reduced its "aircraft warning system [the volunteer aircraft observation posts] to a skeleton" and many were beginning to question "the need for continuing the various protective services which operate under the State Council of Defense and local councils." Attempting to bolster his case for maintaining the civil defense structure, Blood added, "The possibility of enemy bombing is only one reason for preserving our civilian defense protective services. On numerous occasions they have proved invaluable in helping to fight fires, handle train wreck tragedies, and giving aid in other emergencies." Nevertheless, the governor admitted a greatly reduced probability of enemy bombing, and suggested that routine police, fire, and other emergency services might soon be able to handle such non-war-related events. The argument for a continued civilian defense service was weak and waning.[69]

Facing mounting pressure to relax the civilian defense program, the Army stood its ground. Lieutenant General George Grunert, commander of the Eastern Defense Command, on 26 October 1943 declared: "Twenty-four hour maintenance and operation of an adequate system for warning and mobilizing the civilian defense protective forces in the Eastern Defense Command must be maintained." According to the general, "No one but the German High Command knows whether our East Coast will be bombed. It would seem very regrettable and inadvisable to discontinue or make ineffective the fine citizen protective organization in which over three million patriotic Americans have so loyally participated along our Eastern Seaboard."[70] The U.S. Army was not going to stand down without a fight.

On 1 November 1943, Governor Blood succumbed to the inevitable and signed an executive order suspending the dimout regulations in New Hampshire, the first step toward phasing out the civilian defense service.[71] A few days later, Gerald Foss alerted the governor to rumblings of discontent in his council; some of the volunteers in the Portsmouth warning and report centers were questioning whether "they are doing a worthwhile job." Several volunteers had already left "because they do not believe they are doing their bit toward the prosecution of the war."[72] Slowly but surely, the guard of the Portsmouth Council of Defense was being lowered.

After two more months of resistance, Governor Blood announced on 7 February 1944 "certain modifications and relaxation of Protective Services Organizations and Activities effective 15 February 1944 [subsequently changed to 20 February]"[73] that put the Portsmouth council on a greatly reduced status. Post observers could retire their flash cards depicting German airplane silhouettes. The lights could be turned on; seacoast residents could remove the blackout shades from their windows and the black tape from their car headlights. The threat had subsided, the war was under control, and the civil defense system could be dismantled. Life could resume. Yet the war would continue for another eighteen months.

CHAPTER 5
LIBERTY TOWN

We have to furnish entertainment for the soldiers . . . and sailors at the Navy yard . . . besides trying to keep the army, the navy, the marines, the Free French and the British sailors from getting into trouble with each other and with us.

Frederick D. Gardner
Portsmouth City Councilman
14 November 1941

Put thousands of sailors, soldiers, and marines within walking distance of downtown Portsmouth, and what results? The transformation of the once-peaceful city into a bustling liberty town, seamy and sunny by turns. In fact, Portsmouth became something of a "tale of two cities" — two different cities unto itself, depending on the time of day.

The military was everywhere in wartime Portsmouth. Recalls Harold Whitehouse in *Home by Nine: The Real Story of Portsmouth's South End*:

In 1944 there was so much military and so much patriotism in the city of Portsmouth, it was really unbelievable. Marines, sailors, Army soldiers, jeeps, rack trucks, and two-and-a-half ton trucks were going up and down Sagamore and South Streets, through down town, heading toward Fort Dearborn down in New Castle, toward Odiorne's Point in Rye, or to Fort Foster in Kittery. There was the downtown shore patrol working with the local

police on a Saturday night. There were sailors and
Marines in the different bars.[1]

The burgeoning military presence boosted liquor sales,
challenged local police, and attracted women of questionable
morals. The Navy blamed the latter for an alarming spike in
the venereal disease rate, triggering a hot debate between
navy yard and city officials. The Navy saw rampant
prostitution; city officials balked at the idea — their fair city,
they suggested, *might* have a much more benign "girl
problem." While the debate raged, Portsmouth's undersized
police force, augmented by military shore patrols, struggled
to maintain order when the sun went down and the seedier
side of the city emerged.

Prostitution in Portsmouth before World War II

Prostitution was hardly a new problem for Portsmouth. The
trade had thrived in the notorious Water Street brothel
district around the turn of the century, when a combination
of heightened activity at the shipyard and frequent visits by
fishing boat crews flooded downtown Portsmouth with
young sailors. Prostitution's heyday was reportedly in 1897
around the time of the Spanish-American War, when as many
as 1,500 sailors a day were ferried across the Piscataqua River
from Kittery to land at the head of Water Street, a short walk
to an evening's entertainment at the bordellos.[2]

City officials, inspired by the Progressive movement and
prompted by civic-minded organizations, closed down the
Water Street houses of ill repute in 1912.[3] Local historian Ray
Brighton thought the closings had more to do with economics
than ideology. He attributed the closing of Portsmouth's
brothels to "the Navy's threat to ship all its liberty parties to
Boston." According to Brighton, "It was only after the Navy

marched a liberty party through Congress and old Vaughn Street down to the railroad station on Deer Street [to catch a train to Boston]"[4] that local leaders got religion and cleaned up Water Street.

World War I brought a new wave of sailors, and the loose women weren't far behind. "Civic League Attacks Portsmouth Morals" declared a 14 November 1917 *Portsmouth Herald* article, citing numerous complaints about carousing sailors on the streets of Portsmouth. Lieutenant Robinson, commander of the naval shore patrol, came to the city's defense. He stated, "The police were doing great work in keeping the men of the navy straight by their work against

Photo 12: Portsmouth waterfront (circa 1923), viewed from the north tower of the Memorial Bridge looking toward what is now Prescott Park. Courtesy Portsmouth Athenaeum.

the illegal liquor traffic and immoral women."[5] Implicit in the lieutenant's praise was the admission that liquor trafficking and immoral women were indeed part of the scene in downtown Portsmouth during World War I.

In an effort to whitewash the city's shady past, the infamous Water Street was renamed Marcy Street about 1912, but it was not until the mid-1930s that beautiful Prescott Park, which now adorns Portsmouth's riverfront, began to take shape. With the several million dollars Mary and Josephine Prescott inherited in 1932 from their brother Charles, who had made his fortune from a chain of retail businesses, the sisters purchased waterfront properties not far from their childhood home for the construction of a park, dedicated to the city in their father's name in 1939.[6] That park is the portion of the current Prescott Park closest to Memorial Bridge. The sisters continued to buy nearby properties, which they bequeathed to the city in the 1950s after Josephine's death in 1949, with the stipulation that those and additional properties to be purchased with bequeathed funds be "used for park and recreational purposes." Thus the original Prescott Park expanded into the city treasure it now is. Where once throngs of drunken sailors roved among Water Street's brothels, families with children and other spectators now gather to enjoy musical productions and other acts on the outdoor stage in this beautiful riverfront park.[7]

This unsavory red-light episode was a dim memory by World War II; however, the mobilization that brought thousands of sailors, marines, soldiers, and industrial workers to the seacoast quickly rekindled those memories. This time the Navy was more aggressive in its approach to the problem, not just in the seacoast but nationwide. Spurred by the military's debilitating experience with prostitutes and venereal disease during World War I, Congress passed the May Act in 1941, forbidding houses of prostitution near military bases.

The military vigorously enforced the May Act around its installations, especially in small towns such as Kittery and Portsmouth. One notable exception to this regime was Honolulu, a city surrounded by military bases with 40,000 personnel. Sixteen well-publicized brothels, according to the Honolulu chief of police, were "operated cleanly and efficiently," contributing to an environment in which "women could travel safely in any part of the city at any time."[8] Seventy years later, a street map of Honolulu's World War II theater district, posted at the entrance to the celebrated Hawaii Theater, highlights the popular entertainment centers of the early 1940s. Contained within the four-block theater district were eight theaters and ten brothels, speaking volumes about the popularity of both sources of entertainment during the war years.[9] Photographs of sailors standing in long lines leading to the front doors of the brothels attest that there was no attempt to cover up this lucrative business. In the interest of public safety and national defense, authorities permitted houses of prostitution to operate in the Navy's backyard on the island of Oahu. Portsmouth, however, was not Honolulu.

In October 1941, with the area rapidly taking on the look of a liberty town, the Navy took a proactive approach to controlling prostitution. Following up on the May Act, a 3 October 1941 notice from Secretary of the Navy Frank Knox proclaimed, "No prostitutes will be allowed in or near the Portsmouth Navy Yard from Oct. 3 1941 until Oct. 3 1945."[10] Why the notice declared a four-year moratorium and not an outright ban on prostitutes is curious, but unknown. The four-year suspension was an uncanny estimate of the actual duration of the war that, for the United States, had yet to start. The moratorium's scheduled end date turned out to be only one month after the Japanese surrendered on 2 September

1945. The Navy Department had banned prostitution "in or near" the navy yard. Officials at the yard, soon concerned about rising venereal disease rates, questioned whether or not the ban reached across the Memorial Bridge to the bars in downtown Portsmouth.

Venereal Disease

Venereal disease had a clandestine history in the city of Portsmouth until World War I. Despite an 1883 law that required the Board of Health to report disease statistics, it was not until 1918 that syphilis and gonorrhea appeared in the city's reports. According to a local medical history, "Perhaps the increased activity at the Navy yard during the First World War had seriously increased the incidence of those previously unmentionable diseases or perhaps the Board of Health had merely suppressed them from earlier published reports to spare the public's sensibilities."[11] "Previously unmentionable diseases" became very mentionable during World War I when 400,000 servicemen nationwide were affected, seriously undermining the readiness of the United States military. Lacking penicillin — not discovered until 1928, and only introduced as a treatment for infection around 1943 — treatment of the disease most often required extended hospital stays. Some thought that "venereal disease had been a more dangerous enemy than the Germans."[12]

In an October 1917 speech, Secretary of the Navy Josephus Daniels described the devastating effects VD was having on the U.S. Navy: "During the last statistical year men of the American Navy lost 141,378 days by such diseases. This means that every day in the year an average of 456 men were disabled. Add to that number those required to care for the disabled, and we have enough men constantly on the non-effective list to man a modern battleship. . . . One ship in the Far East last year reported that 44 percent of the crew became infected with venereal disease of some kind during the cruise."[13] In the same speech, Daniels reported, "Within the last three months 'red light' districts have been abolished in eighteen cities. . . . [A]t last the American people are awake to the necessity of facing squarely the social evil that is the greatest foe of military efficiency." Daniels, who had abolished the naval officers' wine mess with his infamous General Order #99 on 1 July 1914, was all in favor of eliminating another naval tradition, namely red-light districts, to reduce the debilitating effects of VD on his Navy.

Lacking any effective antibiotic to combat the disease, the American military sought to gain control through "a combination of education, repression of prostitution, medical treatment of the infected, and rigorous case finding and contact tracing."[14] This strategy, especially the repression of prostitutes and the rigorous recording and tracking of venereal disease, would become the Navy's modus operandi during the next war. During World War II, the Navy vigorously applied this tactic locally to combat Portsmouth's high VD rate.

Table 3, constructed from the annual reports of the Portsmouth Navy Yard medical officer, reveals just how urgent the problem was. (The VD rates shown are for the shipyard's enlisted population; the total absence of any reported cases of venereal disease among the yard's officer corps is certainly curious, and suspect.) The shipyard's VD rates were reasonable early in the war before spiking in 1943 and 1944. At 104.44 per thousand in 1944, the yard exceeded the rates experienced Navy-wide at the close of the war. A postwar Bureau of Medicine and Surgery letter noted, "Within the past few months there has been a gradual lowering of the venereal disease rates [for the overall Navy]

Table 3: Portsmouth Navy Yard VD Rates (1939–1944) (fiscal years: 1 July–30 June)						
	1939	1940	1941	1942	1943	1944
VD Rate / 1000	22.83	33.6	18.82	17.91	68.56	104.44

Source: Portsmouth Naval Yard Medical Officer's Annual Reports for the years 1940 to 1945, NARA Waltham, RG 181, Naval Station General Correspondence, Box 10, Folder A9-1, "Sanitary Reports."

to 95.8 per thousand per annum. However, this rate is still much greater than at the close of the war."[15] The shipyard's annual medical reports attribute the high incidence to the prevalence of prostitution in the Portsmouth area, which prompted navy yard officers to demand of Portsmouth officials that they clean up their city.

Overall Navy VD rates were considerably higher than were those of the Army, and the national average. According to historian Alan M. Brandt, "Although in 1940 the venereal disease rate in the Army had risen to 42.5 per 1,000, by 1943 it had fallen to 25. . . . In fact, Army data for rates of infection within the military were essentially equivalent to civilian rates. For the entire duration of the war the average incidence of venereal disease was 37 per 1,000."[16] While VD rates at the Portsmouth Navy Yard early in the war were lower than the national average, by the end of the war they were more than double the national average. The nation's capital also made significant contributions to the national average. According to historian Richard R. Lingeman, Washington, DC, teeming with servicemen of all types as well as a huge influx of young female workers, had "the highest VD-contraction rate among servicemen of any city in the country."[17] During World War II, Washington, DC, apparently led the free world to victory and servicemen to VD.

It was only toward the end of the war that penicillin

turned the tide in the fight against VD. In early 1943, penicillin research was still limited to experiments with guinea pigs and syphilitic rabbits — but in September, the U.S. Public Health Service announced successful results treating VD in humans; mass production of the antibiotic started almost immediately. The entire initial supply of "the miracle drug of 1943" went to the military. Within a year, more than ten thousand patients had received penicillin for treatment of early syphilis, and rates of cure were an unprecedented 90 to 97 percent.[18] At first, health officials administered the drug by injection or through a salve, powder, or topical solution, and not orally, because the stomach's gastric juices destroyed it too quickly.[19] It was not until February 1945 that the medical community solved the problem of taking the drug orally "by suspending the drug in indigestible oil and enclosing it in a capsule."[20] After experimenting with the drug in late 1943, the shipyard hospital received its first million units of penicillin on 4 January 1944.[21] Portsmouth Navy Yard sailors were among the first to benefit from the new drug.

Counterintuitive as it first appears, the dramatic leap in navy yard VD rates later in the war may have been due to the increased availability of a cure, partly thanks to a Navy no-pay provision for sailors hospitalized for VD treatment, and partly because the prospect of a quick and effective cure may have caused sailors to take even fewer precautions for prevention.

Prior to the advent of penicillin, treatment of VD at the shipyard hospital required a period of hospitalization for which the men did not receive pay. The medical officer believed once penicillin was available and patients need not stay overnight without pay, "those cases which were formerly treated by the outside practitioner are now reporting to the naval medical officer for treatment."[22] This reasoning, of course, would also argue that the rates earlier in the war were artificially lower than reported in table 3 if the sailors were seeking off-yard treatment.

The Navy's no-pay policy during hospital stays for men with venereal disease began in World War I after the Army reported the practice had resulted in a reduction in VD rates. Secretary of the Navy Josephus Daniels, in a speech entitled "Men Must Live Straight If They Would Shoot Straight," given at the Clinical Congress of Surgeons of North America in Chicago on 22 October 1917, reported: "We [in the U.S. Navy] have tried to meet this indifference [to risk of VD] by regulations providing for stoppage of pay.... The regulation for the Navy went into effect last fall ... [resulting in] a much lower rate of venereal disease since the regulation was passed. In the Army a regulation providing for the stoppage of pay, passed in 1912, resulted in a decrease in the venereal disease rate, of from 145 per thousand in 1911 to approximately 86 per thousand in 1913.... In 1915, the rate was only 84 per thousand."[23] The Army's rate in 1915, in fact, was lower than that experienced at the Portsmouth Navy Yard in 1944 (104.4 per thousand). However, that Army figure was probably artificially low because soldiers were seeking treatment elsewhere to avoid loss of pay, as the yard's sailors did in the early years of World War II.

In 1926 Congress legalized the loss-of-pay policies of the individual branches of the services when it passed a law "founded on the premise that disciplinary measures and loss of pay were deterrents to exposure on the part of military personnel to venereal diseases." While proponents claimed that the no-pay provision was an effective deterrent to the spread of VD, others argued that it merely led to concealment of the disease, clandestine treatment, and potentially serious consequences. Congress put an end to the debate on 27 September 1944 when it repealed the law requiring loss of pay for hospital stays for treatment for venereal disease.[24]

No longer at risk of losing pay, and well aware of the new "miracle drug" cure, VD sufferers at the Portsmouth yard increasingly sought treatment at the shipyard hospital — and relaxed their guard. The shipyard medical officer hypothesized that the apparent effectiveness of penicillin created "a false sense of security" that caused sailors to take a more cavalier attitude toward casual sex. He believed this "lack of restraint and carelessness regarding prompt prophylaxis" contributed to high VD rates and the need for more penicillin. Ironically, the cure was thought to be increasing the rate of the disease.

There are a number of indicators that VD, the previously unmentionable disease, was more prevalent in the local community during the war than revealed at the time. For example, the 1943 health survey summarized diseases reported in Portsmouth from September 1941 to September 1942 as communicable (174), occupational (5), and venereal (34).[25] Assuming that the 34 cases of venereal disease occurred among males aged fifteen to twenty-five years old and that this group included about two thousand people in 1942,[26] a VD rate of 17 per thousand results. This rate closely approximates the VD rate at the navy yard (17.9) for the same period (1942). This is, at best, a rough approximation, but it suggests that venereal disease was probably a civilian health issue in late 1942, when it was beginning to draw the attention of the shipyard medical officer. The survey provides further insight into Portsmouth's VD problem: "For a two-year period, 1941 and 1942 (Oct. 15, 1942), the syphilis rate for the white population, on the basis of actual blood tests and not on a total population, was 1.8 percent [18 per thousand]."[27] Again, the rate is almost identical to the navy yard rate for 1942. However, it is possible that local VD rates were artificially high because civilian hospitals were treating sailors avoiding the loss of pay if they were treated at the shipyard hospital.

Penicillin was available much earlier at the navy yard than in the local community. The navy yard received its first shipments of the drug in January 1944, but Portsmouth hospitals did not use penicillin until the summer of 1944. On 24 March 1945, the *Portsmouth Herald* reported, "A total of 126 patients in 43 different disease classifications have been treated with penicillin at the Portsmouth Hospital during the past 10 months."[28] The article explained that penicillin had been most effective in treating such diseases as pneumonia, cellulitis, and meningitis, with no mention of using it to treat the unmentionable disease.

Table 4: Portsmouth General Hospital Disease Clinics (1941–42)	
Subject / Disease	Frequency of Clinic
Well baby & child health	Weekly
Venereal disease	Weekly
Tuberculosis	Twice a month
Cancer	Twice a month
Mental hygiene	None
Eye and ear	Adults—none / children in schools
Dental	Adults—none/ children in schools

Source: *Survey of Health and Welfare in the Portsmouth Defense Area,* August 1943, 48, Table 9 "Diseases in Portsmouth from September 1941-September 1942

The schedule of weekly clinics (table 4) at the Portsmouth Hospital suggests a civilian concern about venereal disease: the hospital's VD clinic met weekly, more often than all the other clinics except the child health clinic – a strong signal of where the hospital's priorities lay. The hospital would not have conducted weekly VD clinics without the customer base to support such a frequency.

U.S. Navy versus City of Portsmouth

One of the defining characteristics of boomtown Portsmouth was a continual tension between navy yard officials, concerned about the high sailor VD rates, and city leaders. Naval authorities repeatedly brought the problem to the city's attention; they accused city officials of inaction and inordinate delays when it came to policing the bars where sailors and wayward girls congregated for evening entertainment.

The Navy had the upper hand in these encounters as the result of the May Act, which made "vice activities near military installations a federal offense." According to historian Allan M. Brandt, "The May Act provided the legal power necessary for the Department of Justice to assume the policing of areas deemed to be hazardous to the troops by the secretary of the army or the secretary of the navy. . . . [It] served as a prod to local officials to 'clean up' their communities or be deposed by federal officials." This legal advantage should have compelled Portsmouth officials to be responsive to the Navy's requests to "clean up" their city — and if that proved less than persuasive, the millions of dollars in federal funds pouring into the region should have been incentive enough to get the city's attention. Nevertheless, there was a definite give-and-take to the negotiations. This tug-of-war between the Navy and the city was typical of a scene played out in many military communities.[29]

The Navy's aggressive efforts to combat this scourge were a carryover from the previous war; the Navy merely reinstituted the successful anti-VD measures — severe repression of prostitution and rigorous case finding and contact tracing — that had evolved during World War I.[30] But these measures required the attention and cooperation of city officials, which was less forthcoming than the Navy expected.

Portsmouth officials did not agree that their city was overrun with prostitutes. In fact, they went to great lengths to dispute early rumors to that effect. Newspaper articles and citizens often discussed the subject under the veiled label of "vice," allowing them to express alarm at the growth of immoral behavior within their community without the need to delve into the unsavory and uncomfortable details. By the end of the war, however, the words *prostitute* and *venereal disease* were quite prevalent on the front pages of the *Portsmouth Herald*. Early in the war, as shown below, the local press studiously avoided any mention of prostitutes and their accessories.

Shortly after the start of the war, Portsmouth Police Commissioner J. Verne Wood returned from a hygiene conference at Camp Langdon with the news that federal health officials were pleased with "Portsmouth's lack of vice conditions."[31] New England was reportedly better than the rest of the country and Portsmouth was reportedly better than average. This condition did not last long. One month later, in April 1942, Miss Bernadette Connor, New Hampshire's only female probation officer, declared to members of the Women's Community Council, "Portsmouth does have a vice problem and there are houses here that definitively need clearing out." Discussing "the juvenile delinquency problem that has swept across the country with the outbreak of the war," Connor claimed the problem had increased "20 percent in the East and 40 percent in the West." One of the first to speak of Portsmouth's "girl problem," she described the actions of young girls "from dreadfully underprivileged homes" whose "motive is purely a mercenary one wanting things that others more fortunate than they have."[32] Later in 1942, continuing the theme, Mrs. Dorothy Bouvard of the Family Welfare Association declared that "undesirable conditions existed in the city due to the influx of lower-type girls following men in the armed forces."[33] Bouvant described "the streets of Portsmouth around midnight as being unsafe for decent girls," expressing sympathy for the less decent girls "who merely needed a right steer to become useful citizens."[34] Was the city overrun with prostitutes, as the Navy would argue, or did it merely have a wayward girl problem, as suggested by many of Portsmouth's upright citizens?

At a 4 October 1942 meeting of the Catholic Daughters of America, attorney Stanley Burns of Dover told the group that prostitution was widespread on the streets of Portsmouth. He added, "Portsmouth police are trying to get rid of the menace of professional prostitutes but the job is too great for them in view of the tremendous increase in Portsmouth population." Responding a month later to Burns's allegation that Portsmouth was "overrun by vice and venereal disease," the chairman of the Portsmouth Board of Health, Dr. George A. Tredick, declared, "Portsmouth has no noticeable increase in prostitution or venereal disease." He added, "Portsmouth does not live up to the reputation visiting speakers have recently tried to give it of being a den of iniquity due to the influx of defense workers and men in the armed services." The debate raged on.[35]

A *Portsmouth Herald* headline of 9 June 1943 announced, "Portsmouth police act to smash vice rackets." The article noted that Army, Navy, and State Board of Health officials had reported that vice conditions, and the VD rate, had recently soared in Portsmouth. According to Navy doctors, "There are more cases of venereal disease in the city now [during the first five months of 1943] than records show for all of last year." The "smashing of vice rackets" involved routine inspections of beer parlors where the prostitutes congregated to meet enlisted men.[36]

While the Navy suspected rampant prostitution in

Portsmouth, a careful examination of the Portsmouth Police Records reveals no arrests for prostitution during the war years. The records show ten arrests for fornication—possibly a euphemism for prostitution—and two arrests for adultery, involving a total of six sailors and six women. The first instance, on 9 April 1942, involved two sailors, a waitress, and a housewife. Sailor Tucker and waitress Maynard were charged with fornication, sailor Heures and housewife McGill with adultery.[37] The penalties differed for the two offenses. The two charged with adultery were booked in municipal court on "probable cause" and released on $500 bail each pending a trial. Tucker, charged with fornication, paid a $25 fine to avoid a sixty-day sentence, and Maynard, also charged with fornication, received a four-month sentence in the New Hampshire House of Correction.

Several aspects of this incident are noteworthy. Both women appear to have legitimate occupations and are not prostitutes. Also, judging by the penalties, adultery was considered a far more serious offense than fornication. In fact, the punishment for a fornicating sailor ($25 fine), although significant at the time, was hardly a deterrent, while the four-month sentence for a fornicating female was far more harsh. Thus, a night of salacious liberty in Portsmouth would have little lasting consequence for a young bachelor sailor, but serious and far-reaching effects for his date for the evening. These patterns hold true in the following instances as well.

A police log entry for 20 June 1943 notes the arrest of Sadie M. Allis for "maintaining a disorderly house" and the arrests of four individuals there for fornication—two sailors and two female shoe workers, the latter probably referring to employment at the shoe factory on Islington Street.[38] Was Sadie Allis a madam running a house of ill repute? For "maintaining a disorderly house," Allis was booked on probable cause and released on $500 bail pending trial.

Similar to the earlier incident, the two sailors paid fines of $50, while the "shoe workers" received far more excessive sentences of six months in the New Hampshire House of Correction. Were the girls plying their trade as prostitutes or merely young women with respectable jobs experiencing Portsmouth nightlife? This distinction would take on added weight as city and naval officials sought to better monitor liberty hours in downtown Portsmouth.

A 7 July 1943 *Herald* article, "Two Couples Found Guilty in Vice Case," reports the arrest of two young sailors and their escorts for the evening:

> Two sailors and two Portsmouth girls were found guilty in municipal court this morning on a morals charge in the second case to be heard in less than a month. John L. Lutley, one of the sailors who gave his age as 19, pleaded not guilty to the charge of fornication with Jacqueline Demery, a Negress, testifying that he had known her for only 45 minutes before they were arrested. She also pleaded not guilty. Jessee Aldridge, the other sailor, and Madeline E. Rogers, who were involved together in a similar charge, both pleaded not guilty. Sgt. Timothy J. Connors of the police department, who has been assigned by the Portsmouth Police Commission to special duty in a campaign to rid the city of vice, told the court that he found the two couples together in bed when police raided a house at 27 Deer Street shortly after 1 o'clock this morning.[39]

The police records indicate the two women were shoe workers, like the two girls arrested for the same offense a month earlier.[40] One could infer from this that shoe workers, rather than prostitutes, might be the source of the Navy's VD problem in the city of Portsmouth. As with the other cases, the two sailors involved got off with reasonable fines and the women received sentences of six months in the New Hampshire House of Correction. Of all the arrests mentioned above, ten were charged with fornication and two with adultery — none with prostitution.

Portsmouth's bars were subjected to close scrutiny as possible sources of the high VD rates. In researching some recently reported cases of gonorrhea, the Portsmouth *Survey of Health and Welfare* (August 1943) reported that "one tavern had been named once, one twice, and one three times."[41] The report did not provide the names of the taverns; however, it would not be long before the Navy would broadcast the names of the suspected bars and declare them off-limits for enlisted men.

In 1944, with VD rates at the yard climbing at an alarming rate, the Navy redoubled its efforts to identify local sources of the disease. Naval officials advised the State Board of Health in May 1944 that they had traced 24 of the 97 cases reported in Portsmouth in 1943 to contacts at the Dolphin Hotel, located in the heart of the city immediately off Market Square on High Street. During the first quarter of 1944, the Navy traced 8 additional cases to the same hotel.[42] The Dolphin Hotel, nicknamed the Dirty D by those who knew its reputation,[43] apparently did a good business — whatever that business was. In targeting the hotel, the Navy's strategy to control VD through the repression of prostitution and rigorous contact tracing was finding application in the city of Portsmouth.

On 14 June 1944, the *Herald* reported the highlights of a federal health officials' report delivered to Mayor Charles M. Dale by the Portsmouth Social Protection Committee: "These are our facts. . . . Ninety-seven of 200 cases of venereal disease in New Hampshire are attributed to Portsmouth. . . . [There are] definite exposure places; . . . parks on waterfront . . . railroad station . . . taxicabs . . . some hotels . . . some rooming houses. . . . Taxicabs acting as producers . . . transient girls coming to Portsmouth for contacts."[44] Even more damning, the report concluded that "Portsmouth is known as an open city; city officials not interested." The committee's report recommended "that you as mayor, [should] through proper channels bring pressure to bear upon the law enforcement force which would make it possible to correct the deplorable conditions in the community which has been brought to our attention by the navy department, Federal Security Agency, and other social agencies."[45]

Mounting pressure caused the mayor to go on the offensive against the Dolphin Hotel and other alleged VD source sites. Four months later, in October 1944, the city's stepped-up campaign against vice and venereal disease had produced noticeable results. Cecelia T. McGovern, associate social protection representative of the Community War Services, reported that conditions in Portsmouth had improved considerably. According to McGovern, the venereal disease control officer of the First Naval District had indicated to her that, "due to the alertness of the local police and increased vigilance on their part, Portsmouth has not been named as the source of venereal disease as often as it was previous to the formation of the committee last spring."[46] Thus, with this backhanded compliment, Portsmouth received praise with faint damnation for its relative progress in controlling venereal disease.

Prostitution Problem or Girl Problem?

The May Act, which forbade houses of prostitution near naval bases, may have resulted in a classic case of unintended consequences. Some thought the closing of the establishments forced girls to walk the streets or operate out of automobiles, trailer homes, and other movable locations, where they passed on VD at a much higher rate than before as house-based girls. The United States Health Service reported in November 1941 that only 6 percent of soldiers with venereal disease had received infection from professionals.[47] "The girls and madams of the houses had been much more cooperative with authorities and easier to police than their free-lance counterparts," according to historian Richard Lingeman.[48] The report is consistent with the conclusion of the Honolulu chief of police mentioned earlier, that the sixteen houses of prostitution in his city "operated cleanly and efficiently," contributing to a more wholesome environment and much lower incidence of venereal disease.[49]

Portsmouth officials argued strongly that their city had no brothels. In their defense, as was noted earlier, no arrests for prostitution appear in the Portsmouth police log during the war years. The Navy argued just as strongly that prostitutes infested the city, citing the soaring VD rates. The national experience with VD suggests both could be right. There may have been no Portsmouth brothels as such, but the numerous bars and hotels that apparently served as hangouts for prostitutes, near-prostitutes, and wayward girls facilitated interactions with sailors, contributing to high VD rates.

While the Navy continued to raise concerns about prostitution, city officials and the local newspaper continued to define the issue in more benign terms. They attributed the rampant venereal disease not to prostitutes but to large numbers of young females, including many adolescents, who frequented the local bars to meet servicemen. Portsmouth's "girl problem" was by no means unique: nationwide it was known as the Victory girl or V-girl problem. Richard

Lingeman wrote, "The V-girl was next door to being a prostitute, yet there was about her at least a certain refreshing lack of cold professionalism. She offered the lonely GI transitory fun and excitement. . . . She could also, of course, offer him VD, for there was a higher incidence among the amateurs than among the professionals."[50] In 1943, a study made in the Third Naval District (Texas and the Southwest) found that 80 percent of the cases of VD were attributable to girlfriends or pickups. The preamble to a New York state bill stated that "four times as many soldiers are infected from contact with willing girls in their teens as from prostitutes."[51] VD could obviously thrive in areas free of prostitutes. Was Portsmouth one of those areas?

The West Coast had a serious girl problem as described by Maury Klein in *A Call to Arms*: "In San Francisco venereal disease shot up 75 percent in 1942 and 1943. Uniform-struck teen-aged girls, known as 'V-girls' or 'khaki whackies,' clustered around train depots, bus stations, drugstores, or anywhere else they might encounter soldiers or sailors, offering themselves in exchange for a date as simple as a movie or a dance."[52] The World War II girl problem was a coast-to-coast phenomenon, with the East Coast contingent apparently well represented in Portsmouth.

The Portsmouth *Survey of Health and Welfare* (1943) devoted considerable space to the issue, which it considered to be centered on "unsupervised opportunities for unaccompanied women and girls to meet servicemen on leave. . . on the street as casual meetings or pickups, at beer parlors or taverns or juke joints." [53] The survey indicated that "a frequent method of handling girls who are apprehended, and this is only as a rule when an individual remains in the city roaming the streets, is either to send the girl back to where she came from or to have her get out of town."[54] While the girl problem sounds a lot like a prostitution problem, the report was quick to deny the existence of any brothels in the city and point the finger of blame at promiscuous teenagers: "With respect to prostitution, there are no known 'houses' existing in Portsmouth. It was rumored that of late, in several scattered areas throughout the city, women have allowed seduction. This matter is under investigation. . . . The chief problem with respect to sexual promiscuity seems to be with the younger girls of teen ages . . . whose general attitude seems to be that they are working for the cause and are providing entertainment for the servicemen."[55] This explanation implies that Portsmouth's woes were more associated with patriotism than prostitution. The truth probably fell somewhere between the Navy's hard stand on prostitution and the locally defined "girl problem." Portsmouth demographics during the war took a definite turn toward the younger set, and there is no doubt that there were a great many adolescent girls available and attracted to the sudden abundance of young servicemen, and vice versa.

In *No Magic Bullet*, Allan M. Brandt discusses the military's ineffective control of venereal disease by concentrating on the prosecution of prostitutes when the promiscuous girl-next-door was a more likely contributor: "Despite the incarceration of thousands of prostitutes, it soon became clear that this could not in itself solve the venereal disease problem. . . . The military soon turned its attention to the 'promiscuous' girl. Women of loose morals, eager to support the war effort, were determined to be the primary locus of the infection. . . . The harlot with the painted face had stepped aside for the girl-next-door."[56] Portsmouth city officials may have been more accurate in their assessment of the problem than officials at the navy yard, who were rattling their sabers to force the expulsion of professional prostitutes from local establishments.

A May 1943 *Reader's Digest* article, "Trouble on the Street

Photo 13: World War II VD poster.
Courtesy author's personal collection.

Corners," expressed concern about the contribution of amateur girls to the high VD rates:

A year ago 75 percent of the venereal infection of the armed forces of the United States could be traced to professional prostitutes. Today, 80 percent of it comes from young casuals and amateurs—these "Victory girls" and "cuddle bunnies" who go uniform hunting in railroad stations and wander down Main Street late at night looking for pickups are just ordinary kids who have been swept along by a torrent of wartime excitement and free spending.... When they run afoul of the law and are asked why they are delinquent their answers are amazingly naive. The most common are: "because there's nothing else to do in this town," or "because it's patriotic to comfort the poor boys who may go overseas and get killed."[57]

The editorial explained, "In Portland, Maine, the police blotter coldly records that 14, 15, and 16 year old girls are openly soliciting and that they are just average cases among the more than 100 teen age girls arrested in six months." [58] Portland was facing up to its girl problem, and Portsmouth eventually did the same.

Although enlisted men were typically identified as the victims of venereal disease, it is important to highlight the double standard of the times noted by Allan M. Brandt: "The word 'promiscuous' was firmly anchored to 'girl'—a promiscuous man was, by definition, an oxymoron. Women in this view, were the keepers of sexual mores. . . . They infected the soldiers. In this view, venereal disease could only be transmitted in one direction."[59] Brandt's logic suggests that navy yard officials may have misidentified the victims and that, perhaps, infected enlisted men were spreading the disease to previously uninfected local girls. While the sources of the disease may have been varied and debatable, the increased rate of disease toward the end of the war was an undeniable fact.

The 14 May 1943 *Herald* editorial declared, "Portsmouth

has its teen age problem along with other important defense areas and armed service centers, and it is no time to be a namby-pamby about calling a spade a spade."[60] The editorial accurately reported that the teenage girl problem was prevalent in many boomtowns across the United States. In a departure from some of its past veiled reporting of the issue, the *Herald* proclaimed, "The day of the 'hush, hush' method of attacking problems of this nature ceased along with bustles and hoop skirts. Today as never before, such problems can be handled only by 'calling a spade a spade' and fighting them in the open."[61] To the city's credit, local leaders eventually did exactly that. The initial tepid response to the requests of shipyard medical officers for community assistance to solve the rampant VD problem evolved into a much more cooperative effort by the end of the war. Aggressive actions by city officials, increased shore patrols, out-of-bounds signs, penicillin, and a greatly reduced military presence toward the end of the war reduced the shipyard's venereal disease rates as well as the disputes those rates had caused.

The Bar Scene

The extent of prostitution in Portsmouth may have been debatable, but there was no doubt about the buzz of activity in the city's streets and bars. Portsmouth was not just a Navy liberty town: hundreds of marines guarded the yard and naval prison, more than two thousand Army personnel operated the harbor defenses, Coast Guard personnel fulfilled harbor and beach patrol responsibilities, and visiting merchant seamen occasionally came ashore.[62] This collection of young men looking for adventure and evening entertainment frequently made for an explosive mixture.

Late in 1941, Portsmouth City Councilman Frederick D. Gardner voiced concerns about the forthcoming mobilization and the related problems the city would face. He was particularly concerned about the need to "keep the army, the navy, the marines, the Free French and the British sailors from getting into trouble with each other and with us."[63] Gardner's forecast was quite accurate as local authorities assumed the challenge of maintaining the peace and tranquility that residents had come to expect. At times, it appeared to be a losing battle.

It was Harold Whitehouse's impression that there were "sixty-five or seventy beer joints" in downtown Portsmouth, "buzzing with activity on the weekends . . . scattered throughout the city, every side street, every main street, State Street, Daniel Street, High Street—all of them had a beer joint." Some of the more popular bars he recalls were the Starlight, Leary's, the Club Café, and the Golden Horseshoe. Whitehouse's mother cautioned him to stay away from "any side streets or downtown places where there were many beer joints." If he went downtown, he was to stay on Congress Street and warned not to "venture down Daniel Street, Market Street, Penhallow, or any of the side streets where the beer joints are." Only two private clubs, the Forest Club and the Fleet Reserve Club, Whitehouse says, sold liquor. However, the servicemen were not much interested in purchasing memberships to the private clubs to obtain hard liquor. They wanted beer, and they apparently found a lot of it.[64]

In December 1942, local restaurant owners complained of servicemen's brawls that destroyed tables, chairs, crockery, and fixtures almost nightly. The expense of the breakage was one thing, but "the proprietors in their complaint pointed out that much of the property destroyed by sailors and marines cannot be replaced at any price because of war shortages." One owner, Andrew Jarvis, said he would rather have all sailors and marines barred from his premises than continue to suffer these losses. He and his fellow restaurateurs were unanimous in their complaints about sailors and marines, but were quick to exclude soldiers from the list of troublemakers.[65] Shipyard officials added shore patrol officers in response to a request from city officials, and worked with the same officials to have known trouble spots declared out-of-bounds for enlisted men of the Navy and Marine Corps, but not soldiers.[66] Clearly, the authorities considered sailors and marines to be the culprits.

Portsmouth resident Lester Stevens remembers servicemen on liberty in downtown Portsmouth as a mixed blessing. On one hand, those in uniform were welcomed and, according to Stevens, often could not buy a drink because the local residents insisted on treating the young men. On the other hand, Stevens remembers State Street as being a "lively place," the site of "many inter-service competitions." Barroom brawls occasionally poured out to the street, he says, resulting in there being "more blood on State Street than anyplace else."[67]

According to a *Herald* editorial of 19 March 1943 titled "Drastic Action Needed," the Portsmouth Police Department had been ineffective in controlling vandalism afflicting the city's businesses. The *Herald* reported, "Acts of vandalism have been perpetrated upon the city's business establishments in astonishing numbers and little has been done on the part of the police department to cope with the practice. Almost nightly, merchants suffer losses due to broken glass, destroyed signs, and from acts of indecency. . . . There is little doubt that Portsmouth's police force has neither sufficient numbers nor the proper training to cope with wartime problems of the city."[68] Though the editorial did not single out any particular military personnel, there was little doubt that sailors on liberty were contributing to the woes of a troubled police department.

As the result of mounting criticism, the Portsmouth police

commissioners, on 5 April 1943, appealed to Rear Admiral Thomas Withers, commandant of the navy yard, and Colonel Raymond Watt, commander of the harbor defenses, for the assignment of additional military police on the streets of Portsmouth. The request read, "Due to the present unsatisfactory conditions in Portsmouth, we find it necessary to request your assistance in the matter of police protection. Our Police Department, at present, consists of eighteen patrolmen. According to nationally recognized statistics, the present situation would require at least thirty-five men and, on account of the manpower shortage in the community at the present time, it is impossible for us to secure additional men who have the necessary qualifications to serve in the Police department."[69] The commissioners were looking for help during the peak liberty hours, 6 p.m. to 2 a.m. Conditions were chaotic, and because the selective service had first dibs on qualified candidates, the grossly understaffed police department stood no chance of expanding.

A review of the annual arrests of sailors, marines, and soldiers for various offenses in table 5, constructed from the city's police records, confirms the guilt assigned them by Jarvis and other local merchants. With young servicemen doing their best to uphold a well-deserved reputation for alcohol-fueled carousing, drunkenness was by far the most frequent offense they committed. These arrests often occurred in clusters, suggesting that shipmates who went on liberty together were also arrested together when things went awry. Drunkenness was by no means restricted to sailors and marines. It was also the most common offense among the civilian population: about half of the approximately one thousand arrests made annually in Portsmouth during the war were for drunkenness. For example, in 1944, 43 percent of the arrests were for drunkenness, and in 1945, 50 percent.

Table 5: Annual Arrests: Sailors, Marines, and Soldiers (1940–45)

		Sailors	Marines	Soldiers
1940	Drunk	32	10	4
	Disorderly*	1	4	0
	Auto-related**	17	5	1
	Other***	1	1	1
1941	Drunk	40	7	22
	Disorderly	5	0	0
	Auto-related	19	5	17
	Other	4	1	1
1942	Drunk	59	27	29
	Disorderly	2	5	1
	Auto-related	15	9	4
	Other	2	1	1
1943	Drunk	47	15	20
	Disorderly	7	3	2
	Auto-related	16	0	13
	Other	4	3	0
1944	Drunk	47	15	10
	Disorderly	6	3	0
	Auto-related	17	4	9
	Other	6	0	3
1945	Drunk	44	17	9
	Disorderly	17	0	1
	Auto-related	15	5	8
	Other	3	0	0

* Disorderly conduct, assault, fornication, etc.
** Speeding, running traffic lights and stop signs, reckless driving, etc.
*** Larceny, safekeeping, non-support, liquor laws, etc.

Source: City of Portsmouth Police Records, 24 January 1940 to 23 June 1953.

Surprisingly, servicemen represented only about 15 percent of those arrests. Many civilians obviously joined servicemen in consuming alcohol to a fault in Portsmouth's bars and taverns. Offenders' occupations, listed in the police logs, include many trades typical of shipyard employment (welder, chipper, and laborer, for instance), suggesting that shipyard workers were possibly arrested more often for drunkenness than were shipyard sailors. However, the servicemen's numbers would be artificially low if active shore patrols sent inebriated servicemen back to their duty stations before the local police had an opportunity to make an arrest.[70]

At first glance, the military arrests for disorderly conduct appear to be surprisingly low, judging from the picture of nightly chaos and general rowdiness painted by merchants' complaints, the *Portsmouth Herald*, and Lester Stevens.

Consider, however, that the hundreds of arrests annually for drunkenness were probably the result of police observations of disruptive behavior (staggering, boisterous arguments, scuffles, and other troublesome conduct), heading off the brawls and property damage that would have earned a disorderly conduct charge. With the background din of drunkenness a nightly reality, an occasional street brawl reported on the front page of the *Herald* would complete the impression that near-chaos reigned after hours in downtown Portsmouth. Unlike drunkenness, the disorderly offenses recorded in the police logs usually involved sailors or marines, frequently in groups. For example, disorderly conduct arrests were made on 21 December 1940 (four marines), 1 July 1941 (five sailors), 10 February 1942 (five marines), and 18 January 1945 (seven sailors). These group arrests conjure images of unruly sailors and marines, probably in uniform and fueled by alcohol, celebrating their night of liberty with brawls and hooliganism, similar to the scenes described earlier by Jarvis and other restaurant owners. As with arrests for drunkenness, shore patrols probably defused many potential conflicts before local police made arrests for disorderly conduct. [71]

Readers of the *Herald's* coverage of the 18 January 1945 arrests would have had little doubt that their city had become a rowdy Navy liberty town. That evening it took all nine police officers on the night shift to break up a brawl on Congress Street among navy yard sailors. The fight started at 1:30 a.m. in a local diner, spilled into the street, and continued for several blocks before the police could bring the melee under control. Seven sailors were arrested for drunk and disorderly conduct; two other sailors were arrested for drunkenness at the police station when, incredibly, "they sought to liberate their comrades."[72] It was not an easy job to be a Portsmouth policeman on the night shift during the war.

Why were the submarine sailors and marines such troublemakers, when there were at least as many soldiers in the area? The number of enlisted men stationed at the yard peaked at about 1,300 in late 1942 and early 1943, including several hundred marines. Hundreds of these off-duty men were free every evening to enjoy liberty in Portsmouth's bars. This was also true of the soldiers at the forts — but the streets of Portsmouth were not as accessible to them, posted farther away, while the sailors merely needed to walk across the Memorial Bridge from the yard. Another factor was the high turnover of sailors at the yard. Crews departed the area with their completed submarines, and new crews were constantly arriving to operate the next submarine delivered. The yard was completing submarines so fast that a new crew member might only spend a few months at the yard before his submarine was finished. New arrivals were eager to explore the area looking for entertainment and excitement. Soldiers were, for the most part, permanently assigned to the forts and much more likely to reside locally with families, integrating themselves into the communities. On the other hand, perhaps World War II submarine sailors were, by nature, a more troublesome lot when on liberty.

As the war went on, many of the submarine sailors at the yard were veterans of war patrols who returned to the yard to put their next submarine in commission. Likewise, the marine guards may have experienced combat. Nightly, this battle-tested cohort frequented the bars downtown, looking to take full advantage of their respite before going back to war—a recipe for drunkenness, disagreements, and occasional brawls. The local police had their hands full.

The Portsmouth bar scene apparently peaked with a spontaneous V-J Day parade and celebration in Market Square. Harold Whitehouse missed the celebration because his mother refused to let him go downtown, telling him that "there would be too much drinking: all the servicemen would be out on the street." From his home in the South End,

Photo 14: Portsmouth's spontaneous V-J Day celebration (August 1945). Courtesy Strawbery Banke Museum.

Whitehouse "could hear the noise and the people yelling and screaming and the horns and the bells." When he and his friends walked the streets of Portsmouth a few days later, they found much evidence of partying, including "beer bottles all over the place." The V-J Day celebration marked the end of the war, but not the end of Portsmouth as a liberty town.

Submarine sailors continued to frequent Portsmouth's bars well after the war ended. Mel Low, who lived on High Street within sight of the notorious Dolphin Hotel in the mid-1950s, recalls many evenings when police had to break up disturbances in his neighborhood. Quarrels that started in the hotel bar and O'Leary's Bar, across the street from the hotel, often met in the middle of the street. Despite not having a television set, Low says, he never lacked for evening entertainment: during prime time, he merely had "to open his curtains to watch the Friday night fights on High Street."[73] Portsmouth remained a liberty town well into the 1960s, when renovations and restorations began to replace sailor watering holes with upscale restaurants and shops.

The Other Social Scene

Servicemen did not spend all their time in beer joints: many found entertainment at the USO and in Portsmouth homes. Alice Sussman remembers her mother preparing home-cooked meals for lonely servicemen: "We had more soldiers going through our house than you could shake a stick at." Referring to gas tanks across the street from her house that required a twenty-four-hour military guard, she said, "There wasn't a [Navy] sailor or a Coast Guard [sailor] that wasn't fed while they were on duty." Sussman's family made many long-term friendships because of her mother's caring and generosity.[74]

Eileen Dondero Foley, a young woman residing in Portsmouth during the early years of the war, also saw a wholesome side of Portsmouth's social life. Foley recalled dances occurring almost every night of the week at one of several military locations where young women could meet and mingle with servicemen. As she described the scene: "We had Marines . . . Army . . . Navy . . . Coast Guard . . . had every branch of the services here. Every unmarried person in the city was busy. . . . Navy yard dances . . .[dances at] Rye . . . Odiorne Point . . .USO. . . .[We were] thrilled with all the people here. . . . All of the city became alive with the military."[75]

These dances started as early as April 1941 when the 22nd Coast Artillery chaplain at Fort Constitution sent a request to the women of Portsmouth to help him develop a dance program to boost the morale of the young servicemen at the fort.[76] The dances, held several times a week at various sites, soon attracted large numbers of local girls, many bused in from outlying communities. According to Foley, "You were never at a loss for something to do at night. Either at one of the bases or at the USO there were things to do."[77]

The opening of the USO on Daniels Street on 16 January 1942 expanded recreational opportunities for servicemen. In addition to weekly dances, the USO offered game rooms, a gymnasium, a library, and music and religious activities. Sailors walking a direct route from the navy yard to the downtown Portsmouth bars had to pass by the USO. Many sailors stopped and expended their energy and enthusiasm at the USO, instead of walking a few blocks farther and getting into trouble with the local authorities. However, as discussed earlier, many kept right on walking.

Foley remembered the dances being extremely popular, well attended, and strictly supervised: "We went and had instruction on going to the dances. You had to go in as a group, you had to come home in a group, and you could not have anybody walk you home. You could not go out with any of them while you were there."[78] She and her friends often attended more than one dance a week; sponsors conveniently scheduled the dances not to interfere with each other. In addition, the military provided bus service from the downtown USO to the dances on the military bases. According to the Portsmouth War Records, "Dances are conducted by the Portsmouth Recreation Committee or other non-commercial groups. These are held at the USO every Thursday evening, at Camp Langdon once a week, and at the American Legion on Wednesday and Friday evenings. Every Saturday a dance is held at a favorite restaurant. Public dances are also held at various times."[79] At Camp Langdon, sponsors attempted to invite Catholic and Protestant girls in equal numbers to approximate the distribution of the servicemen attending the dances. There was apparently no effort to accommodate minorities. Girls had to be eighteen years old to attend the dances, which were chaperoned and ended in time to comply with the curfew in effect.[80] Bea Randall, a resident of Portsmouth's South End, had no problem gaining entrance to the dances at Camp Langdon: she played trumpet for a six-piece dance band that entertained there many Saturday nights.[81]

One photo showing more than twice as many girls as servicemen attending a dance class at the Portsmouth USO (photo 15) attests to the support given these dances by local girls. Claire Flanagan Papatones, who worked at the IRS office in the post office building at the corner of State and Pleasant Streets, just a few blocks from the Portsmouth USO, was a frequent attendee at the dances. She remembers fondly, "The USO was the favorite place for our generation. We loved music, dancing to a live band, and everything about it."[82]

Photo 15: Folk dance classes at the Portsmouth USO (September 1942). Courtesy Portsmouth War Records, Portsmouth Library.

The swimming pool at the Wentworth Hotel was another favorite entertainment spot. According to Foley, the Army took over the hotel to use it as an officer candidate school, but soon abandoned that idea because the hotel was unheated. However, she adds, "they fixed the pool. For many of us who had gone by and seen this beautiful place . . . [now] we were allowed, with the soldiers and the sailors, to go swimming down there."[83] Of the many opportunities for the young women of Portsmouth to socialize with servicemen, the Wentworth Hotel swimming pool was one of the better choices. The social scene that Foley and Papatones recall was much more innocent and wholesome than the boisterous nightlife that frequently made the front page of the local newspaper. When asked about the bar scene and Portsmouth's prostitution problem, Foley confirmed that seamy side of the Portsmouth social scene: "Oh, yes. They were there. They lined the bridge waiting for the boys to leave the shipyard."[84] Liberty began for some sailors before they even completed the short walk across the Memorial Bridge.

An active group of young women such as Foley and Papatones, who worked hard during the day and socialized with servicemen in supervised social settings in the evenings, balanced the shady side of Portsmouth's social life. These women rarely saw the darker side of the city, and, in some cases, did not even know it existed. For example, Papatones, who worked mere blocks from the notorious Dolphin Hotel during the height of the Navy's campaign to rid it of prostitutes, was not even aware of its existence. When interviewed at the age of ninety-three, she was surprised to learn of the shenanigans that were going on just across Market Square from her workplace on Pleasant Street. Similarly, Bea Randall, who also worked near the Dolphin Hotel, was unaware of its existence and had no knowledge of the hotel's infamous reputation.

It is difficult to reconcile the newspaper reports of the city's problems as a liberty town with the recollections of those who lived and worked there at the time. It appears that Portsmouth itself was two cities in one—depending on the time of day. During the daylight hours, it was a bustling place filled with hardworking people going about their business, finding reasons to celebrate the best of challenging times, and enjoying life despite inconveniences and hardships. At night, the seedier side of the city emerged when the bars opened and young servicemen escaped the confines of the shipyard and other local bases seeking diversions.

The Portsmouth *Survey of Health and Welfare* in 1943 alludes to the changing personality of Portsmouth: "During the day, the movies and USO are the chief centers of attention [for servicemen]. During the evenings, dance halls, beer restaurants, and USO are frequented. For overnight leavers, the men patronize several hotels and lodging houses. . . . From 10 p.m. on, a few beer parlors are crowded while many are visited by small groups, about 160 men visit the USO every night and on dance nights about 200 to 260 are present."[85] As innocent as all that sounds, disturbances were far too common at the beer joints, and wayward girls were much too often involved with the hotel overnights.

Occasionally the wholesome and the shady sides of life in downtown Portsmouth converged, as the author discovered when interviewing Eileen Dondero Foley. In the process of providing background material about the notorious Dolphin Hotel, which burned to the ground in 1969, she confirmed the suspect activity that took place on the premises. When asked if she ever visited the hotel, the ninety-year-old matriarch and eight-time mayor of the city responded, with a pause and a twinkle in her eye, "Oh, yes — but I was *never* upstairs."[86]

Such was the dichotomy of life in the Portsmouth during the war — on the shady side, alleged prostitution, high venereal disease rates, and barroom brawls; on the bright side, dedicated workers turning out submarines at phenomenal rates, patriots volunteering endless hours to the war effort, and residents befriending thousands of servicemen passing through their city en route to war. The city was alive with young people committed to doing their part to win a war, while making the best of challenging times. By all accounts, Portsmouth's brief tenure as a World War II liberty town was a very exciting period in the city's four hundred-year history.

CHAPTER 6
HOMELAND PORTSMOUTH

The war was more interesting than the peace had been. The war put an end to Depression America and gave meaning to ordinary lives, since all citizens were to some degree participants in the national effort.

William O'Neill
Democracy at War, 1993

The attack on Pearl Harbor changed everything. No longer did the public cherish lingering thoughts of remaining on the sidelines of the war; all of a sudden, the choices were clear, the needs were obvious, and the spirit was willing. Men eager to return to work after the Depression relocated great distances to gain employment in one of the nation's mobilizing industries, women assumed industrial jobs vacated as men went off to war, and Americans purchased war bonds in astounding amounts. The home front became a battlefield where, according to documentarian John Gfroerer, citizens armed themselves with "weapons [that] included conservation, recycling or just plain going without."[1] Portsmouth resident Morris Levy noted, "People on the home front were just as willing to support the war as the guys in the service."[2] And the citizens of Portsmouth proceeded to do so in earnest.

The same patriotism that motivated young men and women to enlist in the armed services also inspired those they left behind to honor their departure with ceremonious sendoffs. Portsmouth dignitaries routinely met with the young men (and women, later in the war) in Market Square at 7 a.m. on the day they were scheduled to depart by train to report to their first duty stations—usually Fort Devens, Massachusetts, or Fort Drum, New York, for the soldiers, and Bainbridge, Maryland, or the Great Lakes Naval Training Station in Illinois for the sailors. After presenting each recruit with gifts—fountain pens, stationery, cigarettes, and chocolate—the mayor and council members would lead the group, flag in hand, on a march to the train station in the North End. Emotions ran high as the enlistees waved to and greeted friends along the route. Onboard the train, the local officials walked the aisles shaking hands and wishing the recruits well as several hundred friends and relatives gathered on the departure platform to see the draftees off.[3] Harold Whitehouse, who was often in the crowd at the train station, remembers, "Draftees were leaving by the hundreds. We would go down to the railroad station every other Saturday morning and see another group of draftees leaving by train to Fort Drum in New York for training. The band would be playing, the mayor would be down there, flags waving, and all the draftees—maybe thirty or forty of them—would be given small ditty bags. In the bag there's a shaving kit, a bar of soap, toothpaste, a tooth-brush, and a little packet of cigarettes, with six in the package. The ditty bag was made of canvas with a drawstring at the top."[4]

Such displays of patriotism were quite common. New Hampshire native Stephen Hatch recalls attending a movie in a small New Hampshire town where the audience spontaneously stood as one for the national anthem.[5] Patriotism drove shipyard workers to achieve unprecedented production heights, encouraged citizens to readily accept rationing, and motivated volunteers to devote seemingly endless hours to the war effort. Staggering numbers of people volunteered for civil defense jobs and Red Cross workshops. Citizens considered these homeland commitments a small price to pay when compared to the sacrifices the troops were making overseas.

Volunteerism

Almost everyone, it seemed, felt a personal sense of responsibility to get the job done. People did the expected and a bit more. Barbara McLean Ward's *Produce and Conserve, Share and Play Square: The Grocer and the Consumer on the Home-Front Battlefield during World War II* describes the various ways in which Portsmouth volunteers did a bit more: "Housewives, USO hostesses, Y.M.C.A. 'girls,' and 'office girls,' after their regular workday was completed, turned up in large numbers to work at Morley when a government contract was due [see chapter 9 for a discussion of Morley Company]. . . . Portsmouth residents turned out in large numbers to staff the wartime committees. . . . Thousands of others did their part by participating in scrap drives, rubber drives, and numerous other salvage efforts."[6]

In many cases, citizens organized themselves. Historian William L. O'Neill wrote, "Most Americans believed that government did not have to be overly effective because the people themselves could manage. . . . [V]olunteerism was a fact of life. . . . Towns convened meetings to discuss ways of aiding the war effort. Citizens' committees sprang up. Neighborhoods organized."[7] At a quickly organized Hampton defense meeting on the Wednesday evening after the Sunday attack on Pearl Harbor, "more than 300 people had already signed up for various defense units, such as the first aid, auxiliary police and fire, motor-corps, air-raid wardens, nursing and medical corps, Red Cross, canteen, and registration and clerical."[8] Once Americans realized there was no turning back, they charged full speed ahead.

The service division of the local civil defense council

organized many of the community action programs. A 17 June 1942 letter from the state council directed the Portsmouth council to appoint a consumers'-interest chairman to arrange the participation of local households.[9] As a result, the service arm of the local council assumed responsibilities for coordinating childcare, consumer affairs, housing availability, nutrition standards, salvage drives, the sale of war bonds and stamps, and interfacing with the Red Cross. Forty-two block leaders, corresponding to the forty-two sectors of the city, kept residents apprised of current issues and upcoming events. Among the most popular of the volunteer activities were the Red Cross, USO, scrap drives, and war bond campaigns.

Red Cross. Red Cross volunteer work appealed to women who could join with friends and family members in a social setting to receive medical training, roll bandages, and perform other tasks and services that benefited the war effort. According to social historian William O'Neill, "With 3.5 million female volunteers, [the Red Cross] was by far the most important outlet for patriotic womanhood. . . . The hottest literary property of 1942 was the Red Cross first aid manual, which, though not considered a book and therefore omitted from best-seller lists, sold 8 million copies."[10]

Sandra Goss Munsey of Rye, New Hampshire, remembers receiving her own copy of the manual during one of her trips to the local Red Cross office with her grandmother: "I learned to fold and roll bandages, tie on a splint, and make an arm sling, practicing at home with my dolls or on myself. I was given my own Red Cross First Aid book, but I was too young to attend the classes."[11] Hampton Red Cross volunteers met every Wednesday afternoon to make surgical dressings. The women, dressed for the occasion in a "white smock or dress and a white head covering of some type," made more than 7,500 surgical dressings from February through April 1942.[12]

In June 1942, Sheridan County, Wyoming, reported that more than seven hundred people had taken the Red Cross first-aid course, and several hundred more were on a waiting list for the training.[13] There was clearly no shortage of first-aid volunteers nationwide.

Since Pearl Harbor, a Red Cross pamphlet published in April 1943, quantified the cumulative efforts of its army of national volunteers. The numbers were astounding—5.5 million first-aid certificates awarded, 200,000 surgical dressings produced, 16 million relief garments made, and 4 million pints of blood collected.[14] These accomplishments, reported sixteen months into the war, would grow significantly before the war was over.

USO. Founded in 1941 to provide morale-boosting and recreation services to U.S. uniformed military personnel, the United Service Organizations (USO) brought six civilian organizations together under one umbrella to support U.S. troops: the Salvation Army, the Young Men's Christian Association (YMCA), the Young Women's Christian Association (YWCA), the National Catholic Community Service, the National Travelers Aid Association, and the National Jewish Welfare Board. The USO's goal was to promote the "development of friendly contacts between persons in civilian life and military life directed toward helping men in uniform to adjust themselves to their new environment with enthusiasm and high morale"[15] By all reports, the Portsmouth USO achieved this goal — and much more.

The Portsmouth USO was located on Daniel Street near the Memorial Bridge. The building that housed it had been constructed in 1916 just before the United States entered World War I. Owned by the Army-Navy Association, it offered recreational options for young military men other than those available in the nearby waterfront brothels and beer joints. The Army-Navy Building closed in 1920 following World War I and reopened in 1937 at the onset of World War II. In 1942, it became the USO Building, complete with a new wing containing a gymnasium and auditorium.[16]

Here, within easy walking distance across the Memorial Bridge, the shipyard's sailors and marines had access to a basketball court, pool tables, Ping-Pong tables, card games, and other activities catering to a young man's interest. The young servicemen, however, were probably most interested in the young hostesses who volunteered endless hours at the USO to escort and entertain the troops. Portsmouth High graduate "Mickey" McWilliams-Hussey frequently made her

Photo 16: Portsmouth USO social (circa 1943).
Courtesy Portsmouth Athenaeum.

way from her workplace near Market Square to the USO, just a few blocks away. Eileen Dondero Foley and Claire Flanagan Papatones also volunteered there. Sometimes volunteering meant merely interacting and passing time with a young sailor. Other times, the hostesses shared coffee and snacks, took in a movie, or attended dances in the gymnasium.[17] In addition to recreational activities, servicemen could get a bed for the evening and a shower in the morning before going back to their submarine or duty station the next day.

Volunteer mothers did their best to make the Portsmouth USO a home away from home. Sometimes they just listened and offered advice; other times they helped the young servicemen make phone calls or encouraged them to write letters home. Mothers also assisted in the chapel, staffed the library, and kept the USO well supplied with fresh baked goods, constantly reminding the young men of home and family. Serving at the USO was one of the most popular and rewarding of the homeland volunteer activities.

Scrap and Salvage Drives. The salvage unit made up 65 percent (178 of 278 volunteers) of the service arm of the Portsmouth Defense Council, making scrap and salvage drives one of the most important council activities. Many drives were organized and conducted locally, but some were national in scope. President Roosevelt himself initiated one such drive, a nationwide scrap rubber salvage campaign. FDR asked "each family to collect all available Scrap Rubber and deliver it to the nearest gasoline station" between 12:01 a.m. on Monday, 16 June 1942, and midnight on Tuesday, 30 June 1942. Members of the local council salvage unit informed every family in Portsmouth about the drive and assisted families with the transfer of scrap rubber to the filling stations. Participants were reimbursed a penny a pound for the scrap rubber."[18] One did not get rich from scrap drives.

In 1941, with aluminum in short supply, the call went out for housewives to turn in pots and pans. In response, women nationwide "stripped their kitchens and donated 70,000 tons of aluminum."[19] The same housewives turned in their kitchen oils and greases at the local grocery store for recycling to extract glycerin for mixing with the black powder needed for artillery shells.[20] Early in the war, federal government advisories alerted women about the glycerin shortage and pleaded for housewives to save lives by saving kitchen fats: "Before the war, many of the fats and oils from which glycerine [sic] is made — almost two billion pounds of them — were imported from the Far East; from the Philippines and the Jap-held islands of the Pacific. That important source has been cut off. At the same time, the military needs of this country and our Allies have tremendously increased the need for glycerine [sic]. . . . *Enough fats and greases are thrown away or poured down the sink drains every year to equal the total of fats and oils we formerly imported from the Far East.* If every housewife in America would save and turn in only one pound of used cooking fats and greases every month, it would produce enough glycerine [sic] to make over half a billion pounds of smokeless powder. A pound a month is only a tablespoonful a day. A tablespoonful a day — to help shorten the war and save the lives of thousands of boys who are fighting so that we may survive. Just a tablespoonful a day — it isn't to [sic] much to ask, is it?"[21] With this and similar pleas, housewives in kitchens all over America began to do their part to shorten the war — one tablespoonful of fat at a time.

Children turned in untold amounts of tinfoil, rags, tin cans, and old overshoes to collection centers. One youngster in Maywood, Illinois, collected one hundred tons of scrap paper.[22] In Portsmouth, Harold Whitehouse gathered tinfoil, string, rags, and all "kinds of brass and copper." Whitehouse described his technique for collecting tinfoil from cigarette packages: "If we opened a package very carefully, we could tear off this foil and make balls as big as a football and then somebody came and collected it."[23] Papatones, then a teenager in Somersworth, remembers being so very proud of her father for donating "our black wrought iron fence to the effort."[24] Bill Tebo recalls that he and his friends volunteered for Portsmouth High School–sponsored scrap drives, rag drives, and clothing drives for which they often received no compensation.[25] The personal satisfaction of contributing to the war effort was payback enough.

On 1 September 1942, the *Portsmouth Herald* reported that the navy yard had made a tremendous contribution to a local salvage drive. The yard had contributed more than 2,500 tons of scrap iron—more than the average displacement of a typical Portsmouth-built submarine during the war. With the yard's help, the final total of more than 3,500 tons almost tripled the original goal for the eight-week drive. There had apparently been some criticism of the yard, because the *Herald* article quoted Rear Admiral Withers as saying that the report of the scrap drive "will materially assist in putting a stop to the vicious rumors that have sprung up about the scrap salvage program at the yard."[26] There were no amplifying remarks about the vicious rumors, leaving one to speculate about what might have happened to that shipyard scrap iron otherwise; perhaps the yard's prewar practice of dumping barge-loads of heavy scrap metal at sea or using it for landfills (discussed in chapter 12) was the issue.

In addition to recapturing tons of valuable resources and raw materials for the military, scrap drives were social events that rallied citizens and gave them the personal satisfaction of making a hands-on contribution to the war effort. Posters such as "Slap the Japs with Scrap" aggressively suggested that citizens were carrying the war to the enemy by participating in such drives. The nation's industrial machine quickly transformed the household items turned in at local collection centers into instruments of war and bullets. An old jalopy, on its way to be recycled, cleverly displayed the sign, "Praise the Lord, I'll Soon be Ammunition."[27] Scrap drives that turned old cars and cooking fats into ammunition also enabled Americans to attack the far-distant enemy from their own backyards — and kitchens.

War Bonds. FDR's administration challenged Americans, reaping the benefits of a newly healthy economy, to help finance the war through taxes and the purchase of war bonds. Both had the additional benefit of limiting inflation, the likely consequence of inflated paychecks chasing too few goods. Income taxes became a way of life for most of the population. According to Maury Klein, "In 1940 about 7 percent of the population paid income taxes; by 1944 the figure would top 64 percent."[28] In addition, each wage earner had a 5 percent surcharge, dubbed a "victory tax," added to his federal income tax. To put more funds immediately at the government's disposal, employers were required to withhold taxes from workers' pay instead of allowing them to make a single payment each March.[29]

Mandated taxes brought in much of the revenue needed to fight the war; war bond campaigns brought in the rest. In *Mobilizing the Home Front: War Bonds and Domestic Propaganda*, James J. Kimble noted that war bonds, in addition to raising massive amounts of money for the war effort, also raised the nation's morale and support for the war. Through the purchase of war bonds, millions of citizens got directly involved and cast a vote in support of the war. Kimble wrote, "In theory, Roosevelt could have used involuntary war taxes to offset the full cost of World War II — at $350 billion the most expensive war in American history. Yet he realized that such efforts would defuse the national morale so necessary to the war effort. . . . His solution was a massive crusade inviting Americans to loan the U.S. government their money while simultaneously — and surreptitiously — using the Treasury's bond publicity machine to target public morale."[30] The program vastly exceeded all expectations, bringing $135 billion into the national treasury.[31] This massive outlay of public dollars helped win the war, but it also helped Americans add significantly to previously nonexistent personal savings accounts.

Kimble argues that the Roosevelt administration used the war bond program as a propaganda instrument to promote "unity and a heightened national spirit" while advancing "its vision of the struggle to unsuspecting Americans." He wrote, "Influenced by the Treasury Department's ubiquitous advertisement programs that dehumanized the enemy and glorified our military, the average citizen believed he was doing his part to win the war when he purchased war bonds." Thus FDR, who'd had difficulty swaying Americans from their isolationist stance before the attack on Pearl Harbor, received continuous endorsement of his administration's prosecution of the war through the business of war bonds.[32]

Many national celebrities supported the war bond campaign. Recounts James Wensyel, "War heroes, entertainers, sports heroes and other home front celebrities volunteered to sell the bonds. With national idols such as Lana Turner, Bing Crosby and Bugs Bunny selling war bonds, how could anyone not participate? Actress Betty Grable donated her nylons to the top bidder at a bond rally; Man O' War's horseshoes rewarded another; comedian Jack Benny's $75 violin brought a $1 million bid; and starlet Hedy Lamarr promised to reward any buyer of $25,000 worth of bonds with a kiss. Singer Kate Smith outdid all rivals when she sold $40 million in bonds during a sixteen-hour radio marathon."[33] Some of these luminaries found their way to Portsmouth to push war bonds. Harold Whitehouse remembers, "Celebrities from Hollywood came in by train, and they had war bond drives where just about half the city would line up. There would be a long line of people down

Parrott Avenue waiting to buy an $18.75 war bond that could be worth $25 after the war ended."[34]

Actress Dorothy Lamour's appearance at a war bond drive downtown on 15 September 1942 was one of the highlights for many. Eileen Dondero Foley recalled Lamour, attractively attired in a green suit with a mink collar, drawing a large

Photo 17: Dorothy Lamour at Market Square war bond drive (15 September 1942). Courtesy Strawbery Banke Museum.

crowd to Market Square.[35] Although only five or six years old at the time, Sandra Goss Munsey also had vivid memories of the occasion: "Probably the biggest [war bond drive] locally was one held in Portsmouth in Market Square. Grandmother Drake took me to see it. A stage was built at the east end of the Square. We stood near the corner next to North Church. The usual endless parade of speakers participated. The only important thing that happened as far as I was concerned was the visit by movie star Dorothy Lamour. Having seen some of the famous 'Road' movies in which she, Bing Crosby, and Bob Hope starred, this was a big moment for me!"[36] According to Foley, local restaurateur Andrew Jarvis stepped forward that day to announce his purchase of a $1,000 bond. Many in the crowd cheered and then followed his example by making purchases of their own.[37]

Portsmouth Navy Yard employees set a record for war bond participation in November 1942 when 100 percent of the yard's more than 17,000 employees pledged an average of 13 percent of their gross pay. The Philadelphia Navy Yard had held the previous record at 98 percent participation and 12 percent of gross pay.[38] The yard's managers solicited maximum employee support; once the employees realized that 100 percent participation was possible, peer pressure and pride drove the final record-setting results. New Hampshire, with a population of about half a million people, contributed about half a billion dollars to the war bond effort between 1942 and 1945.[39]

While those at home were rallying to support the war in any manner they could, flags in the front windows of families of servicemen served as constant reminders of the more serious commitments and sacrifices being made by Portsmouth's sons and daughters overseas. The front window of Leslie Hayes Garner's house had a flag with six blue stars, meaning he had six sons serving in the military.[40] The flag in the front window of the Hersey family's Puddle Dock home had four blue stars and one gold star: a gold star signaled the supreme sacrifice—a son or daughter lost in combat. The family's youngest son, a marine, had been lost off New Caledonia in the Pacific Ocean.[41] Volunteering to serve at the local USO or Red Cross was one thing; volunteering to risk your life while serving in the jungle of a remote South Pacific island was something else entirely.

Rationing

Recycling was vital, but rationing touched ordinary citizens' lives even more directly. Doing with less or going without many comforts became a way of life in order to ensure the military got needed resources. Rationing of foodstuffs and manufactured items served two purposes: it provided for the fair distribution of scarce goods, and it prevented runaway inflation, a major concern to those who remembered the soaring 62 percent inflation rate during World War I.[42] The World War II controls resulted in a cost of living increase of only 28 percent between 1940 and 1945.[43] Rationing was a sacrifice readily accepted by most Americans—and it worked.

The Office of Price Administration (OPA), established in April 1941, initially introduced programs for the conservation of critical materials— rubber, fuel, and silk—in the summer of 1941, followed by the first federal rationing programs in early 1942. Nationwide, purchases were controlled through 5,500 local ration boards staffed by volunteers, whose number eventually grew to 30,000.[44] The rationing program required a huge administrative bureaucracy and a willing and cooperative public. Pollsters "found that an overwhelming 89 percent of Americans preferred rationing to taking a chance of being able to obtain a product."[45] The small percentage opposed to the practice included some who hoarded scarce items and others who participated in an active black market.

Four different programs rationed consumer goods: 1) certificate rationing for items issued on the basis of a one-time or infrequent need, such as tires, automobiles, stoves, and rubber boots; 2) differential coupon rationing for items consumed on a regular basis with differing priorities of need, such as gasoline and fuel oil; 3) uniform coupon rationing for items shared equally in the shortage, including shoes, sugar, and coffee; and 4) point rationing for food purchases using color-coded ration stamps issued by quota to families and dispensed in accordance with individual preferences, which covered meats, butter, margarine, canned fish, cheese, canned milk, fats, oils, and most canned and bottled foods. It was the latter, the point rationing system, that challenged the mettle of housewives to make the best use of ration stamps to meet their families' needs.

One way of maximizing the return on ration stamps for both the customer and the local grocer was to skirt the rules by establishing a cooperative relationship that benefited both. For example, loyal customers of grocery store manager Rodolphe Blais at the People's Market in downtown Portsmouth would have him "clean their book" at the end of each rationing period, meaning he would take all the remaining coupons in the book before they expired. In return for the extra coupons, which would help Blais get more supplies from his distributors, he would accommodate future purchases with fewer than the required number of coupons.[46] There was a definite advantage to being a loyal and favored customer of your neighborhood grocery store.

The OPA never rationed fresh fruits and vegetables.[47] Victory gardens, cultivated by millions of would-be farmers in backyards and on every available tract of land, produced astonishing amounts of vegetables, supplementing the nation's vast agriculture resources. Across the nation, notes James Wensyel, "The 20.5 million Victory Gardens cultivated in 1943 provided more than thirty percent of all the vegetables grown in America that year. Growing food was something the ordinary citizen felt good about—a tangible and tasty way to help the war effort."[48] Victory gardens kept fruits and vegetables on consumers' tables and off the rationing lists.

The service arm of the Portsmouth Defense Council managed the local victory gardens cultivated on government and donated lands. Landowners with suitable acreage for gardens received reimbursement from the city through the council, which divided the land into lots for which the gardeners paid a small fee. In 1943 and 1944, 140 lots were made available yearly for a fee of three dollars each to cover plowing and harrowing the field. Hundreds of other property owners planted gardens on their own land without the council's direct involvement.[49] An undated report in the council archives indicates that a survey of 148 Portsmouth neighborhood leaders found 1,098 home gardens.[50] A similar survey of 150 Hampton families in the spring of 1943 showed that 143 families planned to plant victory gardens.[51] There was certainly no shortage of fruits and vegetables during the war for the Randall family residing on Ridge Court in the South End of Portsmouth. Bea Randall's father maintained a large fruit orchard and a vegetable garden that kept her family well supplied with these items.[52]

Everyone was involved in the conservation of critical materials—even children. On 30 October 1942, the local radio station, WHEB, urged the "younger citizens of Portsmouth" to tone down their wasteful Halloween pranks:

> For many years it has been the custom to observe Halloween by soaping windows, breaking light bulbs and causing other [minor and easily repairable] damage to property in general. . . . This

year is different. We are in the middle of a war the outcome of which is far from certain. . . . Fats used to make soap are also used in ammunition. The metal used to make electric light bulbs, it is also used in ships and planes; metal used to make ash cans and garbage cans is also used in making ships and ammunition. . . . Do not waste or destroy these precious articles on Halloween night.[53]

The children were sternly reminded that wasteful Halloween pranks would only serve to "help the Japs and Nazis" and that "such acts constitute sabotage" during wartime.

When asked about their most vivid wartime memories, interviewees for this book most often mentioned rationing. For example, Portsmouth resident Marion Adams recalled, "You'd be walking up the street in Portsmouth during the war and people who were perfect strangers would come up to you and say, 'They got butter at Ames,' and gee you'd go running up there just to get a pound of butter, and another thing was silk stockings, everybody would run to the store that was carrying them."[54] Paradoxically, these rationing and conservation programs actually enriched the American homeland experience: the camaraderie of standing together in long lines to buy rationed products and the ingenuity called for to make best use of limited items were not soon forgotten by most Americans who were there.

Foodstuffs. Just a few years earlier during the Depression, many families had gone unfed for lack of jobs and income. The wartime situation was completely different: Incomes were soaring, and it was not money but the availability of food items that was the issue. Housewives carefully managed quotas of food stamps to feed their families. Most accepted the sacrifices required by rationing as a mere inconvenience, compared to the all-too-recent hardship of struggling to feed one's family at all.

Sugar, one of the first items rationed, was also the one missed most keenly by Americans. A Gallup poll near the end of the war asked respondents which of four rationed commodities they would choose if forced to select only one: fifteen gallons of gas, twenty-five pounds of sugar, five pounds of butter, or five pounds of beefsteak. Nearly half of those surveyed — 47 percent — opted for the sugar.[55] This was not surprising, given that twenty-five pounds represented a windfall of about a year's supply of rationed sugar. The sugar ration was a mere eight ounces a week and grocers often did not have sugar in stock. [56]

Leslie Clough, a grocery store clerk in Puddle Dock, could vouch for the scarcity of sugar and its preferential distribution by some stores: "Sugar, of course, was impossible. . . . Every day that we'd have sugar come in, we'd put a paper in the window: 'Sugar.' Everybody'd get a chance. . . . Many of the stores uptown, they'd save it for 'special customers' . . . influential people, like the beach people and Middle Street [residents]. . . . But with us, we gave it to all our customers. . . . I think that was fair."[57] Fairly distributed or not, sugar was always in short supply.

Housewives found sugar substitutes in saccharin, corn syrup, honey, and molasses. Consider this wartime recipe for icing for an eggless victory layer cake: "½ cup honey, ½ cup white corn syrup, ⅛ teaspoon salt, and 1 egg white." Recognizing that honey might also be in short supply, a note at the end of the recipe added, "1 cup corn syrup may be used — omitting the honey — in which case, add 1½ teaspoons vanilla." [58] Less tasty desserts were one of many wartime sacrifices.

Meat rationing began on 29 March 1943. The number of points required to purchase meat varied with the type and cut, as well as the availability. Unlike sugar, coffee, and other rationed foodstuffs, meat was not an import; consequently, it was not subject to shortages according to the fortunes of war. In fact, American farmers produced "a wartime supply much larger than in the past." [59] Much of the increased supply went to the military; however, the weekly civilian allotment of twenty-eight ounces (later increased to two and a half pounds) was quite reasonable compared to other rationed items. Historian Doris Weatherford wrote, "Meat rationing was primarily a problem of how to fairly distribute a reasonably large supply, and its objective was to hold down prices."[60] But meat rationing was woefully ineffective; some estimated that "as much as 40 percent of meat mysteriously ended up in black markets."[61] Rodolphe Blais, manager of People's Market, attributed his inability to get enough meat to satisfy his customers to the black market, a condition that forced him to close his store.[62]

Although disgusted with the black market, Blais did not hesitate to stretch the rules when it was to his benefit. He told of a wealthy man from Rye who would send his chauffeur to People's Market to purchase steaks for large barbecues he held at his house. The chauffeur would present Blais an envelope with enough loose coupons, apparently collected from invitees to his barbecue, for a dozen steaks—plus a "little extra" for Blais. Regulations required merchants to accept ration coupons only from intact booklets, but Blais would accommodate the customer in return for the extra coupons.[63]

Meat rationing was less of a problem on the seacoast of New Hampshire, where fresh fish and shellfish were plentiful, than other inland regions. Valerie Cunningham recalled humorously the privations of being a young girl growing up in Portsmouth during the war: "When meat was rationed, one of the neighborhood friends who worked on the lobster boats would come by with extra lobsters and leave them on the back steps. A bag of lobsters! We got so tired of eating lobsters."[64] Feasting on lobsters was one of many ways Portsmouth residents found good times during bad times.

Although sugar was the most sorely missed rationed item, Portsmouth residents placed butter, essential for baking and cooking, a close second.[65] An artificially colored margarine, developed as a substitute for butter, played to mixed reviews. It "took the form of white lard-like cakes that came with an envelope of vegetable food coloring."[66] Homemakers emptied the yellow coloring into the bag of margarine and kneaded it until the contents resembled butter—yellow-streaked butter. No matter the care taken with the preparation, it was the opinion of Somersworth native Claire Flanagan Papatones that "it still tasted like lard."[67]

Rationing categories were assigned to processed foods as well, listed below in order of the number of ration points required, from highest to lowest:

a) Canned soups, fruits, and vegetables.
b) Commercially frozen fruits and vegetables.
c) Dried or dehydrated fruits.

Ration points went much further purchasing dried fruits. Canned foods required higher numbers of ration points because the metal containers were more prized than the contents. Frozen fruits and vegetables were a little risky, considering the state of home refrigeration, but dehydration was a very popular and near-perfect solution to the homeland's food needs. Maury Klein wrote, "The war had turned dehydration into a big business. . . . In 1941, vegetable dehydration plants numbered fewer than 20 and produced about 15 million pounds of food; three years later 141 plants operated with a capacity of 170 million pounds. Two vegetables that lent themselves best to the process were potatoes and onions."[68] The dehydration process minimized spoilage and greatly reduced the volume of foodstuffs shipped, freeing cargo space for more critical wartime needs.

Although fresh fruits and vegetables were never rationed, a scarcity of agricultural workers and food shipments to Europe raised occasional concerns about possible shortages. In September 1943, the New Hampshire Defense Council, responding to a large predicted crop yield and a dearth of farmers, many of whom were now soldiers, alerted local councils that people having time to do so should "assist with the fall harvest to relieve the acute and serious shortage of agricultural labor." Although state officials expected "large crops of certain vegetables and fruits," they predicted that "lend-lease shipments next spring may actually produce a shortage." The same Lend-Lease Act that brought British submarines to the Portsmouth Navy Yard early in the war sent food shipments from New Hampshire to Europe throughout World War II.[69]

As the war wound down in the summer of 1945, after Germany's surrender on 8 May, the *Portsmouth Herald* reported that the nation's large cities faced "mounting shortages of granulated sugar, margarine, lard and some canned goods and vegetables" because of the need to increase food shipments to Europe. According to the *Herald*, "Relief shipments to Czechoslovakia, Greece, Italy, Poland and Yugoslavia in June and July will more than double the total sent to the end of May." The number of big-city grocers without granulated sugar "increased from nine to 21 percent from mid-March to mid-June" and bakeries were curtailing production or closing because of the shortage. With the end of the war in sight, American housewives continued to be challenged to feed their families.[70]

Manufactured Goods. "Use it up, wear it out, make it do,

168

or do without."[71] That was the dictum Americans heard again and again. Numerous booklets and pamphlets offered helpful hints to extend the life of just about everything. *Make and Mend for Victory* provided patterns to turn worn men's shirts into little girls' dresses, blouses, and pajamas.[72] *Make It Do Until Victory* cautioned women to "be careful with your girdles" — wash in lukewarm water, take tucks in fabric and not in elastic inserts, and never iron them.[73] The same tips appeared in the chapter titled "How to Be Well Dressed on a Rational Budget" in *800 Ways to Save and Serve,* which provided instructions for extending the life of hundreds of items.[74]

Conservation was especially vital for rubber products. Japan's expedited conquest of Southeast Asia, the source of most of the world's rubber supply, made rationing of rubber products a necessity early in the war. Klein wrote, "Ninety-eight percent of the rubber used in the United States was imported from the Far East over a 12,000 mile route that took more than two months to travel. By 1939 it had become the largest single commodity in dollar value imported into the United States."[75] The burgeoning automotive industry and rapidly increasing defense needs spiked the demand for rubber to new heights.

Synthetic rubber, under development in research laboratories, was still several years away from large-scale industrial applications. The country's first two synthetic rubber plants opened in April 1942. The nation eventually built fifty-one synthetic rubber plants as production soared from 22,000 tons in 1942 to 250,000 tons in 1943 to 750,000 tons in 1944.[76] It would be several years into the war before synthetics could help curb the military's voracious appetite for rubber. Until then military weaponry gobbled up every scrap of rubber collected during countless salvage drives across the nation.

As noted earlier, in June 1942 the president made a personal appeal to the nation to turn in all available scrap rubber to service stations. The public responded eagerly, noted Klein, "bringing their scrap to 400,000 gas stations around the country. . . . The final tally neared 450,000 tons."[77] Despite those impressive numbers, the rubber crisis remained acute, leading to a total ban on the sale of automobile tires. Richard and Sharon Hanes wrote, "To conserve the remaining rubber supply, President Roosevelt froze the sale of tires and then banned recapping. . . . Car owners could possess no more than five tires. Any extra tires had to be turned in at gas stations for industrial reuse. . . . To further conserve rubber, Roosevelt reduced the national maximum speed limit to 35 miles per hour."[78] Wensyel described the desperate measures taken by some to extend tire life: "To prolong tire use drivers tried recapping and sometimes wrapped plastic, paper, or cornsilk between a worn inner tube and the tire itself." [79] Synthetic rubber could not come too soon.

Local rationing boards strictly applied the OPA's directives concerning the conservation of car tires. For example, in May 1942, the Haverhill, Massachusetts, rationing board denied a petition, signed by many of the five hundred Haverhill residents who worked at the navy yard, to rescind its decision denying them tire retread certificates or supplementary gas allotments. Adequate bus service, the board pointed out, was available to transport the workers to and from the yard. The men argued that using the shipyard bus service, run by the Hill Transportation Bus Company, instead of car pools would cause them to spend three additional hours a day away from home. Long commuting times were one of many sacrifices expected on the home front.[80]

The shipyard workers' commutes were not just long, they

were also very crowded and uncomfortable. Shipyard worker A. I. Harriman expressed his dissatisfaction with the Hill bus system in a poem titled "Public Service:"[81]

Transportation's a problem
To that we agree
Nevertheless tempting the public
"Travel by bus" signs we see.

Remember *over-crowded buses*
Conserve neither gas nor rubber
We pay for a seat
Not standing room brother.

Why *drape us like monkeys*
From the roof of the bus?
Just a case of survival of the fittest
And man you've got to be tough.

So get into the scrimmage
Push, shove and haul.
Try and be a gentleman
And you're out of luck — that's all.

The way *workers are herded*
'Tis a crime and a sin.
We pray for the Transportation Company
And brother — we're not singing hymns.

Just defense workers trapped
Like rats in a cage
Re-route half filled buses
Lives and rubber can be saved.

A crack-up surely
Will be the answer some say
The time to investigate
Is not then—but today.

If they can't do the job
Give us gas for the old hack
She got us there before
And by gosh we got back.
[emphasis added throughout poem]

The Hill Transportation Bus Company transported thousands of shipyard employees to and from work daily from as far away as Manchester, New Hampshire, and Portland, Maine.[82] Employees living closer to the yard walked, rode bicycles, or commuted in car pools. Harold Whitehouse found the occupants of these crowded buses and cars to be excellent customers for his extra papers: "Sometimes I had four or five papers left over from my route. . . . I'd try to catch the Navy Yard traffic coming off the shipyard by bus and car. . . . Busses came down Daniel Street and cars came down State. When a car came from the shipyard it was with five passengers—I never saw just a single person in a car, because they had to carpool."[83]

It was not just shipyard transportation that was overcrowded. With rubber, fuel, and metal at a premium, airline travel was inaccessible to all except the military, greatly increasing civilian use of buses and trains, making for uncomfortable traveling conditions. It was nothing to have to sit on a suitcase or stand for an eight-hour trip.[84] One Portsmouth resident reported, "So great was the demand for transportation that buses were jammed, buses running to Boston carried double their seating capacity, the aisles crowded with standees."[85] On one occasion, a woman traveling with her twelve-year-old son to Boston lost contact with him on a crowded bus. When it came time to get off, she found him perched on the luggage rack at the back of the bus. According to the mother, "The passengers kept crowding him back into the bus until there was no place to go but up."[86] Despite the occasional complaint, Americans generally accepted overcrowded public transportation as just another home-front sacrifice.

As early as August 1941, the OPA ordered gas station owners to curtail their hours in order to discourage overconsumption. The day gasoline sales were curtailed was a memorable one for Portsmouth residents. According to the Portsmouth War Records, "The decree went into effect on Aug. 2, 1941, and all stations were required to close at 7 o'clock."[87] The *Herald* reported, "Portsmouth citizens who own cars prepared to retrench on driving miles and yet to stock up with enough gas before 7 o'clock tomorrow night to survive the fuel blackout."[88] Gasoline rationing, introduced in some areas as early as the spring of 1942, took effect nationally in December of that year. During the first half of 1942, German submarines had a heyday sinking coastal traffic, much of it being northbound tankers. By one estimate, "nearly 95 percent of all gasoline and fuel used in the Northeast came up the coast."[89] As the gasoline supply slowed to a trickle, severe shortages resulted, and New England states were among the first to face gasoline rationing.

The rationing process attempted to prioritize an individual's fuel allotment based on his contribution to the war effort. Wensyel described the alphabetized process as follows:

Each car and truck was assigned a colored sticker

emblazoned with a large letter to be affixed to its windshield. The letter indicated the quantity of gasoline the vehicle's driver could buy each week. An "A" sticker, the one most Americans received, authorized the purchase of from three to five gallons per week. "B" stickers went to war workers, entitling them to exactly as much as they needed to get back and forth to work; those who required automobiles for their jobs but could not estimate precisely how much driving they would have to do (doctors, clergymen, and telegram deliverers) were issued a "C" sticker. Almost unlimited fuel went to emergency vehicles with "E" stickers, trucks marked with a "T," and a few civilians who qualified for an "X" sticker.[90]

The X sticker, which assured the owner of an unlimited supply, included congressmen, who were "exempt from gas rationing, but not widespread criticism."[91] Stickers entitled the holders to gas *if* it was available, which was often not the case. Long lines of cars at gas stations, or following delivery trucks to their destinations, were a common sight. With automobiles averaging less than fifteen miles per gallon, whatever the allotment of gas, it did not go far.

Unpopular as gas rationing initially was, wrote William O'Neill, most people complied "despite the inevitable chiseling and the rise of black marketers and forgers of gas ration permits."[92] Morris Levy experienced the gasoline black market firsthand when he came home to Portsmouth on leave in the middle of the war: when he asked a friend how he could get some gas, the friend drove his car to a local station and the attendant filled the tank, "no coupons or anything."[93] It was obvious to Levy that his friend had a friend who could help him work around any gas rationing. About the effectiveness of gas rationing, O'Neill wrote, "It helped that most people walked to work (40 percent) or took public transportation (23 percent). Even the 36 percent who commuted by car ultimately accepted gasoline rationing. Though only 49 percent of Americans saw a need for it when first proposed, by the end of 1942 the great majority of motorists (73 percent) supported gasoline rationing."[94] Reduced speed limits conserved fuel as well as tires: "The 35 mph speed limit won almost universal approval, 89 percent of car owners backing it." The low limit, for the most part, applied to the work commute because "in January 1943 pleasure driving was banned completely on the East Coast."[95]

New Hampshire police enforced the pleasure-driving ban by monitoring suspicious weekend or holiday traffic. Over the weekend of 4 July 1943, they stopped 1,400 cars on their way to holiday outings in New Hampshire. Many drivers reportedly had letters from their doctors prescribing a trip to New Hampshire for health reasons. Those lacking doctors' letters were subject to fines and the loss of gas rationing stamps. During the winter months, authorities monitored ski areas to search out drivers making "frivolous use of gas." State officials were not above suspicion: on one occasion, police stopped and questioned Governor Blood because he had ski racks on the roof of his car.[96]

Automobile production, which had been booming following record sales in 1940 and 1941, became one of the first casualties of the war. Many of the raw materials needed to build a car were the same ones needed to produce weapons of war. With the attack on Pearl Harbor came the instant realization that everything associated with the automotive industry — raw materials, plants, labor — required immediate conversion to armament production. On 2 February 1942, the last wartime civilian automobile authorized by the OPA rolled off a Detroit assembly line; the factories quickly converted to the manufacture of war vehicles and airplanes for the remainder of the war.

Americans drove less in order to make their cars last longer. Garages found plenty of work keeping the old cars running, and "people tinkered more with their prewar vehicles, making the aging roadsters last for the duration until postwar auto production could resume."[97] Gas rationing drove Rodolphe Blais to jack up his car for two and a half years and carpool to his new job at the shipyard after closing his market.[98] Similarly, Harold Whitehouse's father put his 1937 Dodge in storage each winter, removing the battery, draining the radiator, and setting the car on blocks to spare the tires.[99] In April 1942, the Automobile Association of America (AAA) reported, "Long-trip travel by passenger automobile in the United States already has dropped by almost 40 percent owing to nation-wide tire rationing and gasoline restriction."[100] This contributed to "markedly reduced traffic, lower revenues from gasoline taxes, and fewer automobile accidents and fatalities."[101]

The significant effect of the rationing of gas, tires, and automobiles on Portsmouth traffic is evident in figure 7. A study conducted by the Maine–New Hampshire Interstate Bridge Authority tallied total vehicles using the newly opened interstate Sarah Long Bridge for the same seven-month period (1 December to 1 August) during each of the war years. (Although the seven-month survey period overlaps calendar years, each figure is assigned to the calendar year in which the majority of the survey took place.) Interstate traffic, high in 1941, dramatically decreased in 1942 and 1943 with the mandated limits on gas and tires. After increasing slightly in 1944 and 1945 with the assurance of victory, traffic jumped to higher than prewar levels in 1946.

Rationing of gas, tires, and food was one thing. The rationing of women's silk stockings and, later, nylon

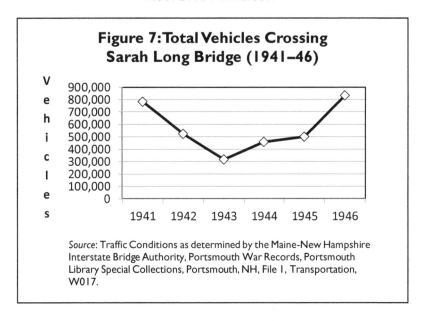

Figure 7: Total Vehicles Crossing Sarah Long Bridge (1941–46)

Source: Traffic Conditions as determined by the Maine-New Hampshire Interstate Bridge Authority, Portsmouth War Records, Portsmouth Library Special Collections, Portsmouth, NH, File 1, Transportation, W017.

stockings and undergarments, was something else. Wensyel provides this short history of women's wartime hosiery plight:

> Before the war women clothed their legs with silk or lisle (cotton-threaded) stockings. . . . The Dupont Company developed a new fiber called nylon from the prewar plastics revolution. . . . On May 15, 1940, [Dupont] placed nylons on the counters for throngs of approving female customers. . . . Silk stockings began to be rationed in August 1940 [with the limiting of Japanese imports], followed by silk slips and panties. Finally, in 1942, nylon joined silk as a war industry, and that November women were enjoined to donate their older silk and nylon stockings to the war effort.[102]

Silk and nylon parachutes were urgently needed to support the war effort. Women's silk and nylon undergarments, although considered a critical need by some, were assigned a much lower OPA priority than parachutes.

The *Portsmouth Herald*'s announcement of a curtailment of silk stocking sales generated a lot of excitement. The 2 August 1941 headline reported, "Silk Stocking Stampede Forces Local Merchants to Restrict Sales." Panicked women stormed the hosiery departments of the local stores as soon as they opened in the early morning hours to purchase silk stockings, limited to three pairs per customer. According to the article, "The overwhelming stocking demand resulted from an order of the Office of Production Management in Washington forbidding the processing of raw silk, effective at midnight tonight. The drastic step was the result of restrictions on trade with Japan." The desperate women reportedly purchased "ill fitting sizes and all available shades as they tried to beat the shortage." Such "stocking stampedes" were not at all uncommon. [103]

As the war progressed and silk hosiery became unobtainable, women aggressively pursued limited opportunities to purchase the new hosiery fashion—nylons. New Hampshire native Doris Elkhorn recalled arriving at a local store at 4:30 a.m. to join a line that grew to several city blocks long to purchase an allotted single pair of nylons when the store opened at 5:30 a.m.[104] One author wrote, "Women have cause to remember the nylon hosiery shortage and what it did to consumer etiquette at the hosiery counter."[105] The scene of women purchasing nylons often resembled a spirited athletic competition more than a pleasant shopping experience.

As a last resort, some women resorted to painting their legs to create the appearance of nylons. According to Claire Flanagan Papatones, who worked at the Portsmouth Internal Revenue Office, "We girls missed our silk stockings. Some genius came to our rescue—semi-fluid jars of various tan colors to paint our legs. It worked well unless we were caught in the rain, in which case we often ended up with streaked or muddy legs." Some women completed the nylon look by painting dark seams up the backs of their legs. Papatones never went to that extreme because, she said, "it required too steady a hand to avoid wiggly seams." [106]

Americans used it up, wore it out, made it do, did without, or found a substitute. Federal rationing and conservation programs provided the guidelines and set the goals, but it was the commitment and sacrifice of individuals across the nation, including the determined residents of seacoast New Hampshire and southern Maine, that guaranteed the success of those programs.

Despite all the sacrifices, few admitted truly suffering as a result. Portsmouth resident Morris Levy said, "I don't think the rationing was too severe. . . . I don't think anybody was hurt badly by it. . . . It didn't affect living, maybe it affected a few luxury items, like, for example, butter and maybe sugar. . . . But I don't think it affected the staples that much."[107] Another Portsmouth resident, Alice Sussman, expressed the feelings of many when she said, "That was tough, the rationing. . . . Things were getting scarce, and you would save your ration coupons for real necessities . . . [but] I don't remember suffering. . . . [You] made do with what you had."[108]

Increased National Attention

War bond drives, USO tours, and the importance of the Portsmouth Navy Yard to the war effort brought numerous VIPs to the seacoast area. A presidential visit on Saturday, 10 August 1940, was a highlight of the early stages of the shipyard mobilization. President Franklin Delano Roosevelt, Secretary of the Navy Frank Knox, and New Hampshire Governor Francis P. Murphy were escorted by ten motorcycle officers of the New Hampshire State Police and a dozen others of the Maine State Police in a parade of thirty-one cars from the Portsmouth train station to the shipyard (photo 18). Rodolphe Blais, then manager of the People's Market on Daniel Street, recalled that "security men came into his store and asked if they could use the second floor of the building which was vacant at the time, during the parade."[109] Harold Whitehouse was in the crowd lining Daniel Street: "My mother took me downtown to see him come by train and be

Photo 18: President Roosevelt in an open car on Daniels Street, accompanied by New Hampshire Governor Francis P. Murphy and Secretary of the Navy Frank Knox (10 August 1940). Note the two Secret Service agents standing on the rear bumper. Courtesy Frank Henry Collection, Thayer Cumings Library and Archives, Strawbery Banke Museum.

motorcaded down Daniel Street to go to the shipyard for a meeting. I'll never forget standing on the corner of Daniel and Pleasant at Market Square and his motorcade passed right by me. I saw Roosevelt in the back of an open car with his hat and his cigar holder. Just like he always did."[110] At the yard, the presidential party met briefly with the commandant, department heads, and others, followed by a short tour of the yard (far quieter than usual, since the shipyard had closed at 7:30 a.m. to all but selected employees and visitors). Although the president made several stops to inspect work, ships, and shops, he never left his car. At the completion of the tour — just fifty-five minutes after arriving at the train station, and forty minutes after entering the shipyard — FDR boarded his barge, the *Potomac*, which had docked at the yard the previous evening, and sailed for the Boston Navy Yard.[111] As short as it was, the visit was an important reminder to shipyard employees that the Navy's expectations of them were on the rise.

In the fall of 1941, with the help of local radio station WHEB, Colonel Dunn, commanding officer of the 22nd Coast Artillery, brought film and radio star Tallulah Bankhead to Camp Langdon Theater for an evening program titled "Let's Join the Army at Camp Langdon," which was broadcast over the radio in order to promote community relations. She was followed in the summer of 1943 by the far less photogenic but endlessly entertaining Jimmy Durante, who had been performing in Boston. Accepting the spontaneous invitation of a camp private to perform at Camp Langdon, he took the next train to Portsmouth intending to make a quick two-hour appearance — but reportedly played the piano and entertained the troops for six hours before returning to Boston.[112]

Another unscheduled appearance was made by Elsa Maxwell, the gossip columnist, songwriter, and hostess of high-society parties; while visiting in Ogunquit, Maine, Maxwell accepted an invitation to attend an enlisted men's party at Camp Langdon. Locals could plan ahead, however, for Vaughn Monroe and his popular orchestra, who entertained at the Hampton Beach Casino on numerous occasions, often in conjunction with the Navy Relief Society to raise money for families of local servicemen.[113] In addition, as reported earlier, Dorothy Lamour led a memorable war bond rally on Market Square.

Toward the end of the war, on 24 November 1945, Helen Keller visited Portsmouth Naval Hospital as part of a goodwill tour of Army and Navy hospitals. While at the yard, she insisted on touring the USS *Tuna*. Keller maneuvered down and up the ladders of the *Tuna*, toured the submarine from the bow to stern compartments, and marveled at the vibration of a 1600 horsepower diesel engine. When told about the pinup girls adorning the walls of the crew's galley, she promised to send the crew a picture of herself for their wall. Keller marveled at the crew's ability to "get along though in such close quarters," suggesting "women would be pulling each other's hair out" if forced to live under similar conditions. While touring the *Tuna*, she learned of German U-boats tied up nearby and added U-873 to her tour schedule. Never one to be told what she could not do, Keller kept a very ambitious schedule during her day at the yard.[114]

Secretary of the Navy Frank Knox was a frequent visitor to the Portsmouth Navy Yard, and not only because of his position: Knox, a Rough Rider and veteran of San Juan Hill, was in fact a Manchester, New Hampshire, native and the founding editor of the city's *Manchester Leader* (1912)— forerunner to the *New Hampshire Union Leader*—as well as a longtime part-owner and editor of the *Chicago Daily News*. Knox was appointed secretary of the Navy on 11 July 1940 and served in that office until he died of a heart attack on 28

April 1944.[115] It was Knox's phone call at 1:40 p.m. on Sunday, 7 December 1941, that alerted FDR about the attack on Pearl Harbor. Prior to his death, Knox was a staunch supporter of Portsmouth's efforts to secure a substantial postwar workload to preserve the city's wartime economic gains.

Long accustomed to attracting summer visitors, the city had the welcome mat out year-round during the war. Celebrities and thousands of new residents flocked to the seacoast. The program cover for the New Hampshire Music Festival, held in Portsmouth on 13 May 1944, welcomed attendees to the "City of the Open Door." Indeed, Portsmouth's doors were open wide, welcoming all.

A New Hampshire Gas and Electric Company advertisement on the back cover of the same program, reproduced below, speaks volumes about what was on the minds of Portsmouth citizens one month before D-Day: victory gardens, conservation, purchasing war bonds, and giving blood to "Keep America American."[116] Three and a half years into the war, the message remained clear and the commitments remained strong.

Homeland Portsmouth was not an "all work and no play"

Plant a Victory Garden
**

Save Fats, Metals and Paper
**

Contribute to all Community and National War Fund Drives
**

Donate your Blood for Plasma
for that Boy whose Life it may Save
**

All to
KEEP AMERICA AMERICAN
**

New Hampshire Gas & Electric Co.
Portsmouth   Newmarket

---

environment. Claire Flanagan Papatones remembers the city's war years as a bittersweet experience: "This period of time, though fraught with fear for our loved ones, was surprisingly beautiful. People were unselfish, generous, and patriotic. . . . It was a marvelous time. There was a lot of love going around."[117] Similarly, Eileen Dondero Foley recalled the exceptional patriotism and goodwill that flooded the area, punctuated with a spirit of oneness and a "we-are-all-in-this-together determination to prevail."[118]

The war changed Portsmouth, as it did many other towns across the nation. Leaving economic hard times behind and welcoming prosperity, as well as thousands of new workers and military personnel, Portsmouth took on a new look. Eager to do their part, residents actively supported the new wartime activities and dedicated themselves to whatever it took to win the war. Nevertheless, these same residents were apprehensive about how their city would emerge from the war. Addressing unprecedented challenges daily, the city forged into a future of unknowns with mixed emotions and many questions. Could the residents of Portsmouth preserve longtime New England values and quality of life while seizing the economic and industrial opportunities that mobilization had wrought? Would mobilization leave its permanent scar on the city or transform the area for the better? Simply stated — would Portsmouth boom or bust.

CHAPTER 7
POPULATION BOOM

Portsmouth is a boomtown with all the challenges that come with that title.

Survey of Health and Welfare
in the Portsmouth Defense Area,
August 1943

Sheer volume was the most visible sign of the overarching change as the wartime activity described above turned Portsmouth into a boomtown, one of many that that sprang up near mushrooming shipyards during World War II. The populations of Mobile, Alabama; Hampton Roads, Virginia; San Diego, California; and Charleston, South Carolina—all with large shipyards—increased anywhere from 38 to more than 64 percent.[1] Portsmouth and Kittery experienced similar growth spurts: the population of Portsmouth and its contiguous towns grew 41 percent, and tranquil Kittery's population exploded by a whopping 76 percent.[2] Portsmouth's wartime experience compared favorably with some boomtowns, less so with others, as all scrambled to provide adequate housing and expand critical infrastructure, while coping with deteriorated living conditions and unprecedented environmental damage caused by massive industrialization and overpopulation.

Portsmouth's World War I Population Boom

This wasn't the first time Portsmouth had experienced such a surge: some twenty years earlier, expanded shipyard operations during World War I had triggered significant population growth in Portsmouth and the neighboring communities of Rye, Greenland, New Castle, Newington, Kittery, and Eliot, from 19,324 to 22,807 people.[3] This mini-boom of about 3,500 people was modest when compared to the influx of more than 10,000 people during the next war, but it certainly brought its share of challenges, opportunities, and prosperity.

A 17 June 1918 *Portsmouth Herald* article, written by a Boston reporter, described the crowded conditions and newfound prosperity in Portsmouth: "If a man thinks he knows Portsmouth because he spent a pleasant week there a summer or two ago, he deceives himself. . . . Business? Nothing like it. . . . 'Money is in the air.'. . . This new war-time wealth in Portsmouth is evenly distributed, and most of it is on the go. . . . Portsmouth alone cannot house and feed them. They come in by crowded trolley cars from York villages. They fill special trains from Dover and Rochester, even from Newburyport, Haverhill, and Lowell."[4] Portsmouth Navy Yard was not the only local shipyard with new workers in need of housing and services. Employees at the newly constructed private Newington shipyards, Shattuck Shipyard and Atlantic Corporation Shipyard, also needed homes. Both yards would have life spans of less than three years.

Shattuck built wooden cargo ships and Atlantic built steel cargo ships for the U.S. Shipping Board. Both shipbuilders came late to the party. Shattuck launched its first three 2,500-ton wooden-hulled cargo steamers on 4 July 1918, four months before the end of the war. The yard delivered one ship before the end of the war and seven more during the following year. The yard closed in late 1919 when the U.S. Shipping Board canceled seven hulls under construction and contracts for three more. It did not take the government long

Photo 19: Launching USS Portsmouth *at Atlantic Corporation Shipyard (4 July 1919). Courtesy Portsmouth Athenaeum.*

to decide wooden-hulled cargo ships had no future.

On 23 May 1918, Atlantic Corporation Shipyard laid the keel of the first steel ship launched from a New Hampshire shore. Three 5,500-ton cargo ships completed before the end of the war, and the last of a ten-ship order was finished on 9 October 1920, at which time the yard folded.[5] On the other side of the river, the navy yard was also late to the war effort. The yard's first submarine, L-8, was completed on 25 May 1918, followed by a second, O-1, on 11 October 1918, just one week before the end of the war. Neither submarine saw action during the war. Despite their minimal contributions to the war effort, the three yards generated boosts in the region's population and economy.

Unfortunately, the economic mini-boom was swiftly followed by a postwar recession that lingered in the minds of many during the next war. In short order, both the Shattuck and Atlantic shipyards closed. Employment at the navy yard, which had increased more than 300 percent between 1914 and 1919, shrank to the prewar level by 1924.[6] Recalling those times, James Tucker, the secretary of the local chamber of commerce during World War II, remembered "committees of Portsmouth citizens rushing to Washington for relief after the armistice had been declared and practically all work discontinued at the local navy yard."[7] He also recalled servicemen selling pencils and peddling apples on the streets of Portsmouth. These unpleasant World War I memories weighed heavily on the minds of Portsmouth's civic leaders during World War II. Recalling the worst from the last war, they were determined not to relive the experience.

World War II National Migration

More than fifteen million civilians moved across county lines during World War II. The general flow was from country to city and from east to west. Home-front historian Richard R. Lingeman summarized the grand scope of the wartime migration:

> In sum the general pattern of the great national migration seemed to be this: Deep South po' whites to the shipyards around the Gulf crescent and in the Hampton Roads–Newport News– Norfolk complex, and further North to the Michigan manufacturing complexes . . . Southern Negro sharecroppers and tenant farmers to the shipyards and factories of the West Coast; up the East Coast and to the factories of the Middle West . . . Arkies, Okies, Tennessee and West-by-God Virginia hillbillies to Illinois and Indiana and

188

Michigan or to the Southern oilfields and shipyards . . . Kansas, Nebraska, Iowa, North and South Dakota plowboys to the great aircraft factories of the West Coast . . . New York and other urban small-manufacturing workers to the Mid and Far West.[8]

Noticeably absent in the above description is any reference to a heavy relocation of outsiders into New England—especially into New Hampshire and Maine. Unlike the Gulf Coast and West Coast shipyards, Portsmouth Navy Yard did not attract large numbers of ethnic and minority workers from great distances.

According to Richard Polenberg's *America at War: The Home Front 1941–45*, the ten most congested areas because of wartime influx were as follows:[9]

Location	Population Increase (1940-45)
Mobile County, Alabama	64.7%
Hampton Roads, Virginia, area	44.7%
San Diego County, California	43.7%
Charleston, South Carolina, area	38.1%
Portland-Vancouver, Wash.-Ore.	31.8%
San Francisco Bay area	25.0%
Puget Sound area	20.0%
Los Angeles area	15.1%
Muskegon County, Michigan	14.4%
Detroit–Willow Run area	8.2%

The numbers certainly show that the seacoast area was part of this phenomenon: as noted earlier, the population of Portsmouth and its contiguous towns grew 41 percent, and Kittery by 76 percent. In fact, tiny New Castle, New

Hampshire, swelled from only 500 residents at the start of the war to a peak of about 2,000, thanks to the hundreds of Army personnel manning the town's harbor defense forts. But in terms of sheer volume, the boom areas listed above far outdid the seacoast. Mobile's population grew by 92,000, Hampton Roads by 153,000, and Los Angeles by 440,000, compared to an increase of 10,000 for Portsmouth and its environs. Nevertheless, the resulting problems caused by the invasion of thousands of migrant workers — congestion, overloaded services, inadequate infrastructure — were strikingly similar.

Historians have written many books about World War II boomtowns, but few about East Coast shipyard boomtowns.[10] Lorraine McConaghy's article "Wartime Boomtown: Kirkland, Washington" examines the economic, political, environmental, and social transformation of a small West Coast town.[11] Kirkland's experience building Liberty ships was so negative that community leaders rejected a continued shipyard or military presence after the war. Portsmouth's leaders, on the other hand, committed themselves to maintaining as much of the wartime shipyard employment as possible to preserve the prosperity that mobilization had wrought.

Wayne Bonnett's *Build Ships! Wartime Shipbuilding Photographs* tells the story of the San Francisco Bay area shipyards.[12] On a larger geographic scale, Marilynn Johnson's *The Second Gold Rush: Oakland and the East Bay in World War II* argues that new war defense industries, including commercial shipbuilding, sparked a mass migration to the Bay Area that resulted in lasting social, cultural, and political changes.[13] On an even grander scale, several studies, including *The American West Transformed: The Impact of the Second World War* by Gerald Nash, have shown how federal spending during the war transformed the entire West Coast by generating unprecedented economic growth and prosperity.[14] All of the above studies primarily focused on large communities and West Coast industries; this book's focus on a small New England shipyard boomtown provides a different perspective.

Portsmouth played its own variations on the overall trends. The national migration was characterized by movement toward the big industrial centers—the shipbuilding yards on both coasts, the auto manufacturers of Detroit, and the airplane factories on the West Coast. The population of Richmond, California, for instance, mushroomed from 23,000 in 1940 to 100,000 in 1943 as workers flocked to the local shipyard to build Liberty ships. Mobilization historian Frederic Lane wrote, "Workers came from all over the Midwest and Southwest—the Okies, Arkies, and Texans were most evident."[15] The Puget Sound area shared many of the same experiences: "Labor shortages replaced unemployment lines and a great migration developed as Americans moved from poorer areas, particularly in the South, to areas with major war industries. Census takers in 1940 counted slightly more than 1.7 million Washington residents. The war effort quickly added a quarter-million more—including thousands of African Americans."[16] Unlike Richmond and the Puget Sound area, employment at Portsmouth Navy Yard swelled primarily from nearby New Englanders relocating closer to the shipyard. The workers who migrated into the Portsmouth area traveled much shorter distances and represented much less diversity. Many merely commuted long distances from hometowns in New Hampshire, Maine, and Massachusetts, accommodated by a fleet of forty buses operated by the yard.[17]

Many elements of the Portsmouth experience are echoed in *The Social History of a War-Boom Community* by Robert J. Havighurst and H. Gerthon Morgan, a study of the small shipyard boomtown of Seneca, Illinois. The Seneca boom was the result of a new shipyard built by the Chicago Bridge and Iron Company on the banks of the Illinois River, which delivered 157 oceangoing landing ship tanks (LSTs) to the Navy. Havighurst and Morgan wrote, "Similar to and yet different from these large congested areas were the cases of . . . many small towns and small cities that boomed on a miniature scale. . . . In Illinois, Indiana, and Wisconsin there were a dozen booms in which a village became a small industrial city almost overnight."[18] Seneca was one of those villages; its population grew from 1,235 in June 1942 to a peak of 6,600 in late 1944, before dropping precipitously to 1,370 in mid-1945.

The Seneca shipyard opened in the summer of 1942 and employment reached 9,000 eight months later, before peaking at 10,600 in late 1944. The yard's employment remained high through 1944 because the Navy needed LSTs to support its island-hopping drive toward Japan in the western Pacific. About the time employment peaked at Seneca's shipyard in 1944, employment at the Portsmouth Navy Yard plummeted from 20,000 to 10,000, because the Navy needed fewer submarines at that stage of the war. The submarine force had put to such good use the vessels built at phenomenal rates by Portsmouth and other yards, ridding the Pacific Ocean of Japanese warships and merchant shipping, that the Navy actually had an excess of submarines at that point.[19]

As victory in the Pacific became more certain, massive reductions followed at the Seneca shipyard, which closed in mid-1945. Most of the thousands of people who'd come to work at the shipyard moved away at the end of the war. The town's economic boom was as fleeting as its population boom, leaving it with "little more than a temporary period of hectic prosperity." Few lasting effects remained. Portsmouth, however, emerged from the war a transformed city, determined to preserve the best, and shed the worst, of its wartime experiences. [20]

Portsmouth's World War II Population Boom

Portsmouth was by no means a perfect city prior to World War II. One author described the prewar state of the city this way: "There are many problems of long standing in Portsmouth, which existed prior to the war [including] housing, government, and pollution. They should be distinguished from emergency problems growing out of the rapid influx of workers and of their families into the area. Wartime problems . . . include the need for more school facilities, insufficient recreational equipment, and increasing loads on utilities."[21] The author concluded, "Portsmouth is a boomtown with all the challenges that come with that title." Portsmouth's exploding population aggravated a prewar housing shortage, overloaded existing schools, and challenged marginal public utilities. Meanwhile, shipyard operations polluted the Piscataqua River and contaminated Seavey Island. The region did not escape the pitfalls experienced by other boomtowns.

Portsmouth Herald editor Franklin E. Jordan sounded the alarm when he wrote, "It is no exaggeration to state that Portsmouth now has the greatest problem in its 318 year history and that its future for the next 318 years will be affected by the way the problem is handled."[22] One might assume that Jordan was writing near the end of World War II, concerned about how the city would adjust to the postwar era. Not so: he wrote these words in the summer of 1941, four months before the attack on Pearl Harbor. Jordan and other leaders had the city's World War I civic issues and its negative postwar experience fresh in mind when they expressed concerns about how Portsmouth would emerge from the war that was yet to start.

In the summer of 1941, shipyard employment had grown from 5,722 to 8,500 in one year and continued to climb. Who knew what problems the community would face if the shipyard grew to 15,000 or 20,000 employees, which it eventually did? Jordan conducted a comprehensive analysis of the mobilization then under way with emphasis on how it would affect the city's utilities, schools, hospitals, police and fire protection, government, recreational facilities, and other resources. With memories of the Great Depression still fresh, and the conviction that another postwar recession was inevitable, he concluded, "Relief will be the greatest problem in a postwar depression."[23] Thus, even before World War II began, Portsmouth's leaders fretted about the peace that would follow. Left unsaid was the assumption that the United States would win the war.

Jordan's primary concern was the aftermath of the anticipated flurry of home building, infrastructure improvements, and expansion of municipal services that would accompany the forthcoming population boom. The city had struggled with the same issues during the last war, and no one was looking forward to traveling down that road again. How would the city maintain the new and enlarged Portsmouth after the war when the inevitable shipyard cutbacks occurred and federal funding expired? How would the city fund the relief effort needed to support its burgeoning population when the inevitable postwar recession arrived?

Table 6 confirms Jordan's worst fears about the predicted population boom.[24] With the rationing of automobiles and gasoline, the communities within walking distance of the shipyard, especially Portsmouth and Kittery, experienced

	1940	1944	Increase
Table 6: Portsmouth Area Population Booms (1940–1944)			
Portsmouth and contiguous towns (Kittery, Eliot, Greenland, New Castle, Newington, Rye)	25,039	35,294	41.0%
Portsmouth	14,821	20,029	35.0%
Kittery	5,374	9,475	76.0%
Rockingham County	58,142	60,276	3.6%
Other local towns York, Durham, Exeter, etc.	18,127	20,410	12.0%
New Hampshire	491,524	459,250	**-6.6%**

Sources: There are three sources for this table: 1) for Portsmouth and contiguous towns: *Survey of Health and Welfare in the Portsmouth Defense Area*, August 1943, table entitled "Population-Total Trends"; 2) for Rockingham County: *Portsmouth Herald*, 15 February 1944, "Survey Shows Trends," 1; and 3) for New Hampshire: Philip N. Guyol, *Democracy Fights: A History of New Hampshire in World War II*, 104 and note 3.

tremendous growth. Proportionally speaking, Kittery's population boom was even larger than that of Mobile County, Alabama, and Portsmouth with its contiguous towns grew more than Charleston, South Carolina.

Between 1940 and 1944, two hundred counties of the United States increased in population by 20 percent or more.[25] Perhaps surprisingly, Rockingham County, where Portsmouth is located, was not one of those, experiencing only a 3.6 percent gain in population. While the entire county remained relatively stable, it appears there was a great migration out of the southern and western parts of the county into the Portsmouth area. This is in sharp contrast to the San Francisco Bay and Puget Sound regions, where a massive influx of minorities and workers arrived from distant parts of the United States. When asked about new shipyard employees who had not grown up locally, William Tebo responded, "There were a lot from towns in Down East Maine."[26] In general, outsiders who migrated to the Portsmouth area seeking wartime employment did not cause the cultural turmoil that roiled other boomtowns. The folks from Millinocket and Damariscotta shared many of the same values and agendas as the folks from Kittery and Portsmouth.

This comparative tranquility is somewhat surprising, given how active the Ku Klux Klan had been just twenty years earlier. In the 1920s, the Klan had large followings in

Photo 20: Ku Klux Klan parade in Kittery, Maine, outside Portsmouth Navy Yard main gate (circa 1923). Courtesy Harold Whitehouse personal collection.

New England: Maine had 150,141 members; Vermont, 75,000; New Hampshire, 65,690; Massachusetts, 13,078; and Rhode Island, 21,321.[27] Klan members were typically Anglo-Saxon Protestants worried about the growing number of French-Canadian Catholics moving into the region seeking low-paying jobs. By the early 1920s, the Canadian immigrants were a substantial percentage of the population in Maine and New Hampshire.[28]

Maine, the first stop for French-Canadians migrating south, was a hotbed of Klan activity in 1923; the first Klan rally in New England and the first daylight KKK rally ever took place in Milo, Maine. A dozen other rallies followed in the state that year, including one in Kittery immediately outside the main gate of the shipyard (photo 20). The rallies moved south into New Hampshire over the next few years: one attended by more than two thousand people was held in Hampton (10 September 1925), followed by rallies in Rye (21 June 1926) and Portsmouth (4–5 September 1927). These gatherings were less aggressive than the typical KKK rallies in the South, generally taking the form of field days with religious services, picnics, clambakes, baseball games, band concerts, fireworks, etc. However, hooded parades and cross burnings served as grim reminders to the communities that the outings were, in fact, KKK events. After minimal violence, and more hype than harm, the New England KKK faded in the late 1920s as the Great Depression brought bigger problems to the area than did the French-Canadians.[29]

Considering that history, it is remarkable that the region absorbed in excess of 10,000 immigrants in the early 1940s with so little consequence and so few disturbances. There were numerous French-Canadian enclaves in the region, but sufficient cultural assimilation had caused any remaining differences to fade, especially given the importance of the war effort. In addition, jobs were plentiful; new immigrants were no longer "stealing" low-paying jobs from longtime residents. Jobs were available for all who wanted them in the seacoast region and even more plentiful out west.

In *The U.S. Economy in World War II*, economist Harold G. Vatter compared the dynamic migration of workers westward in search of jobs in the war-related industries to the static or declining populations in eastern regions not favored with booming industries:

> The great migration wave regionally was to the Pacific Coast . . . the three Pacific Coast states

increasing their population by over 34%. . . . Of the net national migration of about 3.5 million people between April 1940 and November 1943, nearly 1.5 million went to California. . . . Almost all other regions experienced arrested population growth or losses. The New England, Middle Atlantic, and East North Central regions containing the old manufacturing belt barely held their own during the war.[30]

In fact, New Hampshire not only failed to "hold its own," its population decreased 6.6 percent during the war. Philip N. Guyol attributed the loss to an outflow of workers to manufacturing centers in Massachusetts and Connecticut, as well as to the selective service.[31] In February 1944, the *Portsmouth Herald* reported that 10,000 New Hampshire residents were working in Connecticut war plants.[32] Although more than 12,000 new residents relocated to the New Hampshire seacoast during the war, the state lost 30,000 residents overall. Compared to the rest of the state, the seacoast became a hotbed of dynamic growth and activity. The center of the state's population and manufacturing moved sharply in the direction of Portsmouth, pulling with it the economic center as well.

This eastward shift was clearly the result of the increased tempo of operations at the shipyard, as the figures in table 7 show. In 1944, one out of every five local residents and nearly 3 percent of the state's entire population worked at the Portsmouth Navy Yard. Some 7 percent of the state's active labor force of 185,000 worked at the yard. [33] Moreover, in late 1944, when there were 12,981 people working at the shipyard, only 73,000 people were working in all the other manufacturing jobs throughout the state, including the textile, leather, paper, machinery, lumber, and other

	Population	Employed by Shipyard	Percentage Employed
Table 7: Portsmouth Navy Yard Employment Distribution by Towns (1944)			
Portsmouth and contiguous towns	35,294	7,382	20.9%
Portsmouth	20,029	4,355	21.7%
Kittery	9,475	2,188	33.8%
Other local towns – York, Durham, Exeter, etc.	20,410	2,220	10.8%
New Hampshire	459,260	12,981	2.8%

Sources: The table has three sources: 1) for towns: *Survey of Health and Welfare in the Portsmouth Defense Area,* August 1943, table 17, Box 2, Folder 1, "State Council of Defense, Local Committees: Portsmouth"; 2) for New Hampshire: Philip N. Guyol, *Democracy Fights,* 104, note 3; and 3) New Hampshire shipyard employees: Portsmouth Chamber of Commerce, 1, MS 96, Box 1, Folder 5, "Business and Industry," Thayer Cumings Library and Archives, Strawbery Banke Museum, Portsmouth, NH.

industries.[34] The manufacturing boom centered on the shipyard, but it also encompassed many small firms, which supplied the myriad of components and services needed to build submarines. Manufacturing had quickly overtaken farming and tourism as the chief industry of the seacoast.

The wartime invasion of workers with families caused a sharp drop in the average age of seacoast residents. Prior to the war, the region's age distribution skewed heavily toward the shipyard's age-hiring range, while the proportion of children and adolescents was considerably below the state average. According to the 1943 *Survey of Health and Welfare,* "In 1940 the percent of people under 25 years of age or over 54 was smaller for this area than for the entire state. This may have been due to the civil service regulation, which limited the age of most navy yard workers from 18 to 45 years."[35] The area's 41 percent increase in population between 1940 and 1944 included a significant shift toward children and teenagers, as shown in table 8. The large number of adults with families rushing to the seacoast to find employment at

Table 8: Portsmouth Defense Area Age Distribution (1940–1943)			
Age	1940 Census	1943 Estimated	Percentage Shift
< 5	2,003	3,000	49.7%
5-14	4,331	5,950	37.3 %
15-24	4,650	5,450	17.2 %
25-34	4,427	4,825	8.9 %
35-44	4,047	4,500	10.9 %
45-64	6,134	6,975	13.7 %
>65	2,715	2,450	-9.8 %

Source: Survey of Health and Welfare in the Portsmouth Defense Area, August 1943; table is constructed from graph titled "Portsmouth Defense Area Population-Age" in the Appendix. Box 2, Folder 1, "State Council of Defense, Local Committees: Portsmouth." The 1943 numbers in this table were obtained from the hand-drawn graph cited. Accuracy can be assumed to be within 25 people.

the yard more than compensated for the young people going into the armed forces.

These families had many children, bumping up the under-five cohort by about one thousand children. Portsmouth's population boom between 1940 and 1944 (shown earlier in table 6) was fueled by a simultaneous baby boom. The 1942–43 birth rate at Portsmouth Hospital was more than twice the

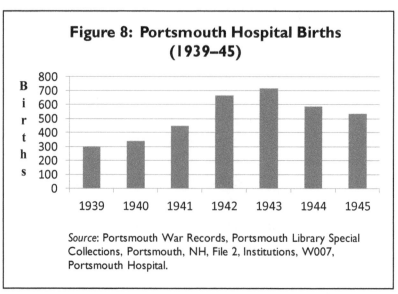

Figure 8: Portsmouth Hospital Births (1939–45)

Source: Portsmouth War Records, Portsmouth Library Special Collections, Portsmouth, NH, File 2, Institutions, W007, Portsmouth Hospital.

1940 birth rate (figure 8). (It should be noted that figure 8 includes births in towns other than those in the Portsmouth Defense Area.[36])

The increase in other activities at Portsmouth Hospital between 1940 and 1944 more closely approximated the area's 41 percent population increase—the number of patients admitted grew by 32 percent, operations performed increased 48 percent, and accidents treated increased 48 percent (figure 9). The more than 200 percent increase in births can probably be attributed to the economic boom that mobilization brought. After a decade of struggling to feed and raise children, all of a sudden the future for families looked much brighter.

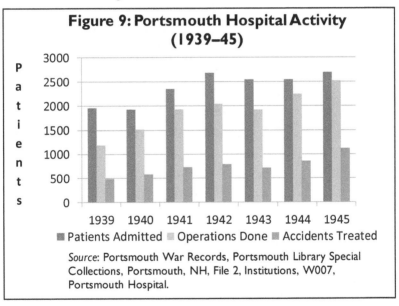

Figure 9: Portsmouth Hospital Activity (1939–45)

Patients

Patients Admitted   Operations Done   Accidents Treated

Source: Portsmouth War Records, Portsmouth Library Special Collections, Portsmouth, NH, File 2, Institutions, W007, Portsmouth Hospital.

The nationwide demographic shift toward higher percentages of youth and adolescents was not without its consequences. Often both parents worked, and they worked long hours, freeing juveniles to get into mischief. Many believed the sharp increase in the number of working mothers, which resulted in less adult supervision at home, contributed to a rise in juvenile delinquency. During the war, noted James Wensyel, "the number of families headed at least temporarily by women jumped from 770,000 to more than 2.7 million."[37] Richard R. Lingeman wrote, "Juvenile arrests increased 20 percent in 1943; in some cities it was even higher—San Diego, for example, reported an increase of 55 percent among boys and 355 percent among girls. This was not a reflection of a nationwide crime wave, for crime on the whole—at least according to FBI figures—dropped during the war." The delinquency among boys "was largely theft and a striking incidence of acts of vandalism, destruction and violence." The alarming increase in girls' delinquency primarily "took the form of an aggressive promiscuity." Portsmouth did not record any significant increase in juvenile crime during the war, but, as discussed in chapter 5, aggressive promiscuity made an appearance on the streets of Portsmouth.[38]

As might be expected with men going off to war, the ratio of females to males increased in most communities during World War II. This trend was under way in the Portsmouth Defense Area as early as 1940: the number of men per 100 females dropped from 108.4 in 1930 to 101.4 in 1940. In 1940, Kittery had the highest number of males per 100 females (123.2), the direct result of thousands of newly hired male shipyard employees relocating to within walking distance of their jobs. On the other side of the river, the city of Portsmouth had fewer males than females (94.8) in 1940. Figures are not available for the war years, but the trend probably accelerated as the selective service took more and more young men into the military. Thus, Portsmouth became decidedly younger and more feminine during the war years. This demographic shift supports the profile of the city presented in this book: that of an active city, full of vitality, with a social life centered on energetic young people. It may also have contributed to the election of the city's first female mayor in 1944 (see chapter 13).

———————————————

The mobilization that brought ten thousand new residents to Portsmouth and its environs between 1940 and 1944 also brought benefits and challenges. The benefits included economic prosperity and a remarkable increase in the number of skilled and female workers. The challenges were primarily those Frank Jordan had predicted: the need for nearly instantaneous home building, massive infrastructure development, and rapid expansion of municipal services. In the process of meeting those challenges, the city experienced a building boom unlike anything it had ever seen before, with long-lasting effects. The environmental consequences of the mobilization, not mentioned by Jordan, also proved challenging. These benefits and challenges are the subjects of the following chapters.

CHAPTER 8
ECONOMIC BOOM

Perhaps the outstanding industrial phenomenon was the surge of Portsmouth Navy Yard to the position of the largest single employer in the state, at its peak employing about as many people [from all states] as the entire textile industry [in New Hampshire].

Philip Guyol
Democracy Fights

As the Great Depression dwindled into a nightmarish memory and the navy yard pumped millions of dollars into the local economy, Portsmouth took on new importance as an engine of prosperity within New Hampshire. For many people, wartime Portsmouth was the best of times and the worst of times: suddenly inflated incomes wielded limited purchasing power in a rationed market and no amount of economic success could buy back the sacrifices of loved ones overseas. Nevertheless, residents welcomed their sudden good fortune after a decade of scarce jobs and abundant financial woes.

When mobilization started in the summer of 1940, the nation's economy was still soft, with more than five million Americans unemployed and seven and a half million workers earning less than forty cents per hour.[1] Economist Harold G. Vatter wrote, " . . . 1940 was the eleventh year of the Great Depression. . . . With a civilian unemployment rate of 14.5 percent, the economy was still far from promising to absorb fully the army of unemployed."[2] According to historian David M. Kennedy, that army of unemployed workers, combined with greatly underutilized industrial facilities, suddenly became an advantage when the country finally decided to mobilize. Unlike World War I, when the nation struggled to recruit soldiers from a fully employed work force and convert near-capacity civilian production to military purposes, the start of World War II found a vast pool of readily available labor and idle factories practically begging to be repurposed.[3] Portsmouth Navy Yard, underutilized during the 1930s, was one of those facilities primed for rapid expansion to support the nation's needs.

The prosperity that Portsmouth experienced during World War II was not without precedent: a lesser economic spike occurred during World War I. A 14 May 1919 *Portsmouth Herald* article, "Portsmouth Leads All New Hampshire Cities in Growth during War," highlighted the

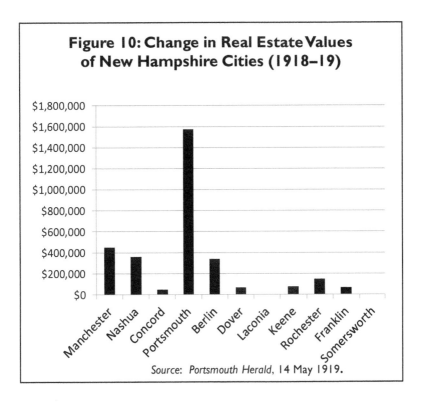

Figure 10: Change in Real Estate Values of New Hampshire Cities (1918–19)

Source: *Portsmouth Herald*, 14 May 1919.

tremendous growth in the value of the city's real estate as compared to the other major New Hampshire cities (figure 10).[4] This real estate boom, driven by the emerging shipbuilding industry at the three local yards — Portsmouth Navy Yard and the two new private enterprises, Shattuck Shipyard and Atlantic Corporation Shipyard — collapsed just as suddenly as it had developed. Postwar employment reductions at the navy yard and the closing of the two new yards left the region with an economic recession and Portsmouth's leaders with memories that convinced them that a similar recession would be inevitable after the next war. These memories heavily influenced Portsmouth's post-World War II recovery plan.

Despite Portsmouth's Great War boom, Manchester maintained a commanding lead in real estate values over all

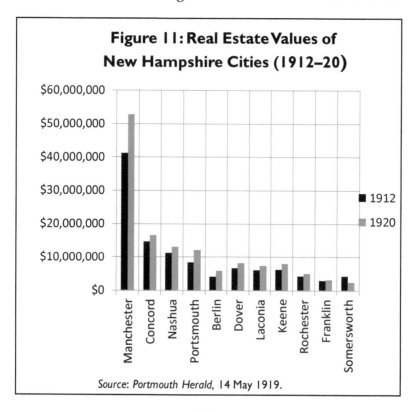

Figure 11: Real Estate Values of New Hampshire Cities (1912–20)

Source: Portmouth Herald, 14 May 1919.

other New Hampshire cities, followed by Concord, Nashua, and Portsmouth (figure 11).[5] The state's economic center remained firmly rooted in central New Hampshire near the traditional manufacturing sites. After the region's brief World War I growth spurt, seacoast New Hampshire and southern Maine reverted to their rural, tourist-oriented ways for the next two decades.

With a preponderance of rural and farming occupations, New Hampshire was not as severely affected by the Great Depression as many areas of the country. According to New Hampshire historian Philip N. Guyol, during the lean years between 1930 and 1939, the state's income per capita was comfortably above the national average, ranking seventeenth in 1939.[6] Consequently, at the start of World War II, New Hampshire had not experienced as drastic an economic depression as other more urbanized states.

As the 1930s came to a close, Portsmouth had a running start into the economic boom that was about to happen. In April 1940, the *Herald* reported very positively that the city had enjoyed increased real estate and retail sales the previous year. With only 3.18 percent of the state's buying power, the city reported 5.7 percent of the state's retail sales.[7] The newspaper attributed these disproportionate sales to recreational and value-minded visitors to the seacoast area; tourism continued to be a driver of the local economy. By any measure, the region was not in dire economic straits at the start of 1940. Portsmouth's economy, already robust relative to the rest of the state, was about to get much better with thousands of workers moving into the area seeking lucrative shipyard industrial jobs.

With the National War Labor Board controlling wage inflation, hourly wages of all workers across the nation increased only 24 percent during the war; however, the wages of high-demand industrial workers leaped by 50 percent.[8] Furthermore, the weekly earnings of industrial workers rose 70 percent because of overtime and longer workweeks. Most of the twenty thousand plus employees driving the phenomenal output at the Portsmouth Navy Yard were industrial workers reaping the benefits of high wages, overtime, and extended workweeks.

A flood of workers rushed into newfound employment — and almost immediately, wartime employers found themselves on the wrong side of a classic supply-and-demand problem, with too few available workers chasing too many jobs. Industrial sectors producing critical products for the military paid well, attracting workers from lesser-paying jobs. One historian wrote, "Too many claimants tugged instantly at the available supply [of manpower]: the draft, the military, the war plants, shipyards, lumber camps, farms, mines, and a host of other, more specialized needs."[9] It was a sellers' market for the in-demand workers — a far cry from the decade of idleness and privation that had preceded the war.

The labor migration from lower- to higher-paying industrial jobs created unprecedented employment opportunities for women, who quickly filled vacated positions. Locally, women found employment at the start of the war in nonindustrial jobs, working as clerks, bus or cab drivers, and the like. The pay for these jobs, although low, was better than the domestic jobs typically held by women. As the war progressed and shipyard jobs became available, women moved to the industrial jobs. Young unmarried women without family obligations were the first to seize the new opportunities. Zina Boulanger, a nineteen-year-old drugstore clerk making fifteen dollars a week in Dover, New Hampshire, increased her wages threefold when she found employment as a navy yard welder.[10] Similarly, Claire Flanagan Papatones, fresh out of high school, greatly boosted her income by leaving a secretarial job to become an auditor at the Portsmouth office of the Internal Revenue Service.[11] It was not long before mothers demanded day-care centers and other child-care provisions to enable them to take advantage of the budding market for women's services.

Among those tempted by lucrative industrial jobs were teachers. In his 1942 report, Kittery's school superintendent warned that unless teachers' salaries increased, the town would not be able to retain current teachers or hire capable new ones to meet the demand of increased enrollments. The superintendent wrote, "During the past two years twelve million factory workers have received an increase of 30 percent in average weekly earnings. Teachers' salaries, for the most part, have remained static."[12] Teacher retention, with high-paying shipyard jobs mere blocks away, remained a challenge for Kittery school administrators for the entire war.

The inflated paychecks brought home by more than twenty thousand workers at Portsmouth Navy Yard were a welcome stimulus to the local economy. At the same time, these paychecks were not free to chase a very limited supply of goods and foodstuffs because of OPA rationing and price controls, which prevented runaway inflation. After years of struggling without "rainy day funds," families were quick to put unspent earnings in the bank. Guyol reported, "Between 1939 and 1945, total deposits of all state and federal banks in New Hampshire grew from $282,000,000 to $462,000,000, and total resources from $323,000,000 to $512,000,000."[13] Similar 60 percent increases in personal savings accounts nationwide would fuel the postwar recovery.

Local communities benefited greatly from the $23 million capital investment at the navy yard between the summer of 1940 and the summer of 1941, as well as from rapidly increasing shipyard payroll and other defense-related spending. During that period, the federal government authorized expenditures of $36.7 million—more than half a billion present-day dollars when adjusted for inflation — for the projects listed in table 9, an exceptional economic stimulus.[14]

Table 9: Portsmouth Area Federal Project Expenditures
(5 July 1940–15 July 1941)

Portsmouth Navy Yard	$23.00M
Portsmouth Harbor Defense	$ 1.50M
Bridges—State and Interstate	$ 3.30M
Housing—Federal and Private	$ 5.00M
City of Portsmouth Facilities	$ 2.50M
Non-municipal Utilities	$ 1.40M
Total	$36.70M ($.601 billion present value)

Source: Franklin E. Jordan, *Portsmouth and National Defense*, 1 August 1941, table titled "Summary Defense Capital Investments," 1862.

The yard received most of the federal money to enhance its capacity to produce submarines as quickly as possible. Other projects brought millions of federal dollars to the city for harbor defense, housing, utilities, facilities, and infrastructure development. The list of harbor defense projects detailed in table 10 offers vivid proof of the Army's increased involvement in the area. By mid-1941, most of the harbor defenses had been activated from caretaker status and were reported to be "practically complete and in use."[15] As

---

Table 10: Portsmouth Harbor Defense Federal Projects
(5 July 1940–15 July 1941)

22 New Barracks and Buildings	$500,000
50-Bed Hospital/Camp Langdon	$150,000
Water and Sewage	$250,000
Roads and Transport	$100,000
Other Improvements	$300,000
Total: 3 Forts and 1 Camp	$1,300,000
	($21.3 million present value)

Source: Franklin E. Jordan, *Portsmouth and National Defense*, 1 August 1941, Table 2, "Portsmouth Harbor Defense," 1871.

---

was the case with the navy yard, the mobilization of harbor defense was well under way long before the nation's entry into the war.

Herald editor Frank Jordan's *Portsmouth and National Defense* (August 1941), provided a summary of the federal dollars received to date for municipal facilities upgrades. The vast majority of the funds were funneled into education/schools ($993,000), utilities/water ($1,011,000), and electrical upgrades ($1,000,000) as the city struggled to come to grips with the heightened demand in these critical areas.[16] This flood of dollars kick-started local markets, swelled merchants' coffers, and set the economic future for seacoast New Hampshire and southern Maine.

In addition to the original $23 million that went into shipyard upgrades, the Navy invested an additional $13 million in shipyard plant additions and facilities during the war, much of which filtered into the local economy.[17] However, it was the shipyard's annual payrolls and ongoing expenditures for local products and services that drove massive dollars into the economy on a regular basis (table 11) — a total of $392 million ($5.46 billion present value, when adjusted for inflation) between 1940 and 1945. The shipyard's annual contribution to the region's economy increased well

Table 11: Portsmouth Navy Yard
Annual Expenditures Excluding Facilities
(1940–1945)

1940	$11 M
1941	$23 M
1942	$43 M
1943	$74 M
1944	$100 M
1945	$141 M
Total	$392 M
($5.46 billion present value)	

Source: Philip Guyol, *Democracy Fights: A History of New Hampshire in World War II*, 162.

over tenfold during the war. It was this high-speed and finely tuned economic engine across the river that local leaders had in mind when they began to consider the postwar economic future of their city. Recalling the post–World War I recession that accompanied the collapse of the shipbuilding industry, authorities were determined not to repeat that experience. Late in World War II, city leaders pulled out all the stops in their efforts to convince the Navy to favor their shipyard with continued high postwar workloads and wages.

The shipyard's windfall contribution to the local economy boosted workers' purchasing power and commercial sales. A 1939 census of 289 retail establishments revealed sales of $10,328,000. A similar survey in 1941 showed the number of establishments had grown to 329 with sales of $12,651,000. With rationing in effect, sales dropped to $11,932,000 in 1942, still considerably above prewar numbers. During the same two-year period (1941–42) the area's purchasing power increased from $18,000,000 to $21,000,000. With disposable incomes on the rise, the OPA's plans to prevent too much money from chasing too few goods through rationing and price controls found good application in the Portsmouth Defense Area. [18]

The local chamber of commerce claimed $15,314,000 in retail sales in 1943. Table 12 shows the strength of the local economy in 1943, midway through the war: with only 4.42 percent of New Hampshire's population, Portsmouth accounted for 6.69 percent of the state's retail sales; likewise, with .016 percent of the nation's population, Portsmouth claimed .024 percent of retail sales nationwide. Portsmouth's retail sales per capita during the war were about 50 percent above both the state and the national averages. Despite rationing and other wartime struggles, life on the seacoast was pretty good.

Table 12: Portsmouth Retail Sales Compared to State and Nation (1943)		
	New Hampshire	United States
Portsmouth Percentage of Population	4.42	.016
Portsmouth Percentage of Retail Sales	6.69	.024

Source: "Portsmouth Chamber of Commerce," 3. Thayer Cumings Library and Archives, MS 96, Box 1, Folder 5, "Business and Industry," Strawbery Banke Museum, Portsmouth, NH.

Zina Boulanger, the drugstore clerk who became a shipyard welder, did her part to increase retail sales. She recalls that one of her first paychecks at the yard, presumably for two weeks' pay, amounted to eighty-eight dollars. Suddenly with more discretionary income than she had ever imagined, she immediately went shopping and bought a fur coat—albeit a muskrat fur coat, not one of the rationed items. Shipyard paychecks enabled many workers to live more comfortably during the war than they had before it.[19] As historian Maury Klein noted in his exhaustive mobilization study, *A Call to Arms: Mobilizing America for World War II*, "To the generation that had endured a decade of the worst depression in American history, the war years seemed a strange and ghastly mixture of the best and the worst of times."[20] This was an oft-repeated theme heard from interviewees for this book.

Arthur Herman, driving home this point, wrote, "Despite rationing and restrictions, the output of consumer goods was larger every war year than it had been in 1939. In 1945 Americans ate more meat, bought more shoes and gasoline, and used more electricity than they had before Hitler invaded France." The miraculous American mobilization, while producing the staggering amounts of munitions needed to win the war, also contributed enough consumer goods to significantly improve living conditions in most parts of the country. "The dream of an economy vibrant enough to produce both guns and butter had been realized thanks to American business."[21]

Claire Flanagan Papatones, who had become an auditor at the Portsmouth office of the Internal Revenue Service, was another who found herself with ample discretionary income in 1943. Papatones recalls that she and her friends "were able to purchase beautiful outfits without too much difficulty."[22] The rationing of items critical to the war effort apparently did not include fashionable women's clothing.

Most families had been fortunate to have even one income earner during the Depression; now a new phenomenon, two-income families, became common as women increasingly filled positions at the yard. According to store clerk Amelia Patch, "They [female shipyard workers] were earning big money, and they didn't care how they spent it. Oh, it was disgustin'. . . . And they'd come in and 'I'll take that and that and I want three of those and that' and oh, they'd have a big roll of bills." In Patch's opinion, "So many women went to work on the navy yard and they had two salaries comin' in and they went crazy. I mean some of 'em I don't think had ever had a dollar before. They didn't know what to do with it."[23] Alice Sussman, who worked in a Portsmouth dress shop during the war, shared similar observations about women spending newfound money on luxuries: "People went out and bought clothes . . . a super-duper dress was $16.95. . . . That was a lot of money, a lot of money."[24] This personal testimony certainly supports the chamber of commerce's figures (table 12) showing Portsmouth's retail sales to be 50 percent higher than those of the state and the nation.

Wartime shortages worked to the benefit of some. The automobile repair shop business boomed, as did the shoe repair shop of Alice Sussman's father. She recalled, "You got ration cards and you couldn't afford to spend ration cards very often for new shoes . . . so everybody was having their shoes fixed. And that was one of the times when he [Sussman's father] was most prosperous. . . . Everybody [in the repair business] made hay at that time."[25] It was not just rationing that drove up the demand midway through the war: the population boom brought tens of thousands more shoes in need of repair to the seacoast area.

Despite the dimming of their normally bright lights, the local beaches and seaside towns attracted large numbers of visitors during the summer months after the first tense year of the war, greatly benefiting seashore attractions and businesses. In his history of Hampton, Peter Randall wrote, "In fact, because gas rationing prohibited distant travel, and because thousands of military men and workers were stationed at the Portsmouth Naval Shipyard, the Beach became a popular destination for New Englanders. The Beach enjoyed record crowds and booming business throughout the war years."[26] Many people found outlets for their new wealth at beach attractions, entertainment sites, and dance halls.

After a decade short on amusement and lightheartedness, Americans sought distraction from past economic woes and current wartime challenges wherever they could find it. As Maury Klein wrote, "Americans pocketed record earnings, paid their debts, amused themselves, and spent freely on whatever they could find. Restaurants and night clubs flourished despite shortages of food and liquor."[27] Portsmouth and the beaches of New Hampshire and southern Maine offered much amusement and many distractions.

While the seacoast prospered, the rest of the state did not fare nearly as well. Although the average Portsmouth resident's annual purchasing power in 1943, as reported by the chamber of commerce, was only slightly above the national average, it was fully 36 percent higher than the state average (table 13). This disparity speaks to the lack of wartime prosperity in the rest of the state.

Table 13: Portsmouth Annual Purchasing Income versus State and Nation (1943)	
	Purchasing Income
Portsmouth	$1,136
New Hampshire	$833
United States	$1,103

Source: "Portsmouth Chamber of Commerce," 3. Thayer Cumings Library and Archives, Strawbery Banke Museum, Portsmouth, NH, MS 96, Box 1, Folder 5, "Business and Industry."

Despite the seacoast's good fortune, New Hampshire was among the states that benefited least economically during the war, more proof of harder times in the rest of the state. Department of Commerce survey data show that even though New Hampshire's per capita income grew by 78 percent during the war years, it increased at a slower rate than the national average (table 14). As Guyol notes, "New Hampshire moved down from seventeenth place [in per capita income] in 1939 to thirty-fifth place in 1945."[28] The state's per capita income dropped from above average in 1939 to only 83 percent of the national average in 1945. This negative trend, which occurred despite the economic boom that occurred in the Portsmouth area, was attributable to the lack of wartime industrialization elsewhere in New Hampshire and the massive growth in industrialization in other states.

Table 14: National versus New Hampshire Annual Incomes (1939–45)

	1939	1940	1941	1942	1943	1944	1945
United States	$539	$575	$693	$862	$1,040	$1,113	$1,177
New Hampshire	$548	$546	$629	$720	$808	$893	$977

Source: Philip N. Guyol, Democracy Fights, 187 and note 2.

Historian Philip N. Guyol wrote in *Democracy Fights*, "The impact of World War II was felt in every segment of New Hampshire's economy. For five years people worked more, produced more, earned more, saved more, and spent more than ever before in their lives."[29] He added, "Perhaps the outstanding industrial phenomenon was the surge of Portsmouth Navy Yard to the position of the largest single employer in the state, at its peak employing about as many people [from all states] as the entire textile industry [in New Hampshire]."[30] By the time the war ended, New Hampshire's industrial center had shifted irrevocably toward the coast and away from the inland mill towns with their textile, leather, and wood industries, while Portsmouth quickly became a prosperous community — albeit an overpopulated one — with challenging problems and legitimate concerns about its future.

CHAPTER 9
SKILLED WORKERS

[Portsmouth] lost not one but several industrial opportunities because we did not have sufficient skilled labor. . . . The tremendous influx of [skilled] workers at the Portsmouth Navy yard can be one of Portsmouth's greatest assets in the future.

Lawrence M. Meyer
New Hampshire Planning
and Development Commission
Portsmouth Herald, 30 January 1941

Speaking to the Portsmouth Rotary Club in January 1941, Lawrence M. Meyer, a member of the New Hampshire Planning and Development Commission, sounded both a cautionary and an optimistic note. In the past Portsmouth had failed to attract industry because of a lack of skilled workers—but with the mobilization at the shipyard, all that was about to change, he noted, and it was in the interest of the city to take advantage of that.[1] Meyer's speech was a testimony to a lack of industrialization in the seacoast area before the war, and an accurate prediction of the abundance of skilled labor that would exist in the postwar era.

The development of skilled labor required good training programs, and as the war geared up Portsmouth had some of the best available. More importantly, local workers eagerly sought out training to qualify for or advance in shipyard jobs or other wartime industries. Three programs provided the needed training: the Shipyard Apprentice Training Program, the Federal War Production Training Program, and the Engineering Science Management War Training Program. The first had very successfully trained shipyard employees for twenty years prior to the start of the war; the other two were new programs, created specifically to address wartime training needs.

The shipyard apprentice program, designed to advance already-employed tradesmen to higher skill levels, provided classroom and hands-on training under the leadership of the shipyard shop masters. The federal training program offered basic courses in welding, pipefitting, shipfitting, and other trades needed to gain entry-level employment at the yard, as well as supplementary courses to increase proficiency in certain trades. The engineering science management program taught college-level courses to augment the training of shipyard engineers, technicians, and managers. These three programs graduated thousands of trainees, reversing the prewar shortage of skilled workers and creating, in Meyer's words, "one of Portsmouth's greatest assets in the future."

Apprentice Program

The shipyard's transition from the construction of wooden-hulled ships in the nineteenth century to steam-powered vessels near the turn of the twentieth century to submarines during World War I required tradesmen with increasingly technical skills and competency. The yard's apprentice program had its roots in the era when Portsmouth first began constructing submarines. An article in the 27 August 1919 *Portsmouth Herald* delighted in the challenging new work at the yard: "The making of submarines was a new kind of work, and work of considerable delicacy, which requires great care and expert knowledge. . . . The submarine is not the alarm clock of the navy, but rather the wrist watch."[2] Implied was that the building of submarines would require skillful tradesmen able to work with precision and accuracy, attributes not typically found in shipyard employees at the time.

At the start of the World War I, in April 1917, the yard had about two thousand employees, of whom only six were skilled shipfitters. Two and a half years later (August 1919), the yard employed four thousand workers, including hundreds of recently trained expert shipfitters.[3] In order to fulfill the Navy's plan to make Portsmouth the nation's premier builder of submarines, the number of skilled workers would have to continue to increase. Lacking other options, and wanting to tailor worker training to specific shop needs, the yard set out to develop its own training program.

In April 1918, according to the *Herald* article, "A trades school was started, the first of its kind in any of the yards, though others copied it at once. The yard offered classes in ship-fitting, chipping and caulking, riveting, drilling, electric welding, acetylene welding, coppersmiths and other trades. The course was for three months."[4] When the yard became the Navy's sole builder of submarines in the 1920s, the classes evolved into an apprentice program to prepare shipyard employees for advancement to journeyman and higher skill levels. The program grew between the wars until it was functioning near full capacity immediately before World War II, having an enrollment of 346 students in August 1941 and 391 students on 2 March 1942.[5] The shipyard apprentice program was annually pumping hundreds of skilled workers into the shops when the war started. It would be a relatively simple matter to expand and tune that program to the shipyard's wartime needs.

The apprentice program consisted of approximately

eighteen classes of about twenty students each; each class met for two hours a day, three days a week, taking advantage of shift turnovers and midday breaks for classes during the workday. A high school diploma was required for entry to the program. Once accepted, each candidate had to accumulate a minimum of 1,816 hours of combined class and selective on-the-job shop training before he or she could take the promotional exam, given twice a year. By October 1941, the frequency of the exam had increased to several times a year to accommodate the growing number of participants.[6]

Percy Whitney, who had hired into the wartime apprentice program after two and a half years at Bates College, described the program as very demanding academically. He recalled being required to pass classroom metallurgy, trigonometry, and other challenging technical courses, while working as an apprentice in the shipyard foundry.[7] With a first-class and time-tested apprentice program attracting candidates like Whitney, the shipyard was well positioned to ramp up its skilled worker population to meet the nation's increasing demand for submarines.

War Production Training Program

The primary purpose of the war production program was to provide free training in those skills needed for entry-level employment at the shipyard and other wartime industries. The state ran the program using machines and equipment provided by the federal government. Supplemental classes also helped workers improve their basic skills or acquire new ones. There were fourteen such training programs in New Hampshire; the Portsmouth program was "praised by the navy vocational officers as one of the finest in the country."[8] Classes convened at Portsmouth High School and at the Morley Company on Islington Street, not far from downtown.

A wordy and rather grammatically challenging description of the start of the program appeared in the 1943 Portsmouth *Survey of Health and Welfare*:

> Through the excellent cooperation of the State Board for Vocational Education, the Portsmouth School Board, under which the work is carried on locally, the Portsmouth Navy Yard and the office of the United States Employment Office, the most varied and extensive program in the state for vocational training for War production Workers (formerly the Vocational training program for defense Workers) has been developed in Portsmouth since its inception in August 1940. . . . The program began with machine shop courses in the shops of the Portsmouth High School, where use of equipment was offered. These shops are still being used, but as a result of the expansion in work, the first floors of four units in the Morley Company Plant were leased in November 1941, and on August 1, 1942, lease was made of more space on the first floor of another unit, and on the second floor and basement of a unit previously occupied on the first floor.[9]

The program offered pre-employment courses in machine shop, sheet metal work, pattern making, and electric and gas welding. Supplementary courses provided more advanced training in some of these topics, as well as instruction in carpentry and woodworking, metallurgy, mold-loft layout for shipfitters, blueprint reading, and mathematics related to shipbuilding. Much of the instruction focused on shipyard trades; however, classes also benefited other local industries

222

requiring skilled labor.

The federal training courses were initially available to anyone seventeen or older, with no maximum age limit. Early on, women were encouraged to participate in the training; the *Herald* cited service wives for "setting records for adaptability from kitchen to war plant." The disabled and handicapped were also encouraged to enroll for the courses because, as the newspaper article put it, "One-armed persons able in all other ways to meet physical standards at the navy yard or at other defense centers can be taught to work an electrical welding torch." All were welcome to receive federal training to support the war effort, regardless of age or capability.[10]

The naval mobilization that began in the summer of 1940 accelerated ship production, expanded shipyard infrastructure, and kick-started the skilled-worker training programs needed to support both. Thus, before the war had even started, the local program expanded to meet the needs of the rapidly growing shipyard. In March 1941, the high school program grew to include a three-shift defense school for welders.[11] The machine shop classes already under way added an extra session from 10 p.m. to 7 a.m. Classes at Morley Company proliferated to include training twenty-four hours a day for welders, sheet-metal workers, pipefitters, shipfitters, machinists, electricians, machine operators, blueprint machine operators, and copyist draftsmen. Nine months before Pearl Harbor, the local program was operating twenty-four hours a day and graduating hundreds of tradesmen.

The Morley Company was a valuable contributor to the war effort as both a federal training site and a manufacturer of war materials for the Department of Defense. The Portsmouth plant, originally a manufacturer of small machines, became famous as a button factory in the 1890s after its founder, James Morley, invented a shoe button sewing machine in an era when button shoes were popular. Realizing that his invention required buttons of uniform size and shape, Morley began manufacturing his own buttons. However, buttons fell out of footwear fashion in World War I, so the company expanded to other types of buttons, becoming the largest supplier of buttons for tufting mattresses and branching out into items as varied as golf tees, collar buttons, ring travelers, fiber shoe soles, and various other fiber products. By the start of World War II, Morley Company had acquired a reputation for the high-quality manufacture of all these items, but especially of buttons of all descriptions.[12]

Photo 21: Morley Company (circa 1940).
Courtesy Portsmouth Athenaeum.

During the war, Morley Company converted from its traditional product line to the manufacture of war materials. A May 1944 Morley advertisement took credit for the "Manufacture of Fiber and Plastic Products and Special War

Table 15: Industrial Plants in Rockingham County with Defense Work
(1 June 1943)

Plant	Town	Product	Employment
Asbestos Products Co.	Exeter	Telephone circuit breakers	3
Brentwood Box Co.	N. Kingston	Packing boxes	9
Chadwick A. Trafathan	Portsmouth	Reamers	22
Exeter Brass Works	Exeter	Aluminum and brass moldings	112
Exeter Handkerchief Co.	Exeter	Handkerchiefs and cotton cloth	359
The Morley Co.	Portsmouth	Gas mask face forms, etc.	372
Sam Smith Shoe Corp.	Newmarket	Shoes	280
Spaulding & Frost	Fremont	Wooden pails	118
G.V. and C.A. Lane Co.	Exeter	Sprocket wheels	2

Source: *Survey of Health and Welfare in the Portsmouth Defense Area*, August 1943, Table 11, Box 2, Folder 14, "S.C.D. Survey of Health and Welfare in Portsmouth."

Products for the Chemical Warfare Service,"[13] which included gas mask face plates and eye shields. Morley was the largest defense contractor in Rockingham County, but there were others (see table 15). Just beyond county lines but not far away in Dover were still others, including Kidder Press Company, which made torpedo parts,[14] and the Marks Brothers Company, which made an extreme conversion from the peacetime manufacture of toys and games to the production of rifle grenades.[15] Federal training programs provided much of the skilled labor needed by these various industries.

The shift of seacoast industries from peacetime products to weapons of war was typical of conversions that occurred in thousands of communities across the nation. Wensyel wrote, "Automobile plants were converted to the manufacture of tanks, jeeps and other war vehicles. Former canneries now made parts for merchant ships; cotton-processing plants produced guns; bedspread manufacturers turned out mosquito netting; a soft drink company loaded shells with explosives; a shoe manufacturer forged cannon; and a former burial-vault builder now specialized in one-hundred-pound bombs." By May 1942, "16,000 new plants [were] operating around-the-clock shifts, and thousands of older factories had been converted to war industries."[16]

A Dover plant, Sylvania Pacific Mills, made the conversion to a critical wartime product with great secrecy. The plant made proximity fuses, a "tiny signaling unit, operated first by light and then by radio" that "could be used in most types of missiles from bombs to rockets to artillery." The Dover plant was one of the few in the nation that manufactured the product. Guyol considered the proximity fuse "the most important product of any New Hampshire factory, and the greatest wartime achievement of the electrical machinery industry . . . one of the three or four extraordinary scientific achievements of the war."[17] According to Maury Klein, "Some deemed [proximity fuses] important enough to remain shrouded in almost as much secrecy as the Manhattan Project."[18] That certainly was true at Sylvania Pacific Mills: its operations were reported to be "conducted in such secrecy that hardly a soul among the eleven hundred persons employed there had the slightest idea what the 'Appliance Department,' as it was referred to, was making."[19] The need for secrecy was so great that the federal government did not permit the plant to display its well-earned Army-Navy E Award for fear it would invite questions about the item manufactured there.

Only 5 percent of the manufacturing companies in the United States received the prestigious Army-Navy E Award, given annually to deserving companies for excellence.[20] Recognized companies received a banner with the first award, and an additional star for the banner for each subsequent award (renewal). Seacoast New Hampshire companies received more than their share of the awards. Morley garnered four awards for the manufacture of a wide variety of products — "gas mask face-pieces, eye shields, gas decontamination bags for the army chemical warfare service, fiber and molded plastic buttons for uniforms, tufting buttons for the maritime commission and medical corps, war workers clothing, fiber board for lunch boxes, and stereotype mats for the newspaper industry."[21] Kidder Press received the award four times for manufacturing high-quality torpedo parts. The Exeter Brass Works won the award five times for production of terminal tubes and fuse cavity formers, among other essential items — one of only 820 manufacturing plants in the entire country awarded the E and four stars.[22] Portsmouth Navy Yard also won the award five times, every year it was eligible. Clearly, there was no shortage of recognition of local industries for their contribution to the war effort.

William Tebo was just fifteen and a high school junior when he took 400 hours of machine operator training at Portsmouth High School, benefiting from a New Hampshire law passed in 1943 permitting fifteen-year-olds to work in war-related industries.[23] Tebo then worked at the yard for about six months beginning in early 1944, receiving training as an electrician in order to perform limited but important shipboard wiring jobs. According to Tebo, there were hundreds of teenagers employed at the shipyard during the war. He and most of the others worked there for less than a year, passing through on their way to military service once they turned seventeen.[24]

The federal training program peaked in 1943. A front-page *Portsmouth Herald* photograph on 23 February 1943 carried the caption, "The defense school at the Portsmouth High School, in which men and women learn to operate the lathes and machines necessary for wartime machine tooling, is typical of those conducted by Ray A. Crosby, supervisor of vocational training for war production workers. Crosby is in charge of 17 instructors at the Morley schools, which operate

24 hours a day, six days a week."[25] A 12 May 1943 *Herald* article titled "School Aids Production of Navy Submarines" heaped credit on the local Federal Vocational Training School, noting that 125 of the 322 students enrolled there were women. The number and percentage of women accepted into the program increased as the war progressed. By one estimate, the Portsmouth federal training program employed as many as eighty instructors who trained more than seven thousand people.[26] This program was largely responsible for reversing the area's shortage of skilled workers.

Engineering Science Management Program

Although receiving far less recognition than the apprentice and federal training programs, the engineering science program was just as vital. Run by the University of New Hampshire, the program provided technical and professional training for shipyard technicians, engineers, and managers that enabled them to stay current with the rapidly advancing technologies stimulated by wartime needs. The curriculum included mechanics, strengths of materials, metallurgy, welding theory, and other courses specifically applicable to submarine construction. More than five thousand employees took advantage of the free training offered by the state and the university.[27] The shipyard benefited greatly from having a nearby state university able to provide courses tailored to the specific needs of its employees.

Employee-Management Relations

Having attracted minimal industrialization prior to the war, the seacoast region also attracted minimal union activity compared to more industrialized areas of the country.

Consequently, the plethora of labor disputes and strikes that often plagued those areas as the war gained momentum were largely absent from the seacoast.

Labor unions had grown in numbers and influence after the passage of the union-supporting Wagner Act (1934), and by 1940 they were exerting powerful pressures on the steel, automotive, coal, and other industries as the nation began to ramp up for war. Despite the looming possibility of war, there was an epidemic of strikes during the two years preceding the attack on Pearl Harbor: "During 1940 a total of 2,500 strikes had created 6.7 million idle labor days; in 1941 the number of strikes soared to 4,300 and the idle labor days to 23.1 million," noted Maury Klein. By the end of 1941, "one out of every twelve workers had gone out on strike." As mobilization gained speed, many communities erupted in strikes, union-organized demonstrations, and occasional violence as workers sought to improve their lot. Strikebreakers and government threats to take over plants frequently fueled the turmoil.[28]

Portsmouth experienced very little of this sort of chaos. There were no labor strikes at the region's major industry, the Portsmouth Navy Yard, during the war: navy yard workers were, in fact, required to take a no-strike pledge. The yard was not only strike-free; it was essentially free of the haggling and contentious relationships between labor and management that disrupted other shipyards and industries. Lacking the challenges of angry workers and aggressive labor unions, Portsmouth's mobilization was more peaceful than most.

The exceptional cooperation that existed between yard labor and management was evident during an incident involving a change in work hours in April 1942. Management moved all shifts back two hours, so that the first shift started at 4 a.m. instead of 6 a.m., believing the new shifts would increase productivity. Members of Ranger Lodge 836 of the International Association of Machinists maintained there would be no productivity improvement and that the change would cause unnecessary inconvenience to workers and their families. While mounting an aggressive effort to have the decision reversed, Ranger Lodge 836 also reaffirmed its support for yard management with the following press release: "We have the utmost confidence in the officers who have been designated by the Navy department to administer the policies at this yard and we pledge our utmost cooperation with their efforts to build our submarine navy quickly and efficiently, but we reserve our inalienable rights to protest any local orders that to us seem unnecessary to our country's war program."[29] Shortly after the machinists had voiced their displeasure with the new shift schedule, a yard-wide poll confirmed that a majority of all yard employees felt the same way. Management quickly relented and restored the old shift hours, and the controversy was settled.[30] Mutual respect and open communications were hallmarks of management-employee relations at Portsmouth Navy Yard during the war.

The wartime training programs produced thousands of workers skilled in shipyard and other trades, turning a shortage of skilled labor into an abundance in just a few years. In 1945, the federal training program gave birth to the state's own program when the city and state took advantage of the existing machinery and equipment at the federal training sites to launch a postwar vocational training program. Striking a deal with Morley Company to continue training classes at the Islington Street plant, the city agreed to rent the first floor and basement of one of the Morley Company buildings, later to include the second floor, in return for the state establishing one of the first state trade schools.[31] Returning servicemen were encouraged to take advantage of the training to acquire the skills needed to compete in the postwar marketplace. In November 1945, thirty-five returning war veterans had already enrolled at the school.[32] Building on that successful start, the vocational program eventually evolved into the New Hampshire Technical College and its successors, which have supplied a never-ending stream of skilled workers to fuel the area's very successful postwar development.

CHAPTER 10
WOMEN STEP UP

The war gave an opportunity to demonstrate that a woman was capable of doing many things, doing them simultaneously, and doing them well. During the postwar period she would finally be recognized as a producer as well as a consumer, and a full human being.

Doris Weatherford
American Women and World War II

R osie the Riveter joined submarine pressure-hull plates at the yard during World War I; Wendy the Welder did the same job during World War II when gas and electric welding had replaced riveting. Welding was one of the many shipyard industrial jobs assumed by women when men went into the services. The war demonstrated a valuable lesson: women were capable of far more than the traditional roles they had been filling.

Some industries and areas of the country caught on more quickly than others. The booming shipyards and aircraft factories on the West Coast were among the first to welcome women into broader employment opportunities; Portsmouth Navy Yard, like the other East Coast shipyards, was among the slow learners. As the war progressed, the yard increasingly recognized the capabilities of women employees; by the end of the war, the percentage of women employed at the yard was consistent with other shipyards As their numbers grew, so did their opportunities to join training programs qualifying them to fill increasingly skilled and responsible jobs.

National Mobilization of Women Employees

During the first six months after the bombing of Pearl Harbor, a wave of some 750,000 women applied for jobs in the defense industry—yet only 80,000 were hired.[1] Women were willing to move into industrial jobs, but it would take some time for managers to break with tradition. Alice Kessler-Harris's seminal study of women employees in America, *Out to Work: A History of Wage-Earning Women in the United States*, described the slow progress made by women in the industrial sector at the start of the war: "As government programs began early in 1942 to 'warm up' the unemployed to heavy industry, twenty men were offered places to every woman. Some workers received training in industrial skills in the last half of 1941. Only 1 percent of those were female. Employers believed women were not suited to most jobs and declared themselves unwilling to hire women for 81 percent of available production jobs. . . . Attitudes began to change after Pearl Harbor. . . . For the first time employers sought out women for nontraditional jobs."[2] As the employment barriers came down and the demand for workers increased, women rushed to claim previously unavailable positions.

Mobilizing shipyards offered excellent opportunities for women. Maritime historian Frederic C. Lane wrote, "The female invasion [of shipyards] began in the fall of 1942" and "reached its maximum in 1944 and 1945 when female workers formed 10 to 20 percent in most yards." According to Lane, female employment during the war was lowest in the Northeast and Gulf Coast shipyards and highest in the West Coast yards. The percentage of females employed at the Richmond Shipyard outside San Francisco was 23 percent in 1944, and the Oregon Shipyard in Portland, Oregon, peaked at 33 percent in 1945. Both were private shipyards.[3]

The Navy's West Coast yards also had higher percentages

of female employees than other government yards. The top two navy yards for female employment in March 1943 were Mare Island, California (19.6 percent), and Puget Sound, Washington (16.8 percent). At that time, Portsmouth Navy Yard's workforce was just 8.5 percent female; of all the government yards, only New York Navy Yard was lower at 8 percent.[4] However, two years later in July 1945, women comprised about 18 percent of the total Portsmouth workforce of more than fifteen thousand.[5] Although the yard had gotten off to a slow start, it had caught up by the end of the war.

Early in the war, New England society was reluctant to fully utilize women employees. In the case of shipyards, this reluctance may have reflected a sincere desire on the part of the managers to protect females from the rigors and unsavory aspects of shipyard industrial work. A directive issued by the commandant of the Boston Navy Yard in January 1942 shows concern about the safety of female employees and the need to limit their assignments in his yard: "The Commandant considers that most clerical positions in the yard can be filled by female employees, except stockman in the storehouse, clerks assigned to night shifts in the shops or in shops where a single clerk is employed, and messengers required to go in the shops or on the ships."[6] In short, the commandant did not want women hired for jobs where they might have to interact with men in out-of-the-way job sites without other women present, especially at night. Without a doubt, shipyard managers were concerned about the introduction of sexuality and its potential repercussions in the workplace.

At the start of the war, women typically held domestic and clerical jobs. The staffing of many offices resembled that of the Portsmouth Internal Revenue Service office shown in photo 22 where Claire Flanagan Papatones and a dozen or

Photo 22: Portsmouth Internal Revenue Service office (circa 1944). Photo courtesy of Claire Flanagan Papatones, the dark-haired girl facing the camera, left of center in the photograph.

more young women worked under male supervision. Clerical work provided welcome income after the Depression years, but many women soon sought the increasingly available and much higher paying industrial jobs. One new sector opened up to local women in May 1942 when the first women were hired as taxi and bus drivers in the city of Portsmouth.[7] In August 1942, the Boston and Maine Railroad employed its first woman crossing-tender for a Nashua crossing and began hiring women for car cleaning, ticket sales, and division office work at the Concord station. About the same time, the railroad opened a school at the Exeter station to train women to become railroad telegraphers.[8] It was a slow start, but the doors were opening.

During the first year of the war, the few women employed

in industry were mostly single. In June 1942, of the three Portsmouth industrial plants engaged in defense work, only the Morley Company employed any women; of the 93 women who worked there, only 3 were married. At the time, the navy yard employed 430 women, only 10 of them married. The situation was not much different at non-defense work sites: the telephone company employed 79 women, 10 with children; and none of the 5 women working at a local brewery had children. Overall, few women had found their way into local industries and almost all were unmarried.[9]

As women slowly filtered into industrial workplaces, a local survey concluded, "Because the Portsmouth Navy Yard is the major industry [in the area], and the only large one, it seems there will be no appreciable increase in numbers of employed women unless, and until, the Navy yard employs women in large numbers."[10] The yard was preparing to do just that. Prompted by a 1 September 1942 directive from the secretary of the navy urging navy yards to expedite the hiring of women, Portsmouth Navy Yard's industrial manager, Captain H. F. D. Davis, ordered his managers to "more aggressively pursue training programs for women—as the West Coast shipyards have done so effectively."[11] With that announcement, employment opportunities for women at the navy yard began to expand and catch up with the rest of the nation.

Women at Portsmouth Navy Yard

Women have made significant progress at Portsmouth Navy Yard since its establishment as the first navy yard in 1800.[12] Progress, however, is relative and depends on the starting point. An 1826 secretary of the navy letter to the commandant of the yard made it obvious that the starting point for women employees at the yard could not have been any lower: they were not even to be hired as servants. The secretary wrote, "It is contrary to the regulations and practices of the service to allow the names of women to appear on the muster role, and however inconvenient it may be to the officers who require servants to employ men, the rule must be adhered to."[13] When one's starting point is lower than servitude, there is much opportunity for progress.

World War I. Women had made considerable progress at the yard by World War I when they were selectively hired for the lesser-skilled positions. According to the 27 August 1919 *Portsmouth Herald*, "To relieve men from certain kinds of labor and allow them to do things that were of immediate great importance, women to the number of 1,000 were employed, and did valiant service in the lighter forms of production, in work especially well fitted to women. The plan is to continue their employment, though not in such a way as to interfere at all with the employment of men."[14] The shipyard positions filled by women in 1919 were similar to the less-demanding jobs later available to women at the start of World War II. The newspaper reported a remarkable achievement by a female riveter performing one of the lighter forms of production: "One of the women claims the championship of the world for women riveters, since she made the remarkable record of placing 264 rivets ½ inch by 3-16ths in two hours."[15] At least one shipyard-employed woman had proved her worth beyond any doubt during the first war. Many women would do the same during the next war.

World War II. When Captain Davis, the yard's industrial manager, encouraged the recruitment of women employees in September 1942, he did so with guarded

Photo 23: Woman worker at Portsmouth Navy Yard during World War I. Courtesy Milne Special Collections and Archives, University of New Hampshire Library, Durham, NH.

optimism about their limitations and potential contributions. Davis wrote, "In view of the increasing demands on the available manpower of the country for defense work and military duty, it is apparent that the services of women must be utilized in every type of work for which they can be trained and for which physically qualified."[16] Implicit in the memorandum is the understanding that women were not to replace certain male employees, given their assumed physical weakness and training limitations. Specifically, Captain Davis emphasized that women were not to be employed onboard ships or as security guards.[17]

Captain Davis further cautioned his managers, "Seeing the trend of the movement, it would behoove Portsmouth to take action to obtain the pick of women available as to avoid the serious dislocations which may occur if action [to hire women] is delayed and later forced upon the Yard in larger numbers and suddenly."[18] At the risk of paraphrasing Captain Davis, he appears to be suggesting that it would be best to expeditiously hire women for two reasons. First, the shipyard could get the pick of the limited female talent available. Second, by boosting the number of female employees, the yard might avoid being forced by the chain of command to hire women en masse at a later date, possibly inundating the yard with great numbers of unqualified and untrained employees.

Despite his reservations, Davis immediately ordered the necessary shop improvements to accommodate large numbers of women. A review of the work orders for toilet facility upgrades, though not scientific, suggests the numbers of women expected in certain shops in the fall of 1942: upgrades were ordered to Building #96 for twenty-five female core and molding workers, Building #55 for fifty female welders, Building #2 for another fifty female welders, Building #74 for fifty female sheet-metal workers, and Building #75 for fifty more female sheet-metal workers.[19] The women hired into the shops at this time were probably helpers, who would eventually get the opportunity to advance to skilled positions via the apprentice program.

The archives do not document exactly what "upgrades" were carried out. Typical improvements at other industrial facilities to accommodate women included turning the old

239

type of plant washroom "into one with fully enclosed toilets, individual wash bowls with mirrors above them, full lockers for complete changes of clothes, and vending machines for sanitary napkins."[20] The times, and the shipyard restrooms, they were a-changin'.

Eileen Dondero Foley started at the yard shortly after the secretary of the navy's directive in September 1942. During an interview with the master of the paint shop on her first day of work, she and another girl were told, "This is dirty work. You are here to paint the boats and not your faces."[21] Such was the no-nonsense approach of shipyard management to the increased hiring of women at the yard. Foley reported to work at the paint shop the next morning, but she never saw the other girl again.

In the paint shop, the master made clear, production trumped appearance—but the opposite was often the case in other industrial settings during the war. Women often "found themselves facing male pressure to be feminine" and personnel managers preferred "the girls to be neat and trim and well put together," claiming that it helped the women's morale and brought prestige to the workplace. There were less welcome workplace consequences, noted Kessler-Harris: "Catcalls, whistles, and hisses faced women who walked onto production floors for the first time."[22] Neither Foley nor any of the other retired shipyard employees interviewed for this book alluded to this type of male behavior in the workplace. Instead, Foley's encounter with the shop master suggests the other extreme.

According to Fred White, a supervisor at Portsmouth Navy Yard during the war, the initial women employees performed secondary operations: punching holes for fasteners or grinding metal for welds, for instance, leaving the primary operation to the male mechanic.[23] Foley confirmed White's observation: as a painter's helper, she applied the primer or first coat of paint topside on a submarine, but experienced male painters always applied the finishing coats.[24] Hazel Sinclair, one of the few African-American woman employees at the yard, worked as a woodworker's helper for more than two years during the war but recalled that "they didn't let women work on the machines"[25] As the war progressed, so did women into more skilled positions.

Foley was permitted to work topside on submarines, but, she says, "never, never, never, in the compartments or tanks. . . They [the shipyard managers] were very strict about that."[26] Jeffery M. Dorwart found a similar reluctance to assign women to worksites aboard ships in Philadelphia: "The Philadelphia Navy yard never appeared entirely comfortable with female employees during World War II. . . . Supervisors would not allow women to work on board the battleship *New Jersey* for nearly a year. . . . Approximately 70 percent of the Navy yard's female employees held clerical, office, or inside shop work."[27] The prohibiting of women workers from onboard sites gradually faded; William Tebo and Dan MacIsaac both remembered women working alongside men in submarine compartments and tanks late in the war.[28]

In May 1943, Assistant Secretary of the Navy Ralph Bard specifically directed Portsmouth and the other East Coast yards to boost employment of women, especially skilled women: "During the past ten months, continental Navy yards have shown a definite increase in the employment of women. . . . The Navy yards at Portsmouth, N.H., Boston, Mass., New York, N.Y., Philadelphia, Pa., and Norfolk, Va., especially should increase their employment of women to at least the average for all yards. The acceptance of women in private industry indicates that the continental Navy yards are not utilizing women on a comparable scale particularly in the skilled Group III."[29] Bard's observation about the dearth of skilled female workers was especially true for Portsmouth Navy Yard: at that point most women at the yard were clerks, administrative assistants, mechanics' helpers, shop cleaners, or operators of less-complex pieces of shop equipment. Bard's directive provided the motivation needed to alter that trend.

Rosie the Riveter was nowhere to be found at Portsmouth Navy Yard during World War II — but that was only because her former job there had vanished along with the rivets as submarine construction moved toward all-welded pressure hulls just before the war. The Portsmouth-built USS *Snapper* (SS-185), commissioned 15 December 1937, was the first submarine with an all-welded pressure hull. In any event, as Fred White maintained, Portsmouth Rosie would not have actually driven the infrequently used rivets; she would have punched the holes for the rivets. Historian David M. Kennedy claims that the emblem of Rosie the Riveter as a "denim-clad, tool-wielding, can-do figure" actually typified very few wartime women employees; Wendy the Welder, Sally the Secretary, or Molly the Mom might have been more appropriate labels, he suggests. [30] Rivets were, however, still widely used in the aircraft industry, so the Rosie the Riveter label persisted for women in these industrial wartime jobs.[31]

The women who worked at the yard were certainly every bit as skilled and industrious as the mythical Rosie. The *Portsmouth Herald* periodically featured front-page articles and pictures highlighting the progress made by local women, beginning with an 18 May 1942 article reporting the advancement of women to positions of taxi and bus driver: "No wonder people are beginning to wonder if it really is a man's world. First Portsmouth had a woman cleaning company driver, then a taxi driver, and now the Hill Transportation company has hired from the government employment agency two women for duty behind its wheels."[32] Six months after Pearl Harbor, this rather dubious distinction was front-page news. While not particularly glamorous or lucrative, these jobs paid better than housecleaning and other domestic jobs. Nevertheless, in the summer of 1942, Rosie was driving a taxi, not rivets, in Portsmouth.

Over the next year and a half, the *Herald* frequently carried pictures of women training for or assuming jobs traditionally held by men at the shipyard. The *Herald*'s coverage provides a chronological summary of the incremental progress made by women toward more meaningful industrial employment. On 18 June 1942, the front page had a picture of several Exeter girls "amid gears and belts of steel lathes," who were among the first women to enroll in defense mechanical training classes with hopes of gaining employment at the shipyard. The 22 March 1943 newspaper showed the first female navy yard machinist to apply for membership in the Ranger Lodge, International Association of Machinists. The article noted that she was currently a "checker of machines and other supplies," but her number one ambition was to become a "full fledged machinist."[33]

On 11 November 1943, a photograph of four shipyard "welderettes" noted that the women "patriotically completed 150 hours of electric welding training" and "have swapped the duties of housekeeping and the tapping typewriter for the glow of a blow torch and the clang of steel. They're laboring, sweating, amid steel beams and plates to build fighting submarines for America's safety."[34] Finally, in May 1944, an important milestone occurred when the first women — 4 out of the 195 graduates — completed the yard's supervisory training program. Rear Admiral Thomas Withers's graduation address praised the class: "Your class is different from any other class in that it is coeducational. I am proud that this navy yard recognizes the fact that women are capable of becoming supervisors and I cannot understand why other navy yards do not take advantage of the capable women employees they must have."[35] Withers's remarks imply that the other navy yards had not yet trained women for supervisory positions. Portsmouth Navy Yard, after a slow start, had made up a lot of ground.

By 1943, so many married women were employed at the yard and in local industries that child-care services were needed. The first child-care center in the region opened at Wentworth Acres in late 1943 at the project's government-built school, caring for 125 children. The mothers' occupations provide an indication of where women were finding employment in late 1943: the mothers of half the children worked at either the navy yard or Morley Company; a quarter of the mothers were professionals, primarily teachers and nurses; and a quarter worked in stores, offices, or small businesses.[36] One year earlier the survey had found only twenty working mothers in local industry. In late 1943, the day-care center accommodated more than sixty such mothers and the need was growing daily as married women found their way to the workplace.

Women had progressed from homemakers at the start of the war to bus and taxicab drivers by May 1942, to machine operators in early 1943, to fully qualified (and sweaty) welders by November 1943, and finally to trained shop supervisors by May 1944. Elsewhere on the yard, military women were also breaking new ground. In May 1943, the first class of fifty WAVES (Women Accepted for Volunteer Service) arrived at the Portsmouth Navy Yard Hospital for four weeks of basic training. The first female doctor at the shipyard reported for duty on 22 February 1945.[37] It seemed women could aspire to practically any job on the yard by the end of the war.

Mary C. Dondero, a clerical helper in the Portsmouth

Navy Yard Supply Department early in the war,[38] progressed further than did any woman employed at the yard: voters elected her mayor of Portsmouth in November 1944. Dondero was the first female mayor ever elected in the state of New Hampshire, and one of the first in the nation.[39] Before one overestimates the progress made by New Hampshire women during the war, it is well to note that a month after Dondero became mayor, the New Hampshire House of Representatives rejected a bill to allow women jurists by a vote of 181 to 174.[40] Thus, in early 1945, women could hold responsible positions at the Portsmouth Navy Yard and govern the city of Portsmouth, but they could not sit on juries in the state of New Hampshire.

Although Portsmouth Navy Yard was not a magnet for large numbers of minorities, it did attract a few African-American women. Hazel Sinclair found employment as a woodworker's helper. Rosary Cooper was another who took advantage of training opportunities to improve her job skills, starting at the shipyard as a file clerk and eventually qualifying as a crane operator.[41] Anna Jones, another African-American, began at the yard as a messenger and was in training to be a drafter when the war ended. [42] These women were part of a national wartime movement that saw African-Americans seize unprecedented opportunities to improve their status and prospects by moving into better-paying jobs.

Late in 1945, supervisor Fred White was faced with the need to terminate about sixty women working in the sail loft of his shop making torpedo straps, mattress covers, cushions, and other leather products for the submarines. The women fell into the category of wartime employees without rights to continued employment after the war. After careful consideration, and with the women's encouragement, White decided to forgo the normal practice of terminating employees individually according to hiring date, and release all sixty on the same day. The women, who did not want to experience individual firings and possible disputes about who should go next, met the decision with universal approval. According to White, the women celebrated together as they walked out of the shop after their last day of employment.[43]

Women were quick to quit their jobs when the war ended. Doris Weathorford wrote, "In the first nine months after VE Day, women's numbers dropped by four million—down from 19,500,000 to about 15,500,000."[44] As was the case with the women in Fred White's sail loft, women left their jobs at double or triple the rate at which they were discharged.[45] The 8 January 1945 *Herald* confirmed the orderly return of women to the home: "There have been many predictions, expert and otherwise, that women who left their homes to work in war factories, or to fill places of men in the service, would be slow to return. The unemployment problem was expected to be complicated by the thousands of women who prefer to work rather than resume the job of housekeeping. Apparently there is little to fear in that respect. Many Portsmouth housewives are among those who have already returned contentedly to their homes after working at the naval shipyard."[46] Many women in the shipyard's industrial shops, like millions of their counterparts nationwide, willingly abandoned their wartime jobs in favor of returning veterans.

Despite their willingness to relinquish wartime industrial jobs, women's attitudes about working outside the home had changed forever. At the beginning of the war, "as many as 95 percent of the women war workers planned to quit as soon as victory was certain." At the end of the war, "two-thirds told pollsters that they intended to keep working."[47] There would be a temporary hiatus of employment for women at the end of the war, but a decade later women returned to the workplace stronger and more determined than ever.

When American men returned from the war, historian James Wensyel noted, they found women "more interchangeable with men than they used to be, better able to fix a tire, or mend a faucet or fix an electrical connection, or preside at a meeting, or keep a treasurer's account, or organize a political campaign than when they went away."[48] Weatherford wrote, "The war gave an opportunity to demonstrate that a woman was capable of doing many things, doing them simultaneously, and doing them well. During the postwar period, women finally achieved recognition as a producer as well as a consumer, and a full human being."[49] Women had proved their worth with long-lasting consequences—and there was no turning back.

CHAPTER 11
BUILDING BOOM

All this [mobilization] means business for Portsmouth—
and business in this case is spelled t-r-o-u-b-l-e. Workers
by the thousands are pouring into the Navy yard—and
the city of Portsmouth—with their families. We have to
house 'em, feed 'em, water 'em, sewer 'em . . . give 'em
police protection and fire protection, schooling, health
service and hospital facilities.

Frederick D. Gardner
Portsmouth City Councilman
14 November 1941

T rue to the summer 1941 predictions of *Portsmouth Herald* editor Franklin E. Jordan, the burgeoning operations at the Portsmouth Navy Yard immediately triggered an array of infrastructure challenges for the city. A few months later, on 14 November 1941, Councilman Frederick D. Gardner bluntly summarized those challenges in an address to the New England Council in Boston, quoted above. Later in the same address Gardner provided a capsule summary of the flurry of activity that had already enveloped the city in its efforts to "house 'em, feed 'em, water 'em, and sewer 'em":

During the past several years the navy yard has
gradually increased its employment. Portsmouth
has absorbed the families of new workers to a great
extent providing housing, schooling for their
children, and other municipal facilities. . . . When

present projects are completed, $33,500,000 will have been poured into Portsmouth and its two small suburbs, Kittery and New Castle. The navy has built new submarine ways, a new drydock, new shops, and new machines at the navy yard. They have built 600 new, small, *cheap houses (with tin chimneys)* at Kittery. The army has built barracks, cantonments, mess halls, administration buildings and what not at New Castle, for Harbor Defense soldiers. Federal Works agency and Defense Homes Corporation have built 959 *houses for better or worse* in Portsmouth, while private builders, using RFC loans for money have built some 500 more for private owners or speculation. A new interstate bridge and by-pass, and three smaller bridges complete the picture of new projects built and building [emphasis added].[1]

Gardner's comments accurately summarized the building boom then under way and raised suspicions about the quality and long-term viability of the federal housing projects then nearing completion. He and other civic leaders thought the "cheap houses (with tin chimneys)" in Kittery's Admiralty Village and the houses built "for better or worse" in Portsmouth's Pannaway Manor and Wentworth Acres had the potential to be postwar maintenance liabilities.

Portsmouth was not alone when it came to shoddy housing projects. Poorly constructed housing, overcrowded neighborhoods, and substandard living conditions often plagued shipyard boomtowns struggling to accommodate burgeoning populations. As the following discussion shows, Portsmouth's difficulties with hastily constructed government housing and accelerated expansion of municipal services were far less of a hardship than in some other locations.

The residents of two of Portsmouth's sister towns with navy yards, Bremerton, Washington, and Vallejo, California, endured some extremely negative living conditions. Describing the public housing near the Puget Sound Navy Yard in Bremerton, one tenant said, "Clothing must be washed by hand in the kitchen sink and dried above the kitchen stove. . . . Due to poor design adequate chimneys are not provided on buildings, causing stoves to fill the homes with smoke. . . . Refrigerators in the buildings consist of a small built-in cupboard with a metal pan for holding the ice. Food will not keep overnight . . . and the danger of eating contaminated food is always present."[2] At Mare Island Navy Yard in Vallejo, living conditions were even worse: "People lived in shacks, stores, trailer camps, or temporary housing units thrown up by the Maritime Commission, or simply camped out. Some 14,000 workers could not find any place to live and traveled more than five hours a day to and from their jobs."[3] Portsmouth's "cheap houses" seem less onerous when juxtaposed with prevailing conditions in Vallejo and Bremerton.

Pascagoula, Mississippi, another shipyard boomtown, also suffered from hastily constructed government housing. Frederic Lane wrote, "They [the poorly constructed neighborhoods] formed a community without adequate sewerage, stores, or pavements. . . . Garbage stood in the streets and the town was overrun with rats."[4] Novelist and mobilization historian John Dos Passos described the deplorable living conditions in Mobile, another shipyard boomtown: "Gutters are stacked with litter. . . . In cluttered backyards people camp out in tents and chicken houses and shelters racked together out of packing cases. . . . Here and there are whole city blocks piled with wreckage and junk . . . heavy with smoke of soft coal, [which] hangs in streaks."[5]

Research for this book found no one living in Portsmouth chicken coops.

The situations experienced by Portsmouth residents were, in most cases, less egregious than those described above. However, living conditions were unsavory enough to disturb longtime residents, who had come to appreciate the city's comfortable, villagelike environment. The *Survey of Health and Welfare* in August 1943 warned of the negative effects mobilization was having: "Increased health hazards of a rapidly expanding community are overcrowding, growth in the incidence of communicable diseases, rise of venereal disease, prevalence of unsanitary conditions attendant upon increased restaurant loads, overcrowding of hospital facilities and recreational centers, and taxing of medical, nursing, and school personnel. Many of these conditions will be found in Portsmouth, Greenland, Newcastle [*sic*], Rye and Newington."[6] Overcrowding was at the root of most of these problems—and adequate housing was the solution.

Housing

As factories and shipyards sprang up in open fields and existing industrial centers expanded into wartime production, housing for the new workers became a nationwide problem. Housing shortages were not new to Portsmouth: the city had faced a similar issue during the last war.

World War I. As employment ratcheted up at the navy yard and the newly built Shattuck and Atlantic Corporation Shipyards during World War I, limited housing created a severe bottleneck. In May 1918, Mr. Shattuck complained to the Dover City Council about the effects of this housing shortage: "If Portsmouth was able to take care of the employees at the navy yard and the shipbuilding plants they would have a city three times its present size. . . . We have from 2,100 to 2,300 or more men employed and we need 1,200 more men. We cannot get them because we cannot find suitable places in which to house them. We have about 25 tents erected at the plant and we are negotiating for 350 more to accommodate the men."[7] The growing "tent city" at the Shattuck Shipyard would be eased by the city's first experience with federal housing, the nearby Atlantic Heights project. Many of the Atlantic Heights homes, however, were not available until the final stages of the war.

Atlantic Heights was constructed between May 1918 and May 1919 adjacent to the Atlantic Corporation Shipyard. Today the I-95 Bridge separates the former site of the yard and the housing area. Unusually appealing and well constructed for a government project, it was the product of Progressive Era concerns about substandard worker housing. Too many hastily and poorly constructed "company towns" had sprouted next to factories and shipyards, the Progressives believed, arrays of row houses and grids of monotonous homes lacking imagination, variety, and landscape that were little more than tenements and instant slums. Congress, seeking to avoid such conditions, assumed responsibility for housing wartime workers associated with government shipbuilding contracts and passed the Emergency Shipbuilders Housing Act in March 1918. Atlantic Heights was one of several projects conceived and funded under that act.[8]

The Atlantic Heights project took on a village atmosphere with a variety of attractive cottage-style houses and a sprinkling of commons and open spaces (photos 24 and 25).

252

ATLANTIC HEIGHTS PORTSMOUTH N H
UNITED STATES SHIPPING BOARD
EMERGENCY FLEET CORPORATION
KILHAM & HOPKINS RETAINED ARCHITECTS BOSTON MASS

*Photo 24: Rendering of the Atlantic Heights federal housing project
(1919). Courtesy Portsmouth Athenaeum.*

*Photo 25: Atlantic Heights cottage-style houses (1919).
Courtesy Portsmouth Athenaeum.*

It consisted of eight long dormitories and 300 cottages. The project met with the unanimous approval of local officials. On 15 August 1918, a *Portsmouth Herald* headline proclaimed, "Atlantic Heights Will be an Ideal Village: Government Housing Plan at Freeman's Point Showing Remarkable Progress — Permanent and Comfortable Houses Provided." According to the article, "The present order is for 300 houses, and at the present time 115 are well underway." In the opinion of A. C. Schenhoff, the government inspector in charge of the work, "The dormitories are more attractive and better built and the houses are far more pretentious and attractive than at any housing plans so far attempted in this country."[9] A couple of decades later, Atlantic Heights set the public's expectations for additional World War II government housing very high; that housing — Wentworth Acres, Pannaway Manor, and Admiralty Village — fell far short of expectations.

World War II. The Lanham Act, passed in October 1940, appropriated $750 million to the Federal Works Agency for the construction of large housing projects in crowded war industry centers. The federal government built approximately 625,000 defense-housing units between 1940 and 1944,[10] including three projects totaling about 1,500 housing units in the Portsmouth Defense Area. Supplementing those three projects, many local residents converted their homes to apartment houses, and the city's hotels were used to the fullest. The wartime housing shortage was never fully resolved. As late as the fall of 1946, according to the Portsmouth War Records, "it was not uncommon for tourists passing through the city to be unable to find a night's lodging available in Portsmouth."[11]

The first signs of the Portsmouth housing problem surfaced at a meeting between yard and city officials in January 1940. At that meeting, Commandant Rear Admiral Cyrus W. Cole advised city administrators, "An increase will practically double the civilian force at the Portsmouth Navy Yard and its officers and men proportionately during the coming year; the lack of reasonable rentals, apartments, and rooms within a 25 mile radius is a serious problem."[12] In the summer of 1940, a *Portsmouth Herald* survey indicated the housing shortage was preventing many shipyard employees from bringing their families to the area. Others reported the housing they were able to secure for their families "was extremely inadequate with many conveniences, which are today considered necessary by most people, unavailable."[13] In August 1940, the *Herald* reported the city needed more than two thousand new homes to accommodate the increased population.[14] If the city needed that many new housing units in 1940, when the shipyard employed eight thousand workers, it would need more than four thousand new units by 1943, when shipyard employment exceeded twenty thousand. The three federal housing projects — Pannaway Manor (159 units) and Wentworth Acres (800 units) in Portsmouth and Admiralty Village (600 units) in Kittery — would fall far short of what was needed.

Horror stories about inadequate boomtown housing are quite common in home-front history books. James Wensyel wrote, "Near San Pablo, a California Navy base, a family of four adults and seven children made do with two cots and a full-sized bed in an eight-by-ten-foot wooden shack. 'Bomber City' near Ford's Willow Run plant housed fourteen thousand workers in trailers, dormitories, and prefabricated family units. At some sites, workers paid twenty-five cents to sleep in a 'hot bed' [still warm from the previous sleeper] during an eight-hour shift, then stood in long lines at restaurants and used shower or restroom facilities wherever they could find them."[15]

In Seneca, Illinois, available housing filled to overflowing within a thirty-five-mile radius of the city; trailers filled vacant lots and backyards. The Federal Housing Authority (FHA) built 1,467 family units and a dormitory for 300 men there, about the same number of federal housing units built in the Portsmouth Defense Area. Shortly after the war, Seneca's leaders elected to demolish all its federal housing.[16] Portsmouth's units remain to this day.

Barbara McLean Ward's *Produce and Conserve, Share and Play Square* speaks to the inadequacy of the limited housing available locally: "The Portsmouth City Planning Board reported that a survey of housing made in 1941 showed that more than half of the 4,021 'dwelling units' in Portsmouth were more than 80 years old, while less than one quarter of the units in Manchester were even 40 years old. The situation in Portsmouth was so bad that the report only considered 28 housing units as 'unfit for use' even though 70 units had no running water, 160 had no gas or electric lights, 162 had no toilets, and 879 had no bathtubs or showers."[17] Having just emerged from a decade during which every available cent went to food and other essentials, Portsmouth's blighted neighborhoods were in dire need of improvements. Portsmouth's substandard housing conditions were, however, actually not that bad when compared to the national average. According to historian Maury Klein, "In 1940 nearly a third of American homes had no running water or indoor toilets. Two fifths lacked bathtubs or showers. Nearly 60 percent had no central heating, and more than 25 percent did without mechanical or ice refrigeration."[18] These national averages are somewhat skewed because they incorporate many rural areas that lacked any possibility to gain the latest advancements in plumbing and electrical services. The marginal living conditions described by the Portsmouth City Planning Board in 1941 do suggest that the region faced a tremendous challenge in finding adequate housing for the thousands of migrant workers flooding in to work at the shipyard.

In June 1941, the Portsmouth Defense Council subcommittee for housing conducted a survey to determine the number of vacant dwellings and rooms available within a fifteen-mile radius of the navy yard. Armed with this information, officials urged residents to convert private homes to rental properties and to register apartments for rent at a centrally located registration site.[19] The Portsmouth War Records note, "Many people who owned homes, [and had] never before rented rooms, did so not because of the need for money, but because there was a big need for the rooms."[20] According to Eileen Dondero Foley, "Everybody in the city took in a boarder—a roomer. If you had a big house on Middle Street or Lincoln Avenue or Richards Avenue [you would] add a sink and stove upstairs and you had an apartment."[21] Twelve hundred such rooms or apartments became available.[22]

Harold Whitehouse recalls, "People were renting upstairs rooms, a room at the back of the house, or a room out over a garage. Any place where people could sleep and use a hot plate to cook was rented." The family sharing a duplex with his family in the South End took in boarders. As described by Whitehouse, "We rented the front part and the back section had six rooms like we had, but the family there only had three people. So they had plenty of space to rent upstairs and rented to two men who were working at the shipyard. . . . [They] cooked their meals on a hot plate in their room. They mingled right in as if they were family, and this happened all over the South End. In fact, it happened all over the city. . . . There were hotels, but they were too expensive for shipyard workers."[23] Despite the city's best efforts to convert homes to boardinghouses, there was a shortage of beds, often requiring a day-shift worker and a night-shift worker to double up by "hot bedding."[24] "Hot bunking" was a familiar concept to the submarine crews in the shipyard; with very limited berths available, relieved submarine watch-standers often collapsed into a warm bunk just vacated by a shipmate who was going on duty. The same practice apparently applied to exhausted shipyard workers in a town with too few beds.

"Quiet—War Worker Asleep" signs appeared during the day in the windows of homes renting rooms to night-shift workers at the yard. Amelia Patch recalled that those signs most often appeared in "the upper part of town where they rented rooms [and] they didn't want any confusion." Patch, who lived in the low-rent South End, added, "Down here you could put signs till God called you and if the kids wanted to go out and bicycle or have a baseball game they were going to do it."[25] An uptown boardinghouse on Middle Street apparently offered better daytime sleeping conditions than a shared family home in the South End.

While residents opened their doors to incoming workers, not all were welcome. According to Portsmouth historian Valerie Cunningham, "Rentals were not easy for black families to come by and discrimination was widely practiced in Portsmouth's boardinghouses."[26] Although ethnic neighborhoods were the norm in Portsmouth during the war, there never was a predominantly black neighborhood.[27] Only three or four black families lived in the South End during the war and, by one estimate, as few as two hundred lived in the entire Portsmouth area by the end of the 1940s.[28] The influx of wartime workers did not include a high percentage of African Americans, and those who did come experienced far more difficulties finding housing than their white counterparts.

While it was challenging for minorities to find housing in Portsmouth's boardinghouses, it was impossible in the federal housing projects, where the covenants excluded all but Caucasians. For example, the Pannaway Manor covenants stated, "No persons of any race other than the Caucasian race shall use or occupy any building on any residential lot."[29] Non-Caucasians could reside in Pannaway Manor on only one condition — a condition of servitude: "This covenant shall not prevent occupancy by domestic servants of a different race domiciled with an owner or tenant."[30] Segregation was alive and well in Portsmouth's federal housing projects.

In late 1940, the government began to acquire the lands needed for the housing projects through eminent domain, precipitating numerous lawsuits. Louise Flynn-McGee, about twenty years old at the time, recalls that a series of legal battles ensued before her family eventually lost twenty-two acres of their Maplewood Avenue farm to the government for Wentworth Acres.[31] Forced sales of prime coastal real estate for the construction of Fort Dearborn had caused bitter feelings and lawsuits — forced sales of family farmland in the Portsmouth suburbs to accommodate federal housing did the same, making the projects even more unpopular.

City officials, in an effort to control what was about to happen, established a planning program to guide and influence the construction of the federal housing projects. Unfortunately, their efforts were fruitless; the federal government largely ignored their recommendations. In his typically brusque manner, Councilman Gardner minced few words when describing the federal government's lack of cooperation:

> At this point, the Public Building administration, *that misbegotten offspring of the Federal Works agency,* announced that it was going to build a few hundred houses in Portsmouth. . . . *[T]he Public Buildings administration went right ahead and did just as they darn well pleased.* They built their 800 dwelling units on more than half of the land we had set aside for future industrial development; instead of the conforming architecture, they built largely six-family units of the barracks or warehouse type; instead of choosing one of the sites recommended by our Board for its ground characteristics, their site demanded the blasting of large quantities of ledge and the felling of large numbers of trees. In short, to our sorrow and theirs, *not one of our recommendations was followed.* Consequently, *it's going to take a lot of planning to make a future asset out of the present cost-plus monstrosity* [emphasis added].[32]

Concluding his outspoken criticism of the federal housing

projects, Gardner said, "With most of them we have tried to co-operate, but we're pretty well fed up, tired and discouraged. In short, we think we're in a terrible mess."[33] From conception to construction, local authorities were concerned about inheriting long-term maintenance nightmares when the "cost-plus monstrosities" were turned over to the city after the war.

Admiralty Village. Admiralty Village was the first of the three federal housing projects completed. In August 1940, Rear Admiral Wainwright wrote the Kittery Board of Selectmen inquiring about the availability of land in Kittery for development because "the Navy Department had authorized the construction of four hundred units to house married and enlisted men and civilian employees attached to the Navy yard."[34] One hundred acres of land, within walking distance of the new Gate #2, were made available on the shores of Spruce Creek. Consistent with the accepted thinking at the time, the Spruce Creek tidal waters were thought to provide excellent opportunities for sewage disposal.

It was subsequently determined that sufficient land and funds were available to expand the project to six hundred homes. Construction bids went out in early September 1940, construction started by mid-November, and the village opened for occupancy in September 1941. One day after the attack on Pearl Harbor, the shipyard commander reported to the Bureau of Yards and Docks, "The construction work at the Naval Housing Project now being done under lump sum contracts is nearing completion."[35] All families moved in by Christmas 1941.

In March 1942, George Michelson, vice president of the Boston construction contractor J. Slotnik Company, described Admiralty Village's hasty construction process in an article titled "Housing Built on the Double-Quick." Emphasizing the prefabrication technique used, he wrote, "On a 600-unit housing development to accommodate personnel at a Navy yard, *practically the only tool the carpenters used in the field was a hammer.* . . [thanks to] complete precutting of all lumber. . . Trim and interior finish came to the work site cut to size and was completely assembled in a job fabricating shop [emphasis added]."[36] The contractor described a labor issue similar to that experienced at the navy yard: "Pre-cutting and assembly line techniques were adopted to conserve material and to meet an expected shortage of skilled help in an area where little construction had been done in the last ten years This solution of the labor problem was based on the expectation that an unskilled man would become efficient quickly by working at the same job day after day."[37] Housing built on the double-quick by unskilled labor would appear to be a recipe for shoddy results. Many shared that opinion, deeming the village poorly constructed from the start. Rumors persisted that the houses were meant to be temporary. Others suspected that the Kittery government housing was ill-designed for cold weather because "it was supposed to go to Virginia or one of the southern states."[38]

As soon as families moved in, "neighbor trouble" began owing to the lack of privacy because of thin walls separating units, no backyards, and insufficient recreational space.[39] There was, however, one positive attribute: in December 1941, the Federal Works Agency authorized $125,000 for a sewage disposal plant for Admiralty Village, one of the first in the seacoast region.[40] Spruce Creek would not become a septic tank for the village.

Contractors had moved quickly to satisfy an urgent need for housing, but with little regard for long-term consequences. The Kittery selectmen, believing there would be little demand for the housing after the war, thought it would be too expensive for the town to maintain. However, many returning servicemen and their families moved into the village immediately after the war when the city set two hundred units aside for families of active-duty enlisted men; the rest of the units sold with priority going to present occupants and veterans. Numerous renovations have altered the buildings over the years, but the village remains.[41]

Pannaway Manor. The smallest of the three federal housing projects, Pannaway Manor, was built on thirty-seven acres of land west of Portsmouth, on the east side of Sherburne Road about a quarter mile from Greenland Road. The Defense Homes Corporation, a subsidiary of the Reconstruction Finance Corporation, funded the construction of 159 family residences for defense workers. Ground was broken in April 1941 and construction completed about a year later, lagging behind Admiralty Village by a few months. The moderately priced single-family homes included garages, electric stoves, and refrigerators. Defense workers immediately occupied the units, paying monthly rents ranging from forty-five to fifty dollars. Extending sewer and water mains to the outer reaches of the city was a major challenge, accomplished at considerable expense to the federal government.[42]

Pannaway Manor also met with the disapproval of civic leaders. Among other things, it was criticized for a lack of diversity and the "monotony created by the unchanged proportions of the houses."[43] Despite the criticism, these homes were more amenable than many of the substandard housing units available in the city. In 1945, the Pannaway Manor homes were sold to individual owners, many of whom were returning veterans under the G.I. Bill of Rights.[44] This housing area has also stood the test of time and

Photo 26: Aerial view of Portsmouth federal housing (circa 1945). Atlantic Heights is in the lower left corner and Wentworth Acres is in the lower right corner. Courtesy Portsmouth Athenæum.

continues to offer affordable suburban housing.

Wentworth Acres. Portsmouth's Wentworth Acres, funded under the Public Buildings Administration of the Federal Works Agency and managed by the FWA's Division of Defense Housing, was the largest of the three federal housing initiatives. The project started construction in April 1941 on 137 acres of land adjacent to Kearsarge Way, Maplewood Avenue, and Woodbury Avenue, near the shoreline of the Piscataqua River. As with Admiralty Village, the site was chosen with intentions to use the swift-flowing tidal river for sewage disposal; however, authorities authorized the addition of a sewage disposal plant shortly after ground was broken. The first tenants moved in on 17 December 1941, about the time the last tenants were settling into Admiralty Village. Some thought the addition of Wentworth Acres' eight hundred units, more than doubling the federal housing available at Admiralty Village and Pannaway Manor, was overkill. This was obviously not the case. In November 1942, Wentworth Acres reached 95 percent capacity, and maintained that occupancy rate for the remainder of the war. At its peak, about three thousand people occupied the project, putting great strain on the city's municipal services and schools.[45]

Although Wentworth Acres was initially intended to serve the navy yard's civilian and enlisted personnel, the federal government later extended eligibility to include civilian and enlisted personnel of the Portsmouth Harbor Defense Units. Monthly rents, which included gas, electricity, and water, varied from $33 for a three-room apartment with one bedroom to $39.30 for a five-room apartment with three bedrooms. Each apartment had an electric refrigerator, a forced warm air coal-burning furnace, a propane gas cooking range, and a propane automatic heater. Toward the end of 1942, a child-care building, a community recreational building, and a project store were added to the development.[46]

It was the opinion of many that Wentworth Acres was also poorly constructed and not designed for long life. Some speculated that the prefabricated housing was actually intended for the Norfolk Navy Yard at Portsmouth, Virginia, and had mistakenly ended up in Portsmouth, New Hampshire. The contractor denied the accusation, maintaining that his company constructed the village as planned, with permanency in mind. Nevertheless, Wentworth Acres showed evidence of hasty construction with inferior materials.

Portsmouth residents quickly dubbed the development Cardboard Acres, referring to the thin walls separating units.[47] City officials were not pleased, questioning the wisdom and cost of running sewers and water lines to what was then the outskirts of town for a project that was only temporary, even though the work was covered by a federal grant.[48] They were particularly miffed that federal officials had ignored their recommendations, proceeding to build the project "against sound advice from local municipalities and against their wishes." Despite much criticism of the quality of construction and concerns about long-term maintenance, Wentworth Acres has survived under a couple of name changes—first as Seacrest Village and now as Mariner's Village.

------ ⁕ ------

Despite the construction of these three government projects, and the conversion of many of Portsmouth's old homes to rental properties, the area's housing remained inadequate for the entire war. As early as September 1943, city officials were debating the postwar fate of the projects. Some urged that they be profitably disposed of in a manner that would "bring the housing market back into balance in the community so as not to depress real estate values." Others argued for keeping the government housing, deeming it superior to "some of the old, dilapidated housing . . . down in the old waterfront area." Another faction pointed out that the government units could help solve the city's prewar housing shortage; if funding intended for the demolition of the federal projects was redirected to the removal of substandard waterfront housing, the city could create an opportunity for new waterfront development for residential or historical park purposes.[49] Elements of this plan prevailed, and Portsmouth's federal housing projects largely remain to this day.

Schools

------ ⁕ ------

The employment boom and the federal projects hastily constructed to accommodate them brought thousands of children to the region, overloading the existing school systems. Kittery's elementary schools were inundated with new pupils while its high school enrollment remained essentially unchanged. In 1942, the school superintendent reported, "There has been a 32% increase in enrollment in the elementary schools and a 2% increase in enrollment in Traip Academy."[50] Because of the serious overload, the federal government funded the construction of the Frisbee School, which opened in 1943 with sixteen elementary classrooms, a gymnasium, and a cafeteria. The Traip Academy superintendent attributed the nearly unnoticeable bump in high school enrollment to a "great demand for defense workers."[51] Many students of high school age were opting for jobs at the yard over the classroom. This was the case nationwide: "Between 1940 and 1944 the number of teenage workers in America increased by two million and the number attending school fell by more than one million," according to one documentarian.[52] Many states suspended, relaxed, or ignored child labor laws to enable teenagers to join the workforce.

Bill Tebo was one of the local teenagers employed at Portsmouth Navy Yard. He and many of his classmates would go to school during the day and then work the 3 to 11 p.m. shift. Students who maintained good grades could earn release from the last two class periods at the high school, giving them enough time to get to the yard for their shift.[53] The days were long, but the pay was good. One mobilization historian observed, "Nothing demonstrated the failure of the educational systems more than the irony that many of these kids earned more than their teachers."[54]

Sadie Dearborn, hired to teach at Kittery's Mitchell Elementary School in 1941, experienced the initial flood of children from the newly opened Admiralty Village. She started with a class of about twenty first-grade students. With the opening of each new street in the village, it was her impression that she got "5 new First Graders each Monday." The trend continued until she had "58 or so at Christmas time." A shortage of desks required the use of orange crates and wooden boxes as substitutes, and students shared the few books available. Over the course of the year, school officials assigned seventy-eight pupils to her class, some of whom were reassigned to less crowded classrooms. Of these seventy-eight, it was Dearborn's opinion that "only 20 were [from families of] so-called natives." Kittery's elementary school population, and the town of Kittery itself, experienced a demographic makeover during the course of a single school year.[55]

The opening of Pannaway Manor and Wentworth Acres in late 1941 had a similar effect on the Portsmouth school system. As at Traip Academy, the existing junior and senior high schools were easily able to handle the upper six grades. There was even room for servicemen convalescing in the shipyard's naval hospital to attend high school classes, and the mechanical arts department provided vocational training under the Federal Training Program. Young children however, inundated the elementary schools. Between 1940 and 1943 the local population of children between the ages of five and fourteen increased 37.3 percent, from 4,331 to 5,950 pupils (table 8). Additional elementary grade schools were needed; federal funding enabled the construction of Sherburne Elementary School (seven classrooms) to accommodate Pannaway Manor children and a similar elementary school, consisting of fourteen classrooms, adjacent to Wentworth Acres.[56]

Utilities

Although discouraged by their inability to influence the construction of Pannaway Manor and Wentworth Acres, Portsmouth officials quickly realized that cooperation with federal authorities would gain them more than continued criticism would. The message was quite clear to Gardner, who wrote, "Finally FWA [Federal Works Agency] indicated more or less subtly that unless we came through on the line for dear old PBA [Public Buildings Administration] we might get considerably less consideration on our applications for Federal assistance on our various projects." Gardner explained that they had "decided that it's THE BANANA [*sic*] that leaves the bunch that gets skinned."[57] Officials decided to stick with the bunch, for the future benefit of their city.

The 11 April 1942 *Portsmouth Herald* recapped the city's progress during the "first year of the emergency." It had been about a year since the president had designated Portsmouth a defense area for federal housing projects; during that year, federal officials had approved most of the $2.5 million of aid the city had requested. As a result, the *Herald* proclaimed, "A new Portsmouth has been born and things accomplished that were undreamed then [one year ago]." Housing projects had been completed; bridges modernized; schools built; telephone, gas, electrical, and sewage service expanded; the water supply greatly increased; and additions made to schools and hospital services. The newspaper explained that preparations started well before the Pearl Harbor attack: "Looking back on the year, it is evident that the bulk of the progress has been made since Pearl Harbor Dec. 7. However, Portsmouth was not idle in the eight months previous, and its preparations for war were well underway when the war hit. One year ago tomorrow, Wentworth Acres, which now houses 200 families, was started. Admiralty Village, where 600 families now live, and Pannaway Manor, where 140 families live, were well under construction." The *Herald* concluded, "Months before war was declared Portsmouth Navy Yard and the Portsmouth Harbor defenses had completed millions of dollars worth of expansion projects and manpower had swelled to war-sized proportions."

Without this running start, the impact of the mobilization would have been far more devastating than it was.[58]

Inadequate telephone service quickly became one of the most obvious infrastructure problems as the burgeoning population's proliferating communication needs overloaded telephone circuits. In July 1942, New England Telephone and Telegraph requested citizens to limit the volume of nonessential calls because "the present emergency is placing a tremendous load of special calls . . . of wartime origin — service men's calls, calls by the armed forces, war industry and government calls." Furthermore, there was no end to the overload in sight because "circuit expansion is limited by the diversion of copper and other basic materials to the war program."[59] As was the case in so many areas, the homeland would have to survive with less to feed the military's need for critical metals and materials.

An inadequate water supply plagued the city throughout the war years. It was editor Frank Jordan's opinion that "Portsmouth had a water problem long before FDR declared an emergency." The federal government began funding upgrades to the city's water system in 1940, but the fifty-three well fields that began operation in late 1941 only served to "relieve a pre-defense shortage."[60] In October of the same year, "the Portsmouth city council agreed that it was no nearer to the solution of the acute water problem than it was six month ago."[61] In February 1942, the Federal Works Agency authorized funding for the drilling of more wells in Rye and Greenland.[62] By the end of the war, Portsmouth's water system had expanded to 108 wells, able to supply about 2.5 million gallons per day.[63] The never-ending struggle to expand water service to the new housing areas and harbor defense fortifications ceased only when the Army began to abandon the harbor fortifications.

The capital outlays of the Portsmouth Water Department,

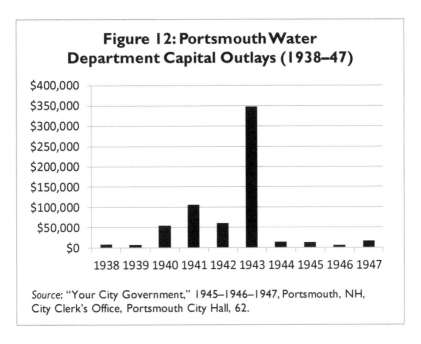

Figure 12: Portsmouth Water Department Capital Outlays (1938–47)

Source: "Your City Government," 1945–1946–1947, Portsmouth, NH, City Clerk's Office, Portsmouth City Hall, 62.

shown in figure 12, illustrate its struggles to maintain an adequate water supply. After spending a few thousand dollars of taxpayers' monies in 1938 and 1939, the department kicked into overdrive; all expenditures from 1940 to 1945 were the result of federal bonds and grants. Thanks to this wartime expansion, the assessed value of the city's transmission mains, pumping stations, and hydrants almost doubled during 1943, from about $500,000 to $900,000.[64]

Assuming figure 12 represents construction activity, the water department was fifty times more active developing upgrades in 1943 than it was in 1939. The capital outlays from 1940 through 1942 primarily involved the expansion of service to Pannaway Manor, Wentworth Acres, and the upgraded harbor fortifications in New Castle. The outlay of nearly $350,000 in 1943 extended service several miles via a 12-inch water main to newly constructed Fort Dearborn in Rye. As victory became more certain and the need for harbor defense waned, the federal government's commitment to funding infrastructure development waned as well. The great reduction in federal grants in 1944 and 1945 attests to this diminishing commitment.

Seeking to ensure that the city received a sufficient allotment of soon-to-be-rationed foodstuffs, the Portsmouth Chamber of Commerce conducted a survey in May 1942 to determine the effect the local population growth was having on food consumption and public utilities. The *Portsmouth Herald* explained why public utilities were included in the survey: "As a double check on the food products figure to be submitted to the federal rationing officials, a survey of public utilities consumption was carried out at the same time. Food figure jumps alone could mean local business had expanded to nearby territory in search of greater markets. A corresponding jump in Portsmouth utilities could only mean the food products jump was necessitated by the growth in Portsmouth's population." The results of the survey, as shown in figure 13, appeared on the front page of the 26 May 1942 *Herald*. The chart shows a slightly exaggerated 48 percent increase in population between 1940 and the spring of 1942, with food products and public utilities struggling to keep up with the population boom. The study concluded, "This is a story of boomtown Portsmouth. War wrote it. War has brought a mushroom growth to Portsmouth similar to those towns that sprang up in our Far West when gold and other precious metals were discovered. At times developments here have been little less hysterical in tempo."[65] Though a bit overstated, the chamber's announcement and chart show a heightened concern about the community's ability to service the booming population.

The *Herald* did not provide the data sources for figure 13; however, the trends give a sense of the city's struggle to service and feed a mushrooming population. Public utilities expanded in fits and starts, consistent with the availability of federal funding. These utilities modestly underserviced the community until early 1940 when mobilization dollars first poured into the region and the infrastructure boom started, resulting in a 50 percent increase in public utilities by January 1942.

The food products graph, showing the availability of foodstuffs to have seriously lagged behind the population increase for most of 1940 and 1941, is a little suspect. With more serious rationing about to start, the chamber wanted to build its case for an allowance of rations commensurate with the expanding population—to ensure the city received its fair share. The chart conveys the message that the area had struggled to feed its growing numbers and only recently

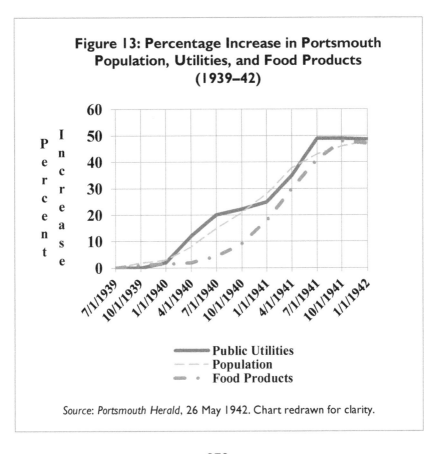

Figure 13: Percentage Increase in Portsmouth Population, Utilities, and Food Products (1939–42)

Source: *Portsmouth Herald*, 26 May 1942. Chart redrawn for clarity.

achieved an adequate food supply,[66] implying that this was the rationing level required. Once rationing began, OPA's administration of the program superseded any local chamber of commerce efforts to influence quotas.

Gregory C. Colati and Ryan H. Madden wrote in *Victory Begins at Home: Portsmouth and Puddle Dock during World War II*, "The war brought changes to all facets of city life. It changed the physical face of the city and the social character of the people."[67] A chamber of commerce report at the end of the war echoed that opinion: "There has also been much private building. There have been tremendous extensions of water and sewer mains, of telephone facilities and of the facilities of other utilities. New schools have been built, [as well as] new streets and sidewalks and roads."[68] The shipyard mobilization had strained public utilities, elementary schools, housing, transportation systems, medical care, and other public services, but not in vain. The wartime infrastructure development set the stage for future development that would propel the city into the latter half of the twentieth century and beyond.

CHAPTER 12
ENVIRONMENTAL IMPACT

With all the new toilet fixtures and with an increase in
personnel several times the former figures, the amount
of sewage now emptying into the river is great. There
have been several complaints about the odor. Some of
it has a tendency to lodge about piers and has to be
cleaned away.

Portsmouth Navy Yard Medical Officer
Annual Report, 1942

From wooden sailing vessels in the nineteenth century
to steam-driven steel-hulled ships at the turn of the
twentieth century to submarines in 1915, Portsmouth
Navy Yard stayed on the cutting edge of evolving
shipbuilding technology, culminating in the production
miracle of World War II. But the dark side of this miracle —
the increasingly harmful by-products of these increasingly
complex technologies — went largely unacknowledged, and
indeed was little understood until long after the war. The
yard's industrial practices and precautions were typical of the
times; they were, however, better documented in general
than those of most other shipyards and industrial facilities.
Therefore the case studies in this chapter primarily involve
shipyard practices, such as uncontrolled dumping of solid
industrial waste in landfills and the direct discharge of
domestic and industrial sewage to local waters. It's important
to remember that no rules were being flouted or broken. The
age of environmental awareness and legislation, although on
the horizon, had yet to dawn.

In fact, it wasn't until half a century later, in 1994, that the Portsmouth Navy Yard first appeared on the National Priorities List (NPL) for Superfund projects.[1] EPA surveys in the 1970s had found numerous hazardous waste sites around the yard that required millions of dollars in cleanup costs. The surveys primarily focused on postwar practices and waste disposal because shipyard management greatly reduced or eliminated record keeping during the war for the sake of production. There was no need for the EPA to extend the surveys farther back; the postwar review produced more than enough evidence to have the yard declared a Superfund site. The EPA studies found that reclamation projects, designed to add acreage to the island shipyard, had dumped tons of hazardous solid waste materials on tidal flats. That waste included chromium, lead and cadmium-plating sludge, asbestos insulation, volatile organic compounds, paint solvents, mercury-contaminated materials, and sandblasting grit containing various metal wastes. Similar practices, discussed below, had been employed during the war when production and the accompanying waste products were much higher. There was little public concern at the time, and even less on the part of the Department of the Navy, about the shipyard's uncontrolled dumping of waste materials and effluents. Rampant pollution was readily accepted as a cost of doing business — and winning the war.

The EPA's analysis of the shipyard's postwar operations also found that tons of raw sewage and industrial waste — a potpourri of acidic and alkaline wastes including battery acid, lead sludge, and spent baths from electroplating — were discharged directly into the Piscataqua River. The EPA studies identified three liquid discharge sites immediately offshore from the shipyard's fitting-out piers with high levels of heavy metals, which included polychlorinated biphenyls (PCBs), cyanide, phenol, oils, and grease.[2] As this chapter shows, the same shipyard industrial sewage system was greatly overloaded during the war; consequently, it is assumed that even higher levels of the same hazardous effluents were discharged to the river and bay.

Precautions were sadly lacking during the war for various shipyard operations involving significant environmental and health risks. For example, it wasn't until late in the war —*after* workers had suffered hearing damage and some had even lost toes, according to Bill Tebo—that earplugs and safety shoes began to appear in the yard. Given this state of affairs, it should not be surprising that other safety precautions were virtually nonexistent, such as protection for employees handling asbestos and dry-dock workers exposed to airborne contaminants. An examination of these and other shipyard operations suggests that the yard was not an environmentally friendly place to work during the war. Again, the yard's wartime practices are highlighted because they are so well documented in the archives, not because they were more egregious than those of other local industries.

Pollution of River and Bay

There was nothing out of the ordinary, unfortunately, in the shipyard's habit of dumping raw sewage and industrial effluents directly into the Piscataqua River. Urban sewage treatment, according to environmental historian Samuel P. Hays, "did not receive much attention until the New Deal public-works programs in the 1930s, and was not taken up by most cities until massive federal funding became available beginning in the 1960s."[3] It was not until after World War II that industrial discharges began to arouse as much interest as did municipal sewage. Pollution dispersion, the dumping of liquid wastes into large bodies of water or fast-flowing streams, was the common disposal practice until the 1950s.

What little environmental conscience the shipyard and other local industries had during the war hinged on the simple belief that the swift, tidal Piscataqua River provided an acceptable, convenient, and effective sewer system.

The efforts of federal and state authorities to gain some control over sewage discharges in the 1930s quickly subsided when the war started. These early state initiatives to regulate discharges from federal navy yards stood on very weak legal grounds. The prevailing legal argument traces back to Chief Justice John Marshall and the 1819 *McCulloch v. Maryland* Supreme Court decision, which invoked the supremacy clause of the Constitution and declared federal facilities immune from state and local regulation.[4] This federal immunity gradually eroded after World War II with the passage of legislation that included the Federal Water Pollution Control Act (1948), the Clean Water Restoration Act (1966), and subsequent Clean Water Acts and amendments, as well as the establishment of the Environmental Protection Agency (1970), which increasingly held federal shore facilities to more demanding environmental standards. However, before and during the war years, the Navy treated all state attempts at regulation with a definite lack of enthusiasm, as evidenced by events at Portsmouth Navy Yard in the mid-1930s and early 1940s.

The first challenges to the dumping of shipyard sewage into the Piscataqua River occurred in the mid-1930s. Prompted by Congress, the chief of the Bureau of Yards and Docks sent a letter to all navy yards in September 1935, requiring them to report any dumping of untreated sewage into local waters. The tasking letter stated, "A resolution adopted by the House of Representatives on 7 August 1935 requested the President to inform the House of the number and distribution of Federal institutions and establishments of every kind and character, which are depositing untreated sewage into the navigable or non-navigable waters of the United States."[5] The House's respect for the supremacy clause of the Constitution was evident in the passive nature of the resolution, which merely *requested* the executive branch to inform the House of the extent of dumping.

In response to the bureau's request, the commandant of Portsmouth Navy Yard reported that a shipyard population of about 2,800 people produced an estimated 18,000 cubic feet of raw, untreated sewage daily that was dumped directly into the Piscataqua River through several sewers.[6] This equated to just under half an acre of raw sewage at a depth of one foot [1 acre = 43,560 square feet] every day. The yard offered no apologies, nor any plan to reduce or treat the sewage. The reports in the fall of 1935 were apparently for informational use only, as the bureau did not contact the shipyard again about its sewage discharge practices until 1940.

The shipyard's 1937 annual sanitary report illustrates a total lack of awareness of the consequences of discharging untreated sewage into the river. The report described the shipyard's sewage system as "excellent," discharging "directly into the Piscataqua River, either into the main channel or back channel," where it was "carried to the ocean by the river current or tide."[7] The yard placed great confidence in the ability of the Piscataqua River to flush itself clean and carry the waste out of sight to a deep and safe place. However, later studies suggest strong incoming tides may also have carried the yard's sewage upriver into the shallow, and vulnerable, Great Bay estuary.

The shipyard's discharge practices escaped challenges in the late 1930s, but local concerns grew about the condition of Great Bay. At a 16 August 1938 meeting of the Public Health and Welfare Committee of the New Hampshire Seacoast Regional Association, Dr. Haven T. Hall reported the results of recent tests and investigations into the growing pollution in the bay. The tests showed that "two hours after low tide there was a considerable number of bacteria in the water." Hall concluded, "The bacteria came in with the incoming tide ... from other places emptying into the Bay." Contrary to the shipyard medical officer's assumption that the yard's waste was being whisked off to the ocean, the navy yard and Portsmouth sewers might well have been generating some of the growing pollution in Great Bay.[8]

At the same 16 August 1938 meeting, Mr. A. M. F. Adams said he "had lived all his life on Great Bay and there wasn't any question about the waters being polluted." Other older residents recalled "when there were beaches along Great Bay where now there is nothing but mud." The bay was becoming increasingly polluted, and very little was being done to reverse that trend. Studies recommended sewage disposal plants for towns discharging sewage into the bay. However, the construction of such plants required state or federal funding, which was about to be consumed in preparations for war. Concerns about the cleanliness of Great Bay were quickly overshadowed.[9]

In 1940, the chief of the Bureau of Yards and Docks received another inquiry, this time from the surgeon general of the United States. The bureau advised the naval shore stations in December 1940 that it had met with state health officials and the surgeon general in Washington, DC, on 16 and 17 September 1940 concerning the discharge of domestic and industrial sewage at industrial plants essential to the national defense. The meeting resulted in a resolution that it be "brought to the attention of the heads of defense agencies" that naval shore stations "should conform to the standards of the Department of Health of the State in which such facilities may be located." Once again, the recommendation merely suggested that naval stations comply with state standards.

The Bureau of Yards and Docks added a lukewarm

endorsement to the surgeon general's initiative: "If there is any question as to the adequacy of the methods proposed or now in use, it is suggested that conferences be arranged with local or state health departments to determine any additional steps in the protection of water supply and disposal of wastes which may be required, and that, where necessary, suitable recommendations be forwarded to the Bureau."[10] The bureau, feeling no obligation to commit immediate resources to compliance, did little more than ask its navy yards to put out feelers and report back. Indicative of the lack of priority given environmental issues at the time, a year went by before the bureau next addressed the dumping of raw sewage. Just a week before the attack on Pearl Harbor, the bureau advised the yards it had "moderate funds" budgeted for "rectifying those faulty conditions [of sewage discharge] of a minor nature." If compliance with state policies required larger projects, the yards were to forward details to the bureau for consideration; the bureau would then attempt to obtain funding through legislation, and then pursue those projects "if funds become available." The bureau's intentions were good, if not aggressive. However, the timing could not have been worse: the nation's need for ships and submarines quickly overwhelmed any concerns about the discharge of industrial sewage.[11]

Despite the yard's focus on more important matters in early December 1941, it found time to query its two border states about their policies and laws concerning sewage discharges. The Maine Department of Health and Welfare responded on 24 December 1941:

> The policy of this Department concerning the discharge of sewage into the Piscataqua River near the Navy yard at Kittery and Eliot is the same as we have had for a number of years

relating to the discharge of sewage along the seashore in that vicinity. We have *recommended* to the various towns that no raw sewage be emptied into such waters and as a result of this, primary settling tanks have been installed at Ogunquit, York, York Beach, and other communities along the shore. We believe that at least this degree of treatment *should be* supplied for any sewage disposal projects emptying into the Piscataqua River or nearby tributaries [emphasis added].[12]

As before, the state of Maine merely recommended that the federal shipyard *should* comply with its long-standing policy.

New Hampshire's response of 16 December 1941 was even more revealing of the times:

As applicable to a case of this kind, *the latter [laws] are nil, except in so far as ground for a charge of nuisance could be found, and this would scarcely be possible here.* That is, there is no legal action this department could take respecting the existent sewage disposals at Dover, Portsmouth, and the Navy yard [emphasis added].[13]

In other words, the state was nearly powerless to regulate shipyard sewage emissions — and, the letter implies, a national defense facility such as the shipyard would never be subject to nuisance laws, the state's only leverage. New Hampshire's response, dated a week after the attack on Pearl Harbor, acknowledged that the shipyard had more important matters at hand than sewage.

Dutifully wrapping up the debate, the yard commandant very unapologetically advised the bureau on 28 December 1941, "The present number of sewer outlets at the Yard is the same as has been in existence for a number of years and the raw sewage is emptied into the Piscataqua River."[14] Once again, no excuses or suggested improvements were offered. However, the report did cite a sewage upgrade then under way at the newly constructed Admiralty Village: "At the Navy yard Housing Development at Kittery, Maine, raw sewage is [at present] emptied into Spruce Creek. . . . A Federal Grant has been issued for a sewage treatment plant and garbage incinerator for the Housing Development."[15] This treatment plant was a start at reducing the contamination of local waters.

In December 1942, the Bureau of Yards and Docks restated its limited intentions to "comply with legitimate requests from local health officials in regard to the treatment of the sewage from naval shore establishments" considering "the current shortage in steel, copper, and mechanical equipment." Furthermore, the bureau directed "that the apparent necessity for sewage treatment at any station be investigated thoroughly before arrangements are made to install sewage treatment structures since there are conditions where, by a reasonable extension of the outfall sewer, the immediate need for sewer treatment may be removed and the treatment plant may be omitted for the present."[16] Although the Navy evidently considered the extension of sewer lines into the swift Piscataqua River a more cost-effective solution than the building of a treatment plant, the Navy did neither.

It is a revealing and sobering exercise to estimate the volume of wartime sewage discharged to the river by extrapolating from the yard's reported discharge in 1935. During the war, the peak daily population of the yard exceeded 25,000, including employees, residents, prisoners, submarine crews, marines, hospital staff and patients, and contractors. The 1935 daily estimate of 18,000 cubic feet of raw sewage for a shipyard population of about 2,800, when scaled to the yard's peak wartime population, equates to roughly 165,000 cubic feet of shipyard waste—about four acres (1 acre = 43,560 square feet) of raw sewage, at a depth of one foot—dumped daily into the Piscataqua River. If anything, this estimate is probably on the low side, considering the breakneck pace of industrial operations during the war and the increased shop industrial waste that must have been generated.

The shipyard medical officer's annual report for 1942 confirms that disturbing amounts of unprocessed sewage were pouring directly into the river: "With all the new toilet fixtures and with an increase in personnel several times the former figures, the amount of sewage now emptying into the river is great. There have been several complaints about the odor. Some of it has a tendency to lodge about piers and has to be cleaned away."[17] The medical officer advised, "Consultation with Public Works resulted in the conclusion that it would be a major task to extend the sewer down the river [as recommended earlier by the Bureau of Yards and Docks]. . . . Since there is apparently no health hazard, such an undertaking is not recommended for the duration of the war." This conclusion speaks volumes about the low priority then given to harbor pollution: even raw sewage sloshing about beneath the piers was quickly dismissed as a health hazard, and no consideration at all was given to the long-term environmental damage. There was a war to win.[18]

The surrounding communities were no more responsible with sewage discharge than was the yard. According to the 1943 *Survey of Health and Welfare*, "All of the sewage from the community is discharged raw into the Piscataqua River with the exception of sewage from the Wentworth Acres section.

The sewage system has grown gradually as the city increased in population. However, as in many instances, little attention has been given to the engineering phases. For this reason, some of the mains are undersized and, under proper tidal conditions, back flooding in the low areas occurs. Also, some of the sewer outlets are not submerged, or have not been extended sufficiently, at times giving rise to localized odor nuisances."[19] Conditions along Portsmouth's shores were not unlike the odiferous and fouled waters around the piers at the navy yard.

Harold Whitehouse can attest to the noisome state of the waterfront during the early 1940s: he and his teenage friends found entertainment shooting rats along the polluted New Castle Avenue seawall during low tide. According to Whitehouse, "The people dumped their garbage overboard thinking this was the thing to do because when the tide went out it took the garbage with it and we understood that you were feeding the fish, helping the marine life. . . . The rats lived under the seawall and they'd come out at low tide and munch on the garbage that wasn't taken out by the tide. And we'd go down and stand by the railing and shoot our BB gun[s] and slingshot[s] at them. So this was a day or afternoon of entertainment, and we'd be there for hours shooting at rats."[20] Portsmouth citizens, like Navy officials across the river, put too much confidence in the ability of the Piscataqua to disperse their detritus; the rats — and teenagers with BB guns — appreciated their oversight.

The 1943 health survey did express concern for the environmental consequences of uncontrolled sewage dumping, noting that the practice added "materially to the pollution of Great Bay, thereby having a direct effect on the shellfish and recreational potentialities of the areas."[21] The authors took some satisfaction in pointing out that Portsmouth was not the only culprit: "There are several other towns and cities bordering on streams discharging into the Bay and they also contribute to the pollution."[22] Unlike the shipyard report, the city survey at least acknowledged the detrimental effects of unrestricted dumping of raw sewage into the river. However, as with the navy yard, the focus of the local communities was elsewhere.

These sewage problems were not unlike those found at other shipyard boomtowns during the war. In some respects, the situation was much better. Lorraine McConaghy's study of the boomtown of Kirkland, Washington, is a horror story by comparison.[23] Kirkland, located on the eastern shore of Lake Washington, doubled in population to about 15,000 during the war when employment at its shipyard grew from a few hundred to 8,000. Lake Washington was not blessed with the strong currents and tidal flushing provided by a river like the Piscataqua, and the uncontrolled sewage dumped into its waters caused a public health catastrophe. In the summer of 1944, Kirkland's authorities declared the town's water supply unfit for human consumption after shipyard workers became ill drinking from fountains in the yard. Sewage leaking into the drinking water supply had raised E. coli bacteria to five times the permissible level. A portable chlorinator alleviated the problem, but residents had to boil drinking water for some time.

On the seacoast, wartime pollution of local waters did not cause any such extreme health crisis; however, as the war wound down, the public became increasingly aware of the importance of maintaining the cleanliness of the harbor and bay, giving rise to the never-ending battle that continues to the present day. In 1944, Dr. Floyd Jackson of the University of New Hampshire assumed a leadership role in documenting the need to clean up the bay. His report, *A Biological Survey of Great Bay, New Hampshire*, measured the increasing pollution of the estuary. Jackson argued that postwar improvement of the bay hinged on several factors, of which proper sewage disposal deserved first priority. He was the first to quantify the pollution problem in Great Bay and offer solutions—many would follow in his footsteps.

Jackson's survey of microbial contamination showed an alarmingly high coliform bacteria count of 2,400 per 100 milliliters of water for the lower Piscataqua River near the shipyard. The U.S. Public Health Service standard for shellfish waters at the time was 70 coliform bacteria per 100 milliliters. According to Jackson, there were two pollution factors, "that resulting from industrial waste dumped into streams and that resulting from sewage." The shipyard ranked high as a contributor of both with its daily discharge of the equivalent of four acres of raw sewage into the river.

Before one is overly critical of Portsmouth's and the shipyard's contributions to harbor pollution, it should be noted that Jackson reported coliform bacteria levels in the tributary Cocheco and Exeter Rivers to be 10,600 and 9,000 per 100 milliliters of water respectively, considerably above the Piscataqua River levels and outrageously higher than the federal standard.[24] Jackson explained, "This bacteria count is sharply reduced as soon as rivers reach tide water and become salt," which he attributed to "the presence of bacteria-eating organisms in the water." The waters near the shipyard, unlike the waters near upriver textile mills, did reap some benefit from a twice-a-day saltwater tidal flushing.[25]

William Tebo remembers local rivers turning colors in the early 1940s when the textile mills changed dye colors. Worse yet, he remembers swimming in the Technicolor rivers.[26] Dr. Jackson confirmed the contamination of local rivers by mill discharges. He wrote, "Much of the material coming from the print mills is colored, and the use of the disc gave a fair idea of the amount of this type of pollution [chemical] that was present." The disc referred to was a Secchi disc, a simple instrument used to measure water clarity. The procedure involved lowering the disc, ten inches in diameter with "alternative quarters painted black and white," into streams and watching to see when it disappeared from sight. Test results showed that the disc disappeared at a depth of about three feet in rivers with a high density of mills, such as the Salmon Falls, Cocheco, and Bellamy Rivers, whereas the disc disappeared at a deeper depth of just over six feet in the Piscataqua River. Given the yard's daily discharge of sewage, the relative clarity of the Piscataqua is another testament to the benefits of tidal flushing.[27]

The growing concern about the pollution of local waters coincided with a similar national movement. Environmental historian Samuel P. Hays observed that, prior to the mid-twentieth century, "Sources responsible for air and water pollution as well as solid waste had long since dumped their waste on the most readily available land, into nearby streams, or into the air."[28] In late 1945, with the war winding down, there was a renewed national interest in cleaning up the nation's waters. This time the federal government assumed a much larger role in the effort. In November, Dr. Thomas Parran, the surgeon general, told the House Rivers and Harbors Committee, "[S]tate and local authorities are unable to solve the [pollution] problem and a clear definition of governmental policy is needed."[29] At the same meeting, Representative Karl E. Mundt (R-SD) asserted, "Water pollution is virtually the last important uncontrolled unregulated and unchecked pagan practice continuing in the United States."[30] With Congress and the federal government finally assuming a leadership role, that "pagan" practice was on its way out.

Hazardous Waste Landfills

The disposal of solid industrial waste presents a serious problem to an island shipyard of limited acreage. Long-term accumulation of the waste is unacceptable because it consumes valuable real estate otherwise available for more productive purposes. Transport to off-yard facilities for storage and eventual disposal is both costly and time-consuming. During the first half of the twentieth century, there were two convenient solutions to this problem: dumping at sea and using the waste for landfill. The yard had a history of both practices.

The dumping of waste products at sea was the subject of a 12 April 1926 memorandum from the shipyard manager, Captain H. W. Osterhaus, to his shop managers. Osterhaus chastised them for their cluttered and untidy spaces and encouraged them to dispose of the excess junk. Referring to unused boilers rusting in the industrial area, he wrote, "The boilers, if of no value, and if they cannot be sold as junk, could be put on the lighter and dumped overboard *as is done at regular intervals* when a load has been accumulated [emphasis added]."[31] In 1926, it had apparently been a long-standing practice to periodically clean up the shipyard by dumping barge-loads of detritus at sea. How far out the lighter traveled is not specified; it is certainly possible that ridding the yard of scrap was a higher priority than ensuring that the barge made a long transit to the deeper depths of the ocean.

It is not known when the yard stopped dumping its scrap at sea. A 12 April 1939 memorandum from Commandant Rear Admiral C. W. Cole to shipyard managers suggests that the use of industrial waste for landfill had replaced dumping at sea. Cole wrote, "It is noticed that considerable burnable material (including food) is being dumped in the Old Timber Basin adjacent to Bldg. 129. All burnable material must be burned and the incinerator is maintained for that purpose. It is also noted that tin cans and drums of various capacities are being disposed of without any effort being made to crush these containers. *This practice not only causes the area to be unsightly but will result in a very unstable fill.* All containers must be crushed before disposal in any fill [emphasis added]."[32] The outdated timber basin was at the northern end of the original Seavey's Island, on the back channel, between the present day hospital and the public works building (figure 14). It is highly probable that the cans and drums used as fill were petroleum containers, which certainly would have had environmental consequences. Cole expressed no concerns about the original contents of the containers, merely that the long-term stability of the fill required crushing the drums.

A review of a 1935 aerial view of the yard and several shipyard maps between 1939 and 1945 shows the timber basin gradually disappearing. In the 1935 photograph, the timber basin is visible as an inlet off the back channel.[33] A 1939 map shows the inlet walled off from the back channel, forming a pond prominently marked Timber Basin.[34] The basin is reduced in size on a 1941 map,[35] and by 1945 it has completely vanished, with the map showing buildings constructed on the reclaimed site.[36] A great many crushed cans and drums must have found their way to the timber basin during the war years. The disposal of industrial waste in landfills was particularly attractive because it killed two birds with one stone: it eliminated waste while adding much-needed real estate to the island shipyard.

Figure 14 shows how reclamation projects have enlarged and joined Dennett's and Seavey's Islands since establishment of the shipyard in 1800 on Dennett's Island.[37] The World War II landfills continued the long-standing practice of enlarging the yard by reclaiming nearby shoal waters — unfortunately, this time with contaminated material in many instances. The yard's two largest reclamation projects during World War II were the twelve acres created on the Pumpkin Island shoals directly across the river from Portsmouth's Prescott Park, and the twelve acres of Jamaica Island landfill in the back channel (figure 14). The former, which extended the shipyard's real estate well out into the Piscataqua River, accommodated the building of a triangular fitting-out pier — 1,100 feet of additional pier space — which became operational in late 1942. The Pumpkin Island project reportedly used uncontaminated off-yard landfill and fill from nearby dredging operations; it never became a

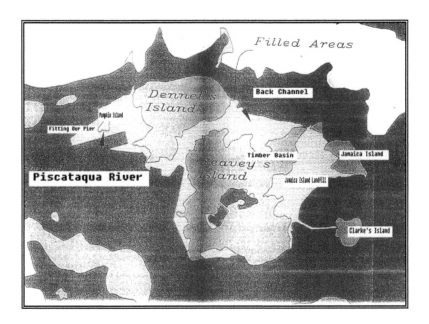

Figure 14: Portsmouth Naval Shipyard Landfills Since Establishment in 1800. *Source: State of New Hampshire v. State of Maine*, Lodging in Support of Motion for Leave to File Complaint, Map 45, 145, Supporting Evidence for Testimony Given to House Judiciary Committee on 24 May 1990 to Introduce H CON RES 337 Regarding the New Hampshire/Maine Border Dispute, Map No. 45, Seavey's Island, Portsmouth Naval Shipyard, 129.

Superfund site.[38] The notorious Jamaica Island landfill, which created additional shipyard acreage on the back channel and provided road access to the Jamaica Island ammunition stowage facility, was another story. This project, which continued well after the war, became the focus of much of the yard's Superfund recovery efforts fifty years later.

Estimates of the amount of hazardous waste dumped at the Jamaica Island landfill during the postwar period from 1945 to the mid-1970s are truly astounding:[39]

Substance	Estimated Quantity
Chrome plating sludge	5,000–10,000 pounds
Lead plating sludge	5,000–10,000 pounds
Cadmium plating sludge	5,000–10,000 pounds
Asbestos insulation	Several thousand pounds
Waste paints and solvents	500,000 gallons
Sandblasting grit	5,000 tons/year

Between 1973 and 1975, shipyard workers buried two concrete vault clusters in the Jamaica Island landfill, the larger of which totaled eight vaults containing twenty-three 55-gallon drums filled with materials contaminated with mercury.[40] Authorities had the contaminated material in these vault clusters removed to a licensed disposal site between 1997 and 2000. If the wastes listed above were routinely dumped in the Jamaica Island landfill after the war, it is reasonable to assume that even greater amounts found their way there during the war when the industrial activity at the yard was several times higher than it has been at any time since.

Additional review of the shipyard maps discussed earlier finds shipyard acreage gradually extending into the back channel during the war. Jamaica Island, purchased at the start of the war for ammunition storage, initially required the construction of a connecting causeway to provide access to the ammunition bunkers. The extensive landfill begun during the war and continued long afterward provided more efficient road access and additional acreage. Jamaica Island does not appear on the 1939 map, as it was not part of the shipyard until late 1941. The 1945 map shows the island fully developed with a substantial land connection to the shipyard proper, the result of dumping tons of industrial waste in the back channel. It is not surprising that the Jamaica Island landfill was one of the most troublesome of the Superfund sites and that millions of dollars were required to clean it up fifty years later.

Shipyard Operations

A shipyard is a potentially dangerous and unhealthy work environment; however, safety procedures, training programs, and protective clothing can minimize many anticipated risks. But not all hazards are immediately obvious, and grievous experience too often provides the motivation for future precautions. During the war, when production reigned supreme at the shipyard, safety and health issues often assumed a secondary role until mishap dictated otherwise. The following examples — those for which enough documentation exists in the archives to construct a narrative — offer evidence of shipyard wartime practices that proved to be harmful to the environment or hazardous to its workers, and eventually became motivators for finding a better way of doing things..

Pickling Tanks.   Pickling operations, which began at the yard in the early twentieth century with the construction of steel-hulled ships, greatly accelerated when the yard began to build submarines during World War I. The process, which involved the chemical removal of iron oxide scale from steel

293

plates prior to rolling the plates to produce pressure-hull sections or framing, was an underappreciated environmental hazard.

Pickling typically required large tanks, approximately 2,000 cubic feet in volume filled with a 10 percent sulfuric acid solution at about 200 degrees Fahrenheit. The acid solution loosened and dislodged scale on steel plates submerged for long periods, forming sludge in the bottom of the tank. The location of the tanks—in underground pits close to the river—permitted periodic flushing of the pits to the river. Many of the early tanks were built of wood, requiring constant repair of the seams and tightening of fasteners to prevent underground leakage of the sulfuric acid. Pickling tanks were accidents waiting to happen.

In 1938, the Bureau of Construction and Repair assigned Portsmouth Navy Yard the task of running a side-by-side evaluation of a new wooden tank and a new steel tank as replacements for two badly deteriorated wooden tanks. The yard subsequently reported, "On 10 October a steel rubber lined pickling tank manufactured by B. F. Goodrich Company . . . and a long leaf yellow pine wooden pickling tank were installed in the galvanizing plant."[41] The letter endorsed the advantages of the rubber-lined steel tank, which was further sheathed in acid-proof brick. Regarding the wooden tank, the commandant noted the difficulty of acquiring suitable lumber, as well as the unsatisfactory performance of the new and previous wooden pickling tanks:

> The securing of lumber for this tank was very difficult, and extended over a period of three years, including three rejections of lumber, before suitable material could be found. . . . Every effort was made to make this wooden tank the very best that could be constructed. . . . *Up to this time it has been*

impossible to make this tank absolutely tight. . . . The leakage of the acid from the wooden tank is particularly undesirable, as *the leakage from the two original wooden tanks so destroyed the concrete foundations of the pickling plant, that a new floor and foundations had to be installed after the old tanks were removed,* and prior to installation of the two subject tanks [emphasis added].[42]

The inability to prevent leakage from a state-of-the-art wooden pickling tank in 1938 invites questions about other long-term consequences of the shipyard's longtime pickling operations. Surely the sulfuric acid solution that ate fasteners and ruined concrete floors contributed other environmental and health hazards.

The conversion from wood to metal pickling tanks reduced leakage; however, the tanks remained an environmental hazard because operating procedures required routine flushing of the pit. In December 1939, the shipyard's production officer wrote the public works officer regarding the design of the pit for the new pickling tanks, "It is further desired that a drain pipe and valve be installed leading from the pit through the adjacent sea wall. It is realized that the bottom of the pit will be below high tide level. The valve will prevent flooding of the pit at high tide and will permit drainage and washing down of the pit at low tide."[43] The shipyard planned to avoid any further concrete deterioration by periodically flushing the pit straight into the river, a practice very consistent with the widespread flushing of other shop industrial waste through the sewer drains. The new steel pickling tanks were installed adjacent to the plate yard in 1942.[44] The extent of pit flushing during the war is unknown; however, the building of seventy-nine submarines during the war, requiring tons of pickled steel, must have resulted in the flow of huge amounts of sulfuric acid wastewater to the river.

Galvanizing Plant. Galvanizing increases the corrosion resistance of steel components by applying a protective coating of zinc through an electrolytic process. This process requires a thorough cleaning of the steel components in acid tanks, not unlike the pickling described above. Historically the yard had its galvanizing done off-yard. As late as 1939, Portsmouth Navy Yard management expressed disinterest in a proposed in-yard galvanizing plant as long as the yard could efficiently and economically contract for outside galvanizing, as it had done for years.[45]

This position changed in late 1942, when wartime needs caused a dramatic spike in the shipyard's galvanizing requirements. Faced with the need to clean 500,000 pounds of metal in calendar year 1943, the shipyard anticipated contractor shortages and opted for a new galvanizing facility. The eventual capacity of the plant exceeded all expectations. In April 1945, Lieutenant Junior Grade William P. Gregory reported to the Bureau of Ships, "It is worth noting in the year 1944, this shop produced 3,680,881 pounds of finished material. . . . For the first quarter of 1945, the shop produced 1,029,596 pounds of finished material."[46] That initial annual estimate of half a million pounds of metal in 1943 had increased to more than four million pounds per year by the first quarter of 1945. There is every reason to believe the eightfold increase in galvanizing operations was typical of the increased output of other operations and processes throughout the yard. Similarly, one might expect an eightfold increase in waste products during the war, with essentially no improvement in the means or efficiency of disposal. This estimate is consistent with the estimated eightfold increase in raw and industrial sewage extrapolated from shipyard reports earlier in this chapter.

The galvanizing plant has had an interesting postwar history. An acidic crystalline growth on the walls of the building that had contained the galvanizing plant caused it to be designated a Superfund site in 1994. In November 2000, the EPA provided an update on the curious crystalline growth:

> The pit was closed for the last time in the 1960s. At that time the pit was filled in and covered over with a concrete floor. And since then the building has been used as a welding school. . . . At various times since the pit was filled, a crystalline substance has been noted to form on the inside wall of the building near the former pit. The crystalline growth was found to be acidic based of a low pH. . . . Investigation at the site indicated that there is a potential risk to people working in the building who come in direct contact (skin contact) with the acidic crystals. The investigation showed that the fill material (including water in the pit) is the likely source of the crystalline growth. In addition, there is a concern that if there were a release from the pit, the high metals concentrations in the pit water could potentially adversely impact ground water under the site.[47]

The pit was subsequently uncovered, the fill material excavated, the site cleaned, and the concrete floor restored. If judged a potential health risk forty years after it was last used, what must the potential risks have been in 1944 when several million pounds of metal passed through the tanks of the galvanizing plant?

As late as October 2006, a letter in the *Portsmouth Herald* reported, "The curious crystals growing along the bottom of the walls in the Welding School building [that previously contained the galvanizing plant] have been cleaned once again and the affected areas covered with protective plastic sheets. The basic problem remains unresolved but the building is now much safer for welder training."[48] The yard's World War II galvanizing plant is the gift that keeps on giving—giving curious crystals that mysteriously reappear on the walls of the building—a reminder of the times when production ruled and workplace safety was a distant second.

Hull Scraping and Painting. The scraping of marine growth and loose paint from submarine hulls in dry dock produces hazardous airborne dust containing chemicals originally included in the paint systems to inhibit marine growth. During the war, these hazards were little appreciated and worker protection was minimal. Foreign submarines visiting the yard presented an additional complication because there was no record of the composition of the paint systems applied to them.

One noteworthy incident of airborne contamination occurred at the dry dock in September 1941 involving the Free French submarine *Surcouf*. During the brush-cleaning of the *Surcouf*'s underwater hull in preparation for renewing the preservation and anti-foulant coatings, workers experienced unusual skin and eye irritation. Seventeen of the men working in the dry dock went to the dispensary complaining of burning eyes, nose, and face. The medical officer suspected some unknown pollutant in the paint to be the cause. Further investigation revealed: "A Frenchman reported that the bottom was last painted in England with English paint. . . . Four men developed skin irritation on August 2nd while working in a ballast tank on an English ship and six men had the same experience on August 19th while working in the battery compartment of a French ship. It has not been possible to determine the composition of the English paint, but it is certain that there is some ingredient in their paint that is not present in ours as we have not had previous similar experiences."[49] The men with the burning symptoms were treated and released, but shipyard authorities did not attempt to determine the composition of the paint. The last of the foreign submarines departed the yard in January 1942, relieving yard workers of the risks involved with removing unknown substances from the hulls of these vessels. There were, however, health risks aplenty on our own submarines.

Asbestos Operations. When Don Ricklefs, a Portsmouth Navy Yard worker, reported for his draft physical, a suspicious spot showed up on his lung that kept him out of the war. When interviewed by Tammi Truax of the *Portsmouth Herald* fifty years later, Ricklefs said he suspected that he had "suffered some damage to his lungs" because "in those days shipyard workers did not wear protective gear."[50] In Ricklefs's case, the damage was obviously not life-threatening, since he enjoyed a long life after the war. Other unprotected workers were not as fortunate, especially those who worked with asbestos. The Navy medical community saw little need for protection, having greatly underestimated the health hazards involved with shipyard asbestos operations, relying on inconclusive studies of the risks conducted late in the war.

The use of asbestos for pipe and machinery insulation in the shipbuilding industry grew consistently throughout the 1930s, peaking immediately prior to World War II with the accelerated shipbuilding programs. The Navy aggressively pursued the use of asbestos because of its affordability, tensile strength, and resistance to heat and chemical damage.[51] High-temperature asbestos pipe coverings, weighing eighteen pounds per cubic foot, replaced older magnesia insulators weighing twenty-six pounds per cubic foot. Because the thermal conductivity of asbestos was much lower than previous insulators, less of it was required. Depending on the size of the vessel, upgrading to asbestos insulation could save tons of displacement, creating opportunities to enhance other features of the ship. Asbestos blocks and blankets found use in insulating steam turbines and other machinery prior to 1930, but it was the development of asbestos felts and cements, applied to valves, fittings, and piping, that greatly expanded its use during the 1930s.

Weight savings, always a critical concern in ship design for reasons of stability and cargo capacity, was even more of a factor in the 1930s because of the tonnage limitations imposed by the various naval treaties. Under these limitations, the greater than 30 percent weight savings that resulted from using asbestos insulation on piping throughout the ship was a significant advantage to the U.S. Navy. In addition, fire-resistant asbestos proved to be a good replacement for the flammable, and sometimes vermin-infested, animal hair insulations previously used on cold water pipes to reduce sweating. Naturally, the use of asbestos in the shipbuilding industries exploded during the latter half of the 1930s. As often happens with rapidly advancing technologies, enthusiasm for the newfound uses far outpaced concerns for the newfound risks. The World War II shipbuilding boom greatly boosted the demand for asbestos as well as the potential for asbestosis among shipyard workers.[52]

In February 1945, the Bureau of Ships, responding to a Bath Iron Works report that several shipyard workers had asbestosis symptoms, requested the Bureau of Medicine and Surgery to investigate allegations that asbestos operations in navy yards might be an occupational hazard.[53] The medical bureau's conclusions, minimizing the hazards, could not have been more wrong. The chief of the Bureau of Medicine and Surgery, Vice Admiral Ross T. McIntire, wrote, "Reports of chest x-rays, which have been made of employees engaged in handling, processing, and applying asbestos to pipe in Boston and Bremerton Navy Yards do not indicate any diseases of the lungs from exposure to asbestos. Repeated observations by personnel of the Yard Safety and Industrial Health Departments indicate that *the exposure of civilian employees in U.S. Navy yards to asbestos do not form an occupational problem as alleged* [emphasis added]."[54] Experience has shown that this dismissal was a bit premature.

Further review of shipyard asbestos operations conducted over the summer of 1945 under the leadership of Dr. Philip Drinker, chief health consultant to the U.S. Maritime Commission, showed a similar disturbing lack of appreciation for the accompanying health hazards. The study concluded, "Asbestos covering is a relatively safe operation. . . . This work, as found in our Navy yards, is most unlikely to cause ill health."[55] Future studies would take a much different view.

The Drinker Study drew its conclusions from a survey of the asbestos operations at Boston and Brooklyn Navy Yards and two private yards, Bethlehem Fore River in Quincy, Massachusetts, and New York Shipbuilding in Camden, New Jersey. The survey included atmospheric sampling of shop and shipboard ventilation for dust count and chemical content, and a review of the medical records of more than one thousand workers at those yards. The survey also included shop and shipboard dust counts provided by Portsmouth Navy Yard, although no members of the Drinker team visited Portsmouth and the medical records review included no Portsmouth employees. The study, however, does permit insight into Portsmouth's asbestos shop and shipboard operations.

According to the Drinker Study, the volume of asbestos work at Portsmouth Navy Yard was small in comparison to the other yards surveyed. In addition, Portsmouth's shop and shipboard environments were cleaner, containing fewer asbestos fibers. The study does note, however, that precautions were almost totally lacking at Portsmouth: only one of Portsmouth's forty asbestos workers, the band saw operator, wore a respirator. In addition, the shop lacked ventilation fans: the cementing station had one small exhaust fan, and all other ventilation was natural.[56] Apparently, open windows and waterfront breezes, like swift river currents, were expected to whisk away environmental hazards.

In retrospect, the 1945 studies looked at much too short an exposure period and were too reliant on lung X-ray markings to draw valid conclusions about the dangers of asbestos exposure. Ships and submarines had only used asbestos for about fifteen years prior to the Drinker Study, and it is now known that "the effects of long-term exposure to asbestos typically don't show up until 20 to 30 years after initial exposure."[57] The Drinker Study had detected only the most severe cases of asbestosis; had the study occurred fifteen or twenty years later, the results likely would have been vastly different. These reassurances from the highest levels of the Navy minimizing the dangers of asbestos delayed the introduction of vital safety precautions. This would change dramatically in years to come.

Portsmouth Navy Yard, the site of a production miracle during the war, was also an environmental liability during its peak production years. Large land reclamation projects filled shoal waters with hazardous industrial waste, raw sewage and industrial effluents spewed directly into the river, and shipyard operations were short on environmental protection and personnel safety precautions. The few examples of environmental abuse presented in this chapter invite questions about other shipyard practices, and the less-well-documented practices of other local industries. It is a disturbing exercise to multiply these abuses thousands of times, to gain an appreciation of the overall effect the World War II mobilization had on the nation's environment.

While it is true that Portsmouth Navy Yard and most industries were guilty of gross environmental and health risk oversights during World War II, it is also true that the lessons learned have contributed to remarkable progress since then. Shipyard work on nuclear submarines, technological marvels that they are, now occurs under the most rigorous of safety standards and environmental scrutiny. Portsmouth and the other nuclear shipyards have an enviable record for personnel safety and environmental protection that is every bit as impressive as was Portsmouth Navy Yard's production miracle during World War II.

CHAPTER 13
WARTIME POLITICS

An aroused Portsmouth citizenry showed its confidence in Mayor Dondero's integrity and administration and repudiated the tactics of the Republican machine by reelecting her by an overwhelming majority and, with the same vote, riding the Republicans out of town on the well known rail.

Portsmouth Herald
7 November 1945

T he far-reaching changes that altered every part of Portsmouth from the economy to the environment transformed its politics as well. In fact, something akin to a revolution galvanized city hall during the last years of the war and the first two years of the peace. In November 1944, while Allied forces were rapidly advancing toward Berlin and island-hopping across the Pacific toward Tokyo, Portsmouth citizens shrugged off many years of Republican domination and elected a Democratic mayor — not just any Democratic mayor, but the first female mayor ever in New Hampshire and one of the first in the nation. Mary Dondero had lost the November 1943 mayoral contest by just one hundred votes; a year later she won election to a one-year term by seven votes, then followed that up by winning a two-year term in November 1945 by the largest plurality in the history of the city. In November 1947, she lost her third bid for mayor by a single vote. The numbers suggest, and the media coverage at the time confirms, several years of contentious partisan politics. Emotions reached a feverish pitch during the two bitterly disputed elections decided by single-digit votes and their recounts. Without a doubt, the Mary Dondero story is an important piece of Portsmouth's World War II history.

Dondero was a highly respected, experienced politician before becoming mayor, having served several terms as a state representative. She also had the distinction of being the first woman to serve on the city council, elected in 1941 while a clerk at the navy yard. Her election as mayor was a watershed in city politics: Democrats, especially female Democrats, have been influential figures in Portsmouth municipal government ever since.

Dondero's election not only broke with the long local tradition of male Republican rule, it ran counter to a wartime national trend of continued male dominance of elected offices. Although women made remarkable progress in the workplace during the war, they seldom advanced in political circles, and rarely in electoral positions. Historian Roger W. Lotchin argues that women should have made more inroads into political office because they represented a "potential majority of the electorate with so many males absent and absentee-voting turnouts light";[1] however, he points out, "there was no labor shortage in politics as there was in the labor force."[2] Younger men vacated industrial jobs to go to war, but few older men vacated political positions for the same reason. While women were quick to fill the newly available higher-paying industrial jobs, there were few job openings in the political arena. Historian Jacqueline R. Braitman agrees with Lotchin's assessment that women made very little electoral progress during the war.[3]

Dondero's election in November 1944 received national attention in the 8 January 1945 *Newsweek*: "Two years ago when Mrs. Mary C. Dondero, Democratic member of the City Council, ran for mayor of Portsmouth (wartime population

23,000) she lost by 100 votes. She ran again in November but again appeared to have lost, this time by eight [actually seven] votes. Last week a recount told a different story. Mrs. Dondero, 50, a former beauty-prize winner and mother of four daughters, had edged Ira A. Brown, Republican, by 7 votes. Mrs. Dondero 2,117; Brown 2,110."[4] The article went on to explain that the new mayor would commute three days a week to Concord because she had also been elected to the New Hampshire House of Representatives for a fifth term. Beauty queen, mother of four, Portsmouth mayor, state representative—Mary Dondero was a local celebrity and a political force to be reckoned with.

Recognizing her unique place in the annals of the city and the state, Dondero said in her inaugural address, "That this election was the closest in the history of the city, that the ensuing results elected a woman as Mayor, a fact unthought of in the records not only of Portsmouth but throughout New Hampshire, has resulted in an avalanche of publicity."[5] She was quick to assure everyone that that avalanche would not distract her from her deep sense of responsibility, and outlined her goals for a "busier, better, cleaner Portsmouth" through a postwar rehabilitation of the city. "The city's business is an open book," she declared, and promised to set aside one day every two weeks "to meet [with] the people of Portsmouth to hear their complaints, their suggestions and to discuss their personal problems." Dondero was determined to be an easily accessible, responsive mayor with a commitment to open and honest government.[6]

Dondero apparently fulfilled her pledges to the people of Portsmouth; one year later, the *Herald* enthusiastically reported her overwhelming November 1945 reelection: "Mayor wins all Five Wards to Rout GOP. . . . Mayor Mary C. Dondero, first woman chief executive in the history of the City of Portsmouth, yesterday won an overwhelming victory in her quest for a second term. The totals: Dondero, 3,997; Ira A. Brown, 1,503. . . . In doing so she won a 2,494-vote victory over the same Republican opponent whom she barely nosed out by seven votes a year ago." The newspaper reported Dondero's victory to be "a definite upset for a normally Republican community" and a changing of the guard: "An aroused Portsmouth citizenry showed its confidence in Mayor Dondero's integrity and administration and repudiated the tactics of the Republican machine by reelecting her by an overwhelming majority and, with the same vote, riding the Republicans out of town on the well known rail." The *Herald* did not foresee the Republicans successfully regrouping and riding the same rail back into town during the next election.[7]

Annual reports for the city of Portsmouth are not available, and probably do not exist, for every year of the war. The two reports issued during Dondero's tenure as mayor, the 1944 report (published 30 June 1945) and a combined report for the years 1945–47, are a departure from previous reports. The pre-Dondero reports are routine financial statements, stark auditor's reports with little explanation of the numbers and no personal message from any city official. In keeping with her personal approach to her mayoral responsibilities, Dondero personalized the annual reports, making them "state of the city" reviews.

In her introduction to the 1944 document, Dondero wrote, "I feel that the people of Portsmouth should have an annual report each year showing, not only the financial condition of the city, but also giving a report of the different city departments. I shall endeavor to have this accomplished during my years in office." [8] She fulfilled this promise with the next report, which includes her inauguration addresses, an introduction outlining her goals and achievements for the city, and numerous pictures of city officials and street scenes.

Written with a warm conversational tone, the report conveys Dondero's compassion for Portsmouth's citizens and her dedication to open and transparent government. It is easy to understand why the *Herald* was so enamored of Portsmouth's first female mayor.

The *Herald's* obvious delight with Dondero's reelection was not an automatic partisan reaction—in fact, the paper repeatedly expressed discontent with FDR's New Deal politics and endorsed Republican Governor Thomas Dewey over FDR in the November 1944 presidential election.[9] The 6 November 1944 editorial endorsing Dewey accurately predicted the future, expressing concern about FDR's health and the unsavory possibility that his running mate would succeed him in the presidency: "Mr. Roosevelt has served three terms as president, but it is obvious that he has aged beyond his years. If Mr. Roosevelt were elected to another term, there is grave danger that Senator Truman would succeed him in the presidency. Few Americans would care to see in the White House a man raised to prominence by the sordid political machine of Boss Pendergast."[10] The paper thought Dewey capable of bringing "sanity to the welter of conflicting agencies now cluttering up the Washington scene and arguing among themselves because of Mr. Roosevelt's lack of ability to organize clearly the administration and federal government."[11] Clearly, given its other views, the newspaper's endorsement of the new mayor had more to do with her fresh approach to city government than the fact that she was a Democrat.

Dondero's 1 January 1946 second-term inaugural address began by acknowledging two important changes. First, she noted, "Last January 1st I entered office in the midst of the great World War II. Today, I enter office in the midst of the great problem of reconversion, with the weary world trying to attain a just peace." Secondly, she added, "Last year, I entered office for a period of one year. Today, the term of office is for two years." Unlike her speech one year earlier, filled with optimism and hope, this address hinted at a past year of frustration and political squabbling: "We must forget party politics. . . . To play politics at a time like this is a form of sabotage and a failing of the trust which was placed in us. . . . [W]e must not fail by the internal bickering of party against party — clique against clique. I would recommend to the City Council that appointments to be made for the coming two years be made on the basis of merit and ability, and not because of party affiliation."[12] The mayor alluded to political sabotage, but newspaper reporter Raymond Brighton addressed the issue more directly in his popular local history, *They Came to Fish*. He accused Republicans of undermining all Dondero's efforts, attempting "to frustrate each of her projects, whether good or bad."[13]

Dondero's unprecedented election prompts several questions, not the least of which is, how much did Portsmouth's wartime challenges and difficulties contribute to Dondero's success? Very little, answers Dondero's daughter, Eileen Dondero Foley. She attributes her mother's victory in November 1944 solely to her popularity with the people of Portsmouth.[14] It is Foley's opinion that her mother's success in Portsmouth politics had more to do with her patriotism, visibility, and acknowledged leadership abilities than any citizen concerns about Portsmouth's wartime environment. While the author shares Foley's assessment of her mother's enormous popularity, the fact that a number of other Democrats won election for the first time in November 1944 seems to point to other factors that may have contributed to the ascendency of Mayor Dondero and her party.

One can argue that the large influx of wartime workers and military personnel stressed city services as never before and made the entrenched Republican administration more vulnerable than in the past. The *Herald* repeatedly criticized Republican incumbents for slow, secretive, and bureaucratic practices when dealing with such challenges as dilapidated housing, a beleaguered police force, a community water shortage, and disputes with navy yard officials. It seems reasonable to assume that as problems mounted, the citizenry would become less tolerant of a business-as-usual government and look for a fresh approach with a change in leadership.

A wartime voter demographic shift may also have favored Dondero and the Democrats. Dondero's landslide reelection in November 1945 attracted the largest voter turnout (5,528) since 1934 (5,743). The high turnout and Democratic plurality were partially the result of a change in voting hours that enabled more shipyard workers to get to the polls. For the first time, the polls were kept open until 6 p.m. instead of closing at 4 p.m. Reportedly, "hundreds of navy yard workers voted after they finished their work for the day . . . lined up in the street waiting their turn to get into the voting place." Previously, day-shift workers "had been forced to vote in the morning before going to work or not at all." Dondero and other Democrats undoubtedly benefited from the change in hours that allowed more blue-collar Democrats to get to the polls.[15]

Two other shipyard boomtowns, Kirkland, Washington, and Seneca, Illinois, experienced Democratic landslides late in November 1944. The Kirkland newspaper, the *East Side Journal*, attributed the change in leadership to newcomers voting for the first time in the state. The paper linked political affiliation with length of residence and social class, implying that the thousands of industrial workers added to the rolls of the local precincts had skewed the vote decidedly in the Democrats' favor.[16] In Seneca, Republicans had outpolled

Democrats 283 to 255 in the 1940 presidential election—but four years later, after an influx of industrial workers, Democrats outpolled Republicans 1,014 to 775.[17] Boomtowns often took a bent toward Democratic candidates—Portsmouth was no exception.

What about Roger W. Lotchin's argument that women often formed the majority of the electorate with so many males absent? Did a preponderance of woman voters facilitate Dondero's election? Table 16, showing a breakdown of Portsmouth residents by gender, suggests the argument may have merit. Portsmouth had slightly more female than male residents in 1930, a larger majority in 1940, and a substantial majority in 1944. The estimated figures for 1944 reflect an average 34 percent increase in wartime population through 1943 and a reduction in the male population by 10 percent to account for military service. Even though the figures represent all residents, and not just eligible voters, it nevertheless appears that women would have been a decided

Table 16: Portsmouth Residents by Gender (1930–44)			
	1930	**1940**	**1944**
Women	7,250	7,610	10,197
Men	7,211	7,245	8,737

Sources: The 1930 and 1940 figures are from *Survey of Health and Welfare in the Portsmouth Defense Area,* August 1943, table in appendix entitled "Population Sex, 1930–1940." As indicated in this chapter, the 1944 figures are based on the 34.3% increase that the survey attributes to the entire area between 1940 and 1943, with a 10% reduction for males to account for military service. "Portsmouth Chamber of Commerce," 3. Box 2, Folder 1, "State Council of Defense, Local Committees: Portsmouth."

majority in the 1944 elections.[18] The research for this study did not find, and Table 16 does not speak to, the number of women registered to vote or the number who actually voted for Dondero. However, the table does support Lotchin's premise that women voters were often in the majority for wartime elections. This demographic may have worked to Dondero's advantage in her successful November 1944 and November 1945 elections. The male voter representation would have increased significantly by the November 1947 election, which may have contributed to Dondero's narrow defeat after her overwhelming victory in the previous election. Then again, her defeat may have been more the result of an aggressive Republican political machine, retooled and rededicated to regaining control of the city.

There is another important consideration when analyzing Portsmouth's female vote. Mary Dondero was enormously popular with families because of the attention she showered on sons and daughters leaving for military service. According to Eileen Dondero Foley, as a council member and later as mayor, her mother presented every recruit leaving for the service with gifts that usually included a carton of cigarettes, a box of chocolate, and writing paper. The presentations took place in the center of town outside Jarvis's Restaurant, after which Dondero, waving a large American flag, would lead the assembled group, accompanied by the small high school band, to the train station.[19] Bea Randall remembers her husband John being the recipient of gifts from Dondero when he left for boot camp in November 1942.[20] Eileen Dondero Foley recalls her mother doing the same for her in 1944 when she left Portsmouth for the Women's Air Corps. William Tebo missed getting Mary Dondero's going-away package because his parents drove him to Concord to catch the train instead; Dondero, determined to show her appreciation, later delivered the package to Tebo's parents to give to him.[21] Harold Whitehouse witnessed many of the ceremonious departures at the train station; it was his impression that "Mayor Mary C. Dondero made sure the draftees got on the train with a real gigantic send-off."[22] Dondero's honoring of departing recruits endeared her to many families and, unquestionably, garnered her many votes.

Her commitment to servicemen was not limited to ceremonial sendoffs. Blanche Washok recalled that Mayor Dondero "came down [to her home in the South End] to see my mother" to offer comfort when the family received a letter from the War Department reporting her brother Roy missing in action. [23] Dondero extended the same commitment and respect to Portsmouth citizens that she did to servicemen and their families. One author wrote, "While Mary Carey Dondero lived no one in this city made the final trip to any of the cemeteries—WASP, Catholic or Jewish—without her in attendance."[24] She was a beloved presence in the community and an acknowledged force on the political scene.

After winning by the largest plurality ever in 1945, Dondero lost the November 1947 election by the narrowest of margins. She initially lost by eight votes and, after several contentious appeals and a recount, lost by one vote to her Republican opponent.[25] Partisan politics ran rampant through the city during this period as the reorganized Republicans fought to regain control of city government. The Republican old guard, although badly shaken, had not been ridden out of town on a rail as the local newspaper reported two years earlier. It was Ray Brighton's opinion that, throughout her tenure, rivals viewed her as "a 'dangerous' Democrat in a town that really wanted to be Republican."[26] Even though the Republicans regained the mayor's office in 1947, the genie was out of the bottle; Democrats—and women—would be a force in Portsmouth politics in the future.

Though boomtown Portsmouth's political scene was contentious, there were, to the credit of both parties, no reported scandals or political graft. That was not the case in other boomtowns where the war brought huge federal contracts and equally large temptations to the public officials administering those contracts. In Kirkland, Washington, the city's treasurer, mayor, attorney, and one councilman resigned after being indicted on grand larceny charges involving government contracts.[27] Portsmouth's scandal-free political scene was mild in comparison. Although the final years of the war involved hotly contested elections and infighting, there was apparently no criminal activity. All had the best interests of their city in mind and were dedicated to securing its future.

Portsmouth historian Raymond Brighton was highly complimentary of Mary Dondero in his writings. His following comments help to complete an understanding of her place in Portsmouth history:

Photo 27: Mayor Dondero leading Portsmouth V-J Day Parade (August 1945). Courtesy Portsmouth Athenaeum.

Mrs. Dondero struck terror in all good Republican hearts. She had all the ruthlessness of any of the tough male politicians around town, and her femininity gave them fits because they never knew quite how to strike back. In her youth, as her later-in-life portraits show, Mrs. Dondero must have been one of the most beautiful women ever born here. She won a Miss Portsmouth pageant in 1918, although already the mother of three children. One of the first of her sex to go to the State Legislature, she became known as the "Sweetheart of the House," but that cognomen merely paid tribute to her looks. She was tough; she had to be to survive in her chosen career. . . . The writer was one of the reporters who covered her administration during the last years. . . . [T]here were few dull moments in Mary's time.[28]

In closing, Brighton paid her the ultimate compliment: "Love her or hate her, Mary Carey Dondero was one of the great Portsmouth personalities of the 20th century. The writer is privileged to have known her."[29] Mary Dondero's legacy in Portsmouth politics is large and secure.

CHAPTER 14
POSTWAR WORRIES

"Can the One Step Which Might Separate a 'Boomtown' from a 'Bust-Town' be Avoided or Must Portsmouth do an Economic Back-somersault."

James Tucker
Portsmouth Herald
4 August 1944

Not least of the challenges facing a wartime boomtown is what happens when the surge of activity subsides — a pitfall with which Portsmouth was all too familiar. Already by late 1943, the city's leaders were anxiously anticipating a postwar recession, perhaps considering it as certain as military victory. One local author wrote, "They did not forget the aftermath of the First World War: the abruptly closed shipyards, the exodus of work, jobs, and population."[1] Fearing a repeat of those conditions, officials realized the fate of their city depended on action — action that would change the expected postwar trajectory of dramatic shipyard cutbacks in production and workers. If the industrial machine across the river slowed — or, worse yet, closed — the local wartime economic gains would be lost forever. The powers-that-be in Washington had to be convinced to keep the shipyard open and active; that is exactly what Portsmouth's leaders set out to do.

World War I. The city's post–World War I recession woes dominated the planning for its future during the final stages of World War II. James Tucker wrote, "Everyone is equally certain that we should begin now and plan for the future. We remember conditions which prevailed locally after the first World war [sic], we have in mind the committees of Portsmouth citizens rushing to Washington for relief after the armistice had been declared and practically all work discontinued at the local navy yard; we remember how servicemen sold and peddled apples on the streets. These things we want to, if humanly possible, avoid after this global conflict has ended."[2] Such grim memories were not to be repeated.

The "cessation" of activity at the yard was, however, apparently in the eye of the beholder. To local leaders, the dramatic postwar employment cuts in 1920 qualified as a cessation of activity. Navy officials, on the other hand, thought the Portsmouth yard had fared better than most, arguing that they had protected it against severe cutbacks over the long haul. Responding to local concerns in May 1945, Vice Admiral E. L. Cochrane, chief of the Bureau of Ships, wrote, "Similar forebodings marked the approach of the end of World War I. Happily those forebodings never came to be realized . . . but on the contrary, while naval construction in almost every other category fell off to the vanishing point as a result of disarmament conferences, we were permitted to carry on a modest but continuous program of submarine development and construction in which the Portsmouth Navy Yard was given the lion's share of the work."[3] Both sides were correct. Portsmouth definitely suffered economically from defense cutbacks immediately after World War I, as did most of the nation. However, the yard was fortunate to have that "modest but continuous" workload during the 1920s when disarmament treaties caused new construction to disappear at one time or another from all other navy yards. Portsmouth enjoyed the most stable employment of any of the yards between 1917 and

1929, holding steady around 1,700 workers while employment levels at other navy yards fluctuated widely.[4] The Navy had similar long-range plans for Portsmouth after World War II, but city officials nervously sought absolute commitments that the Navy was reluctant to give.

For all the dire postwar memories fueling the fears of Portsmouth officials, it is curious that Portsmouth Navy Yard was, in fact, largely the cause of even more serious problems in Bridgeport, Connecticut, after World War I. Bridgeport's population exploded from 114,000 to 166,000 during the first war as its defense industries thrived: Remington Arms was producing rifles and bayonets, the Locomobile Company built trucks, and Lake Torpedo Company manufactured submarines. With the abrupt cancellation of war contracts, the relief rolls swelled to 37,750 people. Lake Torpedo Company closed in 1923 for lack of submarine contracts because the Navy, seeking to develop a government yard as the nation's preeminent builder of submarines, awarded all submarine contracts to Portsmouth during the 1920s. Bridgeport's battered economy — depressed even more by the Great Depression — barely survived until the next wartime boom in 1940.[5]

In 1941, Bridgeport's officials were less than enthusiastic about retooling its factories for armaments; with painful memories from the last war still fresh and ominous, they were "wary of an increase in plant capacity that would come back to bite them. . . . A local chamber of commerce official likened the situation to a cat that is being choked on cream." Cream and war contracts may taste good in the moment, but both could have dire consequences in the long run. Bridgewater officials, much like their Portsmouth counterparts, "rejoiced in their good fortune [of World War II government contracts]," but feared that "evil day when peace breaks out" and "leaves them in the lurch again."[6]

Portsmouth, for its part, was determined not to be left in the lurch.

World War II. Portsmouth's fears about a postwar recession were by no means unique. Historian Doris Weatherford wrote, "A postwar economic crash [nationwide] was widely expected. Many who formed their economic views in the twenties and thirties were fatalists who believed that depression was the capitalistic norm and prosperity the exception."[7] The *Herald* raised the initial postwar recession alarm with Franklin E. Jordan's series of articles in the summer of 1941. However, once the war swung into full gear, other issues pushed postwar concerns to the background for a couple of years. By mid-1943, the progress of the war was such that people became confident of ultimate victory and local concerns began to compete with global issues for attention.

A new term was introduced to the national vocabulary: *reconversion*.[8] Reconversion centered on the challenge of converting national industries from wartime to peacetime production. The questions were many: when to start, how fast to proceed, at what cost to the military's equipment and material needs to successfully conclude the two-front war, and reconversion back to what? One answer to the latter was: certainly not back to the economic conditions that existed immediately prior to the mobilization. The nation, like Portsmouth, sought something better. Mobilization had been a clear and easy decision to open fully the nation's production faucets to get the maximum wartime stream possible. Reconversion required careful considerations about what peacetime streams might be able to flow from the same faucets—and at what flow rates. Some faucets merely required tweaking; others required complete turnoff—with serious reductions in employment and repercussions to communities. The local challenge was to keep the Portsmouth

Navy Yard faucet open with a steady stream of submarines flowing through the yard—and officials in Washington, DC, had their hands on the faucets.

When it came to reconversion, Portsmouth had two advantages over many boomtowns. First, its dominant wartime industry, Portsmouth Navy Yard, had not mobilized to build a new product; it had continued to build submarines—just a lot more of them. Reconversion would involve simply an adjustment to production levels, not a complete retooling to produce something else. Second, and equally important, city officials decided not to leave their fate in the hands of Washington decision makers. Instead, they mounted an aggressive campaign to steer their postwar ship in the direction they wanted it to go. They would not wait for Washington to come to them—they would go to Washington.

In July 1943, with the Allies bombing Sicily and Sardinia in preparation for an invasion of Italy, the Portsmouth Chamber of Commerce launched its own campaign to keep the yard booming after the war. A preliminary plan called for a gradual tapering of submarine construction, the return of all farmed-out work to the shipyard, and private industry's use of whatever yard facilities the government did not plan to use. Local government and business leaders, congressional representatives, and shipyard officials united in commitment to these objectives.[9] The objectives would change over time; the commitment would not.

It was the opinion of the chamber of commerce that the federal government, having brought about the boom, was responsible for the prevention of the much-feared bust: "A further factor is that the Federal Government, having expanded the population and productive powers of Portsmouth, Kittery, and the environs, bears a direct and unavoidable responsibility to see that when contraction occurs, the least possible dislocation of services built to meet the war emergency but no longer needed in peacetime, and a large group of unemployed, should not be left as burdens upon the community."[10] The city should *not* be left — yet again — with blighted housing areas, the struggle to maintain excess services, and untold numbers of welfare candidates on the rolls.

Aggressive pursuit of a Navy commitment for shipyard workload began in late 1943 with another revision of the *Portsmouth Herald's* editorial platform. Having shifted from strong neutrality to a win-the-war stance in March 1941, the newspaper issued a new manifesto in late November 1943. This time the first plank of its platform required "Complete Victory Over the Axis with No Appeasement," while the second plank called for "A Just and Lasting Peace Enforced by a Truly United Nations." Expressing total confidence in the eventual outcome of the war, the editor wrote, "Today we know victory is a certainty, and while the hour may not be in sight, we know we are on the right road."[11] The third plank, "A Postwar Prosperity Plan for Greater Portsmouth," signaled the community's determination to refocus on the postwar era and actively court prosperity. The war by now was under control — Portsmouth's postwar future was not.

Five months before D-Day in Europe, well before the conclusion of the war, local leaders advanced their own D-Day campaign for Portsmouth. On 5 January 1944, the *Herald* editorial laid out a twenty-point plan for development, suggesting, "During the coming year many a cornerstone should and could be laid in the postwar building plans of the city."[12] Curiously, those resolutions included no mention of Portsmouth's ongoing contentious dealings with the Navy or the continuing struggle to upgrade local services and infrastructure. The city seemed eager to close the book on its wartime issues and begin laying the foundation for a brighter future.

Jordan updated his postwar concerns in a fifteen-part series of *Herald* articles in March 1944. This time he was even more emphatic that the shipyard's fate would determine the city's future: "Our navy yard is Portsmouth—whether we like it or not. Portsmouth's future fate will be determined by its dependence on the navy yard." The message was clear: Portsmouth's newfound prosperity would be short-lived if the economic engine across the river stalled—or stopped.[13]

Noting the importance of the shipyard money being pumped into the local economy, Jordan wrote, "Our navy yard provides incomes for almost four out of every five families and, indirectly, about one of every three service workers." There was one important difference between Portsmouth and many communities that had converted peacetime to wartime industries, he pointed out: Portsmouth had no prewar industrial base to resurrect after the war. "The city has practically no converted factories of machinery. This [income on which the city depends] comes from work done on government land, in government buildings, with government machinery, all designed to produce articles of war." So what would happen, he asked, when the navy yard returned to peacetime production and employment levels? Where would the excess employees go and how would the community compensate for the lost incomes? The yard-generated wartime prosperity had the potential to become more of a liability than a blessing. In Jordan's mind, the salvaging of Portsmouth Navy Yard was an all-or-nothing proposition for the city.[14]

Jordan saw no alternative to the chamber's plan to leverage the powers in Washington to ensure maximum workload for the yard. He expressed the plan in terms of tapping the coffers of a rich relative: "Actually, we have a very rich and very much alive uncle, commonly known as Uncle Sam. Our Chamber of Commerce took a look at this staggering amount of capital required and decided last summer that Uncle Sam was our best bet. If he could keep the yard going as near capacity as possible, an otherwise critical situation for Portsmouth would be solved."[15] The plan was simple; the challenge great. Civic leaders would have to get the rich uncle's undivided attention and convince him to buy into their plan.

Jordan properly assessed the area's most valuable postwar resource to be the large skilled workforce, which had grown to service the needs of the shipyard: "Among Portsmouth Navy Yard personnel are thousands and thousands of skilled workers. Most of them would starve to death farming, go bankrupt operating a tourist or restaurant business and, in fact have to be completely re-educated to make a living out of any other endeavor than that involving skill and craftsmanship."[16] This was in stark contrast to the prewar situation, when farming and tourism were the dominant regional occupations and industry had shunned the area because of a lack of suitable workers. The federal training programs had created thousands of welders, pipefitters, mechanics, and other craftsmen. The challenge was to maintain as much shipyard work as possible after the war to employ those tradesmen. A secondary challenge was to create other opportunities for this abundance of skilled workers. It was to these ends that the local chamber, city officials, and congressional representatives would dedicate their efforts.

As the city was pursuing its postwar plan, production intensity peaked at the yard in 1944—the year the yard delivered a record thirty-two submarines. The 17 February 1944 *Portsmouth Herald* announced an increase in work hours from 46 to 50 hours a week to meet the Navy Department's demand for more submarines: "A one half hour boost in the basic work day of Portsmouth Navy Yard workmen was ordered today by Rear Adm. Thomas Withers . . . two main shifts running from 7:30 a.m. to 4 p.m., and from 4 p.m. to 12:30 a.m. The current 10 p.m. to 6 a.m. shift is expected to work from midnight to 8 a.m. and will be limited to maintenance and emergency work."[17] Withers reportedly said, "The navy needs these additional ships; we'll build them."[18] And build them they did. Things looked good at the time, but conditions changed dramatically before the year was out.

The worst fears of city officials were realized in July 1944, when Assistant Secretary of the Navy Ralph A. Bard advised Commandant Withers that recent successes in the Pacific had reduced the need for submarines, requiring the cancellation of a considerable number of submarines from the current building program.[19] Portsmouth and the other submarine-building shipyards had become victims of their own success. Vice Admiral Cochrane, chief of the Bureau of Ships, explained the shipyard's dilemma: "Portsmouth, under Admiral Withers able leadership was just swinging into an astounding rate of production of submarines when three months ago, a review of the needs led to the reduction in the future program. I know this was a bitter disappointment to Admiral Withers as it was to myself. . . . You can readily understand that as our battles move farther westward the distances to be covered by our submarines in their hunt for new victims are correspondingly decreased. Our steadily mounting victories have given us need for fewer submarines and even that need is decreasing."[20] The tremendous success achieved by United States submarines had forced the Japanese navy and shipping to retreat to a smaller ocean area closer to their homeland. Instead of submarines, the Navy now urgently needed aircraft carriers, cruisers, amphibious assault ships, cargo carriers, and tankers to carry the fight to the Japanese. Portsmouth, streamlined for submarine construction, was not equipped, nor easily converted, to build any of the surface ships.

Faced with the first official notice of a shipyard reduction in force, the chamber published a study reiterating the need for the maximum possible postwar shipyard workload.[21] The lengthy and awkward title summarized the community's worst fears: "Can the One Step Which Might Separate a 'Boomtown' from a 'Bust-Town' be Avoided or Must Portsmouth do an Economic Back-somersault." The one step, of course, was continued high navy yard employment. Boomtown or Bust-Town? The question that had been on Frank Jordan's mind in the summer of 1941 continued to be the chief concern of city officials in 1944.

Another chamber study, "The U.S. Navy Yard: Portsmouth's One Big Industry," heightened the public's awareness of its dependency on the yard. Documenting local population and economic changes that had occurred during the war, the study reiterated the need for strong navy yard postwar employment. Citing a total of 12,981 New Hampshire residents employed at the shipyard, and assuming an average family size of four people, the study concluded that about 52,000 New Hampshire residents were dependent on a shipyard paycheck.[22] The chamber's estimate of family size may be high considering the probability of multiple family members working at the yard, but there is no avoiding the conclusion that the local economy was heavily tied to the shipyard.

The war had brought prosperity to many towns that, like Portsmouth, now feared the vacuum that threatened when those wartime industries shut down. Wilmington, North Carolina, was one of those towns. At the start of the boom, one author wrote, "The city became a latter day version of the Alaska gold rush as rural Southern farmers flocked to employment opportunities at the North Carolina

Shipbuilding Company." The yard expanded from an initial "training cadre" sent from Newport News Shipbuilding and Dry Dock Company in the spring of 1941 to a peak of 25,000 employees—about the same size as Portsmouth Navy Yard. Like Portsmouth, the North Carolina Shipbuilding Company made a significant contribution to the war effort, building 243 merchant and cargo vessels, including 126 Liberty ships. Attempts to keep Wilmington's yard open after the war were unsuccessful, resulting in the loss of a $20 million facility and an economic collapse.[23]

Lowell, Massachusetts, was another town that did not fare well after World War II. Marc Scott Miller wrote in *The Irony of Victory: World War II and Lowell, Massachusetts* about the sad postwar fate of that city, "World War II artificially stimulated Lowell's economy, orienting it towards military rather than civilian and human needs. Continued growth depended, in large part, upon continuing war production."[24] Little postwar retooling occurred in Lowell; the faucets were turned off and the city's economy imploded when its war production disappeared.

Local leaders feared Portsmouth might become another such tale of woe. An excerpt from "Taking the Home Front Pledge," a rough draft by an anonymous author found in the Portsmouth War Records, expresses that concern: "Portsmouth was a community profoundly transformed by the war, and became like many other communities in America, reliant upon a military industry for its livelihood. As early as 1943 some in Portsmouth were looking to the future even as they met the challenge of the present."[25] Officials became resolute in their determination to avoid the postwar fate of boomtowns like Lowell and Wilmington.

As the Portsmouth Navy Yard's workload declined, city officials and state legislators became even more zealous in their efforts to avert such a dire fate, accelerating their attempts to convince the Navy to assign the yard plenty of postwar submarine work. During the latter half of 1944, New Hampshire's congressmen lobbied relentlessly to secure work for the yard. Succumbing somewhat to that pressure, Vice Admiral Cochrane clarified the Navy's intention to give Portsmouth and Electric Boat preferential treatment because they were the "two leading yards on matters of submarine design."[26] According to Cochrane, the bulk of the cutbacks would occur at the other four yards building submarines, but Portsmouth and Electric Boat would "carry along on a reduced scale into 1947."[27] Senator Russell Tobey (R-NH) reassured the Portsmouth Chamber of Commerce on 29 August 1944 that he had extracted a pledge from Assistant Secretary of the Navy Ralph Bard guaranteeing the Portsmouth yard a fair share of the postwar submarine overhaul and repair workload. On 27 October 1944, during an address at the yard, Cochrane himself reassured four hundred employees about the Navy's intentions: "A workload of no small proportions is being retained at Portsmouth." The yard would continue "as a going submarine design building yard — to be ready to take us into the next period of development."[28] Yet these repeated verbal assurances failed to satisfy jittery city officials, who wanted ironclad commitments.

Three representatives from Ranger Lodge 836, International Association of Machinists, traveled to Washington in early December 1944 seeking work for the yard. In keeping with the Navy's elevated priorities for the weapons and equipment needed for the final push to Japan, the committee returned with a guarantee of work constructing pontoons for advanced bases — pontoons, not submarines.[29] The shipyard's highly skilled workers and vastly expanded infrastructure, which had produced thirty-two submarines in 1944, would be little challenged with the construction of pontoons. The shipyard was greatly overqualified for this type of work. Was this a telltale sign of the future? Was the yard's efficient, streamlined production of submarines about to be converted to the manufacture of whatever miscellaneous items the Navy might need at the time?

In May 1945, Vice Admiral Cochrane wrote Representative Charles E. Morrow (D-NH), "I can assure you that the navy department definitely has no intention of eliminating Portsmouth from its roster of active navy yards in the postwar period. Whatever the extent to which the navy may be permitted to carry on a peacetime program of ship construction and fleet maintenance, the Portsmouth Navy Yard may count on receiving its fair share of participation in the program."[30] The Navy's assurances kept coming, but always couched in disturbing caveats about an unknown future for its shipbuilding programs. What would Portsmouth's promised "fair share" of that unknown future be? A "fair share" of a drastically scaled back submarine construction program could leave the shipyard a shadow of its former self. City officials remained concerned.

In August 1945, the yard returned to a five-day, forty-hour workweek for the first time in five years. At the same time, yard officials discontinued the third (night) shift and announced plans to return to one-shift operations as soon as possible.[31] Signs of drastic reductions were everywhere. Frequent rumors and fears about employment cuts were rampant in late 1945 and early 1946, followed quickly by more reassurances from the Navy and congressmen that the yard would receive fair treatment. None denied that the reductions were coming; all claimed they would be as gradual as possible. A chamber report at the close of 1945 expressed satisfaction to date with the community's efforts to

328

control the reduction in workforce at the yard: "Because of the continuing efforts which the Chamber of Commerce inaugurated in July 1943 to soften this economic blow and because of like efforts by organized labor at the yard, the local community has not yet suffered severely in a business way. Work has been tapered off, arrangements are being made eventually to return farmout work manufacturing processes to the yard . . . new types of work have been found to help take up the slack and more repair work has been sent to Portsmouth."[32] This expressed satisfaction would wane in the coming months when employment reductions were greater than expected.

Mayor Dondero could not have been more aggressive in her efforts to secure future work for the navy yard. Her trip to Washington in late April 1946 included an audience with President Truman. According to Dondero, "President Truman stated that he was very much interested in the Portsmouth yard and said he was certain that he would see that Portsmouth would get its proportionate share of work." Dondero also met with Assistant Secretary of the Navy John L. Sullivan; Representative John McCormack (D-MA), the House majority leader; Senator David I. Walsh (D-MA), chairman of the Senate Naval Affairs Committee; and Senator Styles Bridges (R-NH). All pledged their assistance and promised Portsmouth would get its fair share of future work. Dondero's final meeting was with the president's labor advisor, John R. Steelman, who reportedly told the mayor that she had "apparently already met with all the Washington officials in a position to be of assistance. These important people were made aware by you that there is such a place as the Portsmouth naval shipyard." Following Dondero's example, in future years many would make the

Photo 28: Portsmouth V-J Day Parade at Market Square (August 1945). Courtesy Portsmouth Athenaeum.

trip to Washington to remind officials that "there is such a place" as the Portsmouth Naval Shipyard.[33]

After Dondero's visit, Vice Admiral Cochrane, in a letter to Bridges, sought once again to allay concerns about the shipyard:

> As a result of the favorable turn in the war the Portsmouth naval shipyard . . . received one of the earlier cutbacks in the navy shipbuilding construction program. . . . Submarines were among the first vessels of which the rate of production could be slowed down, and cancellation of orders for the construction of 98 submarines of which only four had actually had the keels laid was ordered in July of 1944. . . . This cutback coming earlier than

330

the general postwar cutback makes it understandable that the Portsmouth employees might have felt that there was discrimination against them. . . . [S]ubmarines will be among the first type upon which postwar construction is resumed. . . . It is the plan of the navy department to utilize the experience and skill of the employees of the Portsmouth naval shipyard in this work.[34]

As promised, submarine construction did return to the yard after the war, albeit at a greatly reduced rate. Instead of building dozens of submarines annually, the yard returned to the prewar levels of delivering one or two submarines a year, including nine nuclear submarines between 1959 and 1971. Lacking a significant new construction workload, the yard shifted instead toward submarine repair, maintenance, and overhaul work.

City officials had gotten Uncle Sam's attention and convinced him of the need to maintain Portsmouth Navy Yard as an integral part of the nation's defense arsenal. The glory days of building dozens of submarines a year were long gone—never to return. Instead, as repeatedly promised by Navy officials, the yard has received a steady flow of submarine work over the years, to the mutual benefit of both the U.S. Navy and the city of Portsmouth. The yard has compiled an enviable record of successes in submarine design, construction, and, most recently, overhaul and repair work. Concurrent with those accomplishments, as hoped by those who spearheaded the postwar drive to secure a future for the yard, Portsmouth has prospered.

CONCLUSION

Our navy yard is Portsmouth—whether we like it or
not. Portsmouth's future fate will be determined by its
dependence on the navy yard.

Franklin E. Jordan
Portsmouth Herald
Managing Editor
21 March 1944

Portsmouth's World War II legacy is well hidden. The
city's narrow streets, which offer frequent glimpses
into its heyday during the era of sailing ships and
colonial struggles, reveal little of the events that occurred on
those same streets during World War II. The restoration
projects, which have recaptured eighteenth-century
neighborhoods, attract an increasing number of tourists, who
delight in revisiting that era. Portsmouth is a bustling town
that thrives on its past—primarily its colonial past. Yet it is
the transformation that occurred during World War II that
revitalized the city and equipped it to move so boldly into the
future that it enjoys today.

Where is the evidence of that wartime transformation? It
is certainly not on the streets of the city where hordes of
sailors once roamed. Today tourists browse quaint shops and
linger in gourmet restaurants near—or possibly in—the same
buildings that were once sailors' watering holes. There is no
sign along the Memorial Bridge of the prostitutes and
wayward girls who once lined the span in anticipation of a
productive evening. The notorious Dolphin Hotel, the

destination of many of those sailors and their "dates," burned to the ground in 1969. The attractive and spacious new Portsmouth Library has replaced the small armory where local guardsmen drilled to maintain their efficiency. Landmarks associated with boomtown Portsmouth are gone or are fast disappearing, as redevelopment envelops the city. Others are disguised and not immediately obvious to the casual observer.

The site that offered servicemen wholesome entertainment, the USO Building, still stands, but it ceased to cater to servicemen shortly after the war when the city bought it to use as a community center, which eventually became the Connie Bean Recreation Center. A few years ago, the city sold the property to a developer who is currently erecting a five-story condominium complex on the site of the gymnasium where Portsmouth girls once danced with young sailors and soldiers. The developer must maintain the exterior of the former USO Building because it is a historic site, but the library and game rooms, the pool tables and chapel, all the traces of the submarine sailors who spent endless hours before departing the shipyard en route to war will be lost forever.[1]

Time has camouflaged the forts of the once formidable Portsmouth Harbor Defense System as parks and recreation centers. Fort Dearborn is now Odiorne Point State Park, where the popular Seacoast Science Center resides. The path from the parking lot to the science center passes a large mound covered with shrubbery and undergrowth, which hides the concrete encasement for a pair of 6-inch guns that once helped to protect the seacoast from German raiders. Within sight of the science center are two twin 55mm gun mounts, positioned to attack intruders who ventured too close to shore for the larger guns to engage.

Photo 29: Dolphin Hotel fire (1969). The view on the bottom is looking along High Street from Market Square. Courtesy Portsmouth Athenæum.

The bustle of New Castle's Camp Langdon has given way to an attractive park where picnickers and beachgoers while away the time. Fort Stark and Fort McClary are small state historical parks that offer glimpses of their martial pasts. In Kittery, Fort Foster has become a highly popular town park and recreation area, complete with fishing pier, hiking trails, and beach. Fort Constitution is on the grounds of a U.S. Coast Guard station; the public can visit the fort via a well-marked limited-access path. The fort captures its early American history setting, but shrubs and weeds conceal the concrete encasement for the World War II 6-inch gun battery. All the harbor defense sites are now peaceful seascapes with beautiful views—views that once served as vantage points for searching out surfaced enemy submarines or attacking planes.

One World War II artifact is proudly shown off several times a year by local citizens. Friends of the Pulpit Rock Tower occasionally open the structure and permit visitors to

Photo 30: Harbor Entry Control Post (HECP) at Fort Stark (2015). Courtesy author's personal collection.

climb the concrete steps of the eight-story tower to relive those anxious early days of World War II when watch standers scanned the horizon toward the Isles of Shoals for German raiders and the skies for German aircraft. Similarly, the Friends of Fort Stark open that fort's museum to the public occasionally to remind visitors of the historical significance of the battery remnants and the stained and crumbling Harbor Entrance Control Post (HECP). These "friends" must be applauded for their efforts to keep the public aware of these World War II relics, which otherwise would be abandoned, demolished, or hidden behind locked gates.

The city has a number of war memorials, but none dedicated to its World War II veterans. There are two local monuments to World War I veterans: the Portsmouth Plains memorial on the southern outskirts of the city, and the Kittery Sailors and Soldiers Monument at the approach to the Memorial Bridge. The new Memorial Bridge is dedicated "to all veterans from the two states," unlike the old bridge, which was specifically dedicated to World War I veterans.[2] The Sailors and Soldiers Memorial in Goodwin Park on Islington Street honors Civil War veterans. The city did have a World War II memorial at one time, but it, like many other World War II artifacts, has disappeared—sadly, it was torn down after being allowed to rot, fall into disrepair, and become an eyesore.

This short-lived memorial was the best Mayor Mary Dondero could come up with at the time. Eileen Dondero Foley suggests her mother's efforts to build a suitable World War II memorial lacked the support of the city council: "She always wanted a lot of things for memorials . . . to honor them [the veterans] and the city council wasn't always in back of this kind of thing."[3] In her inaugural address of 1 January

Photo 31: Mayor Dondero dedicating World War II Memorial (1946).
Courtesy Strawbery Banke Museum.

1945, Dondero proposed "a temporary memorial of some sort to honor our fighting men and women until such time as a permanent one will be in readiness."[4] In her next inaugural address, she proposed "a live memorial honoring the veterans of World War II in the form of an auditorium."[5] Her recommendations for a temporary memorial were fulfilled — and no more. In February 1984, the *Portsmouth Herald* explained the sad demise of the city's wooden monument to World War II veterans: "One month after World War II ended a wooden scroll was erected on the lawn of the old court house on State Street with the names of all local veterans inscribed in calligraphic letters. But the ink began to run from the effects of weather, the wood began to rot, and the scroll fell into disrepair. Five years later, Portsmouth was destined to become a city without a monument, when the tablet was torn down as an eyesore and traffic hazard."[6] The city has fallen far short of Mayor Dondero's expectations for a World War II veterans' memorial. How prophetic that time first blurred the names on this short-lived memorial that then fell into disrepair and vanished—so many memories and artifacts of that era have suffered a similar fate.

In 1923, five-year-old Eileen Dondero dedicated the original Memorial Bridge across which thousands of sailors later walked to reach their Portsmouth watering holes. She also dedicated the new bridge in 2013, some ninety years later, after having contributed a lifetime of service to the city. At the start of Mary Dondero's second term as mayor, in January 1946, her twenty-seven-year-old daughter, Eileen, won election as city clerk, making her the first female city clerk in Portsmouth's history. Following in her mother's footsteps, Eileen Dondero Foley went on to serve eight terms, totaling eighteen years, as the mayor of Portsmouth—1968 to 1972 and again from 1984 to 1998. She also served seven terms as a New Hampshire state senator. Her election in 1984 marked the beginning of twenty-two continuous years during which women held the position of mayor in the city of Portsmouth. Since 1944, Portsmouth has been largely a progressive Democratic city with women filling many important political offices, following the trail blazed by Mary Dondero and her daughter. Dondero Elementary School honors the dynamic mayor who boldly led the city into the postwar era. Time should not be permitted to dim the public's appreciation of the woman whose name graces that school nor her wartime contributions to the city that she loved so dearly.

The swift Piscataqua River and serene Great Bay show few ill effects of wartime pollution, but protection of these waters continues to be a challenge. The dawning public awareness of water pollution at the close of the war resulted in enforceable legislation and sewage treatment plants that have curbed the uncontrolled discharge of raw sewage and industrial effluents. The discharges from wastewater treatment plants, however, still add nitrogen to the bay, contributing to the killing of the eelgrass needed by oysters, crabs, and lobsters to spawn and survive. Other environmental threats have emerged: nitrogen-laden runoff from the paved parking lots of gargantuan malls and heavily fertilized fields is now the primary pollutant of local waters. Protection of the bay remains a never-ending battle.

As the numbers of those who were there have dwindled, time has eroded the public's appreciation of the World War II home-front challenges and sacrifices. Rationing remains a distant, nostalgic, and life-changing memory for the members of the Greatest Generation. Having suffered through the Great Depression, followed immediately by wartime rationing, many of them have never taken prosperity for granted. The concept of rationing is difficult to grasp for patrons dining on gourmet meals at Portsmouth's upscale restaurants. In today's world of plenty, the thought of a nation's citizenry doing without for the sake of a universal cause is an unfamiliar concept. Sacrifice and commitment are much less in demand nowadays.

The three government-built housing areas, Pannaway Manor, Wentworth Acres (now Mariner's Village), and Admiralty Village, continue to exist in various stages of completion and renovation. Over the years, owners' upgrades and renovations have camouflaged the homes once criticized for the "monotony created by the unchanged proportions of the houses."[7] Built to critical reviews at the time, many of these homes survived to become World War II artifacts of a sort—visual reminders of the region's urgent housing needs to accommodate an exploding population during its boom years.

The abundance of skilled workers turned out by the federal training and shipyard apprentice programs has attracted numerous industries that had previously avoided

Portsmouth because of a shortage of skilled tradesmen. The federal training courses evolved into state vocational schools, which have expanded over the years to address specific employer needs. The shipyard's need for welders, pipefitters, and other shipbuilding tradesmen has evolved to include employees with computer skills and advanced technical training. The required skill sets have changed, but the commitment to provide state-of-the-art employee training to attract industry and employers to the seacoast has never wavered. Women, who vacated their newly found industrial jobs when the men came home from war, returned to the workplace in large numbers a few years later, assuming positions of ever-increasing responsibility in all trades and occupations.

The shipyard itself is the region's best visual reminder of the World War II boom years. From the Portsmouth side of the river, it looks much as it did during the war. The large triangular fitting-out pier, constructed during the war to accelerate production, still juts into the river toward Prescott Park. The prominent structure containing the building ways, which launched unprecedented numbers of submarines, still dominates the waterfront. The building ways have been inactive since the early 1970s when the yard delivered its last new submarine, the nuclear USS *Sand Lance* (SSN-660). Since then the yard has specialized in the overhaul, repair, and refueling of nuclear submarines. A closer look at the yard's infrastructure within the restricted industrial area would reveal many upgrades to accommodate that mission.

The shipyard's wartime legacy lives on in the minds and spirits of the current employees, many of whom are descendants of the workers who accomplished the production miracles that contributed so much to winning the war. Families with several generations who have worked at the yard are quite common. As the employment torch has been passed from generation to generation, so too has the responsibility to uphold the yard's reputation for excellence. The current employees' pride in workmanship and can-do attitude is deeply rooted in the yard's spectacular performance during World War II when fathers and grandfathers achieved record-setting production.

The yard continues to be the economic engine for the region, although it employs far fewer workers now than it did during the war—currently about 5,000, compared to more than 20,000 in 1944. As promised at the end of the war, the yard has received its fair share of the Navy's submarine work over the years. In return, the yard has established a reputation for excellence in the repair and refueling of nuclear submarines — a reputation that has served it well when faced with occasional threats of reductions in force or closure. The public's reactions to those threats — groundswells of support—are reminiscent of the political lobbying and community activism at the close of World War II. That effort, which began with Frank Jordan's call for action in March 1944 and peaked with Mayor Dondero's audience with President Truman in 1946, has had a very positive and lasting effect on the city.

The postwar years have been very kind to the city of Portsmouth. Building on its industrial base, it has evolved into a working port, business hub, cultural center, and magnet for tourists seeking the charms of yesteryears. This transition was possible, in large part, because there was a strong economic base on which to build—a base rooted in a very competitive and highly respected shipyard. At the close of the war, the city leaders, recognizing the importance of the shipyard to their city's future, fretfully asked themselves, "Boomtown or Bust-town?" Thanks to their efforts, and those of their successors, the correct answer was—and still is—Boomtown!

NOTES

INTRODUCTION

[1] Milton Bracker, *New York Times*, 5 October 1941, "Portsmouth Tries to Adjust Life to an Influx of Men and Money." See Portsmouth War Records, File 1, Miscellaneous, W001, Portsmouth Library Special Collections, Portsmouth, NH.

[2] Philip N. Guyol, *Democracy Fights: A History of New Hampshire in World War II* (Hanover: Dartmouth Publications, 1951).

[3] Barbara McLean Ward, ed., *Produce and Conserve, Share and Play Square: The Grocer and the Consumer on the Home-Front Battlefield during World War II* (Portsmouth: Strawbery Banke Museum, 1994).

[4] *World War II Home Front New Hampshire*, video history documentary, John Gfroerer, producer, NH Humanities Council with Continental Cablevision, 1994. Hereafter John Gfroerer, producer, *World War II Home Front New Hampshire*; a video history documentary.

[5] Harold Whitehouse, *Home by Nine: The Real Story of Portsmouth's South End* (Portsmouth: Peter E. Randall, 2008).

[6] Jack P. Wysong, *The World, Portsmouth and the 22nd Coast Artillery: The War Years 1938–1948* (Missoula, MN: Pictorial Histories, 1997).

[7] Rodney K. Watterson, *32 in '44: Building the Portsmouth Submarine Fleet in World War II* (Annapolis: U.S. Naval Institute Press, 2011).

[8] The series was written by the newspaper's managing editor, Frank Jordan, to alert citizens that the mobilization in progress was about to change their community and their lives forever—and not necessarily for the better. Jordan addressed the impending population and economic booms and the potential effects these changes would have on the community. He predicted far-reaching consequences to public utilities, education, health, government, transportation, fire protection, police protection, recreation, and community welfare. His message was clear: Portsmouth's citizens needed to start planning now, in the summer of 1941, for the city they wanted to have when the rapidly approaching war was over. This booklet is especially valuable in defining Portsmouth on the eve of the war. Jordan was the first to emphasize the need for enlightened planning to avoid a seemingly inevitable postwar recession—an often repeated theme throughout all the sources.

[9] This survey was done at the request of the Advisory Committee on Welfare of the State Council of Defense. The Portsmouth Defense Area

342

included the New Hampshire towns of Portsmouth, New Castle, Newmarket, and Greenland; and the Maine towns of Kittery and Eliot. The report, more than two hundred pages in length, includes chapters dedicated to population changes, government, housing, health, family security, day care, nutrition, religious activities, and recreation. Knowledgeable people in each field, including high-ranking state officials, university professors, and local experts prepared each chapter. More than a dozen tables and graphs conveniently summarize a wealth of data. The result of the survey was a list of eighty-seven recommendations to improve the welfare of the Portsmouth Defense Area.

[10] Portsmouth's records are more complete than are those of most New Hampshire communities; however, they lack structure and organization. That said, the records are a valuable collection of the wartime experiences and remembrances of local residents

[11] The records are especially helpful in understanding the organizational structure that transmitted national policies through the state organization in Concord to the local Portsmouth council, which then relied on the cooperation of city officials for funding to implement civil defense directives. These records reveal an early citizen zeal for civil defense, followed by a gradual diminishing of enthusiasm as the war progressed and victory became more certain. As the threat subsided, seacoast residents longed for a return to normalcy. Local businessmen, in particular, eagerly sought relief from the reduced lighting and other civil defense requirements, which were hindering retail sales.

CHAPTER 1: PORTSMOUTH BEFORE THE WAR

[1] Wallace Nutting, *New Hampshire Beautiful* (Framingham: Old America, 1923), 76.

[2] *Survey of Health and Welfare in the Portsmouth Defense Area*, August 1943. Graph is constructed from figures in table titled "Population-Total Trend" in appendix and population discussion on page 18. Thayer Cumings Library and Archives, Strawbery Banke Museum, Portsmouth, NH, MS 96, Box 2, Folder 1, "State Council of Defense, Local Communities: Portsmouth." Hereafter *Survey of Health and Welfare in the Portsmouth Defense Area*, August 1943.

[3] *Cradle of American Shipbuilding: Portsmouth Naval Shipyard* (Portsmouth Naval Shipyard: Government Printing Office, 1979), 76.
[4] *Survey of Health and Welfare in the Portsmouth Defense Area*, August 1943. Table is constructed from information included in table titled "Population – Location, 1930–1940" in the appendix.

[5] *Portsmouth Herald*, 8 October 1941, "Rural NH Like Topsy–Still Growing," 1.

[6] www.seacoastonline.com/articles, 3 June 2009, "Meet Don Ricklefs: Master Carpenter," Tea for Two *Portsmouth Herald* column by Tammi Truax.

[7^7] www.seacoastonline.com/articles, 4 April 2007, "Louise McGee," Tea for Two *Portsmouth Herald* column by Tammi Truax.

[8] *New Hampshire: A Guide to the Granite State*, American Guide Series, written by Workers of the Federal Writers' Project of the Works Progress Administration for the State of New Hampshire (Boston: Houghton Mifflin, 1938), 223.

[9] *Portsmouth Herald*, 14 November 1941, "Gardner Describes Port City Problems Before N.E. Council," 1.

[10] *Portsmouth Herald*, 2 September 1939, "Let Us Rehabilitate Industrial Portsmouth," 1.

[11] *Portsmouth Herald*, 9 September 1939, "Portsmouth Industrial Associates," 4.

[12] Ibid.

[13] *New Hampshire: A Guide to the Granite State*, 223.

[14] *Portsmouth Herald*, 30 December 1939, editorial.

[15] Maury Klein, *A Call to Arms: Mobilizing America for World War II* (New York: Bloomsbury Press, 2013), 3.

[16] John Gfroerer, producer, *World War II Home Front New Hampshire*; a video history documentary.

[17] Ross Gregory, *America 1941: A Nation at the Crossroads* (New York: Free Press, 1989), 27.

[18] Maury Klein, *A Call to Arms*, 213.

[19] Ibid., 81–83, 341–343.

[20] Harold Whitehouse, *Home by Nine*, 53.

[21] *Portsmouth Herald*, 5 January 1940, "Poll Continues to Show Trend Against British Aid," 1.

[22] Peter Randall, *Hampton: A Century of Town and Beach, 1888–1988* (Hampton, NH: Peter E. Randall, 1989), 663.

[23] Maury Klein, *A Call to Arms*, 214.

[24] David M. Kennedy, *Freedom from Fear: The American People in Depression and War* (New York: Oxford University Press, 1999), 461.

[25] BuShips letter Ser No. 6140 to Commandant Portsmouth Navy Yard forwarding British Purchasing Commission letter of 27 December 1940. National Archives Records Administration Waltham, Massachusetts, RG 181, Portsmouth Naval Shipyard General Correspondence (Central Files), Box 43, Folder EP13/L9-3, "British Empire — Alterations, Repairs, Overhauls 1926–42." Hereafter NARA Waltham.

[26] Kennedy, *Freedom from Fear*, 470.

[27] George Brown Tindall and David E. Shi, *America*, 4th ed., vol. 2 (New York: W.W. Norton, 1997), 898.

[28] Quoted in Walter LaFeber, *The American Age: U.S. Foreign Policy at Home and Abroad Since 1896*, vol. 2 (New York: W.W. Norton, 1994), 395.

[29] Quoted in Ross Gregory, *America 1941*, 20.

[30] *Portsmouth Herald*, 18 March 1941, "This Is War," 4.

[31] Ibid.

[32] *Portsmouth Herald*, 27 May 1941, "Our New Platform," 4.

[33] Robert Dallek, *Franklin D. Roosevelt and American Foreign Policy, 1932–1945* (New York: Oxford University Press, 1979), 260.

[34] *Portsmouth Herald*, 20 March 1941, "New Basin Here Will Be Big Enough for Destroyers as Well as Subs," 1.

[35] Chief of Naval Operations letter Op23GEIK Serial/121523 to Commandant Portsmouth Navy Yard of 5 May 1941, "Request Number 112," NARA Waltham, RG 181, Portsmouth Naval Shipyard General Correspondence (Central Files), Box 43, Folder EP13/L9-3, "British Empire — Alterations, Repairs, Overhauls 1926–42."

[36] Bureau of Ships letter of 18 August 1941, "Items Issued to Foreign Governments Under Provisions of Public Law 11, 77th Congress (H.R.1776)," NARA Waltham, RG 181, Portsmouth Naval Shipyard General Correspondence (Central Files), Box 43, Folder EP13/L9-3, "British Empire — Alterations, Repairs, Overhauls 1926–42."

[37] *Administrative History: Portsmouth Naval Shipyard in World War II*, Portsmouth Naval Shipyard Museum Archives, Kittery, ME, 1.

[38] After the war, it was learned that Japan had three submarines (I-400, I-401, and I-402) larger than *Surcouf*, each equipped to carry three floatplane bombers. However, these submarines, built very late in the war, never saw any action. Under a veil of secrecy, the submarines were thoroughly inspected and then scuttled by the U.S. Navy, keeping the Soviet Union unaware of their existence. See http://combinedfleet.com/ships/i-400.

[39] *Portsmouth Herald*, 3 October 1941, "*Parthian* Once Sank Italian Sub; Free French *Surcouf* Unlucky," 1 and 9.

[40] *Portsmouth Herald*, 24 June 1941, "The Portsmouth of Tomorrow," 4.

[41] *Portsmouth Herald*, 25 September 1941, "It's an Old British Custom," 1.

[42] *Portsmouth Herald*, 24 September 1941, "Six British Sailors Injured in Crash," 1–2.

[43] Harold Whitehouse, *Home by Nine*, 52.

[44] Ibid.

[45] James W. Wensyel, "Home Front," *American History* 30, no. 2 (June 1995): *Academic Search Alumni Edition*, EBSCO *host*, 45.

[46] Ross Gregory, *America 1941*, 282.

[47] Oral interview with Eileen Dondero Foley by Barbara McLean Ward, 7 February 1991 at the Mayor's Office, City Hall, Portsmouth, NH in conjunction with the Strawbery Banke Abbott Store project.

CHAPTER 2: NAVY YARD MOBILIZATION

[1] New Hampshire Music Festival program cover, Portsmouth, 13 May 1944, Portsmouth Athenaeum, E0927.

[2] This chapter draws heavily from Rodney K. Watterson, *32 in '44: Building the Portsmouth Submarine Fleet in World War II* (Annapolis: U.S. Naval Institute Press, 2011) and Rodney K. Watterson, "Top Sub Shop," *Naval History*, February 2013.

[3] James W. Wensyel, "Home Front," 49.

4 Theodore Roscoe, *United States Submarine Operations in World War II* (Annapolis: U.S. Naval Institute Press, 1949). Japanese submarines and tonnage sunk by Portsmouth submarines are the author's counts from the appendix "Japanese Naval and Merchant Shipping Sunk by U.S. Submarines," page 527. Graph inside back cover shows 5,329,000 tons of enemy shipping sunk by U.S. submarines.

5 James W. Wensyel, "Home Front," 49.

6 *Portsmouth Herald*, 27 January 1944, "Four New Subs Launched for World's Record," 1.

7 Secretary of the Navy Frank Knox telegram of 27 January 1944 to Commandant Portsmouth Navy Yard, Subject: Commendation from Navy Department, NARA Waltham, RG 181, Portsmouth Naval Shipyard General Correspondence (Central Files), 1925-56, Box 18, Folder S-6, "Launching General, January 1944–47."

8 *Portsmouth Herald*, 19 July 1945, "Yard Is Tops in Sub Production," 1.

9 David Randall Hinkle, ed.-in-chief, *United States Submarines* (Annandale: Navy Submarine League, 2002); 114–15 provides the building times. The other sources noted under the table provide additional information on dry docks. Electric Boat had 11 building ways in 1940; 10 building ways were added with the Victory Yard in 1941. Manitowac Shipyard in Wisconsin built submarines on cradles and launched them sideways into a river too shallow for endwise launchings.

10 Gary Weir, *Building American Submarines 1914–1940* (Washington, DC: Naval Historical Center, 1991), 5.

11 Robert Connery, *The Navy and Industrial Mobilization in World War II* (Princeton: Princeton University Press, 1951), 266.

12 A. I. McKee, "Development of Submarines in the United States," *Historical Transactions 1893–1943* (New York: Society of Naval Architects and Marine Engineers, 1945), 347.

13 *United States Naval Administration in World War II, Bureau of Ships*, 1946, Navy Department Library, Naval Historical Center, Washington, DC, 7.

14 Local Shore Station Development Board letter to Senior Member of the Departmental Shore Station Development Board of 30 July 1934, NARA Waltham, RG 181, Portsmouth Naval Shipyard General Correspondence (Central Files), Box 1, Folder A1/Y1, "Local Development Boards Package 1."

[15] Ibid.

[16] Commandant First Naval District letter of 10 December 1936 to Commandant Portsmouth Navy Yard, NARA Waltham, RG 181, Portsmouth Naval Shipyard General Correspondence (Central Files), Box 1, Folder A1/Y1, "Local Development Boards."

[17] *Portsmouth Herald*, 16 May 1942, "New Method Puts Subs into Mass Production," 1.

[18] Assistant Secretary of the Navy Ralph A. Bard letter of 6 November 1944, Subject: Survey of Industrial Department, Navy Yard, Portsmouth, NH — Report No. 2 of Industrial Survey Division, National Archives and Records Administration, College Park, MD, RG 19, Bureau of Ships General Correspondence, 1940–1945, Box 785, Folder NY1/ A3, 3. Hereafter NARA College Park.

[19] Navy Department, SOSED (Industrial Manpower Section) letter of 1 May 1943 to Distribution List, NARA College Park, RG 38, Naval Operations General Correspondence, Box 151, Folder NY1, 1 July 1942 to 30 June 1943.

[20] "Naval Expansion Act, 14 June 1940" and "Naval Expansion Act, 19 July 1940," Naval Historical Center, http://www.history.navy.mil/faqs/faq59-21.htm and http://www.history.navy.mil/faqs/faq59-20.htm.

[21] Secretary of the Navy Frank Knox letter of 15 January 1941 to Chief Bureau of Ships and Commandants All Navy Yards, Subject: National Defense Shipbuilding Program — Expedition and Prosecution of Work, NARA College Park, RG 24, Bureau of Naval Personnel General Correspondence, 1941–45, NY1 (66-176) to NY2 (551-661), Box 1601, Folder NY 166-176.

[22] www.navy.mil/navydata/cno/n87/history/pioneers4.html#Thomas Withers.

[23] Oral interview with Fred White, 3 April 2006, at his home in New Castle, NH. White was the master rigger and laborer at the shipyard during the war.

[24] Ibid.

[25] Oral interview with William Tebo, 3 November 2006, at the Portsmouth Navy Yard Museum.

[26] Rodney K. Watterson, *32 in '44*, figure A-4 in appendix.

[27] Oral interview with Dan MacIsaac, 9 November 2006, at the Portsmouth Navy Yard Museum.

[28] David Randall Hinkle, ed.-in-chief, *United States Submarines*, 115.

[29] Theodore Roscoe, *United States Submarine Operations in World War II*, 175.

[30] Chief of Naval Operations Admiral F. J. Horne, letter of 26 April 1944 to Commandant Portsmouth Navy Yard, NARA College Park, RG 38, Naval Operations General Correspondence, Box 1182, Folder NY1, 1 July 1943–30 June 1944.

[31] *Portsmouth Periscope*, 27 August 1945, "72 Port City Subs Launched in 44 Months Play Vital Role,"1, Papers of Harold Caswell Sweetser, Portsmouth Navy Yard Supervisory Naval Architect, 1917–1958, Sweetser Family Papers, Milne Special Collections, University of New Hampshire Library, Durham, NH.

CHAPTER 3: HARBOR DEFENSE

[1] Charles T. McFarlane, *The Present War: Its Background and Related Developments* (New York: American Book Company, 1940), 57.

[2] Richard R. Lingeman, *Don't You Know There's a War On?: The American Home Front, 1941–1945* (New York: G.P. Putnam's Sons, 1970), 42.

[3] www.uboatarchive.net/ESFWarDiaryJan42CH2.htm. "Eastern Sea Frontier, War Diary North Atlantic Coastal Frontier," Chapter II, "The Submarines Arrive," 4–5.

[4] www.uboatarchive.net/ESFWarDiaryJan42CH2.htm. "Eastern Sea Frontier, War Diary North Atlantic Coastal Frontier," Chapter II, "The Submarines Arrive," 1–3.

[5] Ibid.

[6] Jack Rutledge, "U-boat Wreaked Havoc in Gulf of Maine," *Foster's Sunday Citizen*, date not available.

[7] John Gfroerer, producer, *World War II Home Front New Hampshire*; a video history documentary.

[8] Maury Klein, *A Call to Arms*, 514.

[9] Robert G. Kennedy, New Castle, NH, 25 January 1947, Portsmouth War Records, Portsmouth Library Special Collections, File 1, Civil Defense, W002, General Information.

[10] Quoted in Thomas C. and Rosemary F. Clarie, *Just Rye Harbor: An Appreciation and History* (Portsmouth: Portsmouth Marine Society, Peter E. Randall, 2005), 99.

[11] Richard R. Lingeman, *Don't You Know There's a War On?*, 47.

[12] Jack P. Wysong, *The World, Portsmouth, and the 22nd Coast Artillery*, 87.

[13] Portsmouth Defense Area Civil Defense Log Book #1 (1 January 1942–14 April 1942), 2 February 1942, 90, Portsmouth Athenaeum.

[14] www.patriotledger.com. "Recalling Nazi Spies off the New England Coast, and a Mystery on a Scituate Beach," *Wompatuck News*, Jim Rose, posted 11 November 2008,

[15] Assistant Secretary of the Navy John L Sullivan letter of 27 November 1945 to Laurence Shorey, secretary of the Portsmouth War Records Committee, Portsmouth War Records, File 3, WWII Records Ships and Submarines, W016, Portsmouth Library Special Collections, Portsmouth, NH.

[16] www.northamericanforts.com/East/New_Hampshire/Portsmouth/harbor.html. "Seacoast Forts of Portsmouth Harbor, New Hampshire – Maine."

[17] Ibid.

[18] Ibid.

[19] Jack P. Wysong, *The World, Portsmouth, and the 22nd Coast Artillery*, 12.

[20] Robert G. Kennedy, New Castle, NH, 25 January 1947, Portsmouth War Records, Portsmouth Library Special Collections, File 1, Civil Defense, W002, General Information.

[21] www.northamericanforts.com/East/New_Hampshire/Portsmouth/harbor.html. "Seacoast Forts of Portsmouth Harbor, New Hampshire – Maine," and Jack P. Wysong, *The World, Portsmouth, and the 22nd Coast Artillery*, 20.

[22] Jack P. Wysong, *The World, Portsmouth, and the 22nd Coast Artillery*, 36–37.

[23] Ibid., 48.

[24] CPO Frank Reda, World War II Journal, Portsmouth Athenaeum, Fld1, S807.

[25] Jack P. Wysong, *The World, Portsmouth, and the 22nd Coast Artillery*, 11–30, 42.

[26] Ibid., 48.

[27] Ibid., 37, 49–50,

[28] Historical narrative on sign at entrance to Odiorne Point State Park.

[29] "Harbor Defenses of Portsmouth," and Jack P. Wysong, *The World, Portsmouth, and the 22nd Coast Artillery*, 62–67,

[30] Jack P. Wysong, *The World, Portsmouth, and the 22nd Coast Artillery*, 82.

[31] Nelson H. Lawry, Glen M. Williford, and Leo K. Polaski, *Portsmouth Harbor's Military and Naval Heritage* (Portsmouth: Arcadia, 2004), 120.

[32] Ibid., 8.

[33] www.uboatarchive.net/ESFWarDiaryFeb42CH2.htm. "Eastern Sea Frontier, War Diary North Atlantic Coastal Frontier," Chapter II, "The Submarines Arrive,"1.

[34] Jack P. Wysong, *The World, Portsmouth, and the 22nd Coast Artillery*, 62.

[35] www.seacoastonline.com/articles, 3 May 2006, "Keep a Cool Head," Tea for Two *Portsmouth Herald* column by Tammi Truax.

[36] CPO Frank Reda World War II journal, Portsmouth Athenaeum, Fld1, S807.

[37] Robert G. Kennedy, "Harbor Defenses of Portsmouth."

[38] Oral interview with William and Eva Marconi by Valerie Wayne, 28 March 1990 at his home on Shapleigh Island.

[39] Portsmouth War Records, Portsmouth Library, Special Collections, Portsmouth, NH, File 2, Organizations W009C, U.S. Coast Guard, "Duties of the U.S. Coast Guard."
[40] Philip N. Guyol, *Democracy Fights*, 39–40.

[41] Robert G. Kennedy, "Harbor Defenses of Portsmouth."

[42] Ibid.

[43] Ibid.

[44] Jack P. Wysong, *The World, Portsmouth, and the 22nd Coast Artillery*, 90.

[45] CPO Frank Reda World War II journal, Portsmouth Athenaeum, Fld1, S807.

[46] Ibid.

CHAPTER 4: CIVIL DEFENSE

[1] Industrial Officer memorandum of 24 December 1941 to Shop Masters, NARA Waltham, RG 181, Portsmouth Naval Yard General Correspondence (Central Files), Box 14, Folder A3-2/LC Pkg #6, "Orders to Shop Foremen."

[2] Commandant Portsmouth Navy Yard John D. Wainwright memo of 5 February 1942 to Manager and Captain of the Yard, NARA Waltham, RG 181, Portsmouth Naval Base General Correspondence, Box 18, Folder S-7, "Docking — General."

[3] Harold Whitehouse, *Home by Nine*, 54.

[4] Quoted in Richard R. Lingeman, *Don't You Know There's a War On?*, 35.

[5] Quoted in Peter Randall, *Hampton: A Century of Town and Beach, 1888–1988*, 662.

[6] Jack P. Wysong, *The World, Portsmouth, and the 22nd Coast Artillery*, 10.

[7] Gary Skoloff et al., *To Win the War: Home Front Memorabilia of World War II* (Missoula, MT: Pictorial Histories, 1995), 84.

[8] John Gfroerer, producer, *World War II Home Front New Hampshire*; a video history documentary.

[9] James W. Wensyel, "Home Front," 47.

[10] "Taking the Home Front Pledge," a rough draft by an anonymous author, Thayer Cumings Library and Archives, Strawbery Banke Museum, Portsmouth, NH, MS 96, Box 1, Folder 5, "Business and Industry."

[11] New Hampshire State Council of Defense General Memorandum No. 1 of 28 October 1942, Portsmouth Defense Council Records, Box 1, File 4, Milne Special Collections, University of New Hampshire Library.

[12] Portsmouth Defense Council, Civilian Defense Report, Statistical Section, of 31 October 1942, Portsmouth Report Center memorandum of

22 November 1943, Portsmouth Defense Council Records, Box 2, File 11, Milne Special Collections, University of New Hampshire Library.

[13] www.seacoastonline.com/articles, 2 January 2008, "Mickey Hussey Remembers Small-Town Portsmouth," Tea for Two, *Portsmouth Herald* column by Tammi Truax.

[14] Portsmouth War Records, Portsmouth Library Special Collections, Portsmouth, NH, File 1, Civil Defense, W002, Civilian Defense, "Warning District."

[15] Portsmouth Defense Area Civil Defense Log Book #1 (1 January 1942–14 April 1942), 20 January 1942, 50–55, Portsmouth Athenaeum.

[16] Portsmouth Report Center memorandum of 22 November 1943, Portsmouth Defense Council Records, Box 1, File 21, Milne Special Collections, University of New Hampshire Library.

[17] Portsmouth War Records, Portsmouth Library Special Collections, Portsmouth, NH, File 3, Miscellaneous, "Rumored Invasion," W001.

[18] Portsmouth War Records, Portsmouth Library Special Collections, Portsmouth, NH, File 3, Miscellaneous, "Canadian Bombers Land at Greenland," W001.

[19] Ibid.

[20] Ibid.

[21] New Hampshire State Council of Defense letter of 5 May 1942 to Acting Chief Portsmouth Defense Council, Portsmouth Defense Council Records, Box 2, File 10, Milne Special Collections, University of New Hampshire Library.

[22] New Hampshire State Council of Defense letter of 5 May 1942 to Acting Chief Portsmouth Defense Council, Portsmouth Defense Council Records, Box 1, File 1, Milne Special Collections, University of New Hampshire Library.

[23] New Hampshire State Council of Defense Protection Memorandum No. 1, "Personal Protection Against Gas," of 23 June 1942 to All Local Defense Chairmen and Chief Air Raid Wardens, Portsmouth Defense Council Records, Box 1, File 1, Milne Special Collections, University of New Hampshire Library.

[24] New Hampshire State Council of Defense Operations Letter No. 46 of 4 November 1942 to All Local Defense Chairmen and Chief Air Raid Wardens, forwarding "New Procedures for Bomb Reconnaissance,

Unexploded Bombs" of 1 October 1942. Portsmouth Defense Council Records, Box 1, File 5, Milne Special Collections, University of New Hampshire Library.

[25] New Hampshire State Council of Defense letter of 20 March 1944 to Local Defense Chairmen and Chief Air Raid Wardens, Portsmouth Defense Council Records, Box 1, File 11, Milne Special Collections, University of New Hampshire Library.

[26] Oral interview with Harold Whitehouse, 5 November 2014, at the Portsmouth Library.

[27] *Portsmouth Herald*, 29 January 1942, "Cannon to Warn of Air Raids on Great Bay Ice," 1.

[28] Peter Randall, *Hampton: A Century of Town and Beach, 1888–1988*, 666.

[29] Air raid warden's World War II poster, Portsmouth Athenaeum, MS081 Box 1, F18.

[30] Portsmouth City Planning Board Report of 2 November 1942, Portsmouth Defense Council Records, Box 3, File 11, Milne Special Collections, University of New Hampshire Library.

[31] Acting Chairman Civilian Defense Portsmouth letter of 13 August 1943 to Director State Council of Defense, Portsmouth Defense Council Records, Box 1, File 11, Milne Special Collections, University of New Hampshire Library.

[32] Ibid.

[33] Quoted in Thomas C.and Rosemary F. Clarie, *Just Rye Harbor,* 103.

[34] John Gfroerer, producer, *World War II Home Front New Hampshire;* a video history documentary.

[35] Quoted in Thomas C. and Rosemary F. Clarie, *Just Rye Harbor,* 98.

[36] Tebo interview, 3 November 2006.

[37] Gary Skoloff et al., *To Win the War: Home Front Memorabilia of World War II.*

[38] Harold Whitehouse, *Home by Nine,* 55.

[39] Helena Huntington Smith, "Are America's Civilians Ready for Attack?" *Reader's Digest,* 1942. Quoted in Sharon M. Hanes and Allison McNeill,

American Home Front in World War II: Primary Sources (Detroit: Thomson Gale, UXL, 2006), 59.

[40] James W. Wensyel, "Home Front," 48.

[41] Ibid., 47.

[42] Thomas C. and Rosemary F. Clarie, *Just Rye Harbor,* 101.

[43] *Portsmouth Herald*, 8 December 1942, "Defense Official Gives New Dimout Rule for Stores," 1.

[44] Headquarters First Service Command Dimout Regulations for New England Revised and Amended as of May 31, 1943, Section III, 2, paragraphs a and b, The Dimout Area, New Hampshire, Portsmouth Defense Council Records, Box 1, File 35, Milne Special Collections, University of New Hampshire Library.

[45] Ibid., 1.

[46] Acting Chairman Civilian Defense Portsmouth letter of 11 May 1942 to Chairman Rockingham County Defense, Portsmouth Defense Council Records, Box 1, File 20, Milne Special Collections, University of New Hampshire Library.

[47] Rockingham County Chairman Alvin F. Redden letter of 14 May 1942 to Governor Blood, Portsmouth Defense Council Records, Box 1, File 2, Milne Special Collections, University of New Hampshire Library.

[48] Headquarters First Corps Area letter of 19 May 1942 to Governor of the State of New Hampshire, Portsmouth Defense Council Records, Box 1, File 1, Milne Special Collections, University of New Hampshire Library.

[49] New Hampshire State Council of Defense Protection letter of 17 June to Portsmouth Civil Defense Committee, Portsmouth Defense Council Records, Box 1, File 2, Milne Special Collections, University of New Hampshire Library.

[50] Acting Chairman Portsmouth Civilian Defense letter of 13 May 1942 to Governor of the State of New Hampshire, Portsmouth Defense Council Records, Box 1, File 34, Milne Special Collections, University of New Hampshire Library.

[51] Commander First Corps Area letter of 19 May 1942 to Governor of the State of New Hampshire, Portsmouth Defense Council Records, Box 1, File 1, Milne Special Collections, University of New Hampshire Library.

[52] Acting Chairman Portsmouth Council of Defense letter of 24 May 1942 to Executive Secretary State Council of Defense, Portsmouth Defense Council Records, Box 1, File 1, Milne Special Collections, University of New Hampshire Library.

[53] Headquarters First Service Command Dimout Regulations for New England, Revised and Amended as of 31 May 1943, paragraph 7, pg 5, Portsmouth Defense Council Records, Box 1, File 5, Milne Special Collections, University of New Hampshire Library.

[54] Portsmouth Defense Council Blackout Chairman letter of 28 May 1942 to Chairman Portsmouth Defense Council, Portsmouth Defense Council Records, Box 1, File 20, Milne Special Collections, University of New Hampshire Library.

[55] Chairman Gerald D. Foss letter of 19 February 1943 to Director State Council of Defense, Portsmouth Defense Council Records, Box 1, File 8, Milne Special Collections, University of New Hampshire Library.

[56] Director State Council of Defense, Noel T. Wellman, letter of 16 December 1943 to Chairman Portsmouth Defense Council, Portsmouth Defense Council Records, Box 1, File 13, Milne Special Collections, University of New Hampshire Library.

[57] Chairman Portsmouth Civilian Defense letter of 1 April 1942 to Governor Blood, Portsmouth Defense Council Records, Box 1, File 34, Milne Special Collections, University of New Hampshire Library.

[58] Headquarters First Service Command Dimout Regulations for New England, Revised and Amended as of 31 May 1943, paragraph 17, pg 9, Portsmouth Defense Council Records, Box 1, File 5, Milne Special Collections, University of New Hampshire Library.

[59] Portsmouth Council of Defense letters of 18 December 1942, 2 February 1943, and 12 February 1943 to State Council of Defense, Portsmouth Defense Council Records, Box 1, Files 6 and 8, Milne Special Collections, University of New Hampshire Library.

[60] Headquarters First Service Command, Boston, Massachusetts, letter of 8 December 1942 to Secretary-Treasurer Massachusetts Farm Bureau Federation, Portsmouth Defense Council Records, Box 1, File 6, Milne Special Collections, University of New Hampshire Library.

[61] *Portsmouth Herald*, 3 December 1943, "Street Lights Bright Again," 1.

[62] Peter Randall, *Hampton: A Century of Town and Beach, 1888–1988,* 666.

63 Portsmouth Defense Council, Civilian Defense Report, Statistical Section, of 31 October 1942, Portsmouth Report Center memorandum of 22 November 1943, Portsmouth Defense Council Records, Box 2, File 11, Milne Special Collections, University of New Hampshire Library.

64 Quoted in *Hampton Union*, 9 October 1974, "Auxiliary Police Photo Follow Up."

65 Portsmouth War Records, Portsmouth Library Special Collections, Portsmouth, NH, File 2, organizations, W01009C, U.S. Coast Guard, "Duties of the U.S. Coast Guard."

66 Chairman Portsmouth Civilian Defense letter of 1 April 1942 to Governor Blood, Portsmouth Defense Council Records, Box 1, File 34, Milne Special Collections, University of New Hampshire Library.

67 Portsmouth Council of Defense letter of 4 June 1943 to State Council of Defense, Portsmouth Defense Council Records, Box 1, Files 6 and 8, Milne Special Collections, University of New Hampshire Library.

68 Quoted in statement by Governor Robert O. Blood of 6 October 1943, Portsmouth Defense Council Records, Box 1, File 12, Milne Special Collections, University of New Hampshire Library.

69 Statement by Governor Robert O. Blood of 6 October 1943, Portsmouth Defense Council Records, Box 1, File 12, Milne Special Collections, University of New Hampshire Library.

70 Joint statement by the United States Office of Civilian Defense and East Coast Conference of State Defense Council Directors of 26 October 1943, Portsmouth Defense Council Records, Box 1, File 12, Milne Special Collections, University of New Hampshire Library.

71 Amendment to Executive Order of Governor and Council of 2 June 1943 Suspending the Enforcement of Revised Laws, chapter 119, section 7, and promulgating Certain Dimout Regulations of 1 November 1943, Portsmouth Defense Council Records, Box 1, File 34, Milne Special Collections, University of New Hampshire Library.

72 Chairman Portsmouth Council of Defense letter of 5 November 1943 to Governor of New Hampshire, Portsmouth Defense Council Records, Box 1, File 34, Milne Special Collections, University of New Hampshire Library.

73 State Council of Defense letters of 7 and 10 February 1944 to All Local Defense Chairmen, Portsmouth Defense Council Records, Box 1, File 34, Milne Special Collections, University of New Hampshire Library.

CHAPTER 5: LIBERTY TOWN

[1] Harold Whitehouse, *Home by Nine*, 58.

[2] "Prostitution in Portsmouth (Red Light District)," reprinted from web page Seacoast NH.com, 2004, hard copy on file in Portsmouth, NH, Public Library, Local History Vertical File.

[3] Kimberly E. Crisp, "Water Street Remembered," history honors thesis, University of New Hampshire, 1996, 78.

[4] Ray Brighton, *The Prescott Story* (New Castle, NH: Portsmouth Marine Society, 1982), 59.

[5] *Portsmouth Herald*, 14 November 1917, "Civic League Attacks Portsmouth Morals," 1.

[6] Kimberly E. Crisp, "Water Street Remembered," 2–3.

[7] Ray Brighton, *The Prescott Story*, 53, 72–73.

[8] Ross Gregory, *America 1941*, 42.

[9] The author observed the street map in the box office window of the Honolulu Theater on 31 January 2014.

[10] *Portsmouth Herald,* 2 October 1941, "Knox Issues Order," 1.

[11] J. Worth Estes and David M. Goodman, *The Changing Humors of Portsmouth: The Medical Biography of an American Town, 1623–1983* (Boston: Francis A. Countway Library of Medicine, 1984).

[12] Ross Gregory, *America 1941*, 42.

[13] Josephus Daniels, *The Navy and the Nation: War-time Addresses by Josephus Daniels* (New York: George H. Doran, 1919), 64.

[14] Allan M. Brandt, *No Magic Bullet: A Social History of Venereal Disease in the United States Since 1880* (New York: Oxford University Press, 1987), 162.

[15] Bureau of Medicine and Surgery Circular Letter No. 47-88 of 30 June 1947 to Commandants, All Naval District and River Commands, Subject: Venereal Disease Control Officers and Interviewers, NARA Waltham, RG 181, Portsmouth Naval Shipyard General Correspondence (Central Files),1925-50, Box 8, Folder A2-11/EN10 "Bureau of Medicine and Surgery."

16 Allan M. Brandt, *No Magic Bullet,* 170.

17 Richard R. Lingeman, *Don't You Know There's a War On?,* 100.

18 Allan M. Brandt, *No Magic Bullet,* 170–171.

19 Maury Klein, *A Call to Arms,* 715.

20 Ibid.

21 *Administrative History: Portsmouth Navy Yard in World War II,* Portsmouth Naval Shipyard Museum Archives, Kittery, ME, 86.

22 Portsmouth Naval Yard Medical Officer's Annual Report for 1942 of 19 January 1943, 4, NARA Waltham, RG 181, Naval Base General Correspondence, Box 10, Folder A9-1, "Sanitary Reports."

23 Josephus Daniels, *The Navy and the Nation,* 62.

24 http://history.amedd.army.mil/booksdocs/wwii/communicabledise asesV5/.htm, Chapter X, 143, 146.

25 *Survey of Health and Welfare in the Portsmouth Defense Area,* August 1943, Table 9, "Diseases in Portsmouth from September 1941–September 1942."

26 Ibid., Table 8, "Portsmouth Area Age Distribution (1940–1943)."

27 Ibid., 52, Table 9, "Diseases in Portsmouth from September 1941– September 1942."

28 *Portsmouth Herald,* 24 March 1945, "126 Patients Make Use of Penicillin in 10 Months at Portsmouth Hospital," 1.

29 Allan M. Brandt, *No Magic Bullet,* 162.

30 Ibid., 15.
31 *Portsmouth Herald,* 4 March 1942, "Lack of Vice in Portsmouth Lauded by Federal Men," 1.

32 *Portsmouth Herald,* 14 April 1942, "Civic League Attacks Portsmouth's Morals," 1.

33 *Portsmouth Herald,* 22 September 1942, "USO Council Discusses Need of Policewoman Serviceman's Programs," 1.

34 Ibid.

[35] *Portsmouth Herald*, 10 November 1942, "Health Board Head Denies Portsmouth Overrun by Vice," 1.

[36] *Portsmouth Herald,* 9 June 1943, "Portsmouth Police Act to Smash Vice Rackets," 1.

[37] City of Portsmouth Police Records (24 January 1940 to 23 June 1953), 9 April 1942, Portsmouth Athenaeum. Hereafter City of Portsmouth Police Records.

[38] City of Portsmouth Police Records, 20 June 1943.

[39] *Portsmouth Herald*, 7 July 1943, "Two Couples Found Guilty in Vice Case," 1.

[40] City of Portsmouth Police Records, 6 July 1943.

[41] *Survey of Health and Welfare in the Portsmouth Defense Area*, August 1943, "Health."

[42] *Portsmouth Herald*, 1 June 1944, "Navy, Police Fight Vice, Find Dolphin Hotel Chief Venereal Infection Source," 1.

[43] Whitehouse interview, 5 November 2014.

[44] *Portsmouth Herald*, 14 June 1944, "Mayor Promises Action Here on Vice Conditions," 1.

[45] Ibid.

[46] *Portsmouth Herald,* 20 October 1944, "City's Venereal Disease Record Shows Improvement, Report Says," 1.

[47] Ross Gregory, *America 1941,* 42.

[48] Richard R. Lingeman, *Don't You Know There's a War On?,* 89.

[49] In 1941 the infection rates for the total Army for gonorrhea and syphilis were 28.03 and 6.13 versus 13.04 and 2.56 for Hawaii-based Army personnel.http://history.amedd.army.mil/booksdocs/wwii/communicablediseasesV5/.htm, Chapter X, 472.

[50] Richard R. Lingeman, *Don't You Know There's a War On?,* 89.

[51] Ibid.

[52] Maury Klein, *A Call to Arms*, 533.

53 *Survey of Health and Welfare in the Portsmouth Defense Area*, 50, "Family, Security, and Day Care."

54 Ibid.

55 Ibid.

56 Allan M. Brandt, *No Magic Bullet*, 167–168.

57 *Reader's Digest*, May 1943, quoted in *Portsmouth Herald*, 14 May 1943, "A Spade a Spade," 4.

58 *Portsmouth Herald*, 14 May 1943, "A Spade a Spade," 4.

59 Allan M. Brandt, *No Magic Bullet*, 168.

60 *Portsmouth Herald*, 14 May 1943, "A Spade a Spade," 4.

61 Ibid.

62 John Gfroerer, producer, *World War II Home Front New Hampshire*; a video history documentary.

63 *Portsmouth Herald*, 14 November 1941, "Gardner Describes Port City Problems Before N.E. Council," 1.

64 Harold Whitehouse, *Home by Nine*, 57.

65 *Portsmouth Herald*, 8 December 1942, "Hewitt to Seek Aid of Yard Officials on Disorders Here," 1.

66 *Portsmouth Herald*, 11 December 1942, "Navy Bars Enlisted Men from Some Spots," 1.

67 John Gfroerer, producer, *World War II Home Front New Hampshire*; a video history documentary.

68 *Portsmouth Herald*, 19 March 1943, "Drastic Action Needed," editorial.

69 *Portsmouth Herald*, 5 April 1943, "Army, Navy Asked to Aid Police Here," 1.

70 City of Portsmouth Police Records.

71 Ibid.

[72] *Portsmouth Herald*, 18 January 1945, "Arrest Five Yard Sailors After Brawl," 1.

[73] Oral interview with Mel Low, 26 August 2014, Rye Congregational Church, Rye, NH.

[74] Oral interview with Alice Sussman by Judith Moyer, 19 October 1990, at her apartment in Portsmouth, NH, in conjunction with the Strawbery Banke Abbott Store project.

[75] Foley interview, 7 February 1991.

[76] Jack P. Wysong, *The World, Portsmouth, and the 22nd Coast Artillery*, 41.

[77] Foley interview, 7 February 1991.

[78] Ibid.

[79] *Survey of Health and Welfare in the Portsmouth Defense Area*, August 1943, 49, "State Council of Defense, Local Committees: Portsmouth."

[80] Oral interview with Eileen Foley, 30 August 2006, at her home in Portsmouth, NH; and Jack P. Wysong, *The World, Portsmouth, and the 22nd Coast Artillery*, 49.

[81] Oral interview with Bea Randall at the Mary Wentworth Home, Portsmouth, NH, 5 March 2014.

[82] Oral interview with Claire Flanagan Papatones at her Somersworth, NH, home, 26 February 2014.

[83] Foley interview, 7 February 1991.

[84] Foley interview, 30 August 2006.

[85] *Survey of Health and Welfare in the Portsmouth Defense Area*, August 1943, 49–50, "State Council of Defense, Local Committees: Portsmouth."

[86] Foley interview, 30 August 2006.

CHAPTER 6: HOMELAND PORTSMOUTH

[1] John Gfroerer, producer, *World War II Home Front New Hampshire*; a video history documentary.

[2] Oral interview with Morris Levy by William D. Moore, 12 Februatry 1991, at his home in conjunction with the Strawbery Banke Abbott Store project.

[3] Foley interview, 30 August 2006.

[4] Harold Whitehouse, *Home by Nine*, 56.

[5] John Gfroerer, producer, *World War II Home Front New Hampshire*; a video history documentary.

[6] G. Colati and Ryan H. Madden, "Victory Begins at Home: Portsmouth and Puddle Dock during World War II," in Barbara McLean Ward, ed., *Produce and Conserve, Share and Play Square*, 59, 68.

[7] William O'Neill, "The People Are Willing," in Frederick M. Binder and David M. Reimers, *The Way We Lived: Essays and Documents in American Social History, Volume II: 1865–Present* (Boston: Houghton Mifflin, 2000), 197.

[8] Peter Randall, *Hampton: A Century of Town and Beach, 1888–1988*, 666.

[9] State Council of Defense letter of 17 June 1942 to Chairman Portsmouth Defense Council, Portsmouth Council of Defense Records, Box 1, File 2, Milne Special Collections, University of New Hampshire Library.

[10] William O'Neill, "The People Are Willing." 197–8.
[11] Quoted in Thomas C. and Rosemary F. Clarie, *Just Rye Harbor*, 103–104 .

[12] Peter Randall, *Hampton: A Century of Town and Beach, 1888–1988*, 663.

[13] Helena Huntington Smith, quoted in Sharon M. Hanes and Allison McNeill, *American Home Front in World War II: Primary Sources*, 59.

[14] "Since Pearl Harbor: The American Red Cross Reports to the People," 1 April 1943, back cover, Thayer Cumings Library and Archives, Strawbery Banke Museum.

[15] *Portsmouth Herald*, 15 January 1942, "USO Opens New Hall Tomorrow," 1.

[16] http://www.seacoastonline.com/article/20090201/NEWS, "Connie Bean Stood Strong in Wartime, at Dances," Adam Leech, posted 1 February 2009.

[17] www.seacoastonline.com/articles, "Mickey Hussey Remembers Small-Town Portsmouth"; Whitehouse interview, 5 November 2014; Papatones interview, 26 February 2014; and Foley interview, 30 August 2006.

[18] Executive Secretary New Hampshire State Council of Defense Notice of 16 June 1942 to All Local Defense Chairmen, Portsmouth Council of Defense Records, Box 1, File 2, Milne Special Collections, University of New Hampshire Library.

[19] William O'Neill, "The People Are Willing," 198.

[20] Ibid, 52.

[21] Quoted in Gary Skoloff, et al., *To Win the War,* 112.

[22] James W. Wensyel, "Home Front," 55.

[23] Harold Whitehouse, *Home by Nine,* 52.

[24] Papatones interview, 26 February 2014.

[25] Tebo interview, 3 November 2006.

[26] Quoted in *Portsmouth Herald*, 1 September 1942, "Navy Yard Ups City Total," 1, 5.

[27] James W. Wensyel, "Home Front," 55.

[28] Maury Klein, *A Call to Arms,* 441.
[29] James W. Wensyel, "Home Front," 56

[30] James J. Kimble, *Mobilizing the Home Front: War Bonds and Domestic Propaganda* (College Station: Texas A&M University Press, 2006), 5.

[31] James W. Wensyel, "Home Front," 56.

[32] James J. Kimble, *Mobilizing the Home Front,* 6–7, 131.

[33] James W. Wensyel, "Home Front," 56.

[34] Harold Whitehouse, *Home by Nine,* 54.

[35] Foley interview, 30 August 2006.

[36] Quoted in Thomas C. and Rosemary F. Clarie, *Just Rye Harbor,* 103.

[37] Foley interview, 30 August 2006.

[38] *Portsmouth Herald,* 9 November 1942, "Portsmouth Navy Yard Bond-Buying Record Set as Goal for Hub Drive," 1.

[39] John Gfroerer, producer, *World War II Home Front New Hampshire;* a video history documentary.

[40] Portsmouth War Records, Portsmouth Library Special Collections, Portsmouth, NH, File 3, Personalities, W012.

[41] Oral interview with William Hersey by Judith Moyer, 16 November 1990, in the Puddle Dock neighborhood in conjunction with the Strawbery Banke Abbott Store project.

[42] Doris Weatherford, *American Women and World War II* (New York: Facts on File, 1990), 201.

[43] Harvard Sitkoff, "The American Home Front," in Barbara McLean Ward, ed., *Produce and Conserve, Share and Play Square*, 39. Also see Maury Klein, *A Call to Arms*, 596.

[44] James W. Wensyel, "Home Front," 53.

[45] Doris Weatherford, *American Women and World War II*, 201.

[46] Oral interview with Rodolphe Blais by Barbara McLean Ward, 13 February 1992, at the Strawbery Banke Library in conjunction with the Strawbery Banke Abbott Store project.

[47] Richard C. and Sharon M. Hanes, *American Home Front in World War II: Almanac* (Farmington Hills, MI: Thomson Gale, 2005), 45.

[48] James W. Wensyel, "Home Front," 56.

[49] A statement titled "Victory Garden Funds," undated, Portsmouth Council of Defense Records, Box 3, File 4, Milne Special Collections, University of New Hampshire Library.

[50] Ibid.

[51] Peter Randall, *Hampton: A Century of Town and Beach, 1888–1988*, 669.

[52] Bea Randall interview, 5 March 2014.

[53] WHEB Broadcast Sheet, 30 October 1942, Portsmouth Council of Defense Records, Box 1, File 24, Milne Special Collections, University of New Hampshire Library.

[54] Oral interview with Charles and Marion Adams by Barbara McLean Ward, 16 April 1992, in Eliot, Maine, in conjunction with the Strawbery Banke Abbott Store project.

[55] Doris Weatherford, *American Women and World War II*, 203.

[56] James W. Wensyel, "Home Front," 53.

[57] Oral interview with Leslie Clough by Judith Moyer, 18 July 1990, at the site of the Abbott Store in conjunction with the Strawbery Banke Abbott Store project.

[58] Gary Skoloff et al., *To Win the War*, 111.

[59] Ibid.

[60] Doris Weatherford, *American Women and World War II*, 204.

[61] Ibid., 205.

[62] Blais interview, 13 February 1992.

[63] Ibid.

[64] Oral interview with Valerie Cunningham by Judith Moyer, 7 March 1990, in Durham, NH, in conjunction with the Strawbery Banke Abbott Store project.

[65] Randall interview, 5 March 2014, and Papatones interview, 26 February 2014.

[66] James W. Wensyel, "Home Front," 54.

[67] Papatones interview, 26 February 2014.

[68] Maury Klein, *A Call to Arms*, 701.

[69] New Hampshire State Council of Defense letter of 8 September 1943 to Portsmouth Defense Council, Portsmouth Council of Defense Records, Box 1, File 11, Milne Special Collections, University of New Hampshire Library.

[70] *Portsmouth Herald*, "Nation's Food Problem Does Not Look Too Good," 27 June 1945, 1.

[71] Richard Polenberg, ed., *America at War: The Home Front, 1941–1945* (Englewood Cliffs, NJ: Prentice-Hall, 1968), 17.

[72] *Make and Mend for Victory*, Book No. S-10, copyright 1942, The Spool Cotton Company, 40, Thayer Cumings Library and Archives, Strawbery Banke Museum.

[73] *Make It Do Until Victory: Your Wartime Handbook*, Editorial Offices of Life and Health, undated, 171, Thayer Cumings Library and Archives, Strawbery Banke Museum.

[74] *800 Ways to Save and Serve: How to Beat the High Cost of Wartime Living*, ed. Michael Gore (New York: Handbook Library, 1943), 16, Thayer Cumings Library and Archives, Strawbery Banke Museum.

[75] Maury Klein, *A Call to Arms*, 78.

[76] Ibid., 509.

[77] Ibid., 410.

[78] Richard C. and Sharon M. Hanes, *American Home Front in World War II: Almanac*, 48.

[79] James W. Wensyel, "Home Front," 54.

[80] *Portsmouth Herald*, 27 May 1942, "Navy Yard Men Denied Extra Gas in Haverhill," 1.

[81] Portsmouth War Records, Portsmouth Library Special Collections, Portsmouth, NH, File 2, Organizations, W009A, Civic Organizations, "Public Service."

[82] Laurence Shorey, 12 September 1946, Portsmouth War Records, Thayer Cumings Library, Strawbery Banke Museum, MS 96, Box 1, Folder 18, "Transportation."

[83] Harold Whitehouse, *Home by Nine*, 41.

[84] James W. Wensyel, "Home Front," 54.

[85] Laurence Shorey, 12 September 1946, Portsmouth War Records, Thayer Cumings Library, Strawbery Banke Museum, NH, MS 96, Box 1, Folder 18, "Transportation."

[86] Ibid.

[87] Ibid.

[88] *Portsmouth Herald*, 2 August 1941, "Women Invade Local Stores, Portsmouth Drivers Ready for Gas Curfew," 1.

[89] Maury Klein, *A Call to Arms*, 406.

[90] James W. Wensyel, "Home Front," 54.

[91] Clark G. Reynolds, *America at War, 1941–1945: The Home Front* (New York: Gallery Books, 1990), 188.

[92] William O'Neill, "The People Are Willing," 201.

[93] Levy interview, 12 February 1991.

[94] William O'Neill, "The People Are Willing," 201.

[95] Ibid, 197, 201–202.

[96] John Gfroerer, producer, *World War II Home Front New Hampshire*; a video history documentary.

[97] Ibid.

[98] Blais interview, 13 February 1992.

[99] *Portsmouth Herald*, 7 December 2010, "City Answers Call of War," 1.

[100] *Portsmouth Herald*, 12 April 1942, "Long-Trip Auto Travel Drops 40%," 1.

[101] Clark G. Reynolds, *America at War, 1941–1945*, 188.

[102] James W. Wensyel, "Home Front," 58.

[103] *Portsmouth Herald*, 2 August 1941, "Women Invade Local Stores, Portsmouth Drivers Ready for Gas Curfew," 1.

[104] John Gfroerer, producer, "*World War II Home Front New Hampshire*; a video history documentary.

[105] Philip N. Guyol, *Democracy Fights*, 185.

[106] Papatones interview, 26 February 2014.

[107] Levy interview, 12 February 1991

[108] Sussman interview, 19 October 1990.

[109] Blais interview, 13 February 1992.

[110] Harold Whitehouse, *Home by Nine,* 41.

[111] The details of the president's visit are from the *Portsmouth Herald,* 10 August 1940, "Crowds Line Streets to Greet Chief Executive," 1, and an untitled one-page summary of the visit held at NARA Waltham, RG 181, Portsmouth Naval Base General Correspondence, Box 20, Folder EE "President's Visit, 1940."

[112] Jack P. Wysong, *The World, Portsmouth, and the 22nd Coast Artillery,* 71–72.

[113] Laurence Shorey, Portsmouth War Records, Thayer Cumings Library, Strawbery Banke Museum, MS 96, Box 1, Folder 5, Business and Industry, "Social Activities."

[114] *Portsmouth Herald,* 24 November 1945, "Helen Keller Thrilled by Tour of Sub, U-boat; Brings Cheer to Patients at Naval Hospital," 1.

[115] According to Robert Dallek, President Roosevelt "brought Henry Stimson and Frank Knox, two of the country's most pro-Allied Republicans, into his Cabinet as Secretary of War and Secretary of the Navy, respectively. Replacing the two most isolationist members of his Cabinet, Harry Woodring and Charles Edison, the appointments were not only a fresh demonstration to London of Roosevelt's intentions, but also an attempt to create a bipartisan consensus for all aid to Britain short of war and strengthen his bid for another presidential term." Robert Dallek, *Franklin D. Roosevelt and American Foreign Policy, 1932–1945,* 232.

[116] New Hampshire Music Festival program, Portsmouth, 13 May 1944, Portsmouth Athenaeum, E0927.

[117] Papatones interview, 26 February 2014.

[118] Foley interview, 30 August 2006.

CHAPTER 7: POPULATION BOOM

[1] James W. Wensyel, "Home Front," 51.

[2] Franklin E. Jordan, *Portsmouth and National Defense,* 1 August 1941, Table 1. The population figures are for 1940 and 1943; see Table 6 in this book for details. This booklet compiles a series of 13 articles that appeared in the *Portsmouth Herald* in the summer of 1941, published in pamphlet form by J.D. Hartford of the *Portsmouth Herald* on 1 August 1941; Thayer Cumings Library, Strawbery Banke Museum, Portsmouth, NH, MS 96,

Box 2, Folder 1, "State Council of Defense, Local Committees: Portsmouth." Hereafter Franklin E. Jordan, *Portsmouth and National Defense*, 1 August 1941.

[3] *Survey of Health and Welfare in the Portsmouth Defense Area*, August 1943, table entitled "Population-Total Trends" in the Appendix. The contiguous towns are Eliot, Greenland, Kittery, New Castle, Newington, and Rye.

[4] *Portsmouth Herald*, 17 July 1918, "How Our City Looks in Eyes of Stranger," 1.

[5] Richard M. Candee, *Atlantic Heights: A World War I Shipbuilders' Community* (Portsmouth: Peter E. Randall, 1985), 42, 50.

[6] *Survey of Health and Welfare in the Portsmouth Defense Area*, August 1943, Box 2, Folder 14, "Population Changes."

[7] *Portsmouth Herald*, 8 July 1943, "Portsmouth Hopes to Keep Yard Booming after Victory," 1.

[8] Richard R. Lingeman, *Don't You Know There's a War On?*, 69.

[9] Richard Polenberg, ed., *America at War: The Home Front, 1941–1945*, 124.

[10] Clarence Andrews, "Sheldon, Iowa during World War II," *Palimpsest* 70 (1989), 146–165; Lonnie E. Maness, "A West Tennessee Town and World War II," West Tennessee Historical Society Papers, 110–119; Perry Duis and Scott LaFrance, *We've Got a Job to Do: Chicagoans and World War II* (Chicago: Chicago Historical Society, 1992); Marc Scott Miller, *The Irony of Victory: World War II and Lowell, Massachusetts* (Chicago: University of Illinois Press, 1988), Robert J. Havighurst and H. Gerthon Morgan, *The Social History of a War-Boom Community* (New York: Longmans, Green, 1951).

[11] Lorraine McConaghy, "Wartime Boomtown: Kirkland, Washington, a Small Town during World War II." *Pacific Northwest Quarterly*, vol. 80, 1989, 42–51.

[12] http://www.cr.nps.gov/nr/travel/wwIIbayarea/mar.htm. "Mare Island Naval Shipyard: World War II in the San Francisco Bay Area." This site is an essay excerpted from Wayne Bonnett, *Build Ships! San Francisco Bay Wartime Shipbuilding Photographs 1940–1945* (Sausalito, CA: Windgate Press, 2000).

[13] Marilynn S. Johnson, *The Second Gold Rush: Oakland and the East Bay in World War II* (Berkeley: University of California Press, 1996), 116.

[14] Gerald D. Nash, *The American West Transformed: The Impact of the Second World War* (Bloomington: Indiana University Press, 1985); Gerald D. Nash, *World War II and the West: Reshaping the Economy* (Lincoln: University of Nebraska Press, 1990); Roger Lotchin, "The Historians War or the Home Front War?: Some Thoughts for Western Historians," *Western Historical Quarterly* vol. 26, no. 2, (Summer 1995), 185–196; Roger W. Lotchin, ed., *The Way We Really Were: The Golden State in the Second Great War* (Chicago: University of Illinois Press, 2000).

[15] Frederic Chapin Lane, *Ships for Victory: A History of Shipbuilding under the U.S. Maritime Commission in World War II* (Baltimore: Johns Hopkins University Press,1951), 437.

[16] http://www.historylink.rg/essays/output.cfm?file_id=1664, "World War II Home Front on Puget Sound: A Snapshot History."

[17] Rodney K. Watterson, *32 in '44*, Chapters IV and VIII.

[18] Robert J. Havighurst and H. Gerthon Morgan, *The Social History of a War-Boom Community*, xiii.

[19] Ibid., 323.

[20] Ibid., 330, 12.

[21] *Survey of Health and Welfare in the Portsmouth Defense Area*, August 1943, Conclusion.

[22] Franklin E. Jordan, *Portsmouth and National Defense*, 1 August 1941, 5.
[23] Ibid., 84.

[24] The estimating of shifting populations during the war is iffy, at best. In this table, the 1940 figures are census-based and presumably accurate. The 1944 town figures are based on ration book distribution. The sources for this table: 1) For Portsmouth and contiguous towns, *Survey of Health and Welfare in the Portsmouth Defense Area*, August 1943, table entitled "Population-Total Trends" in the Appendix. The contiguous towns are Eliot, Greenland, Kittery, New Castle, Newington, and Rye. 2) For Rockingham County, *Portsmouth Herald*, 15 February 1944, "Survey Shows Trends," 1. The 3.6% gain is based on a comparison of the 1940 census with ration book distribution in 1944. 3) For other local towns, same source as 1). 4) Philip N. Guyol, *Democracy Fights: A History of New Hampshire in World War II*, 104 and note 3. The 1944 state figure is Guyol's estimate, exclusive of those in the armed services. Based on registrations for War Rations Books for May 1942 (470,000) and October 1943 (445,000), Guyol concludes that the decrease (25,000) reflects the loss of population to the armed forces. All of this is to say that, if one uses the October 1943

ration book figure of 445,000, the decrease in the state's population could have been as great as 9.5%. I chose to keep the 6.6% because that is the figure commonly seen in the literature.

[25] Robert J. Havighurst and H. Gerthon Morgan, *The Social History of a War-Boom Community*, xiii.

[26] Tebo interview, 3 November 2006.

[27] https://aha.confex.com/aha/2011/webprogram/Paper5193.html, "The Ku Klux Klan Confronts New England Catholics in the 1920s."

[28] Ibid.

[29] www.mainememory.net/artifact/23229, "The First Daylight KKK Parade and the First Klan Parade in New England;" Peter Randall, *Hampton: A Century of Town and Beach, 1888–1988*, 654–655; *Portsmouth Herald*, 6 September 1927, "Ku Klux Klan Holds Two Day Konklave Here;" *Portsmouth Herald*, 8 September 1925, "Klan Holds Field Day."

[30] Harold G. Vatter, *The U.S. Economy in World War II* (New York: Columbia University Press, 1985), 114–115.

[31] Philip N. Guyol, *Democracy Fights*, 131.

[32] *Portsmouth Herald*, 15 Febuary 1944, "Survey Shows Trends," 1.

[33] Philip N. Guyol, *Democracy Fights*, 131.

[34] Ibid., 126, Chart II.

[35] *Survey of Health and Welfare in the Portsmouth Defense Area*, August 1943, Box 2, Folder 14, Population Changes.

[36] Portsmouth War Records, Portsmouth Library Special Collections, Portsmouth, NH, File 2, Institutions, W007, Portsmouth Hospital.

[37] James W. Wensyel, "Home Front," 52.

[38] Richard R. Lingeman, *Don't You Know There's a War On?*, 87.

CHAPTER 8: ECONOMIC BOOM

[1] James W. Wensyel, "Home Front," 44.

[2] Harold G. Vatter, *The U.S. Economy in World War II*, 7.

[3] David M. Kennedy, *Freedom from Fear*, 617.

[4] *Portsmouth Herald*, 14 May 1919, "Portsmouth Leads All New Hampshire Cities in Growth during War," 1.

[5] Ibid. One of the article's tables used to construct the graph has a typo error. The table near the end of the article showing Portsmouth realty for 1912 as $29,349 should read $8,297,349. The typo is obvious when this table is compared to the previous table in the article.

[6] Philip N. Guyol, *Democracy Fights*, 187.

[7] *Portsmouth Herald*, 27 April 1940, editorial, 4.

[8] Harvard Sitkoff, "The American Home Front," 39.

[9] Maury Klein, *A Call to Arms*, 542.

[10] Oral interview with Zina Boulanger, 14 June 1996, at her home in Dover, NH. Interviewed by Judith Moyer in conjunction with the Portsmouth Music Hall Project.

[11] Papatones interview, 26 February 2014.

[12] 294th Annual Report of the Town of Kittery, Maine, for the Year Ending February 1, 1942, 92, Maine Room, Rice Library, Kittery, ME.

[13] Philip N. Guyol, *Democracy Fights*, 189.

[14] All present day calculations in this chapter use www.usinflationcalculator.

[15] Franklin E. Jordan, *Portsmouth and National Defense*, 1 August 1941, Table 2, "Portsmouth Harbor Defense," 1871.
[16] Ibid.

[17] Philip Guyol, *Democracy Fights*, 162.

[18] *Survey of Health and Welfare in the Portsmouth Defense Area*, August 1943, "Health, Nutrition," footnote 7 on page 65, Strawbery Banke Museum, Portsmouth, NH.

[19] Boulanger interview, 14 June 1996.

[20] Maury Klein, *A Call to Arms*, 298.

[21] Arthur Herman, *Freedom's Forge: How American Business Produced Victory in World War II* (New York: Random House, 2012), Kindle, Conclusion, 77%.

[22] Papatones interview, 26 February 2014.

[23] Oral interview with Amelia Patch, 19 June 1990, at her house. Interviewed by Judith Moyer in conjunction with the Strawbery Banke Abbott Store project.

[24] Sussman interview, 19 October 1990.

[25] Ibid.

[26] Peter Randall, *Hampton: A Century of Town and Beach, 1888–1988*, 669.

[27] Maury Klein, *A Call to Arms*, 599.

[28] Philip N. Guyol, *Democracy Fights*, 187.

[29] Ibid., 131.

[30] Ibid., 139.

CHAPTER 9: SKILLED WORKERS

[1] *Portsmouth Herald*, 30 January 1941, "Navy Yard Workers Asset for City's Future," 1.

[2] *Portsmouth Herald*, 27 August 1919, "Record Made by the Portsmouth Navy Yard during World War Receives High Praise from Officials," 1.

[3] Ibid.

[4] Ibid.
[5] Shop Superintendent memoranda of 26 August, 27 November, 30 December 1941 and 25 February 1942, NARA Waltham, RG 181, Portsmouth Naval Shipyard General Correspondence (Central Files), Box 14, Folder A3-2/LC, PKG #6, "Orders to Shop Foremen."

[6] Ibid.

[7] Oral interview with Percy Whitney, 23 March 2006, at his home in New Castle, NH.

[8] *Portsmouth Herald*, 12 March 1944, "Free Training Courses Offer Top Opportunities," 1.

[9] *Survey of Health and Welfare in the Portsmouth Defense Area,* August 1943, Box 1, Folder 14, Education.

[10] *Portsmouth Herald,* 12 March 1944, "Free Training Courses Offer Top Opportunities," 1.

[11] *Portsmouth Herald,* 20 March 1941, "Start School for Welders Next Week," 1.

[12] *Apparel Manufacturing,* May 1944, "The Story of Morley," Thayer Cumings Library, Strawbery Banke Museum, Portsmouth, NH, MS 96, Box 1, Folder 5, "Business and Industry."

[13] New Hampshire Music Festival program cover, Portsmouth, 13 May 1944, Portsmouth Athenaeum, E0927.

[14] Philip N. Guyol, *Democracy Fights,* 158.

[15] Ibid., 161.

[16] James W. Wensyel, "Home Front," 49.

[17] Philip N. Guyol, *Democracy Fights,* 159.

[18] Maury Klein, *A Call to Arms,* 651.

[19] Philip N. Guyol, *Democracy Fights,* 160.
[20] Ibid., 148.

[21] Laurence Shorey, "The Morley Company," Portsmouth War Records, Thayer Cumings Library, Strawbery Banke Museum, Portsmouth, NH, MS 96, Box 1, Folder 5, "Business and Industry."

[22] Philip N. Guyol, *Democracy Fights,* 147.
[23] John Gfroerer, producer, *World War II Home Front New Hampshire;* a video history documentary.

[24] Tebo interview, 3 November 2006.

[25] *Portsmouth Herald,* 23 February 1943, 4A.

[26] Ibid.

[27] *Administrative History: Portsmouth Naval Yard in World War II,* Portsmouth Naval Shipyard Museum Archives, Kittery, ME, 47.

[28] Maury Klein, *A Call to Arms,* 141.

[29] *Portsmouth Herald*, 16 December 1941, "Ranger Lodge Machinists Hit Navy Yard Hours," 1.

[30] Ibid., "Navy Yard Shift Goes into Effect," 6.

[31] *Portsmouth Herald*, 21 July 1945, "Portsmouth Is Chosen Site for Trade School," 1.

[32] *Portsmouth Herald*, 20 November 1945, "Act to Gain More Room at Trade School," 1.

CHAPTER 10: WOMEN STEP UP

[1] James W. Wensyel, "Home Front," 50.

[2] Alice Kessler-Harris, *Out to Work: A History of Wage-Earning Women in the United States* (New York: Oxford University Press, 1982), 275–276.

[3] Frederic C. Lane, *The Navy and the Industrial Mobilization in World War II*, 343.

[4] Navy Department, Industrial Manpower Section, letter of 1 May 1943 to Distribution including All Navy Yards, Subject: Employment of Women—Continental Navy Yards, NARA College Park, RG 38, Naval Operations General Correspondence, Box 151, Folder NY1, 1 July 1942 to 30 June 1943.

[5] *Administrative History: Portsmouth Naval Shipyard in World War II*, Portsmouth Naval Shipyard Museum Archives, Kittery, ME, 33.

[6] Boston Navy Yard Commandant's Circular No. 398 of 13 January 1942, NARA Waltham, RG 181, Portsmouth Naval Shipyard General Correspondence (Central Files), Box 2, Folder A2-11/NY2, "Circular Letter Navy Yard—Boston."

[7] *Portsmouth Herald*, 18 May 1942, "Feminine Detail Takes Over Bus Service to Navy Yard," 1.

[8] Philip N. Guyol, *Democracy Fights*, 181.

[9] *Survey of Health and Welfare in the Portsmouth Defense Area*, August 1943, 35, Box 2, Folder 14, "S.C.D. Survey of Health and Welfare in Portsmouth." Another survey, between June 1942 and August 1943, found 470 female clerical workers at the yard and 400 women employees at the Somersworth plant. *Survey of Health and Welfare in the Portsmouth Defense Area*, 67.

[10] *Survey of Health and Welfare in the Portsmouth Defense Area*, August 1943, 16, S.C.D.

[11] Manager memo of 30 September 1942, NARA Waltham, RG 181, Portsmouth Naval Shipyard General Correspondence (Central Files), Box 8, Folder A2-11/NY2, "Circular Letter Navy Yard."

[12] Portions of this chapter referring to Portsmouth Navy Yard female employee are taken from the author's *32 in'44: Building the Portsmouth Submarine Fleet in World War II*, 65–72.

[13] Quoted in *Cradle of American Shipbuilding, World War II*, no page numbers.

[14] *Portsmouth Herald,* 27 August 1919, "Record Made by the Portsmouth Navy Yard during World War Receives High Praise from Officials," 1.

[15] Ibid.

[16] Manager memorandum of 15 September 1942, NARA Waltham, RG 181, Portsmouth Naval Shipyard General Correspondence (Central Files), Box 8, Folder A2-11/NY2, "Circular Letter Navy Yard."

[17] Manager memorandum of 30 September 1942, NARA Waltham, RG 181, Portsmouth Naval Shipyard General Correspondence (Central Files), Box 14, Folder A3-2LC Pkg #7, "Orders to Shop Foremen."

[18] Ibid.

[19] Industrial Manager memorandum to Public Works Officer of 2 September 1942, Subject: Toilet Facilities for Women in Shops and Shop Offices, NARA Waltham, RG 181, Box 36, Folder N4-14, "Latrines."
[20] Alice Kessler-Harris, *Out to Work*, 260.

[21] Foley interview, 30 August 2006.

[22] Alice Kessler-Harris, *Out to Work*, 268.

[23] White interview, 3 April 2006.

[24] Foley interview, 30 August 2006.

[25] Valerie Cunningham and Mark J. Sammons, *Black Portsmouth: Three Centuries of African-American Heritage* (Durham: University of New Hampshire Press, 2004), 168.

[26] Foley interview, 30 August 2006.

[27] Jeffery M. Dorwart, *The Philadelphia Navy Yard: From the Birth of the U.S. Navy to the Nuclear Age* (Philadelphia: University of Pennsylvania Press, 2001), 178.

[28] Tebo interview, 3 November 2006, and MacIsaac interview, 9 November 2006.

[29] Assistant Secretary of the Navy Ralph A. Bard letter of 25 May 1943 to Commandants All Continental Navy Yards, NARA College Park, RG 24, Bureau of Naval Personnel General Correspondence, 1941–45, Box 1601, Folder NY January 11, 1943.

[30] David M. Kennedy, *Freedom from Fear*, 776–779.

[31] Maury Klein, *A Call to Arms*, 699.

[32] *Portsmouth Herald*, 18 May 1942, "Feminine Detail Takes Over Bus Service to Navy Yard," 1.

[33] *Portsmouth Herald*, 22 March 1943, "Woman's Place is Back of the Monkey Wrench Say Lady Machinists," 1.

[34] *Portsmouth Herald*, 11 November 1943, caption under the picture reads, "And More are Needed." 1.

[35] Quoted in the *Portsmouth Herald*, 10 May 1944, "Yard Graduates Largest Group; Four Women," 1.

[36] Philip N. Guyol, *Democracy Fights* 215.

[37] *Administrative History: Portsmouth Naval Shipyard in World War II*, Portsmouth Naval Shipyard Museum Archives, Kittery, ME, 89.

[38] Foley interview, 30 August 2006.

[39] *Portsmouth Herald*, 1 January 1945, 1.

[40] Ibid., 10 February 1945, "Women Juror Bill to Get New Action," 1.

[41] Valerie Cunningham and Mark J. Sammons, *Black Portsmouth*, 170–171.

[42] Ibid.

[43] White interview, 3 April 2006.

[44] Doris Weatherford, *American Women and World War II*, 307.

[45] Alice Kessler-Harris, *Out to Work*, 286.

[46] *Portsmouth Herald*, 8 January 1945, "Women Back Home," 4.

[47] Doris Weatherford, *American Women and World War II*, 307–8.

[48] James W. Wensyel, "Home Front," 44–67.

[49] Doris Weatherford, *American Women and World War II*, 313

CHAPTER 11: BUILDING BOOM

[1] *Portsmouth Herald*, 14 November 1941, "Gardner Describes Port City Problems Before N.E. Council," 1.

[2] Gerald D. Nash, *The American West Transformed*, 39.

[3] Frederic Chapin Lane, *Ships for Victory*, 58.

[4] Ibid.

[5] John Dos Passos, "Gold Rush Down South," *State of the Nation* (Boston: Houghton Mifflin, 1944). Reprinted in Richard Polenberg, ed., *America at War*, 125.

[6] *Survey of Health and Welfare in the Portsmouth Defense Area*, August 1943, Health, 46.

[7] *Portsmouth Herald*, 22 May 1918, "2000 Men Employed at Newington Plant," 1.
[8] Richard M. Candee, *Atlantic Height*, 56–57.

[9] *Portsmouth Herald*, 15 August 1918, "Atlantic Heights Will Be an Ideal Village," 1.

[10] Sharon M. Hanes and Allison McNeill, *The American Home Front in World War II: Primary Sources*, 137.

[11] Portsmouth War Records, Portsmouth Library Special Collections, Portsmouth, NH, File 1, Civil Defense, W002, General Information, "Housing."

[12] *Portsmouth Herald*, 17 January 1940, "Housing Needed for Yard Workers," 1

[13] *Portsmouth Herald*, 16 July 1940, "Proposal Believed Likely to Materialize; Navy Yard Co-operating on Project," 1.

[14] *Portsmouth Herald*, 23 August 1940, "Plan Simple Procedure for Housing Survey," 1.

[15] James W. Wensyel, "Home Front," 51.

[16] Robert J. Havighurst and H. Gerthon Morgan, *The Social History of a War-Boom Community*, 61, 325.

[17] Gregory C. Colati and Ryan H. Madden, "Victory Begins at Home," 65.

[18] Maury Klein, *A Call to Arms,* 141.

[19] *Portsmouth Herald*, 19 June 1941, "Present Projects Still Would Leave Housing Shortage," 1.

[20] Portsmouth War Records, Portsmouth Library Special Collections, Portsmouth, NH, File 1, Civil Defense, W002, General Information, "Housing."

[21] Foley interview, 30 August 2006.

[22] *Portsmouth Herald*, 19 June 1941, "Present Projects Still Would Leave Housing Shortage," 1.

[23] Whitehouse interview, 5 November 2014.

[24] John Gfroerer, producer, *World War II Home Front New Hampshire*; a video history documentary.

[25] Patch interview, 19 June 1990.

[26] Comments made by Valerie Cunningham at the author's presentation to the Stratham Historical Society, Stratham Fire Hall, 8 November 2010.

[27] www.seacoastonline.com/articles, 7 March 1990, "Clarence Cunningham: ' . . . Always a gentle, quiet person,'" Tea for Two *Portsmouth Herald* column by Tammi Truax, Valerie Cunningham quoted in article.

[28] Oral interview with Valerie Cunningham by Judith Moyer, 25 March 1990, at the site of the Abbott Store in conjunction with the Strawbery Banke Abbott Store project.

[29] Plot Plan Pannaway Manor, Portsmouth, NH, Protective Covenants, April 1941, Portsmouth Athenaeum, M0329.

[30] Ibid.

31 www.seacoastonline.com/articles, 4 April 2007, "Louise McGee," Tea for Two *Portsmouth Herald* column by Tammi Truax.

32 *Portsmouth Herald*, 14 November 1941, "Gardner Describes Port City Problems Before N.E. Council," 1.

33 Ibid.

34 Commandant Portsmouth Navy Yard RADM John D.Wainwright letter to Board of Selectmen, Kittery, ME, of 16 August 1940, NARA Waltham, RG 181, Portsmouth Naval Base Files, Box 10, Folder N1-13, "Lands."

35 Commander Portsmouth Navy Yard letter L1-2/EN5 (O-4) of 8 December 1941 to Bureau of Yards and Docks, Subject: Housing Project at Kittery Maine, NARA Waltham, RG 181, Portsmouth Naval Base Files, Box 15, Folder L24, "Housing Development."

36 George Michelson, "Housing Built on the Double-Quick," *Engineering News Record*, March 26, 1942, 1.

37 Ibid.

38 Cassie Lutts, "History of Admiralty Village, Kittery, Maine, (a presentation to the Kittery Historical Association on April 13, 1988)," Maine Room, Rice Library, Kittery, ME.

39 *Survey of Health and Welfare in the Portsmouth Defense Area*, August 1943, 46, State Council of Defense, Local Committees: Portsmouth.
40 Commandant Portsmouth Navy Yard letter L24 (O-4) of 10 December 1941 to Bureau of Yards and Docks, Subject: Naval Housing Project — . . . Construction of Sewage Disposal Plant, NARA Waltham, RG 181, Portsmouth Naval Base Folder L24, "Housing Development."

41 Cassie Lutts, "History of Admiralty Village, Kittery, Maine."

42 Portsmouth War Records, Portsmouth Library Special Collections, Portsmouth, NH, File 1, Civil Defense, W002, General Information, "World War II History of Pannaway Manor."

43 *Survey of Health and Welfare in the Portsmouth Defense Area*, August 1943, 46, State Council of Defense, Local Committees: Portsmouth.

44 Portsmouth War Records, Portsmouth Library Special Collections, Portsmouth, NH, File 1, Civil Defense, W002, General Information, "World War II History of Pannaway Manor."

[45] Portsmouth War Records, Portsmouth Library Special Collections, Portsmouth, NH, File 1, Civil Defense, W002, General Information, "World War II History of Wentworth Acres."

[46] Ibid.

[47] Whitehouse interview, 5 November 2014.

[48] *Survey of Health and Welfare in the Portsmouth Defense Area*, August 1943, 46, State Council of Defense, Local Committees: Portsmouth.

[49] *Portsmouth Herald,* 9 September 1943, "Must Portsmouth's War Housing Go?, 1.

[50] 294th Annual Report of the Town of Kittery, Maine for the Year Ending February 1, 1942, 92, Maine Room, Rice Library, Kittery, ME.

[51] Ibid.

[52]John Gfroerer, producer, *World War II Home Front New Hampshire;* a video history documentary.

[53] Tebo interview, 3 November 2006.

[54] Maury Klein, *A Call to Arms,* 630.

[55] Sadie M. Dearborn written testimony, undated, Maine Room, Rice Library, Kittery, ME.

[56] Portsmouth War Records, Portsmouth Library Special Collections, Portsmouth, NH, File 3, Schools, W014, Public School History WWII.

[57] Quoted in *Portsmouth Herald,* 9 September 1943, "Must Portsmouth's War Housing Go?, 1.

[58] *Portsmouth Herald,* 11 April 1942, "First Year of Emergency in the Portsmouth Area Reveals Much Progress," 1.

[59] *Portsmouth Herald,* 19 July 1942, "Telephone Circuits Overloaded," 1.

[60] Franklin E. Jordan, *Portsmouth and National Defense*, 1 August 1941, 22.

[61] *Portsmouth Herald,* 12 October 1941, "City Councilmen Have No Solution to Water Crisis," 1.

[62] *Portsmouth Herald,* 14 February 1942, "New Water Project Approved, 1.

[63] "Your City Government," 1945–1946–1947, Portsmouth, NH, City Clerk's Office, Portsmouth City Hall, 47.

[64] Annual Report of the City Auditor of the City of Portsmouth, NH, for the Year Ending December 31, 1943, 44; and Annual Report of the City Auditor of the City of Portsmouth, NH, for the Year Ending December 31, 1942, 44, City Clerk's Office, Portsmouth City Hall.

[65] *Portsmouth Herald*, 26 May 1942, "Boomtown Portsmouth Finds It Has Special Needs," 1.

[66] Ibid.

[67] Gregory C. Colati and Ryan H. Madden, "Victory Begins at Home," 64.

[68] "Portsmouth Chamber of Commerce," 3, Thayer Cumings Library and Archives, Strawbery Banke Museum, Portsmouth, NH, MS 96, Box 1, Folder 5, "Business and Industry."

CHAPTER 12: ENVIRONMENTAL IMPACT

[1] The Comprehensive Environmental Response, Compensation, and Liability Act (CERCLA) is an EPA national program to identify and assess past hazardous waste disposal sites posing a potential threat to human health or the environment. Sites gaining this dubious honor are referred to as Superfund sites in recognition of the costs that are normally incurred to restore the sites; http://yosemite.epa.gov/rl/npl pad.nsf, U.S. Environmental Protection Agency Waste Site, Cleanup, and Reuse in New England.

[2] Frederick T. Short, ed., *The Ecology of the Great Bay Estuary, New Hampshire and Maine: An Estuarine Profile and Bibliography* (Durham: University of New Hampshire, 1992), 85, Table 6.12.

[3] Samuel P. Hays, *Beauty, Health, and Permanence: Environmental Politics in the United States 1955–1985* (Cambridge: Cambridge University Press, 1987), 77.

[4] Commander Charles W. Tucker, JAGC, USN, "Compliance by Federal Facilities with State and Local Environmental Regulations," in *Naval Law Review*, Spring 1986, 87–112.

[5] Chief of Bureau of Yards and Docks letter of 16 September 1935 to Commandant, Navy Yard, Portsmouth, NH, Subject: Disposal of Untreated Sewage into Waters of the United States, NARA Waltham, RG 181, PNSY Central Files, Box 36, Folder 26-7, "Sewers and Sewage."

[6] Commandant, Navy Yard, Portsmouth, NH, letter of 20 September 1935 to Chief of Bureau of Yards and Docks, Subject: Disposal of Untreated Sewage into Waters of the United States, NARA Waltham, RG 181, PNSY Central Files, Box 36, Folder 26-7, "Sewers and Sewage."

[7] Portsmouth Naval Yard Medical Officer's Annual Reports for 1937–1939 to the Commandant, NARA Waltham, RG 181, Naval Station General Correspondence, Box 10, Folder A9-1, "Sanitary Reports."

[8] *Portsmouth Herald*, 2 February 1944, "Discuss Problem of Pollution in Great Bay." 1.

[9] Ibid.

[10] Chief of Bureau of Yards and Docks letter of 5 December 1940 to Commandant Portsmouth Navy Yard, Subject: Water Supply and Discharge of Domestic Sewage at Training Areas and Industrial Plants Essential to the National Defense, NARA Waltham, RG 181, Portsmouth Naval Shipyard Central Files, Box 36, Folder 26-7, "Sewers and Sewage."

[11] Chief of Bureau of Yards and Docks letter of 28 November 1941 to Commandant Portsmouth Navy Yard, Subject: Water Supply and Discharge of Domestic Sewage — Navy Yard Portsmouth, NH, NARA Waltham, RG 181, Portsmouth Naval Shipyard Central Files, Box 36, Folder 26-7, "Sewers and Sewage."

[12] Department of Health and Welfare, Bureau of Health, State House, Augusta, letter of 24 December 1941 to Commandant, Navy Yard, Portsmouth, NH, NARA Waltham, RG 181, Portsmouth Naval Shipyard Central Files, Box 36, Folder 26-7, "Sewers and Sewage."

[13] State of New Hampshire, State Board of Health letter of 16 December 1941 to Commandant, U.S. Navy Yard, Portsmouth, NH, NARA Waltham, RG 181, Portsmouth Naval Shipyard Central Files, Box 36, Folder 26-7, "Sewers and Sewage."

[14] Commandant Portsmouth Navy Yard letter of 30 December 1941 to Bureau of Yards and Docks, Subject: Water Supply and Disposal of Domestic Sewage — Navy Yard, Portsmouth, NH, NARA Waltham, RG 181, Portsmouth Naval Shipyard Central Files, Box 36, Folder 26-7, "Sewers and Sewage."

[15] Ibid.

[16] Chief of the Bureau of Yards and Docks letter of 18 December 1942 to Officer-in-Charge of Construction Bureau Yards and Docks Contracts, U.S. Navy Yard, Portsmouth, NH, Subject: Sewerage and Sewage Treatment Facilities at Naval Stations, NARA Waltham, RG 181,

Portsmouth Naval Shipyard Central Files, Box 36, Folder 26-7, "Sewers and Sewage."

[17] Portsmouth Naval Yard Medical Officer's Annual Reports for 1942 to the Commandant, NARA Waltham, RG 181, Naval Station General Correspondence, Box 10, Folder A9-1, "Sanitary Reports."

[18] Ibid.

[19] *Survey of Health and Welfare in the Portsmouth Defense Area*, August 1943, Health, 56.

[20] Harold Whitehouse, *Home by Nine*, 48.

[21] *Survey of Health and Welfare in the Portsmouth Defense Area*, August 1943, Health, 56.

[22] Ibid.

[23] Lorraine McConaghy, "Wartime Boomtown," 42–51.
[24] C. F. Jackson, *A Biological Survey of Great Bay, New Hampshire, by the Marine Fisheries Commission* (Durham: University of New Hampshire, 1944), 35–37 and Table IV.

[25] *Portsmouth Herald*, 10 August 1944, "See State Sewage Commission Cure for Bay Pollution," 1.

[26] Tebo interview, 3 November 2006.

[27] C. F. Jackson, *A Biological Survey of Great Ba,y New Hampshire*, 32–33.
[28] Samuel P. Hays, *Beauty, Health, and Permanence*, 72.

[29] *Portsmouth Herald*, 13 November 1945, "Stream Pollution Costs Nation $100,000,000 a Year, Congress is Told," 4.

[30] Ibid.

[31] Manager Captain H. W. Osterhaus memorandum of 12 April 1926, Subject: General Appearance in the Vicinity of Shops, NARA Waltham, RG 181, Portsmouth Naval Base Files, Box 15, Folder N1-1, "Grounds 1925–39."

[32] Commandant Portsmouth Navy Yard Rear Admiral C. W. Cole letter of 12 April 1939, Subject: Grounds, and refuse material — care of, NARA Waltham, RG 181, Portsmouth Naval Base Files, Box 15, Folder N1-1, "Grounds 1925–39."

[33] Nelson H. Lawry, Glen M. Williford, and Leo K. Polaski, *Portsmouth Harbor's Military and Naval Heritage*, 24.

[34] Rodney K. Watterson, *32 in '44*, figure A-1.

[35] Map of U.S. Navy Yard, Portsmouth, NH, June 30, 1941, NARA Waltham, RG 181, Portsmouth Naval Base, Central Files, Box 20, Folder A1/Y1.

[36] Rodney K. Watterson, *32 in '44*, figure A-2.

[37] State of New Hampshire v State of Maine, Lodging in Support of Motion for Leave to File Complaint, Map 45, 145, Supporting Evidence for Testimony Given to House Judiciary Committee on 24 May 1990 to Introduce H CON RES 337 Regarding the New Hampshire/Maine Border Dispute, Map No. 45, Seavey's Island, Portsmouth Naval Shipyard, 129. The graph has been annotated to show discussion topics.

[38] According to James Dolph, the Portsmouth Naval Shipyard historian, much of the fill material for the new fitting-out pier was trucked in from off-yard because the Jamaica Island fill was consuming all the shipyard-generated waste then believed suitable for fill material. Telephone interview with James Dolph of 16 March 2007.

[39] Frederick T. Short, ed., *The Ecology of the Great Bay Estuary, New Hampshire and Maine*, 82, Table 6.11.

[40] *Portsmouth Herald*, 17 August 2000, "Landfill Mercury Removed," 1.

[41] Commandant Portsmouth Navy Yard letter of 27 October 1938 to Bureau of Construction and Repair, Subject: Pickling Tanks — Report on, NARA Waltham, RG 181, Portsmouth Naval Shipyard (Central Files), Box 36, Folder 15-5, "Pickling Plant."

[42] Ibid.

[43] Production Officer memorandum of 22 December 1939 to the Public Works Officer, Subject: Pit for Vertical Pickling Tank, NARA Waltham, RG 181, Portsmouth Naval Shipyard Central Files, Box 36, Folder 15-5, "Pickling Plant."

[44] Commandant Portsmouth Navy Yard Rear Admiral Withers letter of 10 November 1942 to Bureau of Ships, Subject: Building for Metal Cleaning Equipment at Navy Yard, Portsmouth, NH, NARA College Park, Record Group 19, Bureau of Ships General Correspondence 1940–45, Box 791, Folder NY1/N5.

[45] Commandant Portsmouth Navy Yard letter of 11 June 1941 to Lcdr. Philip Lemler, Bureau of Ships, NARA Waltham, RG 181, Portsmouth Naval Shipyard Central Files, Box 2, Folder A1-1, "Developments."

[46] Ltjg USNR William P. Gregory (PNY) letter to Cdr. William Spowers (Bureau of Ships) of 21 April 1945, NARA College Park, RG 19, Bureau of Ships General Correspondence 1940-45, Box 791, Folder NY1/N5.

[47] Portsmouth Naval Shipyard Installation Restoration Program Site 30 EE/CA Fact Sheet, contained in Feasibility Study Report for Operable Unit 3 Volume I of II, Portsmouth Naval Shipyard, Kittery, ME, November 2000. Prepared by Northern Division Naval Facilities Engineering Command, Contract Number N62472-90-D-1298, Contract Task Order 0166.

[48] *Portsmouth Herald*, 13 October 2006, A12, "PNS Cleanup Is Paying Off," James O. Horrigan, RAB member, Seacoast Anti-Pollution League.

[49] Medical Officer Portsmouth Navy Yard memo of 10 September 1941 to Commandant, Subject: Special report of injuries of Yard employees investigated by Ltjg J. L. Hatch, NARA Waltham, RG 181, Portsmouth Naval Shipyard Industrial General Correspondence, Box 43, Folder EP13/L9-3 (161), "British Empire *Surcouf* 1941–42."

[50] www.seacoastonline.com/articles, 3 June 2009, "Meet Don Ricklefs: Master Carpenter," Tea for Two *Portsmouth Herald* column by Tammi Truax.

[51] http://www.asbestos.com/navy/ships.php, "Asbestos Exposure on Navy Ships."

[52] Ibid.

[53] Bureau of Ships letter of 24 February 1945 to the Bureau of Medicine and Surgery, Subject: Industrial Health and Safety Survey Concerning Asbestos, NARA College Park, RG 19, Bureau of Ships General Correspondence 1940–1945, Box 18, Folder P2-4 (vol. 3).

[54] Chief of the Bureau of Medicine and Surgery, Vice Admiral Ross T. McIntire letter of 8 March 1945, NARA College Park, RG 19, Bureau of Ships General Correspondence 1940–1945, Box 18, Folder P2-4 (vol. 3).

[55] Philip Drinker, Chief Health Consultant, U.S. Maritime Commission letter of 21 September 1945 to Bureau of Ships forwarding enclosure (1), A Health Survey of Pipe Covering Operations in Constructing Naval Vessel, NARA College Park, RG 19, Bureau of Ships General Correspondence 1940–1945, Box 18, Folder P2-4 (vol. 3).

[56] Ibid.

[57] http://www.osha.gov/SLTC/asbestos/index.html. U.S, Department of Labor, OSHA website.

CHAPTER 13: WARTIME POLITICS

[1] Roger W. Lotchin, "The Historians' War or the Home Front's War?: Some Thoughts for Western Historians," *Western Historical Quarterly*, vol. 26, no.2 (Summer 1995), 191.

[2] Roger W. Lotchin. "California Cities and the Hurricane of Change: World War II in the San Francisco, Los Angeles, and San Diego Metropolitan Areas," *Pacific Historical Review* 63 (August 1994), 414–416.

[3] Jacqueline R. Braitman, "Partisans in Overalls: New Perspectives on Women and Politics in Wartime California," in Roger W. Lotchin, ed., *The Way We Really Were*, 215–235.

[4] *Newsweek*, 8 January 1945, "She Who Laughs Last," 34.
[5] Inaugural Address by Mayor Mary C. Dondero, 1 January 1945, Rare Pamphlet 41332, "Your City Government, 1945–46–47," Portsmouth Athenaeum, Portsmouth, NH.

[6] Ibid.

[7] *Portsmouth Herald*, 7 November 1945, "A Vote of Confidence and Repudiation," 1, 4.

[8] "Your City Government, 1945–1946–1947," Portsmouth. NH; Annual Report of the City Auditor of the City of Portsmouth, NH, for the Year Ending December 31, 1943; and Annual Report of the City Auditor of the City of Portsmouth, NH, for the Year Ending December 31, 1942, City Clerk's Office, Portsmouth City Hall.

[9] *Portsmouth Herald*, 4 November 1945, "Had Enough—More Than Enough?" 4.

[10] *Portsmouth Herald*, 6 November 1944, "Time for a Change," 4.

[11] Ibid.

[12] Inaugural Address by Mayor Mary C. Dondero, 1 January 1946, Rare Pamphlet 41332, "Your City Government, 1945–46–47," Portsmouth Athenaeum, Portsmouth, NH.

[13] Raymond A. Brighton, *They Came to Fish* (Dover: Randall/Winebaum Enterprises, 1979), 415.

[14] Foley interview, 30 August 2006.

[15] *Portsmouth Herald*, 7 November 1945, "Portsmouth's 1945 Vote Largest in 11 Years," 1.

[16] Lorraine McConaghy, "Wartime Boomtown," 43–44.

[17] Robert J. Havighurst and H. Gerthon Morgan, *The Social History of a War-Boom Community*, 107.

[18] At the risk of extrapolating an estimate from an approximation, one could apply age distribution percentages from Table 19 and conclude that there were about 6,600 women and 5,700 men of voting age in 1944.

[19] Foley interview, 30 August 2006.

[20] Randall interview, 5 March 2014.

[21] Tebo interview, 3 November 2006.

[22] Harold Whitehouse, *Home by Nine*, 56.

[23] Oral interview with Blanche Washok by William D. Moore, 12 April 1991, at 232 Bartlett Road, Portsmouth, NH, in conjunction with the Strawbery Banke Abbott Store project.

[24] Raymond A. Brighton, *They Came to Fish*, 417.

[25] *Portsmouth Herald*, 12 December 1946, "Dondero May Continue [State] Senatorial Seat Fight," 1.

[26] Raymond A. Brighton, *They Came to Fish*, 401.

[27] Lorraine McConaghy, "Wartime Boomtown," 45.

[28] Raymond A. Brighton, *They Came to Fish*, 416–417.

[29] Ibid, 401.

CHAPTER 14: POSTWAR WORRIES

[1] "Taking the Home Front Pledge," a rough draft by an anonymous author, Thayer Cumings Library and Archives, Strawbery Banke

Museum, Portsmouth, NH, MS 96, Box 1, Folder 5, "Business and Industry."

[2] *Portsmouth Herald*, 8 July 1943, "Portsmouth Hopes to Keep Yard Booming After Victory," 1.

[3] *Portsmouth Herald*, 5 May 1945, "Yard Is Assured Proper Share of Shipbuilding," 1.

[4] Rodney K. Watterson, *32 in '44*, 12, table 1.

[5] Maury Klein, *A Call to Arms*, 240–241.

[6] Ibid., 241.

[7] Doris Weatherford, *American Women and World War II*, 306.

[8] Maury Klein, *A Call to Arms*, 676.

[9] *Portsmouth Herald*, 23 July 1943, "Admiral Withers Pledges Support to Postwar Plan," 1.

[10] *Survey of Health and Welfare in the Portsmouth Defense Area*, August 1943, 123, State Council of Defense, Local Committees: Portsmouth.

[11] *Portsmouth Herald*, 20 November 1943, "Our New Platform," 1.

[12] *Portsmouth Herald*, 5 January 1944, "Resolutions—1944," 4.

[13] *Portsmouth Herald*, 21 March 1944, "Portsmouth and Peace Number Two, Portsmouth and the Yard," 1.

[14] Ibid.

[15] Ibid.

[16] Ibid.

[17] *Portsmouth Herald*, 17 February 1944, "2 Shifts 7:30 to 4, 4 to 12:30, March 6," 1.

[18] Ibid.

[19] *Portsmouth Herald*, 31 July 1944, "Navy Slashes Sub Construction Next Year at Portsmouth Yard; Pacific Success Causes Cutback; No Discharges Seen," 1.

[20] Quoted in *Portsmouth Herald*, 28 October 1944, "Adm. Cochrane Says Portsmouth Plays Major Role in Pacific," 1.

[21] *Portsmouth Herald*, 4 August 1944, "James Tucker Outlines Five Point Reconversion Plan for City before Rotarians," 1.

[22] Portsmouth Chamber of Commerce letter of 3 July 1944 to Rear Admiral Thomas Withers with enclosure "The U.S. Navy Yard: Portsmouth's One Big Industry," Thayer Cumings Library and Archives, Strawbery Banke Museum, Portsmouth, NH, MS 96, Box 1, Folder 5, "Business and Industry."

[23] Ralph Scott, *The Wilmington Shipyard: Welding a Fleet for Victory in World War II*, (Charleston, SC: History Press, 2007), 33, 67, 91.

[24] Marc Scott Miller, *The Irony of Victory: World War II and Lowell, Massachusetts*, 206.

[25] "Taking the Home Front Pledge," a rough draft by an anonymous author, Thayer Cumings Library and Archives, Strawbery Banke Museum, Portsmouth, NH, MS 96, Box 1, Folder 5, "Business and Industry."

[26] Quoted in *Portsmouth Herald*, 21 August 1944, "Chamber Told of Plans for Navy Work," 1.

[27] Ibid.

[28] Quoted in *Portsmouth Herald*, 27 October 1944, "Adm. Cochrane Says Portsmouth Subs Play Major Role in Pacific," 1.

[29] *Portsmouth Herald*, 12 December 1944, "Union Gets Wash. Agreement of Future Work at Navy Yard." 1.

[30] *Portsmouth Herald*, 5 May 1945, "Yard Is Assured Proper Share of Any Shipbuilding," 1.

[31] *Portsmouth Periscope*, 27 August 1945, 1.

[32] *Portsmouth Herald*, 8 January 1946, "Chamber Official Reports '45 Activities to Members," 1.

[33] *Portsmouth Herald*, 2 May 1946, "Mayor Reports Successful Trip: Talks to Truman on Yard," 1.

[34] *Portsmouth Herald*, 29 April 1946, "Adm. Cochrane Reaffirms Pledge to Keep the Yard Busy," 1.

CONCLUSION

[1] Whitehouse interview, 5 November 2014.

[2] *Portsmouth Herald*, 12 November 2014, "Memorial Bridge to Recognize All Vets," 1.

[3] Foley interview, 30 August 2006.

[4] Inaugural Address by Mayor Mary C. Dondero, 1 January 1945, Rare Pamphlet 41332, "Your City Government, 1945–46–47," Portsmouth Athenaeum, Portsmouth NH.

[5] Ibid.

[6] *Portsmouth Herald*, 27 May 1984, "The World War II Memorial That Isn't."

[77] *Survey of Health and Welfare in the Portsmouth Defense Area*, August 1943, 46, State Council of Defense, Local Committees: Portsmouth.

BIBLIOGRAPHY

Primary Sources

<u>National Archival and Special Collections</u>

National Archives and Records Administration, College Park, MD

>   Record Group 19
>   Bureau of Ships General Correspondence, 1940–45
>   Record Group 38
>   Naval Operations General Correspondence
>   Record Group 52
>   Bureau of Medicine and Surgery General
>   Correspondence, 1842–1951
>   Record Group 24
>   Bureau of Naval Personnel General Correspondence,
>   1941–45

National Archives and Records Administration, Waltham, MA

>   Record Group 181
>   Portsmouth Naval Shipyard General Correspondence
>   (Central Files), 1925–50
>   Portsmouth Naval Base General Correspondence, 1930–1950
>   Formerly Confidential Correspondence, Portsmouth Naval
>   Shipyard, 1930–1950

Navy Department Library, Naval Historical Center, Washington, DC

>   *U.S. Naval Administration in World War II, Bureau of Ships*
>   *U.S. Naval Administration in World War II, Bureau of Yards and
>   Docks*
>   *U.S. Naval Administration in World War II, Commandant First Naval
>   District*
>   "History of the Electric Boat Company 1899–1949," Unpublished
>   Typescript

<u>New Hampshire and Maine Archival and Special Collections</u>

Thayer Cumings Library and Archives, Strawbery Bank Museum,
    Portsmouth, NH

>   MS 96 Portsmouth War Records
>   U.S. Navy Yard, Box 3
>   Transportation, Box 1:18
>   Business and Industry, Box 1:5

Medical, Box 1:6
Survey of Health and Welfare in the Portsmouth Defense Area, August 1943, Box 2, Folder 14
Strawbery Banke Abbott House project
Strawbery Banke Museum Oral History Archives, OH 2, Abbott Store, Transcripts and Documents, SC1-SC41, Working Copies
Frank Henry Photo Collection
Staples-Herald Photo Collection

Fort Stark Museum, New Castle, NH

Pulpit Rock Tower Museum, Rye, NH

New Hampshire Historical Society Library, Concord, NH

World War II Ephemera Collection

Portsmouth Athenaeum, Portsmouth, NH

Portsmouth Defense Area Civil Defense Log Book #1 (1 January 1942–14 April 1942)
Frizzell Collection of Family Papers
City of Portsmouth Police Records, January 24, 1940 to June 23, 1953
CPO Frank Reda, World War II Journal, Portsmouth Athenaeum, Fld1, S807
Athenaeum Photo Collection

Portsmouth Courthouse, City Clerk's Office, Portsmouth, NH

Annual Reports of the City Auditor for the Years Ending December 31, 1942 and 1943
"Your City Government, 1945–1946–1947"

Portsmouth Naval Shipyard Museum Archives, Kittery, ME

U.S. Naval Administration in World War II, Portsmouth Navy Yard
Cultural Resources Survey, Portsmouth Naval Shipyard, U.S. Department of Defense, Legacy Resource Management Program, April 2003. Prepared by the Louis Berger Group for the Engineering Field Activity Northeast Naval Facilities Engineering Command.

Portsmouth Public Library, Special Collections, Portsmouth NH
Portsmouth War Records
Portsmouth Herald microfiche files

Rice Public Library, Kittery, ME

Boyd, David F. "Continuation of Preble's History of the United States Navy Yard, Covering the Years 1878-1930," typescript with handwritten corrections and additions.
Annual Reports of the Town of Kittery, Maine, for the Years 1939-1946.

University of New Hampshire Milne Special Collections and Archives, Durham, NH

Jackson, C. F. *A Biological Survey of Great Bay New Hampshire by the Marine Fisheries Commission*. Durham: University of New Hampshire, 1944.
Portsmouth Naval Shipyard Photographs (Volumes 1-4)
Portsmouth Council of Defense Records (Collection 169)
Sweetser Family Papers
Papers of Harold Caswell Sweetser, Portsmouth Navy Yard Supervisory Naval Architect, 1917-1958, including selected copies of the *Portsmouth Periscope* (Portsmouth Navy Yard's weekly newspaper)
Short, Frederick T. ed. *Biography of Research on the Great Bay Estuary and Adjacent Upland Region*. Durham: University of New Hampshire, 1989.
_____ . *The Ecology of the Great Bay Estuary, New Hampshire and Maine: An Estuarine Profile and Bibliography*. Durham: University of New Hampshire, 1992.
_____ . *Eelgrass in Estuarine Research Reserves Along the East Coast, U.S.A.* Durham: University of New Hampshire, 1993

Newspapers

Portsmouth Herald microfiche files at Portsmouth Library, all front pages and editorial pages for all issues between 1 January 1939 and 31 December 1946.

Portsmouth Periscope, Portsmouth Navy Yard weekly newspaper

Oral Interviews

By Rodney K. Watterson:

Bea Randall, Portsmouth resident during World War II, 5 March 2014, at the Mark Wentworth Home, Portsmouth, NH.
Claire Flanagan Papatones, Portsmouth Internal Revenue Service employee during World War II, 26 February 2014, at her Somersworth, NH, home.

Dan MacIsaac, crew member of USS *Redfish* during World War II, 9 November 2006, at the Portsmouth Naval Shipyard Museum.

Eileen Dondero Foley, shipyard paint shop employee during World War II, 30 August 2006, at her home in Portsmouth, NH.

Fred White, master rigger and laborer during World War II, 3 April 2006, at his home in New Castle, NH.

Harold Whitehouse, lifetime Portsmouth resident, 27 October 2014, at Ceres Bakery, Portsmouth, NH; and 19 November 2014, Portsmouth, NH, Library.

James Dolph, Portsmouth Naval Shipyard historian, 16 March 2006, by telephone.

Mel Low, Portsmouth resident in the mid-1950s, 26 August 2014, at Rye Congregational Church, Rye, NH.

Percy Whitney, apprentice program student and foundry employee during World War II, 23 March 2006, at his home in New Castle, NH.

Stan Davis, grandson of Captain H. F. D. Davis, 25 September 2007, 3 October 2007, and 25 February 2008, via e-mail.

William C. Tebo, apprentice program student and electrical shop employee during World War II, 3 November 2006, at the Portsmouth Naval Shipyard Museum.

In conjunction with the Strawbery Banke Abbott House project; Strawbery Banke Museum Oral History Archives, OH 2, Abbott Store, Transcripts and Documents, SC1-SC41, Working Copies.

By Barbara Ward:

> Charles and Marion Adams, Portsmouth residents, 16 April 1992, in Eliot, ME, SC 31.

> Eileen Foley, shipyard painter's helper and city clerk, daughter of Mary Dondero, 7 February 1991, at the Mayor's Office, City Hall, Portsmouth NH, SC 24.

> Rodolphe Blais, grocery store manager, 13 February 1992, Strawbery Banke Library, SC 33.

By Judith Moyer:

> Alice Sussman, Portsmouth clothing store clerk, 19 October 1990, at her Portsmouth apartment, SC-20.

> Amelia Patch, Portsmouth clothing store clerk, 19 June 1990, at her home, SC-9.

> Leslie Clough, grocery store clerk, 18 July 1990, at the site of the Abbott Store in Strawbery Banke, SC-2/2A.

> Valerie Cunningham, Portsmouth resident, 25 March 1990, at the site of the Abbott Store in Strawbery Banke, SC-10.

> William Hersey, Portsmouth resident, 16 November 1990, Puddle Dock neighborhood, SC-23.

By Valerie Wayne:

> William and Eva Marconi, 28 March 1990, at their home on Shapleigh Island, SC-5.

By William Moore:

> Blanche Washok, Portsmouth resident, 12 April 1991, at 232 Bartlett Road, Portsmouth, NH, SC-29.

> Morris Levy, Portsmouth resident, 12 February 1991, at his home, SC-25.

In conjunction with the Portsmouth Music Hall Project, Portsmouth Athenaeum.

By Judith Moyer:

> Zina Boulanger, shipyard welder during World War II, 14 June 1996, at her home in Dover, NH.

Secondary Sources

Books

Bailey, Ronald H. *The Home Front, USA*. Alexandria, VA: Time-Life Books, 1978.

Baime, A. J. *The Arsenal of Democracy: FDR, Detroit, and an Epic Quest to Arm an America at War.* New York: Houghton Mifflin Harcourt, 2014.

Binder, Frederick M., and David M. Reimers. *The Way We Lived: Essays and Documents in American Social History, Volume II: 1865–Present.* Boston: Houghton Mifflin, 2000.

Bonnett, Wayne. *Build Ships! San Francisco Bay Wartime Shipbuilding Photographs 1940–1945.* Sausalito, CA: Windgate Press, 2000.

Brandt, Allan M. *No Magic Bullet: A Social History of Venereal Disease in the United States Since 1880.* New York: Oxford University Press, 1987.

Brighton, Raymond A. *They Came to Fish.* Dover: Randall/Winebaum Enterprises, 1979.

_____. *The Prescott Story.* New Castle, NH: Portsmouth Marine Society, 1982.

Buckley, Thomas H. *The United States and the Washington Conference, 1921–1922.* Knoxville: University of Tennessee Press, 1970.

Candee, Richard M. *Atlantic Heights: A World War I Shipbuilders' Community.* Portsmouth: Portsmouth Marine Society, Peter E. Randall, 1985.

Clarie, Thomas C., and Rosemary F. *Just Rye Harbor: An Appreciation and History.* Portsmouth: Portsmouth Marine Society, Peter E. Randall, 2005.

Connery, Robert H. *The Navy and Industrial Mobilization in World War II.* Princeton: Princeton University Press, 1951.

Cooke, Alistair. *The American Home Front: 1941–1942.* New York: Atlantic Monthly Press, 2006.

Cunningham, Valerie, and Mark J. Sammons. *Black Portsmouth: Three Centuries of African-American Heritage.* Durham: University of New Hampshire Press, 2004.

Cradle of American Shipbuilding: Portsmouth Naval Shipyard. Portsmouth Naval Shipyard: Government Printing Office, 1978.

Dallek, Robert. *Franklin D. Roosevelt and American Foreign Policy, 1932–1945.* New York: Oxford University Press, 1979.

Daniels, Josephus. *The Navy and the Nation: Wartime Addresses by Josephus Daniels.* New York: George H. Doran, 1919.

Dingman, Roger. *Power in the Pacific: The Origins of Naval Arms Limitation, 1914–1922*. Chicago: University of Chicago Press, 1977.

Dorwart, Jeffrey M. *The Philadelphia Navy Yard: From the Birth of the U.S. Navy to the Nuclear Age*. Philadelphia: University of Pennsylvania Press, 2001.

Duis, Perry, and Scott LaFrance. *We've Got a Job to Do: Chicagoans and World War II*. Chicago: Chicago Historical Society, 1992.

Eiler, Keith E. *Mobilizing America: Robert P. Patterson and the War Effort 1940–45*. Ithaca: Cornell University Press, 1997.

Estes, J. Worth, and David M. Goodman. *The Changing Humors of Portsmouth: The Medical Biography of an American Town, 1623–1983*. Boston: Francis A. Countway Library of Medicine, 1984.

Fussell, Paul. *Wartime: Understanding and Behavior in the Second World War*. Oxford: Oxford University Press, 1989.

Gluck, Sherna Berger. *Rosie the Riveter Revisited: Women, the War, and Social Change*. Boston: Twayne, 1987.

Goldin, Claudia. *Understanding the Gender Gap*. New York: Oxford University Press, 1990.

Goodwin, Doris Kearns. *No Ordinary Time: Franklin and Eleanor Roosevelt: The Home Front in World War II*. New York: Simon & Schuster, 1994.

Gregory, Ross. *America 1941: A Nation at the Crossroads*. New York: Free Press, 1989.

Guyol, Philip N. *Democracy Fights: A History of New Hampshire in World War II*. Hanover: Dartmouth Publications, 1951.

Hanes, Richard C., and Sharon M. Hanes. *American Home Front in World War II: Almanac*. Farmington Hills, MI: Thomson Gale, 2005.
Hanes, Sharon M., and Allison McNeill. *American Home Front in World War II: Primary Sources*. Detroit: Thomson Gale, UXL, 2006.

Hareven, Tamara, and Randolph Langenbach. *Amoskeag: Life and Work in an American Factory City*. New York: Pantheon, 1978.

Havighurst, Robert J., and H. Gerthon Morgan. *The Social History of a War-Boom Community*. New York: Longmans, Green, 1951.

Heckman, Meg, and Mike Pride. *We Went to War: New Hampshire Remembers*. Concord, NH: Monitor Publishing, 2008.

Hays, Samuel P. *Beauty, Health, and Permanence: Environmental Politics in the United States 1955–1985*. Cambridge: Cambridge University Press, 1987.

Herman, Arthur. *Freedom's Forge: How American Business Produced Victory in World War II*. New York: Random House, 2012.

Hinkle, David Randall, ed. *United States Submarines*. Annandale, VA: Navy Submarine League, 2002.

Historical Transactions 1893–1943. New York: Society of Naval Architects and Marine Engineers, 1945.

Hoopes, Roy. *Americans Remember the Home Front*. New York: Hawthorn, 1977.

Hurley, Andrew. *Environmental Inequalities: Class, Race, and Industrial Pollution in Gary, Indiana, 1945–1980*. Chapel Hill: University of North Carolina Press, 1995.

Jackson, C. F. *A Biological Survey of Great Bay, New Hampshire, by the Marine Fisheries Commission*. Durham: University of New Hampshire, 1944.

Johnson, Marilynn S. *The Second Gold Rush: Oakland and the East Bay in World War II*. Berkeley: University of California Press, 1996.

Kennedy, David M. *Freedom from Fear: The American People in Depression and War, 1929–1945*. New York: Oxford University Press, 1999.

Kessler-Harris, Alice. *Out to Work: A History of Wage-Earning Women in the United States*. New York: Oxford University Press, 1982.

Kimble, James J. *Mobilizing the Home Front: War Bonds and Domestic Propaganda*. College Station: Texas A&M University Press, 2006.

Klein, Maury. *A Call to Arms: Mobilizing America for World War II*. New York: Bloomsbury, 2013.

Lane, Frederic Chapin. *Ships for Victory: A History of Shipbuilding under the U.S. Maritime Commission in World War II*. Baltimore: Johns Hopkins University Press, 1951.

Lawry, Nelson H., Glen M. Williford, and Leo K. Polaski. *Portsmouth Harbor's Military and Naval Heritage*. Portsmouth, NH: Arcadia, 2004.

LaFeber, Walter. *The American Age: U.S. Foreign Policy at Home and Abroad Since 1896*, Volume 2. New York: W.W. Norton, 1994.

Lingeman, Richard R. *Don't You Know There's a War On? The American Home Front, 1941–45*. New York: G.P. Putnam's Sons, 1970.

Lotchin, Roger W. ed. *The Way We Really Were: The Golden State in the Second Great War*. Chicago: University of Illinois Press, 2000.

McFarlane, Charles T. *The Present War: Its Background and Related Developments*. New York: American Book Company, 1940.

Milkman, Ruth. *Gender at Work: The Dynamics of Job Segregation by Sex during World War II*. Urbana: University of Illinois Press, 1987.

Miller, Marc Scott. *The Irony of Victory: World War II and Lowell, Massachusetts*. Chicago: University of Illinois Press, 1988.

Muir, Malcolm, Jr., ed. *The Human Tradition in the World War II Era*. Wilmington, DE: Scholarly Resources, 2001.

Nash, Gerald D. *The American West Transformed: The Impact of the Second World War*. Bloomington: Indiana University Press, 1985.

_____ . *World War II and the West: Reshaping the Economy*. Lincoln: University of Nebraska Press, 1990.

New Hampshire: A Guide to the Granite State. American Guide Series. Written by Workers of the Federal Writers' Project of the Works Progress Administration for the State of New Hampshire. Boston: Houghton Mifflin, 1938.

Nutting, Wallace. *New Hampshire Beautiful*. Framingham: Old America, 1923.

Peters, Thomas J. *In Search of Excellence: Lessons from America's Best-Run Companies*. New York: Harper & Row, 1982.

_____ . *A Passion for Excellence: The Leadership Difference*. New York: Random House, 1985.

_____ . *Thriving on Chaos: Handbook for a Management Revolution*. New York: A.A. Knopf, 1994.

Polenberg, Richard, ed. *America at War: The Home Front, 1941–1945*. Englewood Cliffs, NJ: Prentice-Hall, 1968.

Potterfield, Thomas A. *The Business of Employee Empowerment: Democracy and Ideology in the Workplace*. Westport, CT: Quorum Books, 1999.

Purser, Ronald E., and Steven Cabana. *The Self-Managing Organization: How Leading Companies Are Transforming the Work of Teams for Real Impact*. New York: Free Press, 1998.

Randall, Peter E., *Hampton: A Century of Town and Beach, 1888–1988*. Hampton, NH: Peter E. Randall, 1990.

Reynolds, Clark G. *America at War, 1941–1945: The Home Front*. New York: Gallery Books, 1990.

Roscoe, Theodore. *United States Submarine Operations in World War II*. Annapolis: U.S. Naval Institute Press, 1949.

Scott, Ralph. *The Wilmington Shipyard: Welding a Fleet for Victory in World War II*. Charleston, SC: History Press, 2007.

Short, Fred, Clayton A. Perriman, and Stephen Adams. *Bibliography on the Great Bay Estuary and Adjacent Upland Region*. Durham, NH: University of New Hampshire/University of Maine Sea Grant College Program, 1989.

_____ . *The Ecology of the Great Bay Estuary, New Hampshire and Maine*. Durham, NH: Jackson Estuarine Laboratory, University of New Hampshire, 1992.

_____ . *Eelgrass in Estuarine Research Reserves Along the East Coast, U.S.A*. Durham, NH: Jackson Estuarine Laboratory, University of New Hampshire, 1993.

_____ . *Eelgrass as an Indicator of Nutrient Over-Enrichment in Estuaries: A Final Report* Durham, NH: Jackson Estuarine Laboratory, University of New Hampshire, 2003.

Skoloff, Gary, Martin Jacobs, Jack Matthews, Jim Osborne, Ken Fleck, Merv Bloch, and Stan Cohen, from the collections of. *To Win the War: Home Front Memorabilia of World War II*. Missoula, MT: Pictorial Histories, 1995.

Southworth, Katherine, Jack Taylor, Marilyn Wentworth, eds. *The War We Knew: Residents of Riverwoods Remember World War II*. Exeter, NH: Riverwoods, 2011.

Tindall, George Brown, and David E. Shi, *America*, 4th ed., Volume Two. New York: W.W. Norton, 1997.

Vatter, Harold G. *The U.S. Economy in World War II*. New York: Columbia University Press, 1985.

Watterson, Rodney K. *32 in '44: Building the Portsmouth Submarine Fleet in World War II*. Annapolis: U.S. Naval Institute Press, 2011.

Ward, Barbara McLean, ed. *Produce and Conserve, Share and Play Square: The Grocer and the*
        Consumer on the Home-Front Battlefield during World War II. Portsmouth: Strawbery Banke Museum, 1994.

Weatherford, Doris. *American Women and World War II*. New York: Facts on File, 1990.

Weir, Gary. *Building American Submarines 1914–1940*. Washington, DC: Naval Historical Center, 1991.

_____ . *Forged in War: The Naval-Industrial Complex and American Submarine Construction, 1940–1961*. Washington, DC: Naval Historical Center, 1993.

Whitehouse, Harold, Jr. *Home by Nine: The Real Story of Portsmouth's South End*. Portsmouth: Peter E. Randall, 2008.

Whittaker, Robert. *Portsmouth-Kittery Naval Shipyard in Old Photographs*. Stroud, Gloucestershire: Alan Sutton, 1993.

Winslow, Richard E., III. *"Do Your Job!" An Illustrated Bicentennial History of the Portsmouth Naval Shipyard, 1800–2000*. Portsmouth, NH: Portsmouth Marine Society, 2000.

_____ . *Portsmouth-Built: Submarines of the Portsmouth Naval Shipyard*. Portsmouth, NH: Portsmouth Marine Society, 1985.

Wysong, Jack P. *The World, Portsmouth, and the 22nd Coast Artillery: The War Years 1938–1948*. Missoula, MT: Pictorial Histories, 1997.

Articles

Andrews, Clarence. "Sheldon Iowa during World War II." *Palimpsest* 70 (1989), 146–165.

Argyris, Chris. "Empowerment: The Emperor's New Clothes." *Harvard Business Review*, May/June 1998, Issue 3, 98–105.

Bolster, Jeffrey. "Prof," *University of New Hampshire Magazine*, Spring/Summer 2014, 38.

Bracker, Milton. "Portsmouth Tries to Adjust Life to an Influx of Men and Money." *New York Times*, 5 October 1941.

Braitman, Jacqueline R. "Partisans in Overalls: New Perspectives on Women and Politics in Wartime California," in Roger W. Lotchin, ed., *The Way We Really Were: The Golden State in the Second Great War.* Chicago: University of Illinois Press, 2000, 215–235.

Colati, Gregory C., and Ryan H. Madden. "Victory Begins at Home: Portsmouth and Puddle Dock during World War II," in Barbara McLean Ward, ed., *Produce and Conserve, Share and Play Square: The Grocer and the Consumer on the Home-Front Battlefield during World War II.* Portsmouth: Strawbery Banke Museum, 1994.

Fenton-O'Creevy, Mark. "Employee Involvement and the Middle Manager: Evidence from a Survey of Organizations." *Journal of Organizational Behavior*, vol. 19, no. 1 (January 1998), 67–84.

Jordan, Franklin E. *Portsmouth and National Defense*, a series of 13 articles that appeared in the *Portsmouth Herald* in the summer of 1941, compiled and published in pamphlet form by J. D. Hartford of the *Portsmouth Herald* on 1 August 1941.

Lotchin, Roger W. "The Historians' War or the Home Front War? Some Thoughts for Western Historians." *Western Historical Quarterly* vol. 26, no. 2, (Summer 1995), 185–196.

_____ . "California Cities and the Hurricane of Change: World War II in the San Francisco, Los Angeles, and San Diego Metropolitan Areas." *Pacific Historical Review* 63 (August 1994), 414–416.

Maness, Lonnie E. "A West Tennessee Town and World War II." *West Tennessee Historical Society Papers*, 110–119.

Michelson, George. "Housing Built on the Double-Quick." *Engineering News Record*, March 26, 1942, 1.

McConaghy, Lorraine. "Wartime Boomtown: Kirkland, Washington, a Small Town during World War II." *Pacific Northwest Quarterly* vol. 80, 1989, 42–51.

McKee, A. I., Captain, U.S.N. "Development of Submarines in the United States." *Historical Transactions 1893–1943.* New York: Society of Naval Architects and Marine Engineers, 1945.

O'Neill, William. "The People Are Willing" in Frederick M. Binder and David M. Reimers, *The Way We Lived: Essays and Documents in American Social History, Volume II: 1865–Present*. Boston: Houghton Mifflin, 2000, 197.

Passos, John Dos. "Gold Rush Down South." *State of the Nation*. Boston: Houghton Mifflin, 1944. Reprinted in Richard Polenberg, ed. *America at War*, 125.

Rutledge, Jack. "U-boat Wreaked Havoc in Gulf of Maine." *Foster's Sunday Citizen*, date not available.

Sitkoff, Harvard. "The American Home Front," in Barbara McLean Ward, ed., *Produce and Conserve, Share and Play Square: The Grocer and the Consumer on the Home-Front Battlefield during World War II*. Portsmouth: Strawbery Banke Museum, 1994).

Smith, Helena Huntington. "Are America's Civilians Ready for Attack?" *Reader's Digest*, 1942. Quoted in Sharon M. Hanes and Allison McNeill, *American Home Front in World War II: Primary Sources*. Detroit: Thomson Gale, UXL, 2006.

Tucker, Charles W., Commander JAGC, USN. "Compliance by Federal Facilities with State and Local Environmental Regulations." *Naval Law Review*, Spring 1986, 87–112.

Valiela, Ivan, Deborah Rutecki, and Sophia Fox. "Salt Marshes: Biological Controls of Food Webs in a Diminishing Environment." *Journal of Experimental Marine Biology Ecology*, Mar 2004, Vol. 300 Issue 1/2, 131–160.

Watterson, Rodney K. "Top Sub Shop." *Naval History*, February 2013.

Webster, C. M. "Air Raid Defense for Small Towns." *Yankee*, May 1942, vol. VIII, no. 5.

Wensyel, James W. "Home Front." *American History* 30, no. 2 (June 1995), 44–67.

Woodward, Mylinda. "Pod Squad: Children Harvest Milkweed to Aid in War Effort." *University of New Hampshire Magazine*, Fall 2013, 64.

Videos

World War II Home Front New Hampshire, a video history documentary. John Gfroerer, producer. NH Humanities Council with Continental Cablevision, 1994.

Russell Street Reunion. Gould Productions, 1986, VHS Tape, Portsmouth Public Library.

Unpublished Theses

Crisp, Kimberly E. "Water Street Remembered." History honors thesis, University of New Hampshire, 1996.

Dearborn, Sadie M. Written testimony about Kittery schools, undated, Maine Room, Rice Library, Kittery, Maine.

Douglas, Dean C. "Submarine Disarmament: 1919–1936." Ph.D. Diss., Syracuse University, 1969.

Hirshfield, Deborah Ann. "Rosie Also Welded: Women and Technology in Shipbuilding during World War II." Ph.D. Diss., University of California, Irvine, 1987.

Horn, John D. "Submarines and the Electric Boat Company." A.B. Degree, Princeton University, 1948.

Lutts, Cassie. "History of Admiralty Village, Kittery, Maine" (a presentation to the Kittery Historical Association, April 13, 1988). Maine Room, Rice Library, Kittery, ME.

Watterson, Rodney, K. "32 in '44: A Management and Environmental Study of Submarine Construction at Portsmouth Navy Yard during World War II." Ph.D. Diss., University of New Hampshire, 2007.

West, Michael A. "Laying the Legislative Foundation: The House Naval Affairs Committee and the Construction of the Treaty Navy, 1926–1934." Ph.D. Diss., Ohio State University, 1980.

Pamphlets

800 Ways to Save and Serve: How to Beat the High Cost of Wartime Living. S241, Thayer Cumings Library and Archives, Strawbery Bank Museum, Portsmouth, NH.

Make and Mend for Victory. Book S-10, Spool Cotton Company, 1942. SISC 286, Box 16, FF 13, Thayer Cumings Library and Archives, Strawbery Bank Museum, Portsmouth, NH.

Make It Do Until Victory: Your Wartime Handbook. Editorial Offices of Life and Health, undated. SISC 286, Box 16, FF 13, Thayer Cumings Library and Archives, Strawbery Bank Museum, Portsmouth, NH.

Since Pearl Harbor: The American Red Cross Reports to the People, 1 April 1943. SISC S198-S209, Box 13, FF 1-5. Thayer Cumings Library and Archives, Strawbery Bank Museum, Portsmouth, NH.

Electronic

"Asbestos Exposure on Navy Ships,"
http://www.asbestos.com/navy/ships.php.

"Connie Bean Stood Strong in Wartime, at Dances," Adam Leech, posted 1 February 2009,
http://www.seacoastonline.com/article/20090201/NEWS.

"Contamination a Big Problem at the Shipyard," Rebecca Kaufman, New Hampshire Public Radio Commentary, 13 May 2005,
http://www.nhpr.org/node/8782.

"Eastern Sea Frontier War Diary North Atlantic Coast Frontier, chapter II," www.uboatarchive.net/ESFWarDiaryFeb42CH2.htm.

"Gearing Up for Victory: American Military and Industrialization in World War, Naval Historical Center II,"
http://www.history.navy.mil/colloquia/cch5d.htm.
"I-400 Class Submarine," Nihon Kaigun,
http://combinedfleet.com/ships/i-400.

"Mare Island Naval Shipyard: World War II in the San Francisco Bay Area." This site is an essay excerpted from Wayne Bonnett, *Build Ships! San Francisco Bay Wartime Shipbuilding Photographs 1940–1945* (Windgate Press: Sausalito, CA, 2000).
http://www.cr.nps.gov/nr/travel/wwIIbayarea/mar.htm.

"Naval Expansion Act, 14 June 1940," www.history.navy.mil/faqs/faq59-20.htm.

"Naval Expansion Act, 19 July 1940," www.history.navy.mil/faqs/faq59-21.htm.

Portsmouth Herald Tea for Two columns by Tammi Truax,
www.seacoastonline.com/articles:

"Louise McGee," 4 April 2007.
"Meet Don Ricklefs: Master Carpenter," 3 June 2009.
"Keep a Cool Head," 2 May 2006.
"Mickey Hussey Remembers Small-Town Portsmouth," 2 January 2006.

"Clarence Cunningham: '… Always a Gentle, Quiet Person,'" 3 June 2009.

"Recalling Nazi Spies off the New England Coast, and a Mystery on a Scituate Beach," Jim Rose, *Wompatuck News*, www.patriotledger.com.

"Seacoast Forts of Portsmouth Harbor, New Hampshire — Maine," www.northamericanforts.com/East/New_Hampshire/Portsmo uth/harbor.html.

"The First Daylight KKK Parade and the First Klan Parade in New England," www.mainememory.net/artifact/23229.

"The Ku Klux Klan Confronts New England Catholics in the 1920s," https://aha.confex.com/aha/2011/webprogram/Paper5193.ht ml.

"Thomas Withers," www.navy.mil/navydata/cno/n87/history/pioneers4.html#Th omasWithers.

"U.S. Army Medical Department, Office of Medical History, Chapter X, Venereal Diseases," http://history.amedd.army.mil/booksdocs/wwii/communicabl ediseasesV5/chapter10.htm, page 146.

"U.S. Department of Labor, OSHA," http://www.osha.gov/SLTC/asbestos/index.html.

"U.S. Inflation Calculator," http://www.usinflationcalculator.com.

"U.S. Environmental Protection Agency Waste Site Cleanup and Reuse in New England," http://yosemite.epa.gov/rl/npl pad.nsf.

"World War II Home Front on Puget Sound — A Snapshot History," http://www.historylink.rg/essays/output.cfm?file_id=1664.

Index

hiring women, 218, 236-39;
prepares yard for attack, 82
Dearborn, Henry, 69
Deming, W. Edwards Dr., 49
Dewey, Thomas Governor, 308
dimouts, 99-105: controversy
over, 100-01; Maine
enforcement area, 100; New
Hampshire enforcement area,
100; suspension, 105;
violations, 101-05. *See also civil
defense.*
Dolphin Hotel, 142, 146-47:
alleged VD source, 127-28;
burns down, 332-34
Dondero Elementary School, 338
Dondero, Mary C., 11,304-15:
employed at yard, 245; legacy,
315, 338; mayoral elections
245, 304-06, 313; memorial,
336-38; national attention, 305;
political squabbling, 309;
political success, 309-13;
popularity, 309, 312-13;
President Truman meeting,
329, 341; recruits, 286, 312;
Republican opponents, 309,
313; state representative, 305
Dorwart, Jeffrey M.: on restricted
work assignments at
Philadelphia Navy Yard, 241
Dover: coast guard flotilla,78
Drinker Report, 301-02
Durante, Jimmy: visits Camp
Langdon, 181

E

Electric Boat Company, 39, 41,
49: building sites, 48; controls
submarine designs, 40;
preferential treatment, 328;
sectional construction, 44;
struggles to survive, 41
Elkhorn, Doris: on women's
hosiery shortages, 178

Emergency Shipbuilders
Housing Act, 252
Engineering Science
Management War Training
Program, 219, 228
environmental pollution,6, 8,
184, 202, 274-304, 339: Great
Bay, 279-80, 285-86, 339; rivers
and bay, 277-88; shipyard,
caused, 293-302, asbestos
operations, 299-302,
galvanizing plant, 296-98, hull
scraping, 298-99, landfills,
289-03, pickling tanks, 293-96
Environmental Protection
Agency: establishment of, 278
galvanizing plant
environmental hazard, 297;
Superfund Site, 8, 276
Exeter Brass Works, 225: receives
five Army-Navy Production E
Awards, 227

F

federal housing, 249, 269: World
War I, 252-55; World War II,
255-66
Federal War Production Training
Program, 6, 219, 221-228, 339
Foley, Eileen Dondero: on
boarders, 257; Dolphin Hotel,
146; Dorothy Lamour, 159;
memorial, 336, 309; military
dances, 143-44; mother's, gifts,
312; mother's popularity, 309,
312; Paint Shop interview,
240; Pearl Harbor, 34;
Portsmouth's seamy side, 145;
Portsmouth, eight term
mayor, 338; restricted work
assignments, 240-41;
patriotism, 184; Wentworth
Hotel swimming pool, 145;
USO volunteer, 153
Ford, Henry: builds bombers, 37